The Politics and Governance of Basic Education

The Politics and Governance of Basic Education

A Tale of Two South African Provinces

Edited by
Brian Levy, Robert Cameron, Ursula Hoadley, and Vinothan Naidoo

OXFORD
UNIVERSITY PRESS

OXFORD
UNIVERSITY PRESS

Great Clarendon Street, Oxford, OX2 6DP,
United Kingdom

Oxford University Press is a department of the University of Oxford.
It furthers the University's objective of excellence in research, scholarship,
and education by publishing worldwide. Oxford is a registered trade mark of
Oxford University Press in the UK and in certain other countries

First Edition published in 2018

Published in the United States of America by Oxford University Press
198 Madison Avenue, New York, NY 10016, United States of America

British Library Cataloguing in Publication Data
Data available

Library of Congress Control Number: 2018935425

ISBN 978–0–19–882405–3

Foreword I

What is distinctive about both this compelling book and a related (forthcoming) OUP collection[1] (also based on research conducted with the Effective States and Inclusive Development Research Centre) is the insistence that the crisis of schooling without learning is fundamentally a challenge of politics and governance, and that the routes forward must involve changes in these interrelated realms.

This emphasis on politics and governance resonates with wider debates within international development and policy. Indeed, the analysis and findings presented in this book operate at the cutting-edge of a broader discourse on development in the twenty-first century, stretching far beyond the field of education. By bringing high-level debates around the role of inter-elite bargaining in shaping long-term development trajectories into direct contact with pressing issues of service delivery, it starts to breach what Merilee Grindle terms the 'missing middle' of the newly emerging governance agenda.

The book's presentation of a method that enables us to identify and explore how different kinds of reform unfold in different ways in different types of contexts marks a considerable advance on the now-anodyne insistence that 'context matters'. The rigorous comparison between two provinces within South Africa illustrates the power of the method, and offers an approach that can be borrowed for many other such studies. Importantly, this approach uses comparisons between the Western Cape and other settings to reveal the limitations of systems that rely too heavily on hierarchical accountability mechanisms and bureaucratic procedures, as opposed to more flexible systems for governing service provision.

Brian Levy, the lead editor and principal investigator behind the research on which this book is based, has already contributed much to the project of rethinking the politics of development and devising 'best-fit' governance solutions for particular types of context, not least through his 2014 book *Working with the Grain*. This new work builds directly on this wider project—

[1] *The Politics of Education in Developing Countries: From Schooling to Learning?*, edited by Sam Hickey and Naomi Hossain, will be published by OUP in 2018. The book centres on six country case studies, and includes a chapter on South Africa by Brian Levy and colleagues.

both by bringing it right down to the front line of service delivery, and also by further proving the benefits of 'thinking and working politically' for all of those concerned with understanding how injustices such as the learning crisis occur and how they might be challenged.

Professor Sam Hickey
Professor of Politics and Development at the University of Manchester, and Joint Director of Research at the Effective States and Inclusive Development Research Centre.

Foreword II

Three features of this book make it a valuable contribution to the research literature on the governance of schools and the systems which sustain them. First, it engages in ground-clearing scholarship which describes the myriad changes which have occurred in South Africa since the advent of democratic rule in 1994. These include a radical restructuring of the school system and the way it is financed and governed, no fewer than three waves of curriculum reform, and a complete overhaul of the way in which teachers' work is regulated. In 'steady-state' countries, such developments evolved over the span of a century or so; in South Africa they have been crammed into a tumultuous one-quarter of this time. In tracking the details of these changes, many of the chapters of this volume provide a service which will be of inestimable value to scholars, not only in South Africa but to students of social change everywhere.

The second feature of the book which commands attention is the theoretical lens developed to examine school governance. Breaking free of the either/or approach, which pits the power of centralized decision-making against the democratic advantages of local control, the book is premised on a more complex and productive both/and perspective. Two sets of axes define this terrain. Technocratic, impersonal rules of 'best practice' are in tension with politics, patronage and negotiation; predatory elites compete with citizens pursuing their rights to a fair share of social goods.

The third focus, and the heart of the book, puts the first two elements in conversation. The book is an extended reflection on the forces at play between top-down hierarchical processes and horizontal participation by local actors in the governance and management of schools. One after the other, successive chapters examine the interactions between contextual complexities, policy frameworks and institutional competencies in two very different provincial settings: the Western Cape and its eastern neighbour, the two major components of the Cape Province prior to 1994. The book's combination of macro- and micro-perspectives enables novel linkages to emerge that are invisible from either point of view alone. The theoretical framework provides important insights into the unpredictable trade-offs between pragmatic politics and idealistic civil service reform initiatives.

A variety of methodologies—socio-political, econometric, system-level analyses of management practices and micro-level case studies of institutional leadership—produce no easy answers. This in itself is an important result, indicating just how complex these processes are and how stubbornly they resist formulaic solutions. Virtuous cycles of exemplary institutional leadership thrive in the most unpromising provincial circumstances. Exemplary systemic processes are frustrated by ambitious local-level bit-players. Through it all the theory remains robust and, in the end, the most important contribution of the book is to provide novel ways of thinking about public leadership; it enables new perspectives which are likely to produce fresh insights well into the future as we continue to grapple with this recalcitrant problem.

Dr Nick Taylor
Senior Research Fellow at JET Education Services, and formerly CEO of the organization. Between 2012 and 2015, he was seconded to South Africa's Department of Basic Education to establish and lead its National Education Evaluation Development Unit.

Acknowledgements

This book is the product of a sustained collaboration across disciplines; our team includes public administration specialists, educationalists, economists and political scientists. Cross-disciplinary work is never straightforward; the process of producing this book has been more collegial and (we hope) more productive than many such endeavours.

The project would not have been undertaken without the financial, intellectual and moral support of the Effective States and Inclusive Development (ESID) Research Centre, a global partnership based at the University of Manchester and funded by the UK government's Department for International Development. We thank especially Sam Hickey, Julia Brunt, Kunal Sen, David Hulme and others in the ESID team for their sustained engagement.

At the University of Cape Town (where we all are faculty), we are grateful to the Nelson Mandela School of Public Governance for hosting the project, and to the SPADE (Schools Performing Above Demographic Expectations) project, housed in the School of Education, for sharing generously its findings and experience. We also express our sincere thanks to our research collaborators from partner institutions, such as Rhodes University, for their invaluable contributions.

We acknowledge the valuable ongoing encouragement provided by Crain Soudien and Alan Hirsch. We also thank for their feedback the participants at an April, 2016 workshop at UCT's Graduate School of Business at which we shared our preliminary findings, and also the anonymous reviewers of the ESID working papers that comprise the basis of much of this book.

Thanks to the many organizations and individuals (in schools, and within provincial and national government) who opened their doors and shared their insights into the ongoing successes and challenges of improving education outcomes in South Africa. We hope that this work contributes in some measure to that vital and noble purpose.

April 2018

Brian Levy
Robert Cameron
Ursula Hoadley
Vinothan Naidoo

Contents

Part III. Horizontal Governance

List of Figures

List of Tables

List of Contributors

Robert Cameron is Professor of Public Administration in the Department of Political Studies, University of Cape Town. He has published around ninety journal articles and book chapters on local government, public administration, and public service reform. He has also written one book and co-edited two books. He is a Senior Fellow at the Global Cities Institute, University of Toronto. He was a member of the South African Municipal Demarcation Board (1999–2004), which demarcated non-racial local government boundaries for the democratic South Africa.

Luis Crouch is a Senior Economist in the International Development Group at the Research Triangle Institute. He specializes in education policy, decentralized finance, political economy of reform, education statistics, planning, and projections. He has previously worked at the World Bank and at the Global Partnership for Education (GPE). He worked as an advisor to South Africa's education sector in regard to funding and governance reforms, Egypt's decentralization experiments, and decentralization and other policy reforms in Peru and Indonesia. He has worked in more than twenty-five countries in a thirty-year career in education and socio-economic development, and is the author of many reports, technical papers, and books.

Monica Hendricks is the Director of the Institute for the Study of the Englishes of Africa, Rhodes University. She teaches and co-ordinates an undergraduate course for teachers of English as an additional language, mostly in rural schools, and does graduate supervision. She has a long-standing interest in children's writing ability and sense of self, and how teacher education can improve pedagogical writing practices. Recent publications include editing and contributing two chapters to *ISEA 1964–2014—A Research Institute Serving People* (2016).

Ursula Hoadley is Associate Professor in the School of Education at the University of Cape Town. Her extensive published research explores the relation between education and social stratification, and the differential social and academic outcomes engendered through educational processes, with a focus on pedagogy, curriculum and school organisation at the primary level. Ursula participates in multiple professional education associations, fora and boards, including South Africa's Ministerial Review Committee of 2009 which led to the revision of the outcomes-based national curriculum. Her book, *Pedagogy in poverty: 20 years of curriculum reform in South Africa,* was published by Routledge in 2018.

Zukiswa Kota currently heads up the Monitoring and Advocacy Programme of the Public Service Accountability Monitor (PSAM) at Rhodes University, South Africa. She has developed expertise in promoting social justice and in particular advocating for the implementation of law and policy promoting the right to education. Her other areas of work include monitoring of resource management in the delivery of public services. An environmental science graduate, her interests range from food security and ethnobotany, to Ecoliteracy and early childhood development.

Janeli Kotzé is a researcher at the South African Department of Basic Education. She has been involved in evaluations of national education policy and projects related to cross-national comparisons of educational achievement, early childhood development and learning trajectories of children in poorer schooling contexts. Her PhD in Economics focused on the South African education crisis and learning inequalities.

Brian Levy is Professor of the Practice of International Development, School of Advanced International Studies, Johns Hopkins University in Washington DC and Academic Director, Nelson Mandela School of Public Governance, University of Cape Town. He worked at the World Bank from 1989 to 2012. His books include *Working with the Grain: Integrating Governance and Growth in Development Strategies* (Oxford University Press, 2014) and (co-edited with Sahr Kpundeh) *Building State Capacity in Africa* (World Bank Institute, 2004). He completed his BA (Hons) at the University of Cape Town in 1976, and a Ph.D. in economics at Harvard University in 1983.

Eric Matambo is the Training Coordinator at the Public Service Accountability Monitor (PSAM) at Rhodes University. He facilitates and co-ordinates the Fundamentals of Social Accountability Monitoring certificate short course run by the Regional Learning Programme of PSAM. One of his areas of focus has been public integrity management within the public resource management framework. Eric was a school teacher in the Eastern Cape before starting at PSAM in 2009.

Vinothan Naidoo is Senior Lecturer in the Department of Political Studies, University of Cape Town. His research on South African policy analysis spans various fields, including education, public works, agriculture and water and sanitation. He also writes on various public administration subjects such as institutional co-ordination, public sector reform, political-administrative relations, and inter-governmental relations. His most recent research has examined South Africa's changing bureaucratic machinery.

Debra Shepherd is a lecturer and researcher in the Economics Departments at Stellenbosch University. Her research interests lie in the fields of applied microeconometrics, economics of education, and labour economics.

Lawule Shumane holds degrees from the University of Cape Town and Yale University. She currently works for Dalberg Advisors, a global development consulting firm, as an analyst, where her focus is education and other global development challenges.

Shelly Wilburn is an international researcher in education, currently based in the School of Education at the University of Cape Town. Her work focuses on the social organization of teaching, teachers' relationships, and the nature of educational change in under-resourced schools.

Gabrielle Wills is an education economist and researcher at ReSEP (Research on Socio-Economic Policy) in the Economics Departments at Stellenbosch University. With interests in systemic reforms in South African education more generally, her work has been concentrated specifically on school leadership and management and union effects on learning.

Part I
Framing the Issues

1

Improving Basic Education—The Governance Challenge

Brian Levy

1.1 Introduction

The world over, economic inclusion has risen to the top of the development discourse. A well-performing education system is central to achieving inclusive development—but the challenge of improving educational outcomes has proven to be unexpectedly difficult. Access to education has increased, but quality remains low, with weaknesses in governance comprising an important part of the explanation.

'Achieve universal primary education' was adopted unanimously at the United Nations in 2000 as the second of the Millennium Development Goals. Major gains have been achieved. As of 2015, 91 per cent of children in the relevant age cohort in developing countries were enrolled in primary schools, up from 83 per cent in 2000. But 2008 results from the Trends in International Math and Science Study (TIMSS) found that more than half of developing-country students who took the test scored below the 'low' threshold benchmark set for the test. Of the 250 million children worldwide who cannot read, write, or add, more than half are in school (Unesco, 2014).

The reasons for the difficulties in improving learning outcomes are many (Sniltsveit et al., 2016). The 2018 World Development Report, *Learning to Realize Education's Promise,* distinguishes usefully between the proximate and underlying causes of learning shortfalls. The proximate causes include the difficult socio-economic context in which many children live, with the result that many children arrive at school without being ready to learn; the lack of resources to provide teachers, facilities, or schoolbooks; and shortfalls of teaching and managerial skills, and of teacher training. Underlying these proximate causes are shortfalls in the effectiveness with which the human, financial, and physical resources available for educating children are used effectively. This leads to a consideration of governance, and its political determinants.

A burgeoning literature, synthesized by Kingdon et al. (2014) and Hickey and Hossain (2018), identifies a multiplicity of distinct political explanations for lagging quality. These include:

- Incentives of teachers (and teachers' unions) which are not necessarily consistent with the goal of enhancing quality.[1]
- The mediating role of political and bureaucratic institutions, which can undercut the incentives for politicians and public officials to give priority to improving educational quality.[2] One especially relevant political mechanism comprises the use of patronage to sustain political support; this generates strong incentives to expand access, hire more teachers, and build more buildings—but weak incentives to confront inefficiencies within the system.[3]
- Relatively limited demand for skills emanating from employers and the labour market, especially in low-income countries.[4]
- Limitations in the ability of parents to effectively demand quality education.

This proliferation of political explanations is a mixed blessing. As Kingdon et al. (2014: 46–7) put it:

> The literature on the political economy of education is under-developed in geographic scope, robustness of methods utilized, and theoretical richness ... The array of theoretical frameworks developed since the emergence of the 'new institutionalism' of the 1980s has not been well utilized ... Future work needs to develop more nuanced political theories about change and particularly about how alternative structural, historical and institutional conditions determine varied possibilities and constraints.

The need is thus not for more studies which show in general terms that 'politics matters' for educational outcomes, but rather for in-depth work that delineates some specific causal mechanisms through which specific political drivers exert

[1] See, for example, Béteille (2009), Grindle (2004), Hoxby (1996), and Kingdon and Muzammil (2003, 2009).

[2] This is a central theme of the present study, with multiple references throughout this volume. Important contributions from different perspectives than that adopted here include Kosack (2012).

[3] See Grindle (2004), Kingdon et al. (2014), Pritchett (2013), Sharma (2009), and World Bank (2018)—plus additional discussion later in this chapter and elsewhere in this book.

[4] Hickey and Hossain (2018) review this literature. Key contributions include Busemeyer (2014) and Gift and Wibbels (2014).

their influence—and how better insight into these drivers can support better informed and more effective policymaking and implementation.

This book aims to advance the state of the art of political analyses of education policymaking and implementation by exploring in depth a specific policy-related question: What should be the balance between hierarchical and horizontal institutional arrangements for the public provision of basic education? The analysis uses the 'new institutionalism' (defined later in this chapter) as a key theoretical basis, is anchored empirically in a single country and, within that on the public provision of basic education. Choosing South Africa as the case study country anchors the more abstract and academic reflections on governance in a setting, and a sector, where achieving real gains is of vital concern.

Though the focus of the book is narrow, its goals are ambitious. A first goal is to contribute, academically and practically, to the crucial, ongoing challenge of improving educational outcomes in South Africa. A second is to use the South African case to contribute from a fresh perspective to the global literature on some aspects of education sector governance. A third goal is to contribute more broadly from a political and institutional perspective to the analysis of public bureaucracies, and of participatory approaches to service provision. A fourth goal is to illustrate how research approaches which put politics and institutions at centre stage can be applied at a micro level in a way which sheds light on specific practical challenges of policymaking and implementation.

1.2 Horizontal versus Hierarchical Governance

Schools can come in many forms: public schools, private schools, religious schools, secular schools; and hybrids that combine the above: charter schools, not-for-profit schools run by private foundations, voucher-financed schools.[5] The research presented in this book focuses on public schools—that is, schools financed by the public sector, and operated under public auspices. In most countries, public schools remain the predominant mode for the provision of education (including in South Africa where, as of 2015, close to 95 per cent of schoolchildren were in public schools).

In discussion of public school systems, a major controversy worldwide concerns the appropriate balance between hierarchical (top-down, bureaucratic)

[5] Pritchett (2013) is a strong (implicit) advocate of these more market-like options. Ravitch (2010, 2013) offers a more chastened picture—as a former advocate sobered by the many unintended consequences of the American school reform movement. Russakoff (2015) provides an extraordinarily rich depiction of the uphill, contentious struggle to implement a hybrid agenda of school reform from 2010–13 in Newark, NJ, USA.

governance, and more 'horizontal' approaches, which delegate significant resources and responsibility to internal and community stakeholders at the school-level. There are (at least) two distinct variants to this controversy. One question, which is *not* a focus of this book, concerns where bureaucratic control should be located—nationally, subnationally, or at local government level. Here the focus is on the related but different question of the extent to which governance responsibility should be assigned to the school-level itself.

Building on the experience of some countries with strong and effective centralized systems of education (e.g. France, Russia, Japan), some practitioners argue that education should be tightly managed hierarchically—with strong, top-down control of recruitment, promotion, curriculum and the content (almost to the level of individual lessons) of classroom-level instruction. But others argue for greater flexibility at the school level, allowing for quick identification of localized problems, and development of appropriate context-specific solutions (Pritchett, 2013; Sayed, 2002; Lauglo, McLean, and Bray, 1985; Prawda, 1993; Alexander, 2000).

Certainly, a better performing public hierarchy is more desirable than a weakly performing one: The allocation of scarce public funds across the system, the assignment of personnel to the places where they are most needed, building the capabilities of the teachers and other employees who work within the system, monitoring and managing the results achieved by staff, the construction and management of infrastructure, and the provision of furniture, textbooks, and other teaching materials are quintessentially bureaucratic tasks. A school system will surely work better when they are done well than when they are done badly.

What determines whether or not a bureaucracy works well or works badly? Insofar as a bureaucracy works well, might more governance flexibility at the school-level nonetheless be a useful complement, adding to the overall effectiveness of the system? And insofar as the bureaucracy works badly, can school-level governance be at least a partial substitute, sustaining at least some performance-orientation? As will become evident, the answers to each of these questions depends in important part on context.

1.2.1 *Bureaucracies are Embedded in Politics*

Since at least the 1980s, discourse on the performance of public bureaucracies has been predominantly managerialist in orientation. The result, in education and more broadly, was a worldwide wave of reforms (including in South Africa) under the rubric of the 'New Public Management'. But, as Pollitt and Bouckaert (2000), World Bank (2004), Grindle (2013), Levy (2014), and Yanguas (2017) explore in depth, this managerial framing ignores the ways in which bureaucracies are embedded in politics.

The World Bank's (2004) *World Development Report* framed the relationship between politics and bureaucracy as a 'long route' of accountability—a hierarchical chain linking citizens (as principals) to politicians, politicians (as principals) to policymakers, and policymakers (as principals) to the bureaucracy. The long route of accountability is dauntingly complex. For the system to work, each of the links in the chain needs to be robust; such robustness can be achieved only under very distinctive political conditions.

The interface between politics and bureaucracy can undercut the efficacy of the long route of accountability in at least three ways. First, political principals set the goals which bureaucracies should pursue—and politicians are more successful in some settings than in others in reconciling their multiple competing interests and objectives in ways that provide clarity of purpose to public officials (Wilson, 1989). Second, political principals (plus other arm's-length check and balance institutions) are charged with the task of overseeing bureaucracies, and holding them accountable for performance—and, again, there is substantial variation across settings in the extent to which they take on this responsibility. Third, and of particular relevance to the education sector, the ways in which political leaders cultivate and sustain political support may run counter to the kinds of actions needed to improve educational outcomes.

Consider patronage and clientelism—the use by political leaders of public resources and positions as mechanisms for rewarding friends, punishing opponents and, more broadly, sustaining political support. One key consequence of a patronage orientation is to give strong support to expansion of access to education (with all of its associated promises to voters, new jobs in the sector, and new procurement contracts)—but in practice to give low priority to improving quality (for which gains become evident only over the longer term, with many of the required measures likely to meet resistance, insofar as they involve holding public employees and others to account).

Numerous analyses of the politics of education have highlighted how patronage and clientelism shape sectoral decision-making. Grindle (2004) details the incestuous links between teachers' unions and the education bureaucracy in a half-dozen Latin American countries. Kingdon et al. (2014) summarize the voluminous literature on the ways in which patronage-related political considerations have shaped decision-making in education, including Sharma's (2009) analysis of discretionary and patronage-based appointment and transfer processes in India; Kingdon and Muzammil (2003, 2009) and Kingdon and Teal's (2010) exploration of the role of teachers and teachers' unions in shaping education policymaking and implementation in that country; and also (in broader, comparative empirical studies) Hoxby (1996) and Beteille (2009).

Chapters 3–7 of this study analyse comparatively how the political-bureaucratic interface works, and what its effects are on performance in South Africa's education sector, at the national level (Chapter 3) and in South Africa's Western Cape and Eastern Cape provinces (Chapters 4–7). The two provinces operate under similar formal rules, and have similar levels of access to fiscal resources—but differ widely from one another in their modes of operation, their political contexts, and their performance. Building on our analysis of how provincial political dynamics influence the bureaucracy, we explore also what kinds of policy approaches might improve educational outcomes, even in difficult contexts.

1.2.2 *Horizontal Governance—its Potential and Limitations*

Turning to horizontal governance, Bruns, Filmer, and Patrinos (2011) and Westhorp et al. (2014) review the literature on the potential and limitations of a variety of horizontal governance mechanisms. Bruns et al. focus on the results of methodologically rigorous randomized control trials and ex-post impact evaluations of bottom-up, transparency and participation initiatives to strengthen bottom-up accountability. They report a mixed picture. Studies show gains from participatory initiatives in El Salvador, some parts of India, Kenya and Pakistan, but multiple studies (including some conducted in India) show no positive effect. Pritchett (2013) takes a more positive view, with a detailed depiction of how a networked education ecosystem might provide an improved platform for performance.

What might be some reasons for this uneven pattern? In exploring this question, it is useful to begin by laying out some theoretical arguments as to how horizontal governance—delegation of significant authority and thus flexibility to internal and community stakeholders at the school level—might improve educational outcomes. One set of arguments is intrinsic to the educational task—and thus potentially applies both in settings where the bureaucracy works well, and in settings where it works less well. The second is more directly relevant to settings where the bureaucracy works less well.

To begin with the intrinsic arguments, Wilson (1989), Israel (1987), and World Bank (2004) distinguish among sectors according to the heterogeneity and monitorability of their production activities. Top-down hierarchical governance, they argue, is most effective where production can be standardized, and where the monitorability of outputs and/or outcomes is straightforward. By contrast, where production is more heterogeneous, and outputs/outcomes are less readily monitorable, more flexibility needs to be accorded to front-line production units, with a correspondingly greater role for horizontal ('principal-principal'/peer-to-peer) governance arrangements.

In sectors where provision cannot be standardized, delegation of authority is hypothesized to improve performance in three distinct ways:

- By creating scope to customize provision in ways which are responsive to the local context. (In the context of education, this concerns questions of approaches to pedagogy, and adaptation of curriculum—questions which, it is important to note, fall wholly outside the scope of the present study.[6])
- By improving motivation—with the 'zone of autonomy' at the service provision front-line hypothesized to provide the opportunity for internal leaders to motivate their teams effectively, including by fostering an environment of continuing learning on the part of staff as well as students. This is a classic argument for improving the effectiveness of 'street-level' bureaucracies (including schools) which operate at a distance from organizational hierarchies (Wilson, 1989; Lipsky, 2010; Carpenter, 2001).
- By creating scope for the utilization of local-level information of a kind to which higher-level hierarchical authorities lack access—and thereby enhancing processes for the selection of good quality staff and leaders, and the efficacy of efforts to hold staff and leaders accountable for their performance. Sah and Stiglitz (1986), North (1990), and Aghion and Tirole (1997) explore the informational dimensions of organizational governance and decentralization in general terms.

Note that, although all three of the above propositions potentially are relevant regardless of whether or not hierarchies perform well, a necessary condition for their efficacy is that the rules of the game set by higher levels provide some local-level autonomy.

The more context-specific argument highlights the role that horizontal governance potentially might play as a partial institutional substitute for relatively weak bureaucracies—enabling some schools to operate as relative 'islands of effectiveness' within a broader sea of dysfunction. The key channel here is the empowerment of developmentally oriented local stakeholders (including professionally committed teaching staff) to hold school staff accountable for making their best effort. As Levy (2014) explores, a necessary condition for 'empowerment' to be effective as a means of strengthening accountability is that developmentally oriented stakeholders indeed have sufficient influence to be able to 'trump' predatory actors seeking to capture school-level resources (teaching and administrative positions, contracts, other discretionary resources) for private purposes.

[6] For a sampling of the voluminous literature on the impact of pedagogical approaches on educational outcomes, see Snilstveit et al. (2016).

The question as to whether parents and other school-level stakeholders have the potential to hold schools accountable for performance has been the subject of much controversy. Based on their review of the literature, Kingdon et al. (2014) are sceptical: they report multiple studies which show that local power relations disempower poor parents in ways that inhibit them from having an impact—from Indonesia (Chen, 2011), to Ghana (Essuman and Akyeampong, 2011), to Honduras and Guatemala (Altschuler, 2013) and India (Rawal and Kingdon, 2010). A quote from Kingdon et al. (2014: 2) provides a flavour of the criticism:

> while decentralization [to school-level] is a widely advocated reform, many of its supposed benefits do not accrue in practice because in poor rural areas the local elite closes up the spaces for wider community representation and participation in school affairs.

But other studies—undertaken in El Salvador (Jimenez and Sawada, 1999, 2003), India (Pandey, Goyal, and Sundararaman, 2011), Ghana (ESID, 2016), and Indonesia (Pradhan et al., 2014)—report a more positive impact. The mixed evidence lends itself to the interpretation that the relative power of 'developmental' and 'predatory' actors at the local level is indeed key to the effectiveness of horizontal governance. Chapters 8 and 9 of this book explore in detail how these school-level interactions play out in practice in the two South African provinces.

1.3 South Africa as a Case Study

Over the past three decades, one response in many countries to weaknesses in the performance of education bureaucracies has been to try and shift responsibility for delivering (public) education from national to subnational and school levels.[7] As Grindle (2004) details for Latin America, the reform of historically centralized systems often has been difficult to achieve politically; reforms have been scattershot and uneven.

In contrast to Latin America, the 1996 South Africa Schools Act (promulgated two years after the advent of democracy, at a moment of unusual political cohesion) put in place a carefully designed set of institutional arrangements which located very substantial responsibility for delivering basic education at the provincial level, and gave quite broad authority,

[7] It is important to underscore that this volume does not take any normative position as to what patterns of inter-governmental (de-)centralization are preferred. The analytical and normative preoccupation of this chapter concern the balance between hierarchical and horizontal patterns of governance vis-à-vis authority at the level of schools.

including for recruitment, to school governing bodies in which parents comprised a majority. (Chapter 2 reviews in detail the trajectory of education sector reform in South Africa.) This combination of strong delegation to provincial and school levels, and large differences in provincial-level political dynamics creates an ideal opportunity for exploring comparatively the influence of politics on bureaucratic performance—and on the relative efficacy of hierarchical and horizontal governance in public schools.

Taking a long-run view, transforming the system of education is one of the most crucial tasks confronting South Africa's democracy. Notwithstanding the democratic 'miracle' of 1994, the legacy of apartheid left the country saddled with among the highest levels of inequality in the world. The longer-term sustainability of democracy depends on moving the economy in a more inclusive direction—and this, in turn, depends on a transformation of basic education from a system which (as Chapter 2 details) was geared to the reproduction of subservience on the part of the majority of the country's population, to one that builds skills, citizenship, and enhanced economic prospects for all.

As a middle-income country with a clear commitment to redirect policy in a pro-poor direction, South Africa had available relatively abundant fiscal resources for improving education. The country's legacy of economic, social, and political dualism meant that (alongside a dysfunctional educational system for the majority) it also had in place the knowledge, institutions, and track record of a relatively high-performing public education system—albeit one that historically had been targeted only towards elites). And the country's sophisticated bureaucracy seemingly had the capability to effectively use the available money and capacity to address the challenge of providing a quality education for all.

By the early 1990s, South Africa already had achieved near universal enrolment of the relevant age cohort in primary education. The secondary school enrolment rate rose from 51 per cent in 1985 to 91 per cent by 2007. However, a consequence of South Africa's apartheid legacy was that only a very small minority of the country's students have had access to a quality education. Overall, South African students scored lowest among twenty-six low-middle and middle-income countries for which Pritchett (2013) reports comparable data from international standardized tests.

As Chapter 2 details, in the years immediately following its first democratic election in 1994, South Africa embarked on an extraordinarily far-reaching transformation of the governance, fiscal, and curricular arrangements of its education system. Yet for all that the new arrangements enabled the country to distance itself from the unequal arrangements inherited from apartheid, it has proved extraordinarily difficult to reverse the inequality in educational outcomes. Some recent efforts to identify the causes of these continuing difficulties have identified governance as a key contributory factor.[8] A major research project to identify binding constraints, synthesized in Van den Berg, Spaull, Wills, Gustafsson, and Kotze (2016), concludes that the root causes of South Africa's low educational outcomes generally fall into one of two categories: 'a lack of accountability (including weak institutional functionality and undue union influence), and a lack of capacity (including weak teacher knowledge and pedagogical skill, wasted learning time and insufficient opportunity to learn'). Gustafsson and Taylor (2016), using an innovative empirical strategy, quantify the impact on performance of differences in implementation capacity at the provincial level. Zengele (2013) hones in on how teachers' unions influence recruitment in ways which are inconsistent with a commitment to quality. This study complements these findings by drilling down into some specific mechanisms of policymaking, implementation by the bureaucracy, and school-level governance, and their political influences.

Three sets of features of the institutional arrangements put in place by the 1996 South Africa Schools Act are especially relevant for the present research. First, responsibility for policymaking, for resourcing the system, and for setting the overall regulatory framework was retained at the national level. The latter included the negotiation and promulgation of an elaborate system for performance management. How politics shaped the eventual form of this system is the subject of Chapter 3.

Second, responsibility for implementation was delegated to the country's nine provinces, which differed substantially from one another both politically and institutionally. This makes for a natural experiment, where (with policy, regulation, and financing automatically controlled for) the focus can be on the impact of politics and institutions on the operation of the provincial education bureaucracies responsible for policy implementation. Differences in politics and institutions are especially stark between the Western Cape and Eastern Cape provinces, providing a strong platform for comparative analysis of the interactions between politics, institutions, and how bureaucracies operate—and the effect on educational outcomes. Chapters 4 and 5 explore in detail why each of the two provinces' bureaucracies perform the way they do; Chapter 6 examines econometrically the effect of differential bureaucratic performance on educational outcomes; Chapter 7 builds on the case studies to explore comparatively and conceptually how background political and institutional contexts shape the performance of public bureaucracies.

Third, the new institutional arrangements assigned substantial school-level responsibilities (including the recruitment of the school principal and senior teachers) to school governing bodies (SGBs) in which parents are required to

[8] See other chapters in this volume for many references in addition to those highlighted here.

be in the majority. This provides an excellent opportunity for exploring the interactions between education hierarchies, and more 'horizontal' school-level governance arrangements in the divergent Western Cape and Eastern Cape contexts—with the research in both provinces focusing on lower-income communities with limited experience of school-level governance during the apartheid era. Chapters 8 and 9 use in-depth case studies to explore school-level governance dynamics, with a particular focus on how the interplay between developmental and predatory stakeholders affects performance. Integrating the school-level findings and the analysis of educational bureaucracies, Chapter 10 lays out an overarching 'all for education' approach to working at scale, so that the benefits of quality education can be made available to all of South Africa's citizens.

1.4 Analytical Framework

This section lays out the framework used in this book to analyse the relationship between context and the governance of public education—including (but not only) the relative merits of hierarchical and horizontal approaches to governance. The framework builds on an ongoing movement in the development discourse over the past decade—away from technocratic visions of 'best practice', and towards a focus on more 'good fit' approaches to policy-making and implementation.

One task for 'good fit' analysis is to delineate a practical framework for distinguishing among different contexts. There is a burgeoning literature which explores how political context affects educational outcomes. One set of contributions (Ansell, 2008; Bourguignon and Verdier, 2005; Hicken and Simmons, 2008; Stasavage, 2005) focuses on regime type, specifically whether democratic or authoritarian setting lead to better educational outcomes.

Recent work has moved beyond 'regime type' to explore more broadly how a variety of different types of country-level 'political settlements' influence development policymaking, implementation, and outcomes. Contributions include Khan's (2010) pioneering analysis, and North, Wallis, and Weingast's (NWW) (2009) conceptualization of 'limited access orders'. Building on these efforts, Levy (2014) lays out a typology of country-level political settlements, distinguishing between them according to whether their configuration of political power is dominant or competitive, and whether the institutional rules of the game are personalized or impersonal. This two-fold distinction generates four 'ideal types' of political settlement:

- Dominant-personalized—where elite cohesion is high, and power is exercised top-down by the leadership, with limited constraint.

- Dominant with rule-by-law—where elite cohesion is high, and power is top-down, but anchored in rules which institutionalize how it is to be exercised.
- Personalized competitive (or competitive clientelist)—where elite cohesion is low, the settlement revolves around agreement that political power should change hands on an electorally competitive basis, but the rules of the game are personalized.
- Competitive with rule-of-law—where politics is competitive, and impersonal rules prevail.

In a companion volume to this one (also sponsored by the Effective States and Inclusive Development research programme), Hickey and Hossain (2018) and co-authors use this typology for a comparative cross-country analysis of the politics of education quality in Bangladesh, Cambodia, Ghana, Rwanda, and Uganda, plus South Africa.[9] This book extends the typology 'vertically'—it explores how institutional and political contexts shape development policy-making and implementation at each of a variety of distinctive levels.[10]

Figure 1.1 lays out the multi-level framework. As the figure suggests, each level is nested within a set of incentives and constraints shaped in part by the higher level; in turn, each level shapes, in part, the incentives and constraints which prevail at lower levels. At the peak level is the country's national political context—the national political settlement, the national-level

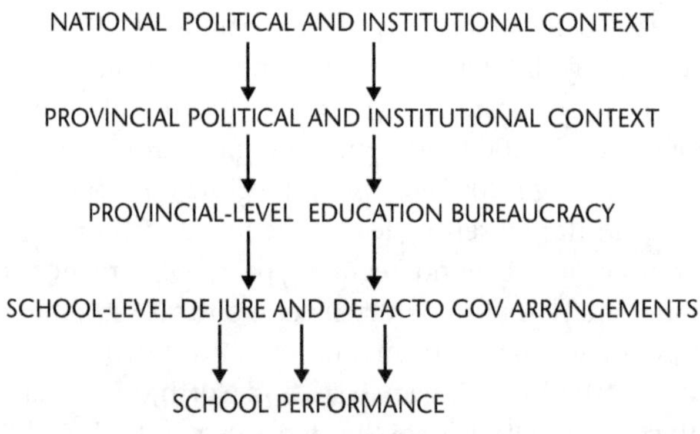

Figure 1.1. The governance of education—a multi-level framework

[9] See also Wales, Magee, and Nicolai (2016) for a comparative review of the results of eight country studies conducted by the Overseas Development Institute which explore the relationship between different types of 'political settlement' and educational outcomes.

[10] Hickey and Sen (2017) adopt a similar approach, introducing a distinction between 'political settlement' and 'policy domain' levels.

institutional arrangements for the education sector derived from that settlement, and national-level policies for the education sector. At the next level down is the subnational context, shaped partly by the national level, and partly by distinctive, provincial-level drivers. The provincial-level political context in turn affects the operation of provincial education bureaucracies. All of this cascades down to the de jure and de facto school-level governance arrangements, and thence to educational outcomes.

A multi-level framework along these lines provides a platform for giving practical content to the idea of 'good fit'. 'Good fit', Levy and Walton (2013) hypothesize, can be framed in terms of the alignment between the political and institutional patterns which prevail at a higher level, and the patterns which prevail at levels beneath that:

- Where the higher- and lower-level configurations are aligned, we can say we have a 'good fit'—and thus potentially the best feasible outcome.
- Where they are misaligned, we can say we have a 'poor fit'—there exists the possibility of improving the development outcome by reshaping lower-level institutional arrangements and policy choices to align better with the political and institutional arrangements which prevail at higher levels.

Based on this formulation, the relative merits of hierarchical and horizontal governance of schools are hypothesized to depend in important part on the specific patterns of incentive and constraint which cascade down from higher levels to the levels beneath them.

The ways in which the two core analytical concepts—institutions and politics—are used to distinguish among contexts varies as one moves from the over-arching country-level political settlement to lower levels. It is thus helpful to spell out carefully each of the core concepts, and the relationships between them.

Institutions can be defined colloquially as 'the rules of the game'. North (1990) provides a more formal definition of institutions as 'humanly-devised constraints which govern human interaction'. He distinguishes between the institutional rules of the game on the one hand, and the players of the game ('organizations' or 'stakeholders') on the other. Building on this distinction, 'politics' is defined here as comprising the stakeholders involved in decision-making, their interactions with one another, and their relative power.

As North (1990), North, Wallis, and Weingast (2009), Ostrom (2005), and Acemoglu and Robinson (2006) explore theoretically, governance arrangements and stakeholder dynamics are interdependent: the rules of the game set the parameters for the interactions among stakeholders; stakeholders, in turn, work to try and (re-)shape the rules of the game to their advantage.

As Levy (2015) explores, in analysing the institutional arrangements for public governance, two sets of distinctions are key:

- The distinction between hierarchical and more horizontal, peer-to-peer modes of structuring authority—with the former organized around vertical relationships between 'principals' and 'agents', and the latter organized around negotiated understandings among multiple principals, who are more or less equal in power.[11]
- The distinction between impersonal and personalized rules, monitoring and enforcement mechanisms—with the former applied equally, by an impartial body, to all who have standing, and the latter structured around 'deals' among influential actors.

Table 1.1 combines the latter two distinctions, giving us four distinct sets of 'ideal type' institutional arrangements for governing public policymaking and implementation:

- The top-right cell delineates the classic impersonal and hierarchical mode of decision-making and implementation.
- The top-left cell delineates a mode of decision-making and implementation which also is hierarchical, and thus governed via nested principal–agent relationships, but is one where compliance on the part of agents follows from the personalized authority of the leadership, rather than a system of rules.
- The bottom-right cell comprises a pattern where multiple stakeholders, each with significant independent authority, agree on how they will work together, and codify these agreements in formal, enforceable rules.
- In the bottom-left cell neither formal rules nor a well-defined hierarchy of authority is in place. Stakeholders may or may not reach agreement as to whether and how to co-operate. Insofar as they do, such agreements are dependent on the shared understandings of the specific parties involved.

In practice, any specific governance arrangement is likely to be a hybrid combination of the four ideal types defined by the cells, with the relative

Table 1.1. A Public Governance Typology

Hierarchical	(i)	(ii)
Negotiated	(iii)	(iv)
	Personalized	Impersonal

[11] For analysis of horizontal governance arrangements, see Ostrom (1990, 2005).

weight varying from setting to setting. (A useful heuristic way of describing these weights, applied throughout this volume, is to allocate 100 points across the four cells.)

The middle column of Table 1.2 summarizes the explanatory variables used to analyse how the institutional context influences South Africa's educational outcomes at each of the multiple levels considered in this book. As the table signals:

- At the national level, higher-level institutions enter in two distinct ways:
  - The overarching 1994 political settlement provided an enabling framework for new sectoral governance and budgetary arrangements, arrangements which were responsive to central concerns of both black and white South Africans vis-à-vis public education (see Chapter 2 for details).
  - The Education Labour Relations Council (ELRC) provides a formal arena for government and organized labour to deliberate and reach agreement on national-level policies for managing the performance of education bureaucracies (see Chapter 3).
- At the provincial level (explored in depth in Chapters 4–7), higher-level (and inherited) institutional arrangements—including those which govern electoral competition and the internal operation of political parties—account for the quality of education bureaucracies.
- At the school level (the focus of analysis in Chapters 8–10), both higher-level and concurrent institutional arrangements account for the observed educational outcomes.

The right-hand column of Table 1.2 directs attention to some key explanatory variables used to analyze how, at each level, 'politics'—stakeholders, their interactions with one another, and their relative power—influences South Africa's educational outcomes. Following North, Wallis, and Weingast (2009) and Khan (2010), it is useful to distinguish between two broad types of stakeholder interactions: interactions among elites, and the ways in which non-elites are incorporated politically.

Consider, first, interactions among elites. Two distinct types of inter-elite interactions are explored in this book's case studies:

- interactions within a political party (governing or otherwise)—illustrated by the strategic interplay among key stakeholders under the African National Congress's governing umbrella at both the national level (Chapter 3) and within the Eastern Cape (Chapter 5).
- electoral contestation between political parties, which emerges in Chapters 4 and 7 as key to understanding political-bureaucratic interactions in the Western Cape.

Table 1.2. How Context Influences Outcomes—A Multi-Level Analysis

Outcome to be explained	Explanatory variables	
	Institutions *('rules of the game')*	Politics *(stakeholders and power)*
National-level (i): *New education sector budgetary & governance arrangements*	*Higher-level contextual variables:* Derived from inclusive political settlement	
National-level (ii): *Quality of performance-based management*	*Higher- and concurrent-level variables:* Formal bargaining arrangements of ELRC	Interactions among key stakeholders under ANC umbrella
Provincial-level: *Quality of education bureaucracies(chapters 4-7)*	*Higher-level contextual variables* (i) Extent of electoral competition (ii) Configuration of power within governing political party (iii) Quality of inherited bureaucratic institutions	(iv) Social composition of non-elite groups
School-level: *School-level educational outcomes*	*Higher-level contextual variables:* (i) Quality of provincial education bureaucracy (ii) De jure arrangements for school-level governance	(iii) de facto interactions with officials from department of education with union officials, and with other political stakeholders
	Concurrent level variables (iv) De facto school-level governance arrangements	(v) Interactions between principal, teachers, school governing body, and other external stakeholders

Turning to the incorporation of non-elites, a first question concerns the mechanisms of incorporation. Especially relevant here is the distinction between broad-based, 'programmatic' approaches, centred around the provision of services to citizens, and more clientelistic modes of incorporation. (In South Africa a third approach, the repression of non-elite stakeholders, has an especially long and sordid history.) Chapters 4–7 explore in depth the divergent mechanisms through which non-elites are incorporated in the two case study provinces.

A second question concerns which non-elite actors are (analytically) relevant. Building on a definition suggested by Kelsall and vom Hau (2017), the relevant non-elite groups can be delineated in terms of the 'social composition', that is:

> all those [elite and non-elite] groups that [can threaten the authority of the political leadership relevant to the problem at hand].[12] The social [composition]

[12] This formulation is broader than Kelsall and vom Hau's framing which focused narrowly on the social *'foundation'* (rather than 'composition') of a political *settlement* (rather than of 'contexts'

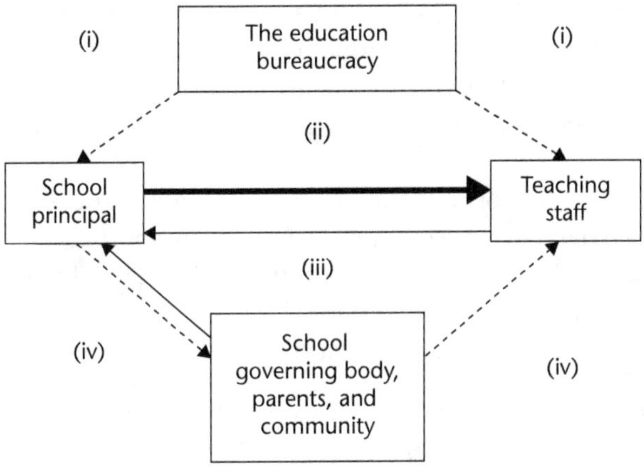

Figure 1.2. Governance interactions

> influences... whether or not incumbent leaders will pursue policies intended to benefit broad or narrow segments of the population. Other things being equal, the broader the social composition, the more inclusive the development outcomes.

Chapter 7 explores how the divergent social composition of non-elite groups in the Western Cape and Eastern Cape influenced the operation of their public bureaucracies, and thus educational outcomes.

One final pattern of stakeholder interaction (identified in the bottom part of Table 1.2) warrants attention—stakeholder interactions at the school level. Figure 1.2 details schematically five distinct causal mechanisms through which a variety of stakeholders potentially can influence school-level governance arrangements, and thereby performance:

- *Causal mechanism (i)*—The influence of hierarchical governance by the education bureaucracy.

As per the earlier discussion, this could have a variety of divergent consequences: it potentially could support efforts to improve educational outcomes; it could be a driver of patronage; or (insofar as the bureaucracy is rendered ineffective by broader political influences) it could be largely without influence.

- *Causal mechanisms (ii) and (iii)*—between the school principal and the school's teaching staff.

more broadly). In Kelsall and vom Hau's variant of political settlement analysis, the relevant social foundation comprises those groups which 'have the power to overturn the settlement, and which are not repressed or resisted by government.'

Causal mechanism (ii) is consistent with a central finding of empirical research on the determinants of school performance—namely that the quality of school leadership is an important proximate explanatory variable (Hallinger and Heck, 1996; Leithwood, Patten, and Jantzi, 2010). As per Figure 1.2, we broaden this hypothesis somewhat by considering also the possibility of a two-way relationship, with the organizational culture among the school's teacher cadre having a (relatively weaker) causal effect on the approach to management of the school principal (Wimpelberg in Stringfield, 1993; Taylor et al., 2013; Leithwood, Harris, and Hopkins, 2008).

Turning to causal mechanisms (iv) and (v), we have:

- *Causal mechanism (iv)*—The role of bottom-up governance—specifically the extent to which SGBs, with the support of parents and the local community more broadly, are able to provide offsetting governance support and oversight.
- *Causal mechanism (v)*—Although not included explicitly in Figure 1.1, the school-level research also probed for the influence on school-level governance of the teachers' unions (SADTU and NAPTOSA) and political parties.

As Chapters 8–10 detail, how the above five causal mechanisms play out varies both across provinces, among schools within each province, and within schools over time. School-level interactions are shaped in the short-to-medium-term by the direction provided by school principals—and, over the longer-term, by the local power dynamics between developmental and predatory stakeholders, and their influence on the de facto governance arrangements within schools. More broadly, the case studies suggest that the school-level outcomes are not foreordained by local context, but are contingent and cumulative—with individual 'agency' by stakeholders playing a significant role.

1.5 A Preview of the Research Findings

The chapters which follow explore in depth the research questions introduced in section 1.2, using the analytical approach laid out in section 1.4. Chapters 7 and 10 synthesize the findings vis-à-vis, respectively, hierarchical and horizontal governance. Major findings include:

- First, *the policies promulgated and the observed patterns of bureaucratic implementation are shaped by distinctive political and institutional drivers—with the causal drivers carefully documented in the research.* As Chapter 3 details, national-level political and institutional drivers account for the limitations of the performance management arrangements negotiated for the education sector. At provincial level, Chapters 4–7 underscore the stark differences between the Western and Eastern Cape educational bureaucracies in the quality of management—and the roots of these differences in the starkly divergent background political contexts of the two provinces.

- Second (and unsurprisingly), *a well-functioning bureaucracy emerges as a valuable asset.* As Chapters 4 and 5 detail, the Western Cape does well (but the Eastern Cape poorly) the core bureaucratic tasks of managing resources; assigning personnel to where they are most needed; monitoring and managing on the basis of performance. Econometric analysis in Chapter 6 reinforces the conclusion that differences in bureaucratic performance, rather than demographic or resource differences, account for the Western Cape's superior educational outcomes relative to other South African provinces. But,
- Third, *a well-functioning bureaucracy does not provide a sufficient governance platform for achieving good educational outcomes*. The Western Cape school-level case studies in Chapter 8 show how a combination of strong, top-down bureaucracy and weak horizontal governance can result in 'isomorphic mimicry'—in which a school seemingly is compliant with formal processes, but in practice is locked into a low-level equilibrium of mediocrity. The comparative econometric analysis in Chapter 6 confirms that, notwithstanding its strong top-down management (and significant resource advantages), the Western Cape school system underperforms that of Kenya—even after socio-economic differences and teacher skills and experience are accounted for. Finally,
- Fourth, *horizontal governance emerges as a partial institutional substitute for hierarchical weakness*. The econometric analysis in Chapter 7 shows a strong, significant positive effect on educational outcomes of 'parental contribution to building construction and maintenance' (high in the Eastern Cape relative to the Western Cape). The Eastern Cape school-level case studies in Chapter 9 detail how pro-active engagement on the part of school governing bodies and parents helped sustain and turn around school-level. But participation is no panacea; the case studies also uncover instances of capture by predatory interests.

As these findings underscore, politics, institutional arrangements, management systems, and stakeholder dynamics are interdependent. There are thus multiple governance constraints to education sector reform. There also are multiple potential governance entry points (both hierarchical and horizontal) for improving educational outcomes—with the efficacy of any of them depending as much on how politics and power interact within specific contexts as on the technocratic expertise of reformers.

Given the urgency of the task of improving educational outcomes, a pre-occupation with institutional and political complexity might, to some, seem unnecessary. Indeed, the temptation can be strong to argue that getting better results is simply a matter of 'political will'. However, as the global experience of efforts at education sector reform underscore, a 'just do it' approach is misguided. All too often, the result can be confrontation, with a high likelihood of negative, unintended consequences. Effective reform requires skilful engagement with stubborn governance realities.

Building on the empirical findings laid out in Chapters 2–9, the book's final chapter lays out an incremental and cumulative strategy for engaging these realities—an 'all for education' approach to reform. The approach combines two complementary aspects of change. One aspect comprises practical initiatives which aim to strengthen governance by working around, and engaging constructively with, reform constraints. The second aspect comprises a broader reframing of the ideas surrounding how the provision of education and other public services might be improved. Especially relevant here is the call for 'active citizenship' in South Africa's 2012 National Development Plan:

> Active citizenship requires inspirational leadership at all levels of society . . . Leadership does not refer to one person, or even a tight collective of people. It applies in every aspect of life . . . To build an inclusive nation the country needs to find ways to promote a positive cycle, where an effective state, inspirational leadership across all levels of society, and active citizens reinforce and strengthen each other. (The Presidency, 2012)

If South Africa were actually to embrace active citizenship as the path to improving outcomes, the consequences for the education system could be far-reaching. In many schools an activated citizenry could shift the balance decisively between developmental and predatory actors in favour of the former. Within the bureaucracy, new momentum could emerge for learning-oriented engagement, surfacing the limits of pre-occupations with 'process compliance' for its own sake. Teacher unions might increasingly embrace a vision of teaching as a profession, as a calling, and move decisively away from a narrow pre-occupation with the rights of teachers as employees. New possibilities would arise for adapting national policies in ways that enhance a focus on educational outcomes. Civil society activism might more systematically target those aspects of education sector governance which have strong impacts on learning. A top-down vision of 'education for all' is insufficient to meet the frontier challenge of improving outcomes. What now is called for is 'all for education'.

References

Acemoglu, D. and Robinson, J. A. (2006) *Economic Origins of Dictatorship and Democracy*. New York: Cambridge University Press.

Aghion, P. and Tirole, J. (1997) 'Formal and real authority in organizations', *Journal of Political Economy* 105, 1–29.

Alexander, R. (2000) *Culture and Pedagogy: International Comparisons in Primary Education*. Oxford: Blackwell.

Altschuler, D. (2013) 'How patronage politics undermines parental participation and accountability: community-managed schools in Honduras and Guatemala', *Comparative Education Review* 57(1), 117–44.

Ansell, B. W. (2008) 'Traders, teachers, and tyrants: democracy, globalization, and public investment in education', *International Organization* 62(2), 289–322.

Béteille, T. (2009) 'Absenteeism, transfers and patronage: the political economy of teacher labor markets in India'. Dissertation, Stanford University, California.

Bourguignon, F. and Verdier, T. (2005) 'The political economy of education and development in an open economy', *Review of International Economics* 13(3), 529–48.

Bruns, B., Filmer, D., and Patrinos, H. (2011) *Making Schools Work: New Evidence on Accountability Reforms*. Washington DC: World Bank.

Busemeyer, M. R. (2014) *Skills and Inequality: Partisan Politics and the Political Economy of Education Reforms in Western Welfare States*. Cambridge: Cambridge University Press.

Carpenter, D. (2001) *The Forging of Bureaucratic Autonomy*. Princeton: Princeton University Press.

Chen, D. (2011) 'School-based management, school decision-making and educational outcomes in Indonesian primary schools', Policy Research Working Paper Series 5809. Washington DC: World Bank.

ESID (2016) 'How politics shapes the quality of education in Ghana', ESID briefing number 17, University of Manchester.

Essuman, A. and Akyeampong, K. (2011) 'Decentralization policy and practice in Ghana', *Journal of Education Policy* 26(4), 513–27.

Gift, T. and Wibbels, E. (2014) 'Reading, Writing, and the Regrettable Status of Education Research in Comparative Politics', *Annual Review of Political Science* 17(1), 291–312.

Grindle, M. (2004) *Despite the Odds: The Contentious Politics of Education Reform*. Cambridge: Harvard University Press.

Grindle, M. (2013) *Jobs for the Boys*. Cambridge: Harvard University Press.

Gustafsson, G. and Taylor, S. (2016) 'Treating schools to a new administration: Evidence from South Africa of the impact of better practices in the system-level administration of schools'. Stellenbosch Economic Working Paper Series WP No. 05/16, Stellenbosch University, Department of Economics.

Hallinger, P. and Heck, R. H. (1996) 'Reassessing the principal's contribution to school effectiveness: A review of empirical research, 1980–1995', *Educational Administration Quarterly* 32(1).

Hicken, A. and Simmons, J. W. (2008) 'The personal vote and the efficacy of education spending', *American Journal of Political Science* 52(1), 109–24.

Hickey, S. and Hossain, N. (eds) (2018) *The Politics of Education Quality in Developing Countries*. Oxford: Oxford University Press.

Hickey, S. and Sen, K. (2017) 'Politics, power and development: Identifying alternative pathways to social justice', mimeo.

Hoxby, C. (1996) 'How teachers' unions affect education production', *Quarterly Journal of Economics* 111(3), 671–718.

Israel, A. (1987) *Institutional Development: Incentives to Performance*. Washington DC: World Bank/Oxford University Press.

Jimenez and Sawada (1999) 'Do community-managed schools work? An evaluation of El Salvador's EDUCO program', *World Bank Economic Review* 13(3), 415–41.

Jimenez and Sawada (2003) 'Does community-management help keep kids in school?' Centre for International Reseach on the Japanese Economy, Discussion Paper F-236. University of Tokyo.

Khan, M. (2010) 'Political Settlements and the Governance of Growth-Enhancing Institutions.' London: mimeo.

Kelsall, T. and vom Hau, M. (2017) 'Beyond Institutions: A Political Settlements Approach to Development', paper presented at ESID research workshop on political settlements, University of Manchester.

Kingdon, G. G., Little, A., Aslam, M., Rawal, S., Moe, T., Patrinos, H., Beteille, T., Banerji, R., Parton, B., and Sharma, S. K. (2014) 'A Rigorous Review of the Political Economy of Education Systems in Developing Countries. Final'. *Education Rigorous Literature Review*.

Kingdon, G. and Muzammil, M. (2003) *The political economy of education in India*. Oxford: Oxford University Press.

Kingdon, G. and Muzammil, M. (2009) 'A political economy of education in India: the Case of Uttar Pradesh', *Oxford Development Studies* 37(2), 123–44.

Kingdon, G. and Teal, F. (2010) 'Teacher unions, teacher pay and student performance in India: A pupil fixed effects approach', *Journal of Development Economics* 91(2), 278–88.

Kosack, S. (2012) *The Education of Nations*. New York: Oxford University Press.

Leithwood, K., Harris, A., and Hopkins, D. (2008) 'Seven strong claims about successful school leadership', *School Leadership and Management* 28(1), 27–42.

Leithwood, K., Patten, S., and Jantzi, D. (2010) 'Testing a conception of how school leadership influences student learning', *Educational Administration Quarterly* 44(4), 455–7.

Levy, B. (2014) *Working with the Grain: Integrating Governance and Growth in Development Strategies*. New York: Oxford University Press.

Levy, B. (2015) 'Governance Reform: Getting the Fit Right', *Public Administration and Development* 35(4).

Levy, B. and Walton, M. (2013) 'Institutions, Incentives and Service Provision: Bringing Politics Back in', Working Paper 18, Effective States and Inclusive Development Research Centre, University of Manchester.

Lipsky, M. (2010) *Street-level Bureaucracy: Dilemmas of the Individual in Public Service*. New York: Russell Sage Foundation.

North, D. W. (1990) *Institutions, Institutional Change and Economic Performance*. New York: Cambridge University Press.

North, D. W., Wallis, J., and Weingast, B. (2009) *Violence and Social Orders*. New York: Cambridge University Press.

Ostrom, E. (1990) *Governing the Commons*. New York: Cambridge University Press.

Ostrom, E. (2005) *Understanding Institutional Diversity*. Princeton, NJ: Princeton University Press.

Pandey, P., Goyal, S., and Sundararaman, V. (2011) 'Does Information Improve School Accountability? Results of a Large Randomized Trial'. South Asia human development sector; discussion paper series no. 49. Washington DC: World Bank.

Pradhan, M., Suryadarma, D., Beatty, A., Wong, M., Gaduh, A., Alisjahbana, A., and Artha, R. P. (2014) 'Improving Educational Quality through Enhancing Community Participation: Results from a Randomized Field Experiment in Indonesia', *American Economic Journal: Applied Economics* 6(2), 105–26.

Pollitt, C. and Bouckaert, G. (2000) *Public Management Reform: A Comparative Analysis*. Oxford: Oxford University Press.

Prawda, J. (1993) 'Educational decentralization in Latin America: Lessons learned', *International Journal of Educational Development* 13(3), 253–64.

Pritchett, L. (2013) *The Rebirth of Education*. Washington DC: Center for Global Development.

Ravitch, D. (2010) *The Death and Life of the Great American School System*. New York: Basic Books.

Ravitch, D. (2013) *Reign of Error: the hoax of the privatization movement and the danger to America's Public Schools*. New York: Alfred A. Knopf.

Rawal, S. and Kingdon, G. (2010) 'Akin to my teacher: does caste, religious or gender distance between student and teacher matter? Some evidence from India', DoQSS Working Paper 10–18, Department of Quantitative Social Science Institute of Education, University of London.

Russakoff, D. (2015) *The Prize: Who's in Charge of America's Schools*. New York: Houghton Mifflin Harcourt.

Sah, R. K. and Stiglitz, J. E. (1986) 'The architecture of economic systems: Hierarchies and polyarchies', *American Economic Review* 76(4), 716–27.

Sayed, Y. (2002) 'Democratising education in a decentralised system: South African policy and practice', *Compare* 32(1), 35–46.

Sharma, R. (2009) 'The internal dynamic'. In R. Sharma and V. Ramachandran (eds), *The Elementary Education System in India*. New Delhi: Routledge.

Sniltsveit, B., Stevenson, J., Menon, R., Phillips, D., Gallagher, E., Geleen, M., Jobse, H., Schmidt, T., and Jimenez, E. (2016) *The impact of education programmes on learning and school participation in low- and middle-income countries: a systematic review summary report*, 3ie Systematic Review Summary 7. London: International Initiative for Impact Evaluation (3ie).

Stasavage, D. (2005) 'Democracy and education spending in Africa', *American Journal of Political Science* 49(2), 343–58.

Taylor, N., Gamble, J., Spies, M., and Garisch, C. (2013) 'School leadership and management'. In N. Taylor, S. van der Berg, and T. Mabogoane (eds), *Creating effective schools*. Cape Town: Pearson.

The Presidency, National Planning Commission (2012) *National Development Plan, 2030: Our Future—Making it Work*. Pretoria.

UNESCO (2014) *Teaching and Learning: Achieving Quality for All*. EFA Global Monitoring Report, 11.2013/14. Paris: UNESCO.

Van der Berg, S., Spaull, N., Wills, G., Gustafsson, M., and Kotze, J. (2016) *Identifying Binding Constraints to Educational Improvement. Synthesis Report for the Programme to Support Pro-poor Policy Development (PSPPD)*. Stellenbosch University: Research on Socio-Economic Policy.

Wales, J., Magee, A., and Nicolai, S. (2016) 'How Does Political Context Shape Education Reforms and Their Success?', https://www.odi.org/sites/odi.org.uk/files/resource-documents/10808.pdf.

Westhorp, G., Walker, B., Rogers, P., Overbeeke, N., Ball, D., and Brice, G. (2014) 'Enhancing Community Accountability, Empowerment and Education Outcomes in Low and Middle-Income Countries: A Realist Review.' London: Department for International Development.

Williamson, O. (2000) 'The New Institutional Economics: Taking Stock, Looking Ahead', *Journal of Economic Literature* 38(3), 595–613.

Wilson, J. Q. (1989) *Bureaucracy*. New York: Basic Books.

Wimpelberg, R. (1993) 'Principals' roles in stable and changing schools'. In C. Teddlie, and S. Springfield (eds), *Schools make a difference: Lessons learned from a 10-year study of school effects* (pp. 165–86). New York: Teachers College Press.

World Bank (2004) *Making Services Work for Poor People*, World Development Report 2004. Washington DC: World Bank and Oxford University Press.

World Bank (2018) *Learning: to realize education's promise*. World Development Report 2018. Washington DC: World Bank.

Yanguas, P. (2017) 'Varieties of state-building in Africa: Elites, ideas and the politics of public sector reform'. ESID Working Paper No. 89. Manchester.

Zengele, T. (2013) 'A critical Analysis on Processes of Filling Promotional Posts in South African Schools: A Transactional Leadership Perspective', *Mediterranean Journal of Social Sciences* (4)3.

2

The Transformation of South Africa's System of Basic Education

Luis Crouch and Ursula Hoadley

2.1 Introduction

Since 1994, South Africa's education sector has undergone a process of far-reaching transformation. The principal goal of the research presented in this book is to explore at the micro level some political and institutional dimensions of this transformation. However, these micro-level dynamics played out within a broader context of far-reaching change—and are best understood in the context of that change. The aim of this chapter is to provide the requisite background on this broader context.

The transformations wrought by the ANC government, and its civil society partners, on South Africa's education system in the mid-1990s could be argued to be among the most far-reaching of the second half of the twentieth century anywhere in the world. Nineteen administrative racial systems had to be joined and then re-shaped into nine geographical provinces; funding had to be put on a rational footing that did not provide white children with ten times as much per-child support as African children; large-scale ambition had to be tempered against fiscal realities; salary scales had to be unified; curricula revamped; boundaries between provinces re-established; capital planning systems streamlined; exam systems re-calibrated; and procurement, tendering, and payroll systems unified. The key changes all took place within a few critical years, between roughly 1995 and 1998.

This chapter describes these transformations, suggests some reasons for the key decisions, and details some of what the results for post-apartheid South Africa have been. We do not purport to assess whether other decisions might have produced a better outcome; rather, we argue that the most important transformation choices were to a large degree driven by circumstances, as perceived at the time. The set of circumstances, to be explored as hypotheses that determined the transformational policy choices, include:

- The felt need to transform education sector governance by decentralizing certain elements of decision-making to both new provinces and schools. As section 2.3 details, these decisions were not always taken for purely technocratic reasons. Some were political compromises needed to keep important social groups involved in governing the country by giving them a share of the governance, especially over their own spheres of action.
- The broader fiscal context which prevailed as of the end of apartheid and the dawn of democracy, discussed in section 2.4. These did not concern only fiscal aggregates, but also the fact that there were other social sectors, affected by apartheid inattention, that were perceived to be in a far sorrier state than education, at least judging from an enrolment criterion and in comparison with other countries.
- The necessity of transforming the education curriculum—both to expunge the apartheid legacy, and in response to strong global trends in professional opinion on 'what works' in education, as mediated by South African intellectuals, sometimes isolated, as they were, by apartheid sanctions and relative lack of intellectual exchange with the rest of the world during the height of the sanctions in the 1980s and early 1990s. How this played out in practice—and some of the implications for learning outcomes—is the focus of section 2.5.

Before turning to the details of these transformations, we first set the stage by describing the legacy of extreme dualism that was a consequence of South Africa's dismal apartheid history.

2.2 South Africa's Education Sector—A Legacy of Dualism

Though it is fairly common to look for the origins of South Africa's education problems under the explicit apartheid policies that were introduced in the late 1940s, and culminating in the Bantu Education Act of 1953, in reality the attitudes, policies, and issue-treatment that determine the dynamics of the system until the end of the twentieth century go back at least three centuries—in fact, nearly all the way back to the founding of the Cape Colony in 1652. In this brief historical sketch we pause at the very beginning, 300 years ago, just to 'prove' how deeply ingrained and historical the problems are; we then 'fast forward' to the formalism of apartheid in the 1940s and 1950s, and end up with a look at the situation towards the end of apartheid, providing a quick snapshot of the result of the dynamics of forces over 300 years.

2.2.1 *Some Deep Background*

The first school in the Cape Colony was started in 1658, just six years after the founding of the colony. As it happens, this coincided with the first arrival of slaves from outside the Cape itself. Already then, van Riebeeck (Commander of the Cape Colony from 1652 to 1662) 'saw the need to establish an institution... [that] would teach slaves sufficient linguistic skills, in order to promote a greater understanding of their master's orders... In addition, these slaves would also be indoctrinated in their master's religion, which would teach them the values of servitude, discipline, and obedience' (Molteno, 1984: 45, cited in Moore, 2015: 20). (Of course, this may not have been so different from how European children were schooled in those days, either in Europe or in the Cape—the influences of Montaigne and Comenius would have been distant indeed. The more interesting point is that this would be done in separate institutions which would presumably allow different *interpretations* for these curricular values—some for citizens, others for slaves—and interpretation is everything.) The first officially separated building would be opened in 1685 (Moore, 2015: 20). Later, (some) missionary schools might have had a relatively more humanistic attitude towards education. But, interestingly, this led to conflict with trekboer policies which forbade missionary activities in the Eastern Cape, as a way to not 'disseminate unsettling ideas of human equality as taught in [one presumes some] missionary schools' (Moore, 2015: 21, citing Welsh, 2000: 109).

2.2.2 *Fast-Forward 300 Years*

Up until the middle of the twentieth century, the 'history' of (African, or in general) education policy in South Africa has to be interpreted as a quilt of various colours, and tendencies, where big 'Policy' can only be seen as the accretion of the policies of many different, localized, time-bound policies of particular bodies, some official, some not (e.g. missions). Even so, the tendency for education for Africans to be distinct and inferior, often by design, was self-evident to even casual observers working from the 1960s onward. But it is only in the early 1950s that 'policy history' becomes much more easily interpretable via the documentary evidence—the historical documentation leaves no doubt as to the intent of policy, and by then one can now mean Policy with a capital 'P'—though even so, academics find ways to disagree about 'deep' motivations. Some ascribe high apartheid policy to be mostly aimed at the limitation of Africans to be providers of cheap, relatively unskilled labour; others ascribe it to serving the needs of apartness first and foremost. But in the end, the impact is similar.

The guiding policy document was the Bantu Education Act, passed in 1953. This Act, while decisive for education, embodied much of what was criticized about apartheid in general. Under the guise of providing the opportunity for separate development in separate 'nations,' it laid out a framework of centralized control, bureaucracy, physical apartness, inferior funding, and paternalism. In the words which many anti-apartheid activists have engraved in their minds, F. W. Verwoerd, one of the architects of apartheid, noted in a Senate speech in regard to the Bantu Education Act: 'There is no space for him [the "Native"] in the European Community above certain forms of labour. For this reason it is of no avail for him to receive training which has its aim in the absorption of the European Community, where he cannot be absorbed. Until now he has been subjected to a school system which drew him away from his community and misled him by showing him the greener pastures of European Society where he is not allowed to graze' (Maree, 1984: 149).

According to one of its key tenets, the Act centralized control of Native Education in the Department of Native Affairs. Mission schools, whose curricular offerings were seen as suspect by the new apartheid government, were brought under the control of the state, and subsidies were eliminated, forcing many to close down. Efforts to create 'Bantustans' (quasi-independent 'reservations' or 'homelands') were initiated in the 1950s. These entities were theoretically able to devise their own education systems, but in fact largely operated in accordance with Bantu Education. Indeed, the intention behind the creation of the Bantustans can be seen as mirroring the Bantu education curriculum: 'to limit and reorient African political, economic and social aspirations away from a common political and economic life and towards a separated, rurally-oriented, ethnically-based life' (Chisholm, 2013: 408). In addition, it would be soon discovered, the Bantustans offered abundant opportunities for populist and patron–client politics. Under the guise of separate development, for instance, high schools were created in the Bantustans, but not so much in the areas where Africans lived within the Republic of South Africa 'proper' (though later this policy was rescinded); similarly, each Bantustan was to be given a teacher training college.

Under this legislative regime, per student funding for black schools was much lower than that for other ethnic groups, school feeding disappeared and the state largely placed the burden of the costs of the expansion of schooling on local black communities themselves. Hartshorne (1981) gives an indication of the inequalities of the system. In 1969, the gap between the unit cost of black and white education reached its widest, at a ratio of 20:1 white to black. At the same time as financing of black education was being squeezed, the government attempted to increase enrolment. In 1972, responding to the crisis in African schooling, the structure of financing changed, and slowly per capita spending differences between black and white children were reduced. However, little additional funding reached primary schools, although in some provinces there was a significant reduction in the number of double-shift schools. Although some gains were made in the retention of children in primary school, quality remained dire. Schooling was further disrupted through the late seventies in widespread student protest action, reaching a climax in the 1976 Soweto school uprising.

In the 1980s, under P. W. Botha, there was an effort to 'modernize' apartheid education, largely in response to human capital demands. This was a period of great expansion of schooling, with large increases in African enrolments in both primary and secondary schools. By 1985 the number of secondary students was four-fold that of 1975; 76 per cent of children aged 5–14 were enrolled in primary school (Unterhalter, 1991: 39). Enrolments, expenditure and the number of African matric passes continued to increase over the 1980s. By the late 1980s the ratio of white to black spending had been decreased to 1:6, although with enormous variations within the 'black' category (see below).

Changes in curriculum over the course of apartheid largely mapped onto the shifts in broader ideological discourses and the shifting economic context of the rising and declining apartheid state. Curriculum broadly moved from a culturally oriented curriculum, with a strong emphasis on content and education for the rural, racially distinct 'native' and manual labourer in the 1930s and 40s, to a progressively more technicist orientation, and an emphasis on vocational education and the development of skills for a modernising economy. From early on, however, different curriculum knowledge was distributed to different race groups less through different syllabuses and more through different institutionalized forms of provision, especially the lack of broad subject offerings, teaching resources, and qualified teachers in schools for black, coloured, and Indian students.

Schools were governed through nineteen racially separated departments of education for different racial and geographical groupings. Information systems were poor, examination systems dysfunctional and often corrupt, and a draconian inspectorate system was the only accountability and performance management mechanism within the system (Swartz, 2004). The Hunter Report (DOE, 1996) showed the dismal state of school infrastructure in 1995 after years of neglect. Increasingly, and especially after 1976, black schools, in particular those in urban areas, were largely dysfunctional, the material conditions deplorable, and teacher morale decimated. The apartheid-based curriculum was rejected, and any progressive or state-driven reform became unacceptable. Inspectors were driven from schools. Exams were regarded as illegitimate. Especially in urban areas, student protest action made many schools ungovernable in this wide-scale rejection of apartheid schooling.

2.2.3 *Educational Inputs and Outcomes at the Dawn of Democracy*

The educational inputs and outcomes at the end of apartheid were a legacy of inequity and, not often noted, also inefficiency. These views influenced important technocrats in the new government. A perspective on both inefficiency and inequity is provided by Figure 2.1, which shows both expenditure per student in 1990, and a simple 'instantaneous' indicator of internal school efficiency, namely the ratio of enrolment in Standard 5 (Grade 7, the last grade of primary) to enrolment in SSA (Grade 1 in the new parlance as an informal measure of the 'survival rate' to Standard 5). The results of the relationship are graphed in Figure 2.1.[1] As the figure shows, there were huge differences in spending per pupil across the systems (far from the '5 to 1' that is often noted with regard to White/African in general)—with the massive additional per pupil spending going to white schools doing nothing to increase 'survival' rates. With no comparative data available at the time on learning outcomes, this led some observers at the time to question whether the 'white windfall' was achieving much beyond providing pleasant surroundings and 'posh' infrastructure.

Aside from the implicit efficiency critique of having to spend so much more on white schools than seemed strictly necessary, there is the equity or equality

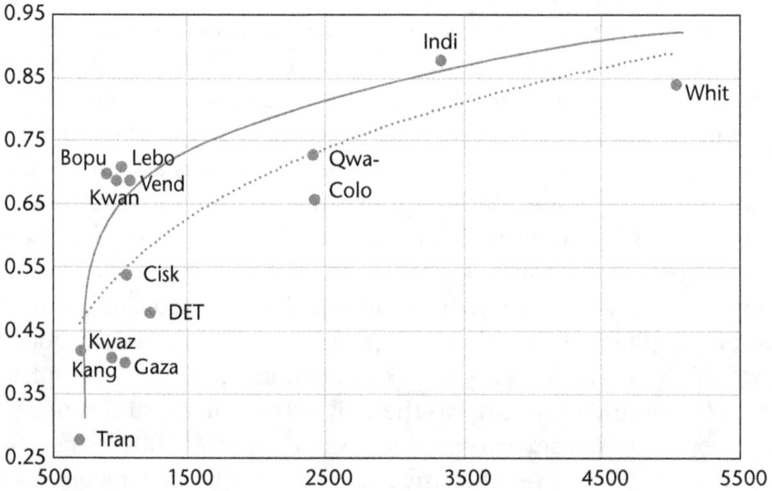

Figure 2.1. School efficiency by racial department towards end of apartheid
Source: Derived from data in Crouch (1996).

[1] The figure uses both a formally estimated semi-logarithmic fit of results (the 'survival' rate to Standard 5) on the vertical axis and inputs (cost per student) on the horizontal axis, as well as a casually estimated 'envelope' or 'near envelope' of the data.

critique of spending so little on the poor schools, an issue to which we return in section 2.3.

Matric exams are also revealing. Cronje (2010), using data from the Institute of Race Relations, tracked the performance of black African matric pupils from 1955 to 2008/09. In 1955, only 598 black Africans sat for their matric exams and only 259 achieved a pass. Through the 1960s, the number of black Africans sitting the matric exam increased rapidly, as did the proportions of those pupils obtaining passes and university entrance passes. By 1970, 2,846 black Africans wrote matric and of this group, 1,865 (or 65.2 per cent) passed and 1,103 (or 35.6 per cent) achieved a university entrance pass. The 1960s had therefore seen significant increases in the number of black Africans writing their matric exams. In 1980, 29,973 black African pupils wrote matric. In 1985, 82,815 wrote and by 1990 the number of black African pupils writing matric had rocketed to 255,669. At the same time, however, and through the 1980s and early 1990s, the pass rate and university exemption rate began to fall. In 1993 the pass rate touched a record low of 37 per cent and the exemption rate bottomed out at 8 per cent. The decline in the pass rate is generally attributed to increasingly disrupted schooling through the 1980s, mainly due to political struggle and the breakdown in the culture of learning and teaching in most schools. Some spoke of a 'lost generation' of youth who had forgone years of schooling in service of the struggle.

Figure 2.2 extends the analysis by trying to compare not just matric pass rates, but by taking into account the percentage of pupils who reached Standard 10 (Grade 12 in modern parlance). In that sense, what cognitive disadvantage had apartheid education created for the least advantaged in society, as measurable towards the end of apartheid (the early 1990s)? This question is more difficult to answer than it might appear at first. Looking only at the matric pass rates (Senior Certificate Examination pass rates) is not enough, because the proportion who even made it through to Grade 12 varies a lot by population group. To get at that, one might rely on data about persistence in school. But surveys tended not to ask, of those attending school, which grade they were in, and asked instead the highest grade achieved ever, which creates a timing issue. It is difficult to derive completely clear answers, but one can derive a range of estimates of advantage, triangulating various sources. Figure 2.2, which focuses on the extremes of whites and Africans so as to unclutter the graphics, shows a range of interpretations. Panel A in Figure 2.2 shows the percentage of twenty-one-year-olds having achieved Standard 10 (Grade 12 in today's parlance), plus various certificates or higher. It shows that for the white population, this was 91 per cent, while for the African population the percentage was 55 per cent: a 1.65 ratio (91/55) in advantage for whites. The 55 per cent strikes us as a little high, but not extremely so, as Panel B confirms. But, in any case, Panel A has the advantage that all the data

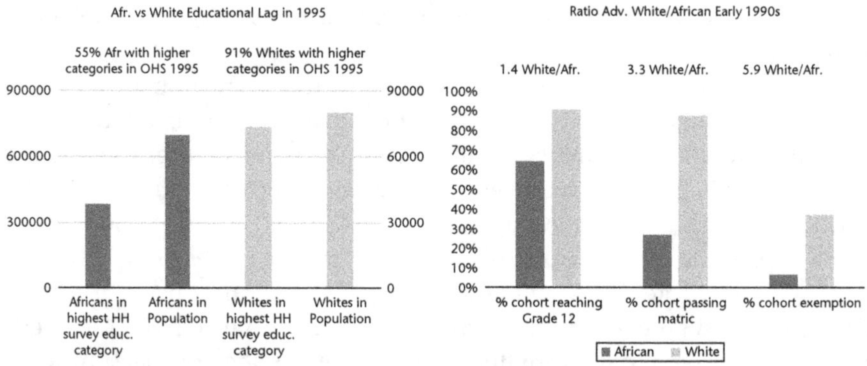

Figure 2.2. Educational success, by race, as proportion of populations

Source: Panel A uses strictly the 1995 October Household Survey (OHS) and shows the percentage of 21-year-olds having achieved Standard 10 (Grade 12 in today's parlance), plus various certificates, or higher. Panel B uses enrollment data provided by the then Research Institute for Educational Planning at the then University of the Free State, which compiled data by race and administrative department in the 1990s throughout the entire SA (including homelands). The population data came from a non-governmental demographic think-tank called the 'Demographic Information Bureau' that, similarly produced information, in the early and mid-1990s, by age, gender, and race, for planning and analysis purposes for a future re-constituted South Africa.

come from a single source. Panel B shows decrements in percentages achieving certain 'bars' according to increments in quality or 'demandingness' of those bars. The first two columns show the ratio of enrolment in Standard 10 in 1994 to population of eighteen-year-olds for Africans and whites. In addition, data for senior certificate passes and exemptions were obtained for the early 1990s. Applying the pass rates to the first two columns and the exemption rates to the same two columns gives all the other values. According to these data, whites had advantages over Africans of 1.41, 3.3, and 5.9 respectively, depending on how high the bar in question was. All this provides less optimistic conclusions than the usual pass/writer conception of the pass rate, as the denominator is not those who sit or write the exam, but the whole population, and thus takes into account dropping out prior to Grade 12. A *grosso modo*, the white/African difference was about 4 to 1 at the end of apartheid.

This disparity cannot be attributed to differential labour market returns from passing matric; numerous studies have shown that rates of return to secondary and tertiary education range from about 10 per cent to 18 per cent, are similar for whites and Africans (actually higher for Africans), and the returns from post-secondary education are relatively high (Bhorat, 2000; Crouch, 1996; Mwabu and Schultz, 1996). The differential access to matric was therefore a socially inefficient and inequitable phenomenon, depriving society and individuals of access to production and income.

Further insight into the South African patterns of access to education at the dawn of democracy is provided by a comparison for 1989–94 with a selected

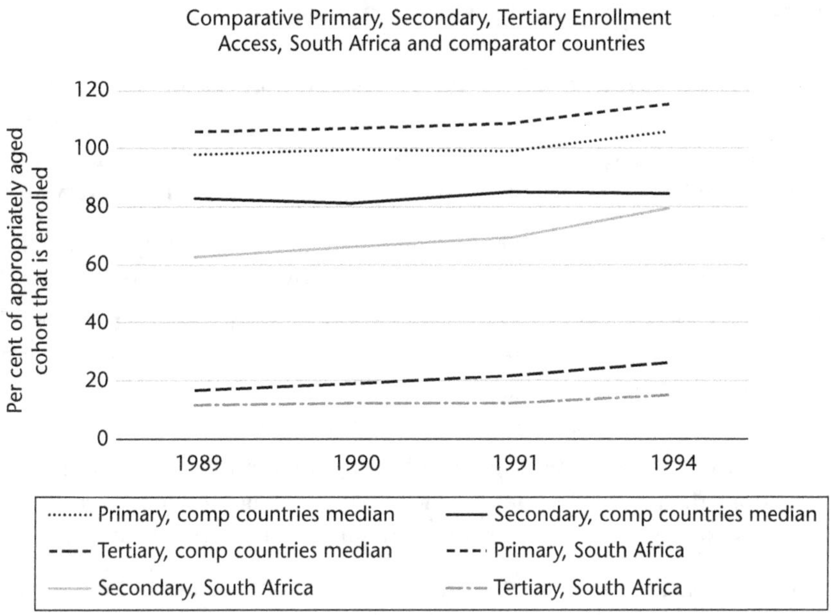

Figure 2.3. Comparative performance of South Africa on access to education
Source: World Bank EdStats data query system.[2]

group of international comparators.[3] As Figure 2.3 shows, relative to these comparators, South Africa was a little—not hugely—skewed, but in ways that are revealing of the racial differences. South Africa's access to primary education was, at 115 per cent, above the 'efficient' maximum for the age cohort—a sign of low quality in the early grades particularly in the African parts of the system, which induced repetition and excess enrolment. Some provinces, largely those where Bantustans had been located, had Grade 1 enrolments which were more than 50 per cent above the age cohort. Secondary enrolment was low in comparison with other countries, but was rapidly (one could say more rapidly than quality could keep up with) catching up (especially in the African portions of the system) and had essentially caught up by 1994. However, the low pass rates highlighted above resulted in a low tertiary enrolment rate relative to the comparators.

[2] For reasons explained below, we prefer to assure the integrity of international comparisons by using one standardized international database, in this case the World Bank's, which derives from data reported by countries to UNESCO. If one debates the SA data, then in principle one could similarly debate the data for every single country, and these kinds of comparisons would become either impossible or very tedious to read. The point of using a large number of comparators is to support fairly general statements such as those we make here.

[3] See n. 7 for a discussion of the comparator countries.

2.3 Transforming Education Sector Governance

The 1996 the South African Schools Act (SASA) and the new Constitution (1996) both transformed radically the institutional arrangements governing the country's system of education. It replaced the pre-existing, fragmented and racially ordered institutional arrangements with a unified, multi-tiered system:

- The national (central) level was assigned responsibility for policymaking, for resourcing the system, and for setting the overall regulatory framework.
- The provincial level was assigned responsibility for implementation—spending the budgetary resources made available from the centre, and employing the teachers, administrators, and other personnel who comprised the vast majority of employees in the system.
- Substantial school-level responsibilities (including the recruitment of the school principal and senior teachers) were assigned to school-governing bodies (SGBs) in which parents were required to be in the majority.

This transformation in the structure of governance seemingly was consistent with both a technocratic and a political logic. The apartheid state was seen by new technocrats as not only unjust, but also inefficient in its racial decentralization combined with administrative centralization. Decentralization of power, in the framework of a new Constitution and, in the education sector, a new Schools Act, along with a fiscal framework to go along with it (the 'equitable shares formula' and the 'school funding norms', on which more in section 2.4), were seen as a way to both load-shed some responsibility for finances, encourage important social groups to 'keep skin in the game', and encourage sub-national levels of government (all the way down to the school) to take substantial responsibility for decisions. Two funding contrasts between SASA and the Bantu Education Act (and its remnants) are especially noteworthy: in the new South Africa, poorer schools would be supported out of the central fiscus (through inter-governmental transfers and the requirements of the school funding norms), instead of depending on supposedly local taxes; and independent schools which attended to the relatively poor and maintained certain quality levels would be funded, instead of deprived of funding as the mission schools had been.

At the time when South Africa's new education sector governance arrangements were put in place, there was a strong reformist impulse worldwide for downward delegation of education governance to subnational and school levels[4] (e.g. Bray, 1996; Fiske, 1996; Patrinos and Ariasingam, 1997). Even

[4] A Google search for 'World Bank interest in education decentralization', for instance, produces, at the top of its search results, five documents, all produced between 1996 and 1998,

so, a narrowly technocratic perspective is misleading. The South African Schools Act (SASA) was promulgated in the same year in which the country's final constitution was formally approved. Indeed, the new institutional arrangements for South Africa's school system aligned well with broader political imperatives which were at the heart of South Africa's 1994 transition from apartheid to constitutional democracy.

South Africa's extraordinary transition from racist, apartheid minority rule to a new competitive, rule-of-law based political settlement was one of the most inspiring democratic miracles of the 1990s (a decade of many inspiring democratic miracles). En route to a democratic election in 1994, and the promulgation of a new constitution in 1996, the apartheid-era governing National Party agreed to give up its stranglehold on power; the exiled African National Congress agreed to end its armed struggle and pursue a negotiated settlement; and multiple other protagonists, including large-scale organized business, played influential roles in facilitating the transition. The complex story of what brought these protagonists to the table, and how they reached agreement, has been well told elsewhere[5] and goes way beyond the scope of the present exercise. For present purposes, the crucial insight is that the institutional arrangements incorporated into SASA were explicitly designed to be responsive to the central concerns vis-à-vis the education sector of both black South Africans who were about to become the majority in the emerging constitutional democracy, and white South Africans who were negotiating away their monopoly control over government.

The African National Congress was a mass-based political party, committed to ending South Africa's system of racial discrimination. In 1994, it received a sweeping electoral mandate, winning almost 63 per cent of the vote nationally. Universal access to education, the move to non-racial institutions in the sector, and the elimination of racially discriminatory practices in the allocation of public funds were all non-negotiable political imperatives. As subsequent sections of this chapter will detail, all of these indeed were achieved under the new institutional arrangement for the sector established by SASA.

For white South Africans, a central concern was agreement on a system of governance which could sustain the quality of the public[6] schools which historically had served their children. The institutional arrangements laid

some by prominent and influential thinkers such as Mark Bray, Edward Fiske, and Harry Patrinos (Bray, 1996; Fiske, 1996; Patrinos and Ariasingam, 1997).

[5] See, for example, Mandela (2004), Sparks (1996), Marais (1998), Seekings and Nattrass (2005), Gevisser (2007), and Welsh (2009).

[6] In South Africa, public education dominates, both historically and to the present day; as of 2016, about 95% of school-going children were enrolled in the public system. See https://www.education.gov.za/Portals/0/Documents/Reports/School%20Realities%202016%20Final.pdf?ver=2016-11-30-111439-223, p. 3.

out in SASA were responsive to these concerns in two ways. First, consistent with the broader constitutional logic of the political settlement, the delegation of substantial authority to nine provinces served as a check on at least some aspects of discretionary decision-making by central government. The second, more direct way in which the concerns of the white minority were addressed was via the delegation of substantial authority to the school level. This delegation included, in subsequent regulation, the ability to vote, at the local level, fees to be paid by parents at school level, and for these fees to stay at school level and to be used there with considerable discretion, including the appointment of extra teachers.

SASA (and the South African constitution more broadly) incorporated an overarching principle of non-racialism in admissions policy—although the details were left ambiguous as to how decisions should be made regarding who had the right to attend individual schools for which there was more demand than available places. But beyond this, parents of children in elite public schools (which historically had served the white minority) were well-placed to leverage the authority granted to SGBs to ensure that the schools would remain well managed. Further, as noted, the autonomy provided by SASA included the right to top up public funds with self-financing by the parent body—ensuring that elite schools need not be starved of resources as a result of the racial equalization (indeed, the pro-poor skewing) of certain public expenditures.

To be sure, keeping middle class and elite children in the system was not only in the interests of the relatively privileged minority. There is strong evidence from around the world that ensuring that multiple classes (not only children of the poor) are served by a public system is a crucial buttress for the system's efficiency and budgetary defence. Further, both delegation to provinces, and participatory school-level governance aligned well rhetorically with the embrace by all parties of the principles of constitutional, democratic governance. In practice, though, as this book explores in detail, the gap was substantial between this rhetorical alignment and the reality of the challenges of governing the education sector in a way which served effectively the disproportionately poor majority of the country's citizens. And the evidence in Chapters 8–10 suggests that efforts to turn this rhetorical embrace of participation into genuine empowerment of parents and communities, beyond the already-empowered elites, were disappointingly scant.

2.4 Transforming Education Financing

Compared to other upper-middle income countries (UMICs), particularly those that went on to grow robustly, South Africa's finances were in a dismal state in the period roughly five years before the new government took power.[7]

- The economy was not growing. In the period 1990 to 1994, immediately preceding the start of the democratic government, South Africa's economy shrank at an average annual rate of −2.2 per cent, while comparators' economies grew at 1.8 per cent: a 4-percentage point difference.
- The fiscal deficit was high. In the same period, South Africa's deficit was, on average, 5.9 per cent of GDP; that of its comparators was 0.9 per cent of GDP. South Africa's deficit peaked at 9 per cent in 1993—it was the highest of any of the comparator countries in that year.
- Because debt was accumulating, interest payments as a proportion of total government expense were high, and rising fast. Payments as a proportion of government expense were 15 per cent in South Africa, only 9 per cent in the comparator countries. What's worse, in South Africa they were rising by half of a percentage point per year, whereas in the comparator countries, interest payments were going down by 1.3 percentage points per year.
- Apartheid had left in its wake some urgent social crises outside the education sector. Under-five mortality rates were 183 per cent higher in South Africa than in the comparator countries, and were worsening rapidly. By contrast, as noted earlier, there was already universal access to primary education, and in education the percentage of the population enrolled in secondary education was only a little lower in South Africa than in comparator countries (70 per cent versus 83 per cent), and was growing rapidly.

In short, as detailed further below, relative to other UMICs, South Africa's fiscal effort in education was relatively high, and enrolment already high. Given the other economic and social challenges, and a pervasive sense (notably including on the part of some influential public officials[8]) that resources

[7] For this section, we constructed a set of comparator countries consisting of countries that were a) upper-middle income in the period 1990–95, according to the World Bank's classification for that period, b) were 'big enough to have complexity and interest' (our judgement—examples include Antigua and Barbuda, Malta, etc.), and c) not oil-rich (Gabon, Saudi Arabia, etc.). The resulting comparator countries were Argentina, Brazil, Chile, Croatia, the Czech Republic, Greece, Hungary, Malaysia, Mexico, Slovenia, South Africa, and Uruguay. As is often the case in using international databases, not all countries have data for all variables in all years, so the medians for the comparators have to be interpreted with caution: only for the overall sense of direction. Note that in principle, it would have been possible to use South African data for the South African case, but we opted to use World Bank data for all countries, as this would provide a standardized set where data would, hopefully, be maximally comparable to each other.

[8] For instance, Andrew Donaldson (1992), who would become a prominent actor in the Ministry of Finance, was already noting in the early 1990s that the education system in South Africa was notoriously inefficient: '"Internal efficiency" is of course not the only aspect of the economic

for education were not well used, it followed that there would be no 'end-of-apartheid' dividend in terms of increases in aggregate public spending on education relative to GDP. The overwhelming fiscal challenge was to put in place new fiscal formulas which could assure high levels of access to education and reverse the stark inequalities in expenditure inherited from the apartheid years, but without putting too much pressure on the fiscus. The subsections which follow detail how this was addressed, and what was achieved.

2.4.1 *New Fiscal Formulas*

The fiscal solutions to this dilemma, arrived at by the new technocracy (with particular relevance to education) were two, which worked to complement each other. First, an 'equitable shares formula' would create a division of centrally sourced revenue and provide those shares to the provinces and local governments. The formula would consider the weight of certain needs (total population, enrolment, the size of the economy, the need for a certain fixed cost to run a province) to create shares of funding. After keeping a certain amount of funds for financing national-level activities, and a certain amount for subnational activities (the 'vertical' break), the central government created a 'horizontal' division for the provinces. From within their share, the provinces were free to allocate to various sectors with considerable freedom. Some chose to devote relatively more funding to education, others to health, and so on, as they saw their needs. This allowed the central government to be perceived as responding strongly to a pressure for equity and transparency, while promising only 'shares' (but *fair* shares) of the fiscal fortune, and thus enabling a certain degree of austerity.

In a similar manner, the norms and standards for school funding, as well as the post provisioning norms for educators, provided policy direction from the national Department of Education as to how provincial education authorities should assign resources to schools in an equal (in the case of teachers) or even pro-poor manner (in the case of non-personnel, non-capital expenditure). Schools would typically not be mandated as to how to spend the funds, and some could even procure their own inputs. Echoing the 'equitable shares formula', the basic idea was to mandate equity in the shares of per student spending going to schools of different levels of poverty, but not to mandate

efficiency of the education system, but it is all too easily neglected... And in South Africa, improved educational opportunities must be afforded to some 10m children... although available financial resources are stretched more or less to their limits. In these circumstances, improving the "internal efficiency" of the education system is the only way forward... I take the view that there is scope for improvements in the way schooling and training are organized and provided in South Africa, that this is an arena in which the post-apartheid state can meet substantially the rising expectations of the new electorate, and that reorganising the education industry will lay an important foundation for sustainable long-term economic growth'.

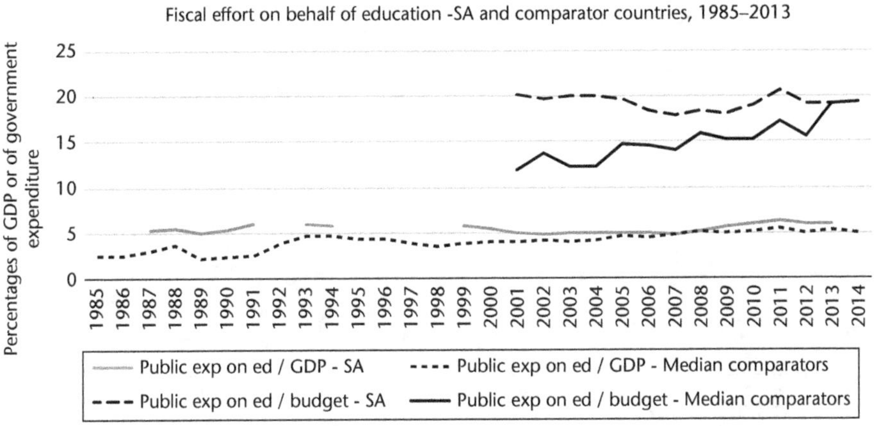

Figure 2.4. Funding for education, South Africa and comparator countries
Source: World Bank EdStats data query system.

absolute amounts of per student spending. At the same time, the funding norms allowed schools to self-assess fees, under certain conditions, to keep the funding at their own level, and to meld this private funding with their public funding into a unified vision of the school's budget under the (presumably) strong supervision of the school governing body. Both 'formula-driven' solutions thus focused on equity and shares, without making promises about absolute levels of expenditure. The results seem to have been pro-equity, encouraged the maintenance of an upward trend in enrolment, and did prevent a privatization of middle-class schooling.

As Figure 2.4 makes clear, funding for education remained reasonably constant as a proportion of GDP, at least over the longer haul. Thus, in that sense, the 'trick' of keeping the middle classes involved in public education 'worked.' Compared to other upper-middle income countries, South Africa spent a high proportion of GDP on education and it maintained this proportion throughout the late 1990s and onwards, as other countries caught up. The result was that by 2015 the expenditure patterns of South Africa and the comparator countries were similar to one another.

2.4.2 *Trends in Access to Education*

After and before apartheid, what did the spending buy for South Africa and for other countries, in terms of access to education (enrolment)? As section 2.2 detailed, as of the end of apartheid, access to primary education was 'raw' ('raw' in the sense that though access was high, quality was highly variable, and almost always poor for low-income black South Africans).

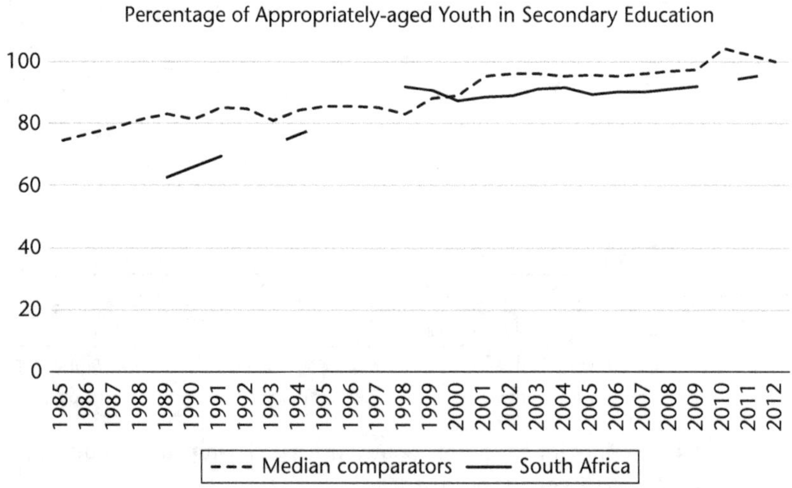

Figure 2.5. Access to secondary education, South Africa and comparator countries
Source: manipulations of data downloads from https://data.worldbank.org/data-catalog/world-development-indicators.

As Figure 2.5 shows, access to secondary enrolment, already high in comparison with other UMICS, continued apace after the end of apartheid. The percentage of South Africa's youth cohorts attending secondary education was known to be rising (though the figure makes it hard to see this precisely in the early 1990s, because South Africa was not and in any case reporting in the late 1980s showed South Africa to be nearly on par with the comparators). The rise in attendance at secondary education in the early 1990s had obviously nothing to do with any policies set in place by the democratic government, and much to do with a sort of populist expansion of investment in the Bantustans (which included also the creation of large numbers of teacher training colleges). But the approaches put in place by the democratic government allowed those trends to continue and for secondary enrolments to essentially catch up to the comparator UMICs by 2010 or so.

Figure 2.6 shows both the growth in enrolment as a proportion of the more-or-less enrolable age groups and, importantly, changes in the pattern of enrolment within those age groups.[9] Given constancy in spending, South Africa showed relative constancy in both enrolment and in composition of enrolment: the end of apartheid had hardly any discernible impact. The comparator countries showed much more growth in total enrolment and

[9] The age groups in question are three to twenty-four, to take into account pre-primary and even pre-Grade 0 pre-primary all the way up to tertiary.

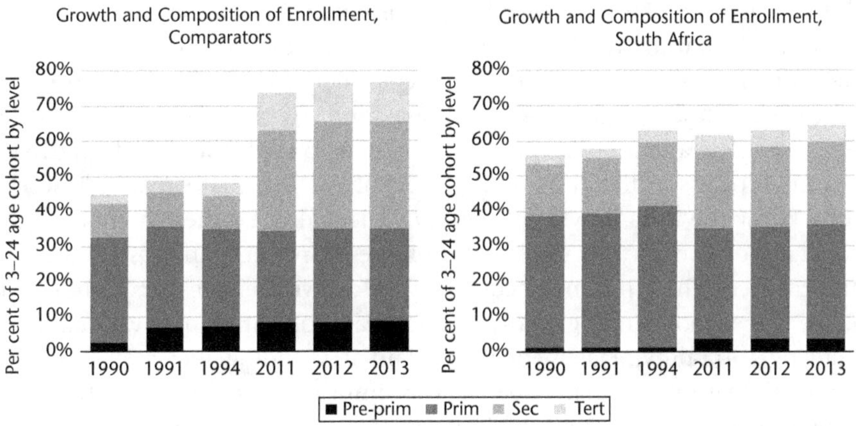

Figure 2.6. Composition and relative size of enrolment by level, South Africa and comparator countries

that enrolment came about both because of more spending, but also because of a reorganization of enrolment between sub-sectors, with a strong relative shrinking of primary education and an expansion in other levels, achieved partly by increasing the internal efficiency of primary education. Countries in other regions, particularly in Latin America, became more and more convinced of the importance of human capital in generating growth and combatting inequality, and spending was stepped up, particularly in sub-sectors such as early childhood. (Also stepped up in South Africa, but not quite as much, and, perhaps, with not—yet—much demonstration of cognitive results.)

2.4.3 *Equity in Resourcing*

It is clear that resourcing came to be far more pro-poor after democracy. Being pro-poor correlates very closely with being pro-African, but note that the funding norms in South Africa (both in the sense of funding from centre to provinces, and from provinces to schools) were (naturally) de-racialized after democracy, and were set in terms of poverty or were poverty- and race-neutral at best (with one proviso: formerly richer schools typically kept more expensive teaching staff, even if the numbers of teaching staff publicly provided were de-racialized). Data can be tracked by province as well, and, with some assumptions, by race. But the important categories are poverty and province. Strong evidence of the fast changes in, for example, public funding, can be found in Department of Education (2006: 36), and is reproduced as Table 2.1.

Two summary measures of inequality are presented in this table: a Gini coefficient and a Coefficient of Variation (CV). Both show radical reductions in the inequality of public funding—roughly 75 per cent to 80 per cent in just fifteen years, with most of the change coming in the space of just ten years (1990 to 2000, roughly). Naturally, the provinces did not exist in 1990, but their constituent 'homelands' and RSA departments did, their enrolments and their per capita expenditures were known, and so it is possible to present a fairly complete and accurate picture of matters towards the end of apartheid and the progress in the years immediately after. Note that we do not necessarily know the intra-provincial spending inequality, so these numbers may overstate (or conceivably understate) progress. Spending increased faster in the provinces whose internal inequality would have been greater; on the other hand, the school funding norms were already operating and were already reducing intra-provincial inequalities, and if spending increased faster in provinces whose internal equality was improving faster, then Table 2.1 could be understating total equalization.

Table 2.1 makes it clear that the apartheid inheritance disproportionately favoured Gauteng and the Western Cape; so the rebalancing meant spreading their 'excess' resources to the other provinces. The Northern Cape, being very small in enrolment terms, did not contribute much in absolute terms to the rebalancing, but gives further evidence that the formula-based cutting back of the 'bigger spenders' worked transparently and without much favouritism. However, note also that because the poorer provinces were also among the largest, cutting back on the spending in the higher-spending ones could not result in big per pupil increases in spending in the lower-spending provinces. (Also, recall that how much to spend on education was, according to the equitable shares formula, a matter for the provinces to prioritize, so these numbers are a result both of equity drivers in the central funding, the equity drivers in the school funding norms, but also of provincial decisions on how much of their fiscal share to spend on education.)

Table 2.1. Public Ordinary School Expenditure, per pupil, by province 1990–2004, and its inequality, national base of 100 in each period

	1990/91	2000/01	2004/05
EC	78	93	95
FS	104	109	116
GP	154	123	108
KN	80	87	92
LP	74	92	92
MP	86	93	102
NC	153	135	112
NW	88	111	112
WC	180	117	109
Total	100	100	100
Gini	0.39	0.09	0.08
CV	0.34	0.15	0.09

Source: Department of Education 2006, p. 36.

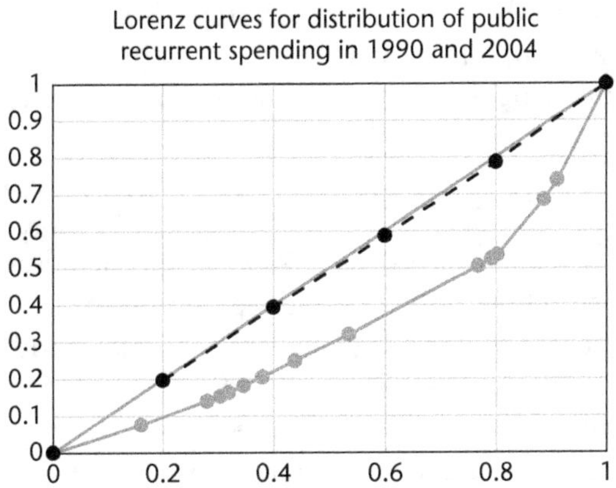

Figure 2.7. Changes in inequality curves for distribution of public resourcing of public schools

Source: calculated for this report from data in Department of Education 2006, pp. 41 and 42. Note that in that report the horizontal axis is sorted by per capita income, not per capita expense, as here.

Another take, using the actual homelands data from Buckland and Fielden (1994) and Department of Education (2006), gives the Lorenz curves shown in Figure 2.7 for inequality of public recurrent expenditure in terms of the fourteen departments that spent money on pupils in a distinguishable manner (i.e. ignoring provincial differences in HoA spending). The curves are approximate, because for the erstwhile administrative departments the curve is plotted with population by expenditure level on the horizontal axis. Nonetheless, the results are striking: the dashed black spending curve for 2004 is nearly exactly equal to the 45-degree line of equality, whereas the lower line for spending in 1991 yielded a Gini coefficient of 0.33.

Naturally, given that the system allowed schools to charge individual fees (determined at local level, and therefore much higher for the higher income groups), these numbers under-state the amount of inequality reduction achieved. Nonetheless, such a rapid reduction in inequality in public spending is unequalled in modern history, to our knowledge. Remaining inequalities, though, surely account for some important differences in performance (van der Berg and Gustafsson, 2017).

2.5 Curricular Trends and Learning Outcomes Implications

Among the many transformations of South Africa's education system, the transformation of the education curriculum was perhaps the most far-reaching in terms of its implications for day-to-day practice in the classroom.

This section describes this transformation, reports on the consequences (of the full set of transformations, curricular and otherwise) for learning outcomes, and also on some recent, perhaps somewhat encouraging trends.

2.5.1 *Curriculum under Apartheid*

Over the forty-eight years of National Party rule, syllabuses, examinations, and prescribed instructional practice changed significantly, adapting to both shifts in political economy and broader international trends in curriculum. The shifts in curriculum can be seen in the changes in the 'imagined' learner of different curricula across time. As outlined earlier, early mission and colonial curricula were concerned with the conversion of the 'heathen indigene'. Industrialisation and the onset of mining focused the curriculum on the development of manual skills and docility (the 'moral' and 'industrious' learner). In the 1930s, in the light of international debates, the notion of the (indigenous) colonial subject became tied up in issues of cultural specificity and questions of the mind of the 'native'. Here, strong culturalist notions of the learner, whose language and traditions should be preserved through education, provided the platform for Bantu education and the apartheid ideology of separate development. With the modernization of the economy, higher skills were sought and the curriculum focus became increasingly vocational. In the later 1980s and early 1990s the imagined learner of the curriculum became something quite different—the individual learner of no determinate race on the one hand, and a worker for a growing and diversifying economy on the other. These last reform attempts of the apartheid government, came, however, late in the day and given the intensified political protest and breakdown of teaching and learning in schools, reached only the minority white sectors of schooling.

Despite these shifts, a number of general points can be made about curriculum, especially from the mid-1950s onwards. Firstly, different knowledge was distributed to different race groups, accomplished less through different syllabuses and more through segregated provision, and differences in the material and symbolic resources available to different race groups in different schools. The fact that the curriculum was very similar on paper was used to mask inequities. The Minister of Bantu Education in the late 1970s proudly claimed that his department 'had not only adopted the same curricula and syllabi as were used by Whites, but Black and White students were now writing the same senior certificate and matriculation exams' (Marcum, 1982: 21, cited in Jansen, 1990: 202). Black students, however, received watered-down, minimal or narrower curricula than children in the white department of education. There were different subjects on offer in white and black schools, more academic in white schools, and more vocationally oriented in black schools.

The distribution of teachers capable of teaching more demanding subjects was also quite different. Secondly, the issue of language was paramount and would become the flashpoint for intense protest in the 1970s. The language issues are complex, and shifted over time, but crucially had to do with the imposition of Afrikaans on African language speaking learners as the language of instruction and testing. Language was also used, especially in the primary school, as a means for establishing the cultural particularity and apartness of black learners; while white, Indian, and coloured children had to learn two languages, African children had to learn three (for long periods, as early as the third grade). Third, curricula contained racial biases favouring whites, and the stereotyping of the black population as tribal, rural and backward. Ideological content was added to the syllabuses specifically for black learners presenting a narrow (largely rural) and static view of 'Bantu society', and referencing some folk and historical heroes as well as contemporary apartheid arrangements and governing institutions for the black population. Fourth, and throughout the period, curricula constructed during apartheid were subject-based and content-driven, with minimal explicit conceptual content-skill relationships made. Knowledge across curriculum reforms was regarded as 'given' and strong boundaries were maintained between different subjects.

Among South Africa's education sector pedagogical thought leaders, there was an enduring progressivist thrust in curriculum, both inside and outside of the state, sustained through the decades up until the transition to democracy in 1994. To be sure, official attempts at curriculum innovation in the 1970s and 1980s were largely piecemeal—often consisting of taking out contents or adding in new contents in different subjects. But there also were ongoing micro-reforms, often influenced by trends in the United States and United Kingdom, notably ideas arising out of progressive reforms there. Galant (1997) gives the example that, between 1974 and 1984, at least five new syllabuses were introduced in South Africa following the 'new maths' movement in Europe. However, these largely had effect in white schools only. There was also a significant amount of curriculum work being done outside of state institutions, as alternatives to the traditional curriculum forms developed during the apartheid era.

2.5.2 *A Radical Curriculum for Democracy*

The first post-apartheid curriculum, Curriculum 2005 (C2005), introduced in 1998, was a radical constructivist curriculum that emphasised a learner-centred, outcomes-based approach to teaching and learning. It backgrounded prescribed knowledge content, leaving it to teachers and learners to select the appropriate content or precise method in order to achieve specified outcomes. Textbooks and testing were regarded as authoritarian and backward-looking, and were dispensed with (apart from the Grade 12 examination). C2005 was framed as a 'radical break' from the apartheid past. It was essentially a reform focused on pedagogy—intent on shifting authoritarian relations of classrooms, defined by bureaucratic routine, deferential ritual and whole class, choral production of knowledge at a very low level of cognitive complexity. In the process of addressing issues of pedagogy, knowledge and its specification was lost.

What is often missed in the accounts of the shift from apartheid to C2005 is that although the changes introduced represented a radical departure from the past for black schools, for white schools (which had been part of the final progressive curriculum reforms of the apartheid era) there was much continuity between the new curriculum and established pedagogic practices (Harley and Wedekind, 2004). Thus, the schools where teachers were in the first place less qualified, were also the schools who were most disadvantaged by the very unfamiliar terms of the new curriculum.

2.5.3 *Reforming the Reform*

The new curriculum, C2005, quickly came under severe criticism. What became clear in its implementation was its complexity, incomprehensible to many, and inappropriate for the majority of classroom contexts (Jansen and Christie, 1999). The system was unprepared for the shift to a radical, learner-centred, outcomes-based curriculum—introduced in a very short space of time, with very little training. A review of the curriculum followed in 2000, presenting the central critique of C2005 as barring access to school knowledge for both learners and teachers. The fact that the curriculum had removed most of subject content, and replaced it with outcomes expressed as generic skills, meant that teachers were expected to select the appropriate content and design 'learning programmes' themselves. Teachers in more advantaged schools were confident, well advised, and could rely on past experience and training in selecting content from their field of specialisation to construct appropriate learning programmes for students. However, in the majority of schools, poor prior training, and a lack of school-level support made this impossible. Pedagogic practices of the past, entailing the communal production of low level, localised content, persisted. The central difference was that learners sat in groups—group work becoming for many teachers a graspable outward form of the curriculum they could implement, masking real change in the classroom.

The 2000 review introduced a second iteration of this curriculum, the National Curriculum Statement. It retained the outcomes-based framework, but delineated more clearly content knowledge and appropriate methodologies for teaching. It also attempted to reassert the importance of summative assessment (tests and examinations). The retention of outcomes, however, would prove politically contentious and pedagogically problematic. Under increasing pressure of poor student academic outcomes and stringent public criticism of the outcomes-based education framework, a further review was initiated in 2009; in 2012 the current curriculum, the Curriculum and Assessment Policy Statement (CAPS) was implemented. In this curriculum, outcomes-based education was abandoned in favour of clear, per grade content stipulation, as well as specified pacing and sequencing requirements for the curriculum. The importance of textbooks as key pedagogical resources for both students and teachers was reasserted. A programme of distributing curriculum-aligned workbooks to all learners was entrenched. CAPS thus established a clear and stable curriculum-based signalling system for teacher training, the development of textbooks, and accountability for classroom practice. The highly specified curriculum would also lay an important basis for experimentation in instructional reform, discussed below.

Teacher training did not receive the same levels of attention as curriculum reform—and was complicated by the under-stipulated nature of C2005. Thus, teachers schooled and trained through Bantu education under apartheid lacked opportunity to overcome the legacy of a very poor preparation for teaching. Without teachers gaining a better content understanding of subjects to be taught, not simply new and complex ways in which to teach them, there was unlikely to be significant change in classroom practices and learning outcomes. Although more recently there has been some shift in instructional practices (Hoadley, 2018), especially in the number of texts in classrooms, many of the practices dominant under apartheid, the communalized, slow pace of learning and low level of classroom content, persist in the majority of classrooms (Hoadley, 2012). The clear specification in the CAPS of *what* content is to be covered *when* and in *what order* has promise to shift these practices both directly in classrooms and through defining subject-specific teacher training requirements more precisely.

2.5.4 *Cognitive Achievement after the Transformation*

This is a complicated story, and much depends on what countries one compares South Africa with, and on what issues. One can start with the most commonly held and alarming part of the story: that South Africa, in comparison with the world as a whole, or at least in comparison with the parts of the world that participate in assessments such as the Trends in International Mathematics and Science Study (TIMSS) or Progress on International Literacy Study (PIRLS) (repeated approximately every three years since 1995), performs badly, in absolute terms (last or nearly last—but noting that most countries that participate in these assessments are wealthy countries with long-established education systems), but also, perhaps more alarmingly, relative to its level of per capita income and the level of fiscal effort devoted to education. In exercises predicting results in TIMSS Grade 4 Mathematics for 2015, and PIRLS 2016, using GDP per capita and public spending on education as a share of GDP as predictors, for instance, South Africa's actual performance is much worse than expected—in fact, South Africa is perhaps one of the 'worst' outliers. Figure 2.8 shows predicted performance on the horizontal axis and actual performance on the vertical axis. South Africa is clearly a negative outlier—and this is at least fifteen years after the end of apartheid, when the system has had at least ten years to 'practice' with improving lives for the children who take this assessment.

In the case of SACMEQ III (2007) data, South Africa appears not so much as an under-performing outlier. Part of the reason for this is that in making comparisons in SACMEQ, the total score achieved by students is affected by the degree to which the country has a high primary school completion rate: countries with a higher completion rate are making a bigger 'access effort' in reaching out to previously un-served portions of their populations, and are thus trying to educate those who are harder to educate (e.g. may be first-generation literates in their families). Once this is corrected for,[10] what is

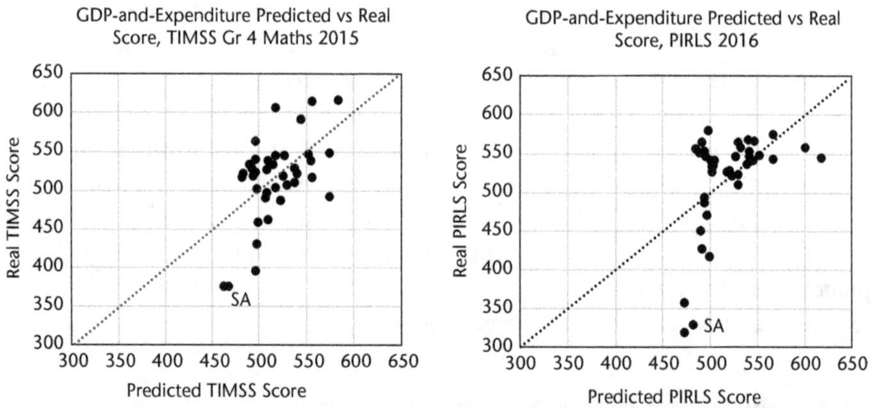

Figure 2.8. South Africa as an efficiency outlier in TIMSS and PIRLS

Source: calculated from https://timssandpirls.bc.edu/timss2015/international-database/, Mullis, Martin, Foy, and Hooper (2017), and data from the World Bank's EdStats database, http://databank.worldbank.org/data/reports.aspx?source=Education-Statistics-~-All-Indicators.

[10] Using SACMEQ data we have corrected for 'access effort' by creating a simple index of human capital contemporaneously produced by the country, by taking the SACMEQ score (averaging reading and mathematics) times the primary school completion rate (divided by 100, to keep the numbers in the same range as the scores). This score is then controlled by the speed with which the completion rate has been improved (increasing the completion quickly would presumably drain

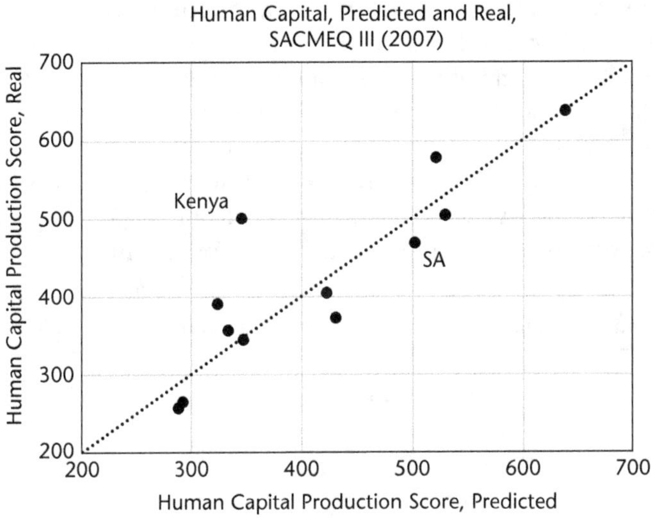

Figure 2.9. Kenya as positive outlier in SACMEQ

Source: calculations and transformations of online materials shown at http://www.sacmeq.org/ReadingMathScores, and the World Bank EdStats database, http://databank.worldbank.org/data/reports.aspx?source=Education-Statistics-~-All-Indicators.

interesting is not so much that South Africa is a negative outlier (as is the case in TIMSS 2015 and PIRLS 2016) but that (as Figure 2.9 shows) there seem to be positive outliers, namely Kenya, from which South Africa could perhaps be learning (but generally has not been, or had not been until recently). Chapter 10 explores this issue further.

Almost any way one looks at it, the internal distribution (the cognitive equality) of South Africa's scores is quite poor, at least in comparison with other countries taking part in assessments such as TIMSS, PIRLS, and SACMEQ. However, using various rounds of TIMSS, inequality has decreased, even markedly if one believes the data. Taking the score produced by children at the ninety-fifth percentile of the score distribution, subtracting the score produced by children at the fifth percentile, and dividing the result by the score produced by children at the middle of the distribution is a reasonable measure of relative inequality. Typically, developing countries with low averages will tend to show higher relative inequality (because the denominator is low). Wealthier, more educationally developed countries will tend to show less inequality, both because they actually apply more effort to improve things at the bottom of their distributions, and because their averages are higher.

resources away from improving learning outcomes), the fiscal effort the country devotes to education (education expenditure as a share of GDP), and GDP per capita.

Table 2.2 shows some examples, and shows South Africa's placement both at a given point in time and over time. The data are sorted from the most equal country in 2003 to some of the most unequal in 2003, 2011, and 2015. It is clear that South Africa is among the most unequal, though there are sometimes one or two that are just a bit more unequal. Table 2.3 shows the data for PIRLS 2016, showing that South Africa, has, if not quite the worst inequality results (using our index), close to it. Some developing countries which have done more work on improving equality are shown. Chile, for instance, in

Table 2.2. Inequality data for South Africa and other countries, TIMSS, various years

Country/year	Score of the child at the following percentiles of the score distribution, TIMSS Grade 8, Various years					Inequality ratio (score at 95th minus score at 5th)/score at 50th
	5th percentile	25th percentile	50th percentile	75th percentile	95th percentile	
Singapore 03	455	556	614	662	723	0.44
Australia 03	368	450	506	561	634	0.53
Chile 15	297	372	427	482	560	0.62
Jordan 03	279	362	427	488	567	0.67
Chile 03	258	328	382	441	531	0.71
Turkey 15	289	385	454	531	634	0.76
Saudi Arabia 03	204	279	331	385	460	0.77
SA 15 (Gr 9)	242	311	364	426	529	0.79
SA 11 (Gr 9)	229	295	343	398	516	0.84
Ghana 03	130	213	274	337	430	1.09
SA 03	117	191	248	316	484	1.48

Source: calculated from Mullis, Martin, Gonzalez, and Chrostowski (2004) for 2003; Mullis, Martin, M., Foy, P., and Arora, A. (2012) for 2011; and https://timssandpirls.bc.edu/timss2015/international-database/ for 2015.

Table 2.3. Inequality data for South Africa and other countries, PIRLS 2016

Country	Score of the child at the following percentiles of the score distribution, PIRLS Grade 4 (Reading)					Inequality ratio (score at 95th minus score at 5th)/ score at 50th
	5th percentile	25th percentile	50th percentile	75th percentile	95th percentile	
Singapore	432	528	570	633	695	0.38
Chile	356	442	489	550	614	0.42
Iran	226	361	420	505	581	0.61
Morocco	180	282	350	436	529	0.66
South Africa	147	246	311	390	498	0.70
Egypt	112	246	319	420	520	0.78

Source: calculated from Mullis, Martin, Foy, and Hooper (2017).

2016, has nearly 40 per cent less inequality as South Africa does in PIRLS 2016. (But note only about 25 per cent less in TIMSS 2015 Grade 4 Mathematics.)

The inequality in South Africa looms particularly large also in comparison with other countries in the SACMEQ region. Figure 2.10 shows each country's average reading and mathematics scores in 2007 (SACMEQ III) in the bars. Differences, in each country, between the performance of high and low SES students are shown as lines. One line (solid) shows the absolute difference, that is the difference in points scored, between the high-SES and the low-SES students. Another line (dotted) shows the difference divided by the average score: a more thorough indicator of inequality, if perhaps a slightly harder one to understand.[11] Countries are shown ranked from left to right in order of overall performance. This helps make it clear, comparing the size of the bars and the slope of the lines, that in general (in the case of SACMEQ—no such assertion can be made for other cross-country assessments) there is an association between increasing average scores and increasing inequality. South Africa is seen to be of middling performance in terms of the total score. But the most striking thing is that in spite of South Africa's average performance being only middling, its inequality as measured using either

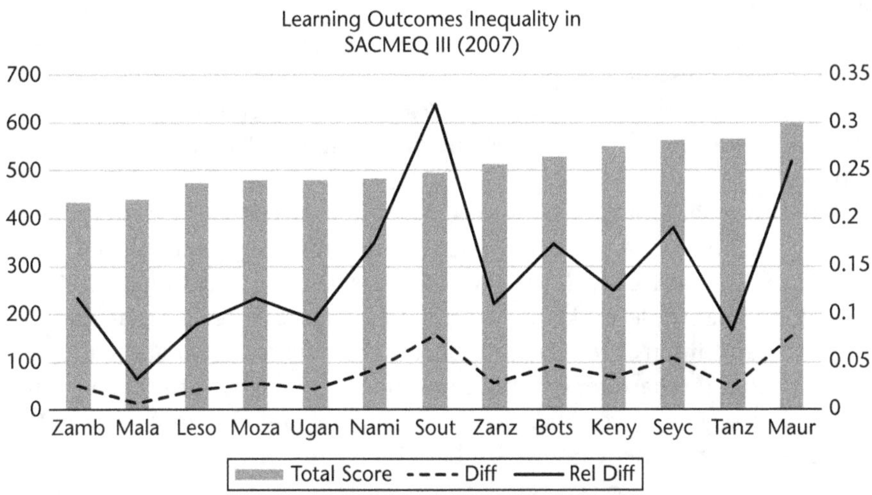

Figure 2.10. South Africa as an inequality outlier, SACMEQ data

Sources: calculations and transformations of online materials shown at http://www.sacmeq.org/ReadingMathScores.

[11] Note that the scores and the absolute differences between the low and high SES levels are shown as bars on the left-hand vertical scale, whereas the relative differences (high minus low divided by the mean) are shown as lines, on the right-hand vertical scale.

of the measures noted, was distinctly the highest, especially taking the relative (dotted) measure into account.[12]

2.5.5 *Recent Upticks in Performance*

The low results for South Africa, especially when one controls for fiscal effort made in favour of education and for GDP per capita, and also the inequality in the results distribution, have been alarming, especially as they are evident ten to fifteen years after the changes that would supposedly benefit the children were crafted. Some, as noted above, foresaw likely low impact from early on. However, more recently there have been some signs of hope. First, as van der Berg and Gustafsson (2017) have shown, recent levels of improvement of South Africa in TIMSS are quite fast, comparable to Brazil's improvements on PISA—themselves quite fast. Table 2.2 shows that, at the fiftieth percentile (the median), South Africa's TIMSS performance between 2011 and 2015 improved by about twenty points. Van der Berg and Gustafsson (2017) explain that Brazil's improvement in PISA, of about 0.06 of a standard deviation per year, is at about the upper limit of how quickly countries can improve, and that South Africa's improvement is on a par with Brazil's. Whether these trends will continue, and how truly solid they ultimately are (they seem to be) would be hard to say. But for now they seem to bode well. The same authors show improved results in the equity of matric results in more or less the same period (roughly 2008 to 2015). And this lines up well with the evidence on the reduced inequality in TIMSS results presented in Table 2.2.

At the same time, at the pilot project level, it seems as if fast improvements are possible and are documented, even in underprivileged schools, via what Fleisch (n.d.), and Fleisch (2016) calls a 'turn to the instructional core' and sometimes the 'triple cocktail' of simplified curricular lesson plans, vastly improved and intensified coaching of teachers, instructional and curricular materials that (perhaps for the first time) are aligned a) with the lesson plans and with vastly improved and increased coaching and b) are available in the home language of the learners.[13] A description of the components of these early grades reading projects is to be found at Department of Basic Education (2017). To some extent, these efforts represent the most serious attempt, perhaps since the end of apartheid, to reverse the litany of cogent critiques

[12] Inequality also happens to have increased between 2000 and 2007, though this is not shown in the graphic. Inequality seems to have increased in all countries, but it increased most for South Africa.

[13] See https://internationalednews.com/2015/06/10/brahm-fleisch-on-building-a-new-infrastructure-for-learning-in-gauteng-south-africa/. Also see Spaull's weblog on the ideas behind Early Grade Reading projects in South Africa, at https://nicspaull.com/.

of classroom instruction presented by Hoadley (2012) and are documented perhaps most succinctly and accessibly in Spaull and Hoadley (2017).[14] Even earlier, however, critics of C2005 had experimented with methods of direct instruction that seemed to work well, at least at imparting basic concepts (Schollar, 2015).

Now, one might over-read into these glimmers of hope, because of the usual 'external validity' problem of pilot projects and randomized controlled trials. However, there is a lot of evidence from other countries that the basic 'formula', elsewhere referred to as 'structured pedagogy', (Snilstveit et al., 2015) used in these particular efforts in South Africa, does work in general, and are thus less of a concern over what one might call pedagogical or cultural external validity.[15] This is part of a broader worldwide trend towards 'teaching at the right level' while eschewing the damage created by curricula and teaching and lesson approaches that are theoretically ambitious but very badly implemented in practice.[16] While strong evidence would suggest that these programs do not suffer from much of a pedagogical or cultural external validity problem, they could suffer from the usual 'exhaustion when taken to scale by government problem', whereby, when a programme is implemented by government, the necessary fidelity which can be guaranteed by good governance and accountability is lost, as has been documented in other cases (see Bold et al., 2013).

But serious concerns remain. The glimmers of hope noted above seem real enough. But they are either not big, or if big, not sustained (yet) over any serious length of time. Or, the changes refer only to pilot projects, sometimes without rigorous randomized controls (though sometimes with). South Africa's educational outcomes are so far behind other middle-income countries, as noted above, that stronger remedies seem necessary, and most commentators on the scene do not see them. Either the lists of remedies scholars provide are very long, or the remedies would seem to require using up quite a bit of political capital. The pedagogical dysfunctionalities observed in the classroom and reported by Hoadley (2012) are many and profound. Nick Taylor, writing

[14] It is important to note that the ineffective techniques noted by these various authors, which the pilot projects are reversing, are not necessarily 'due' to post-apartheid curricular reforms. These practices have been endured by poor South African children for many decades; but the confused idealism of the post-apartheid curricular reforms did nothing to improve on the situation or, in some cases, could have made it worse. This would be especially the case where parents are not able to understand the nature of the transformations and are under-equipped to hold teachers accountable for ineffective practices, teachers found the new practices bewildering, and districts were unable to help.

[15] See literature such as Piper and Korda (2010) from Liberia and Freudenberger and Davis (2017) from Kenya. Kelly and Graham (2017) mention many other country cases. Patrinos describes the Papua New Guinea case (https://hpatrinos.com/tag/papua-new-guinea-education-early-grade-reading/).

[16] Banerjee et al. (2016) and Pritchett and Beatty (2012) discuss the global experience.

for DPME/Department of Basic Education (2017), notes that time management in schools remains poor, teacher content knowledge is way below what is needed to sustain instruction, formative assessment is weak, and teaching and learning materials are not always present. He lays particular blame on corruption, nepotism, and usage of union power to select often inappropriate teachers—in essence, governance and management problems.

2.6 Tentative Conclusions

To speak of the results of the transformation as if they could be causally traced to the transformation would be mistaken. Policy changes as massive as those wrought in South Africa are hardly controlled experiments; any mention of causality therefore should be seen with suspicion. We occasionally lapse into language that seems to assign causality because it is inelegant to be qualifying constantly. But the proviso holds throughout.

The thesis of this section, and hence of the whole chapter, could be put something like this:

1. Governance was reformed and unified in ways which were responsive to both the imperatives of South Africa's broader political settlement, and to normative conceptions of 'good practice' which prevailed at the time, both globally and within South Africa.
2. The government succeeded in transferring resources in a sharp manner. Perhaps not as much as would have been desired by progressive educationists, but to an extent that is unprecedentedly large relative to the international experience and, strikingly, was achieved within a framework of severe macroeconomic constraint.
3. The curriculum was reformed and unified so as to do away with odious apartheid implications and at the same time to 'modernize' it according to the dominant global and national perceptions of the day, recognizing that even under apartheid certain 'modernizing' reforms had already started.
4. Yet, at least by the middle 2000s, or approximately ten years after the formal end of apartheid and the start of the transformations, there seemed not to be much to show for the effort, particularly viewed from the twin lenses of efficiency and equity. Numbers ('access') had increased a little (in some sub-sectors a lot). But learning outcomes, and their inequality, in particular, seemed largely stuck, in spite of some glimmers of hope.

The general view continues to be that the overall effort has been a failure. Indeed, almost immediately upon the announcement of the reforms, especially the curricular reforms, critics such as Jansen (2001) had noted these reforms could not possibly work, or at least not to the extent of the hopes pinned upon them.

The conclusion might be that the better-off segments of the system, at the outset of the transformations, were able to weather the changes in funding, either by self-funding or by becoming more efficient. It is also possible to conclude that they were able to either tune out some of the least useful of the curricular reforms, had already adapted them (given that some of the curricular reforms pre-dated the end of apartheid), or were able to adapt them in light of what they saw as more sensible, given that these segments of the sector had much better-trained teachers, and given that the governance of these schools trusted (and had good reasons to trust) the professionalism of the teachers (and principals). These segments of the system were those where 'good governance' (defined elsewhere in this book) was common.

In other segments of the system, however, neither teachers nor other officials within the education bureaucracy had the training, background, and incentives to put in the hard effort it would have taken to interpret the new curricular and teaching/learning dispensations in a manner that made sense to them and for their environment. Nor, of course, notwithstanding the enhanced role afforded them vis-à-vis school-level governance, were parents in a position to provide support for implementation of the new approaches. Schools on the whole seem unable to make much use of the extra non-personnel funding allocated via the Funding Norms. Informality and maybe even corruption seem to be playing a role in preventing good management.

But things continue to evolve. Some pilot research has shown that, at least in the lower grades, there are sensible ways to simplify and structure the curriculum so that children learn better. These simplified approaches are also easier, in principle, for parents to supervise and in that sense might fit better with a governance model that provides School Governing Bodies considerable power—though the whole notion of the sorts of stable, idealized 'parenthood' envisioned in the South African Schools Act might be problematic in the South African context. In that sense, presuming that additional study and evidence confirms the seemingly compelling evidence from pilot projects, curricular simplification or, at any rate, clearer specification of lesson plans and more direct teaching (along with delivery of more and better learning materials and capacity building for teachers) could be nicely made to coincide with a revamped role for localized parental accountability, if governance could be improved along the lines explored in later chapters of this book.

References

Banerjee, A., Banerji, R., Berry, J., Duflo, E., Kannan, H., Mukherji, S., Shotland, M., and Walton, M. (2016) 'Mainstreaming an Effective Intervention: Evidence from Randomized Evaluations of "Teaching at the Right Level" in India'. NBER Working Paper No. 22746.

Bhorat, H. (2000) 'Wage Premia and Wage Differentials in the South African Labour Market'. Cape Town: Development Policy Research Institute, University of Cape Town.

Bold, T., Kimenyi, M., Mwabu, G., Na'anga, and Sandefur, J. (2013) 'Scaling Up What Works: Experimental Evidence in External Validity in Kenyan Education'. Center for Global Development. Working Paper 321.

Bray, M. (1996) 'Decentralization of Education. Community Financing'. World Bank Directions in Development Paper No. 16167. Washington DC: World Bank.

Buckland, P. and Fielden, J. (1994) 'Public expenditure on education in South Africa: 1987/8 to 1991/2'. Washington DC: World Bank.

Chisholm, L. (2013) 'Bantustan education history: The "progressivism" of Bophuthatswana's Primary Education Upgrade Programme (PEUP), 1979–1988', *South African Historical Journal* 65(3), 403–20.

Cronje, F. (2010) 'Matric: a 50 year review. Independent Education'. Independent Schools Association of South Africa.

Crouch, L. (1996) 'Public Education Equity and Efficiency in South Africa: Lessons for Other Countries', *Economics of Education Review* 15(2), 125–37.

Department of Basic Education (2017) 'Summary Report. Results of Year 2 Impact Evaluation. The Early Grade Reading Study (EGRS)'. Pretoria: Department of Basic Education.

Department of Education (1996) *Report of the Committee to Review the Organisation, Governance and Funding of Schools* (Hunter Report). Pretoria: Department of Education.

Department of Education (2006) '2005 Education Investment Review. Key Trends and Policy Implications'. Directorate: Economic Analysis.

Donalson, A. (1992) *Content, Quality and Flexibility: The Economics of Education System Change.* Spotlight 5/92. Johannesburg: South African Institute of Race Relations.

Fiske, E. (1996) 'Decentralization of Education: Politics and Consensus'. World Bank Directions in Development Paper, No. 1626. Washington DC: World Bank.

Fleisch, B. (2016) 'System-Wide Improvement at the Instructional Core: Chancing Reading Teaching in South Africa', *Journal of Educational Change* 17, 437–51.

Fleisch, B. (n.d.) 'The Instructional Turn and Change Theory.' Manuscript, personal communication.

Freudenberger, F. and Davis, J. (2017) 'Tusome External Evaluation: Midline Report'. Report contracted by USAID to MSI International, https://ierc-publicfiles.s3.amazonaws.com/public/resources/Tusome%20Midline%20evaluation%202017%20final%20report%20from%20DEC.pdf.

Galant, J. (1997) 'Teachers, learners and mathematics: An analysis of HSRC research reports on mathematics education 1970–1980'. Unpublished MEd thesis, University of Cape Town.

Gevisser, M. (2007) *Thabo Mbeki: The Dream Deferred.* Jeppestown: Jonathan Ball.

Hartshorne, K. (1981) 'Private sector involvement in education, 1960–1986'. In C. Millar, S. A. Raynham, and A. Schaeffer (eds), *Breaking the formal frame: Readings in South African education in the eighties*. Cape Town: Oxford University Press.

Hoadley, U. (2012) 'What do we know about teaching and learning in South African primary schools?', *Education as Change* 16(2), 187–202.

Hoadley, U. (2018) *Pedagogy in Poverty: Lessons from 20 years of curriculum reform in South Africa*. London: Routledge.

Kelly, S. and Graham, J. (2017) 'The Case for Investment in Early Grade Reading'. Georgetown University, Global Human Development Program. Final Report.

Jansen, J. (2001) 'Explaining non-change in education reform after apartheid: Political symbolism and the problem of policy implementation'. In Y. Sayed and J. Jansen (eds), *Implementing Education Policies: The South African Experience* (pp. 271–92). Cape Town: University of Cape Town Press.

Jansen, J. and Christie, P. (eds) (1999) *Changing curriculum: Studies on outcomes-based education in South Africa.* Cape Town: Juta and Company Ltd.

Jansen, J. D. (1990) 'Curriculum as a political phenomenon: Historical reflections on black South Africa education', *The Journal of Negro Education* 59(2), 195–206.

Mandela, N. (2004) *Long Walk to Freedom.* Johannesburg: Macdonald Purnell.

Marais, H. (1998) *South Africa: Limits to Change: The Political Economy of Transition.* London and Cape Town: Zed Books and University of Cape Town Press.

Maree, L. (1984) 'The Hearts and Minds of the People'. In P. Kallaway (ed.), *Apartheid Education: The Education of Black South Africans*. Johnannesburg: Ravan Press.

Molteno, F. (1984) 'The Historical Foundations of The Schooling of Black South Africans'. In P. Kallaway (ed.), *Apartheid Education: The Education of Black South Africans*. Johnannesburg: Ravan Press.

Moore, N. (2015) 'In A Class of Their Own: The Bantu Education Act (1953) Revisited'. Master's Thesis, History, University of Pretoria, https://repository.up.ac.za/bitstream/handle/2263/53445/Moore_Class_2016.pdf?sequence=1&isAllowed=y.

Mullis, I., Martin, M., Foy, P., and Arora, A. (2012) 'TIMSS 2011 International Results in Mathematics'. Chestnut Hill, MA: TIMSS & PIRLS International Study Center, Boston College, https://timss.bc.edu/timss2011/international-results-mathematics.html.

Mullis, I., Martin, M., Foy, P., and Hooper, M. (2016) 'TIMSS 2015 International Results in Mathematics'. Chestnut Hill, MA: TIMSS & PIRLS International Study Center, Boston College, https://timssandpirls.bc.edu/timss2015/international-database/.

Mullis, I. V. S., Martin, M. O., Foy, P., and Hooper, M. (2017) 'PIRLS 2016 International Results in Reading', TIMSS & PIRLS International Study Center website: http://timssandpirls.bc.edu/pirls2016/international-results/.

Mullis, I., Martin, M., Gonzalez, E., and Chrostowski, S. (2004) 'Findings From IEA's Trends in International Mathematics and Science Study at the Fourth and Eighth Grades'. Chestnut Hill, MA: TIMSS & PIRLS International Study Center, Boston College, https://timss.bc.edu/timss2003i/mathD.html.

Mwabu, G. and Schultz, T. P. (1996) 'Education Returns Across Quantiles of the Wage Function: Alternative Explanations for Returns to Education by Race in South Africa', *American Economic Review* 86(2), 335–9.

Patrinos, H. and Ariasingam, D. (1997) 'Decentralization of Education: Demand-Side Financing'. World Bank Directions in Development Paper, No. 17047. Washington DC: World Bank.

Piper, B. and Korda Poole, M. (2010) 'Early Grade Reading Assessment (EGRA) Plus: Liberia. Program evaluation report'. (Prepared for USAID/Liberia.) Research Triangle Park, NC: RTI International, https://www.rti.org/publication/early-grade-reading-assessment-egra-plus-liberia-program-evaluation-report.

Pritchett, L. and Amanda Beatty, A. (2012) 'The Negative Consequences of Overambitious Curricula in Developing Countries'. Working Paper 293, Center for Global Development.

Schollar, E. (2015) 'The Primary Mathematics Research Project: 2004–2012. An Evidence-Based Programme of Research into Understanding and Improving the Outcomes of Mathematical Education in South African Primary Schools'. Thesis submitted for the Degree of Doctor of Philosophy in the Department of Sociology, University of Cape Town, https://nicspaull.files.wordpress.com/2016/01/eric-schollar-thesis-final-library-copy-27_may_2015.pdf.

Seekings, J. and Nattrass, N. (2005) *Class, Race and Inequality in South Africa*. New Haven: Yale University Press.

Snilstveit, B., Stevenson, J., Phillips, D., Vojtkova, M., Gallagher, E., Schmidt, T., and Eyers, J. (2015) 'Interventions for improving learning outcomes and access to education in low-and middle-income countries: a systematic review', http://www.3ieimpact.org.

Sparks, A. (1996) *Tomorrow is Another Country: The Inside Story of South Africa's Road to Change*. Chicago: University of Chicago Press.

Spaull, N. and Hoadley, U. (2017) 'Getting Reading Right'. In L. Jamieson, L. Berry, and L. Lake (eds), *South African Child Gauge 2017*. Cape Town: Children's Institute, University of Cape Town.

Swartz, R. (2004) *School Management, Teacher Development and Support: Proceedings of a Conference held at Eskom Centre, Midrand, 18–19 August 1994*. Johannesburg: Education Policy Unit, University of the Witwatersrand.

Unterhalter, E. (1991) 'Changing aspects of reformism in Bantu education 1953–1989'. In E. Unterhalter, H. Wolpe, T. Botha, S. Badet, T. Diamini, and B. Khotseng (eds), *Apartheid education and popular struggles* (pp. 53–72). Johannesburg: Ravan Press.

Van der Berg, S. and Gustafsson, M. (2017) 'Quality of Education. A Report to Working Group 1 of the High Level Panel on the Assessment of Key Legislation'. ReSEP (Research on Socio-Economic Policy), Department of Economics, University of Stellenbosch.

Welsh, D. (2009) *The Rise and Fall of Apartheid*. Charlottesville: University of Virginia Press.

Welsh, F. (2000) *A History of South Africa*. London: Harper Collins.

3

Education Policymaking at National Level

The Politics of Multiple Principals

Robert Cameron and Vinothan Naidoo

3.1 Introduction

Since democratisation in 1994, substantial resources have been allocated to basic education in South Africa. So far, however, outside the top tiers of the income distribution, the results have not matched the resources that have been made available. As Chapter 1 details, governance (the focus of this book) is just one of many variables that account for this exceptionally poor performance. This chapter focuses on one key aspect of governance in the education sector at the national level.

It explores the following puzzle. At first sight, when one looks at the arrangements that have been put in place for managing public sector performance since 1994—across the public service as a whole, and specifically within the education sector—they are enormously impressive. Indeed, in the early 2000s, South Africa was hailed as a global leader in the introduction of tools of new public management (NPM) (Miller, 2005; Cameron, 2009; Levin, 2009). But these efforts did not translate into strong performance.

The hypothesis explored in this chapter is that the answer to the puzzle can be found in the disconnect between, on the one hand, the technocratic orientation of the performance management systems which were introduced and, on the other, a political environment characterized by strong contestation over policy amongst competing stakeholders in the education sector. Notwithstanding the seemingly strong commitment by political leadership to improving public performance, the political and institutional arrangements that govern the sector have resulted in efforts to institute robust performance management being heavily watered down. As always, the devil lay in the details, which this chapter sets out to explore.

The ANC has governed South Africa as a 'ruling alliance'. One key partner[1] in this ruling alliance was the Congress of South African Trade Unions (COSATU), and its various affiliates—including, in the education sector, the South African Democratic Teachers Union (SADTU). SADTU actively supported the ANC in the run-up to the 1994 general elections. Some of its most prominent officials stood as ANC MPs, including its president and general secretary (Govender, 1996).

The institutional arrangements governing conditions of service in the education sector were formally centralised, yet incorporated a high degree of overlap. As Figure 3.1 illustrates, the initial intent to introduce performance management in practice has depended on the relative influence of three sets of actors:

- Public officials in the Department of Basic Education (DBE)—within which many champions of performance management were to be found, and who formally take their lead from the Minister of Basic Education and the Cabinet more broadly.
- The union representatives involved in negotiating the conditions of service—both SADTU (the majority union), and other, smaller unions also represented in the negotiating process.
- The ANC in its dual role as the governing political party and the *primus inter pares* within the 'ruling alliance', as well as the shaper of education policy through the DBE bureaucracy.

After the ANC's election into government, SADTU's ability to influence education policy strengthened through securing key positions in the new

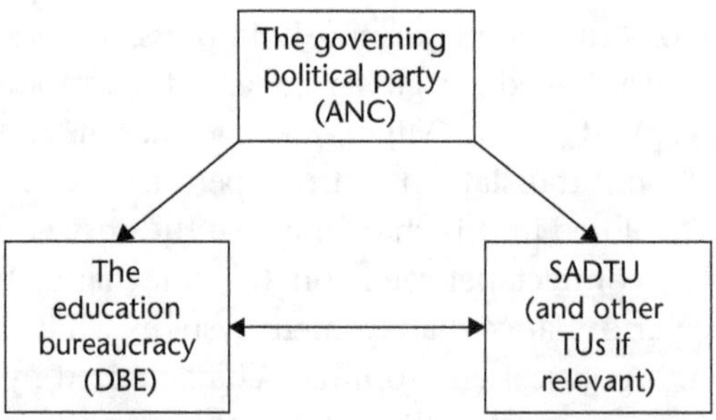

Figure 3.1. SA's education stakeholder 'triangle'

[1] The other partner is the South African Communist Party.

Department of Education (DoE), the Education Labour Relations Council (ELRC), and the South African Council for Educators (SACE). Thus, both Reg Brijraj, the CEO of SACE, a public entity, and Dhaya Govender, the CEO of the ELRC, are former SADTU officials. Govender (2012) recalls that Thami Mseleku, a former SADTU vice-president, was appointed as political advisor to Education Minister Sibusiso Bhengu in 1994, and later held the position of director-general in the DoE. SADTU leaders Shephard Mdladlana, Randall van den Heever, and Ismail Vadi also served as ANC MPs on Parliament's Portfolio Committee on Education. In addition, Duncan Hindle, a former SADTU president and also former director-general in the DoE, left little doubt about the strategic importance that an ANC government held for the union, in this interview with Govender (2012):

> We've put our own people in Parliament, in the Department, it's our Minister, our Thami [Mseleku] is advising the Minister... there was a degree of confidence stemming from the realization that we've finally elected a democratic government, we've got people in Parliament, in the bureaucracies, and so on... we knew that our government had our particular view on the issues...

As we shall see, the intentions to introduce robust performance were repeatedly thwarted by the political exigencies of sustaining the 'ruling alliance'.

The chapter proceeds as follows. Section 3.2 sets the context for the analysis of performance management in education, with an overview of both South Africa's seeming embrace of performance management, and of the institutional arrangements established for governance of basic education. Section 3.3 focuses on performance management in education; it explores in detail what happened en route from the general enunciation of the goals of performance management, to the detailed promulgation of performance measures. Section 3.4 examines in detail the negotiation of one particular performance management initiative, the Occupation Specific Dispensation. Section 3.5 reflects more broadly on the interactions between a country's 'political settlement', its governance arrangements for public service provision, and the observed service provision outcomes.

A central theme of the ESID research programme is that where the political settlement and the governance arrangements are well aligned, good results can be achieved; but where there is misalignment, the results will be poor. This chapter will show that in South Africa there has been a misalignment between the approach to policy at national level for improving basic education, on the one hand, and the realities of the underlying political settlement on the other. The result has been that, for all of their ambitious intent, the national policies may have misdirected attention away from practical options for improving educational performance—and thus complicated, rather than accelerated, South Africa's ability to address effectively the formidable challenges confronting the sector.

3.2 Setting the Stage

This section will set the stage for the chapter's analysis of performance management in education, by providing a brief descriptive overview of two key background developments: how a democratic South Africa (seemingly) came to embrace performance management across the entire public sector; and the overall institutional arrangements which were put in place for the governance of basic education.

3.2.1 *Democratic South Africa's Seeming Embrace of Performance Management*

Table 3.1 lists some key steps in the establishment of South Africa's performance management system. Why was the South African government so enthusiastic in embracing NPM reforms? Friedman and Kihato (2004: 142) argue that South Africa, as is often the case in developing countries, adopted fashionable ideas from developed countries, not because they were gullible to the latest trends, but because the fashion seemed to offer local elites a way out of real dilemmas and to provide solutions to real problems. More specifically, the former minister for public service and administration, Geraldine Fraser-Moleketi, stated in a 2008 interview that public service reforms were not influenced by NPM ideology. The government wanted to borrow NPM skills

Table 3.1. Some steps in shaping South Africa's national performance management system

Year	Measure
1995	***Labour Relations Act:*** establishes a public sector co-ordinating bargaining council (PSCBC) for most parts of the public sector
1995	***White Paper on Transformation of the Pubic Service:*** embraces some central tenets of NPM
1998	***Presidential Review Commission of Inquiry on Transformation and Reform in the Public Service:*** deepens commitment to new public management
1997–99	***Public Service Laws Amendment Act, Public Service Regulations and subsequent resolutions in the PSCBC:*** details roll-out of NPM system, including performance contracting
2003	***Senior Management Service Handbook*** *and* ***Performance Management Development System:*** issued by Department of Public Service and Administration; lay out framework for performance agreements and assessments of senior staff
2007	***Framework for Managing Programme Performance Information:*** issued by National Treasury as a basis for clarifying relationship between budgetary and performance management
2009	***Improving Government Performance:*** report issued by the presidency, as a platform for strengthening performance management at the highest (ministerial) levels
2011	***Management Performance Assessment Tool (MPAT):*** introduced by the Department of Performance Monitoring and Evaluation in the Presidency, as a flagship tool for improving performance via a structured, evidence-based approach

Table 3.2. Establishing a governance framework for the education sector

1995	***Labour Relations Act:*** establishes an ELRC to manage collective bargaining in the education sector
1996	***National constitution:*** defines co-responsibility for education between a national-level department of basic education and nine provincial-level departments
1996	***South African Schools Act:*** details a central role for school governing bodies (SGBs) in school-level governance. SGBs are not involved directly in performance evaluation, but one of their functions is to support the principal, educators, and other staff of the school in the performance of their professional functions
1998	***Employment of Educators Act:*** deals with appointment, promotion, transfers, and other service conditions of educators

and techniques to modernize the public service without buying into the ideological framework (Cameron, 2009).

3.2.2 *Transforming the Institutional Arrangements for Basic Education*

As Table 3.2 details, within the first three years of South Africa's democratic era, far-reaching measures were promulgated that put in place a comprehensive set of institutional arrangements for the education sector. Looking beyond the specific measures listed in the table, two broad patterns are worthy of note:

- Education was defined in South Africa's intergovernmental system as a shared responsibility—with national government responsible for policy and financing, and implementation delegated to nine provincial governments.
- The terms and conditions of employment of education sector workers were to be negotiated at the national level, in a sector-specific ELRC.

As the next section will explore in depth, the last of these turned out to have profound implications for the evolution of performance management within education. It has been pointed out that SADTU successfully lobbied to widen the scope of the ELRC to include matters pertaining to teacher performance—all collective agreements in respect of teachers' performance were now negotiated nationally with the unions. SADTU's next target was the inspection system which had existed in all education departments in the apartheid era. Teachers rejected the inspectorate system because it functioned in a coercive manner and enforced compliance with rules and regulations—accountability was geared to the bureaucracy, rather than the education system, with compliance with standard procedures, policy directives, and rules (Mosoge and Pilane, 2014: 7; De Clercq, 2013). In particular, inspectors were seen as the frontier of apartheid control in black and coloured schools.

3.3 Performance Management in Basic Education—from Vision to Practice

As Figure 3.2 outlines, within a decade after their establishment—and paralleling the broader efforts described in section 3.2 to introduce performance management throughout South Africa's public sector—the new, national-level educational governance institutions promulgated an increasingly robust array of performance management instruments for the sector, resembling a continuum.

From the start, the influence of SADTU was evident. Consistent with SADTU's preferences, the scope of the ELRC was expansively defined, to include agreements on all issues pertaining to teachers' work (Swartz, 1994; de Clerq, 2013). As a consequence, all collective agreements in respect of teachers' performance were negotiated nationally with the unions. From the start, tensions were evident between the aspirations of technocrats in the department of national (subsequently basic) education and teacher unions. These tensions culminated in a massive strike in 2007—not only in education, but across the public sector. Section 3.3.1 explores what happened to efforts to introduce performance management into education prior to 2007; the section then considers the far-reaching reforms of the measures that were introduced after the strike.

3.3.1 *Establishing a Performance Management Platform, 1996–2006*

This section considers first the evolution of the negotiated salary structure for teachers (the backdrop to performance management). Thereafter it considers

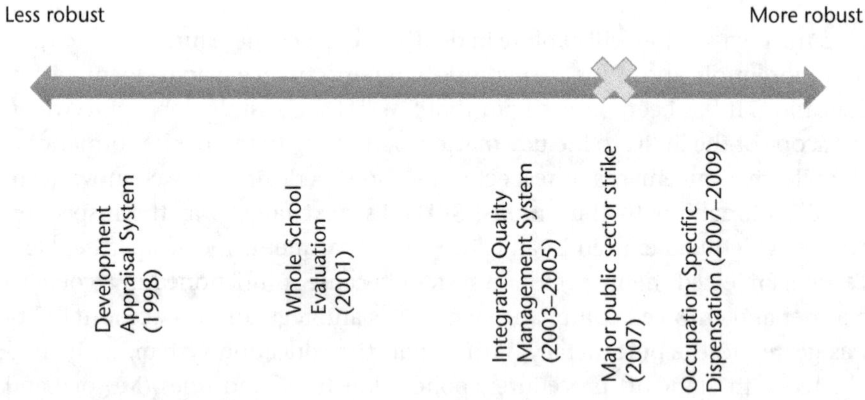

Figure 3.2. Performance management continuum in South Africa's basic education sector

in turn the three performance management measures promulgated successively, as per Figure 3.2, in 1998, 2001, and 2003.

SALARY STRUCTURE FOR TEACHERS

The transition to democracy in 1994 was followed in short order by a major restructuring of salaries. Teacher salary scales were equalised, so as to bring the salaries of female and black, coloured and Indian teachers in line with those of male white teachers, who had enjoyed a privileged position during apartheid (Hosking, 2000). Salaries thus increased significantly in the mid-1990s for most teachers (Gustafsson and Patel, 2008), or amounted to what Armstrong (2009: 6) referred to as an 'abrupt increase in the unit cost of teachers post-1994'.

As part of this general effort to equalise remuneration, SADTU also bargained for salary compression during the 1990s. This involved advocating disproportionately higher salary increases at the lower end of the scale relative to the higher end. Van der Berg and Burger (2010: 10, 11) explain the motives behind SADTU's salary compression strategy by observing that the organisation supported an effort in 1995 to suspend the use of qualifications and experience-based increments relative to general increases, because the latter disproportionately benefited its membership, who were concentrated at lower levels of qualifications and experience, compared to the membership of other unions. The effects of this salary compression are also illustrated in Van der Berg and Burger's (2010: 25) analysis, which, drawing on data between 2000 and 2006, notes that relative earnings of teachers is similar to their private and other public sector counterparts at the age of twenty-two, but are progressively overtaken the longer they remain in the profession, representing a career disincentive. Moreover, the earnings-age profile of teachers is 'flatter' than is the case with private and other public sector workers. As we shall explore further below, in important ways salary compression and performance management turned out to be at odds with one another.

THE 1998 DEVELOPMENT APPRAISAL SYSTEM

During the apartheid era, performance was managed through an inspection system (which existed across all racially separate departments). It has been pointed out that teachers rejected the inspectorate system because it functioned in a coercive manner and enforced compliance with rules and regulations.

In response, SADTU and the DBE jointly agreed in 1998 to a new development appraisal system (DAS), to replace the previous fault-finding evaluation of inspectors and school managers. DAS was hailed as a major step in breaking the long-standing impasse between teachers and employers over acceptable evaluation procedures. Instead of linking evaluations to salary determination or working conditions, the plan was to rely heavily on peer evaluation and to focus on professional skill development. DAS is a process for determining how a teacher performs in his/her job and then to establish an appropriate improvement plan. The principle implies that a teacher can only be evaluated once attempts have been made to make him/her more proficient and effective in his/her job (Fiske and Ladd, 2004: 195; Mosoge and Pilane, 2014: 2–3).

The 2004 study by Fiske and Ladd (ibid.) reported that the early implementation of development appraisal was slow, with teachers viewing the evaluations as time-consuming and cumbersome. It was pointed out that many of the appraisals were based on casual conversations between teachers, rather than classroom observations. Most importantly, the authors noted, with appraisal having been decoupled from professional advancement, the system was weak.

THE 2001 WHOLE SCHOOL EVALUATION

The whole school evaluation (WSE) policy was promulgated by the then Minister of National Education, Kader Asmal, in 2001 (Republic of South Africa, 2001). WSE processes, based on the United Kingdom's OFSTED (Office for Standards in Education), include school self-evaluation, ongoing district-based support, monitoring and development, and external evaluations conducted by the supervisory units. Provision was made for input, social, and output indicators which had to be measured. While the policy stated that it would not interfere in any way with existing activities and agreements, including the DAS, in practice it shifted attention away from focusing on teacher development towards greater monitoring and control measures over office staff, schools, and teachers (De Clercq, 2013).

The WSE policy was promulgated without any consultation with unions. SADTU resisted the introduction of a 'whole school evaluation programme' as 'managerial', 'punitive', and containing 'minimal developmental content for teachers' (SADTU, 2009a); it encouraged its members to boycott WSE supervisors and to refuse them access to schools (SADTU, 2002, as cited in de Clercq, 2009: 99). Reasons cited for the resistance to the WSE was that it adopted a 'fault finding' approach (de Clercq, 2009: 99); with De Clercq (2013: 43–4) adding that SADTU's position was that the WSE 'erod[ed] the autonomy of schools and teachers' and conflicted with the teacher-driven spirit of the DAS; amounted to an 'unfairly judgemental inspection system', and failed to take into account underlying causes of poor performance at a school level caused by decades of under-investment by the state. WSE was never implemented at scale, and was superseded by the 2003 IQMS.

THE 2003 INTEGRATED QUALITY MANAGEMENT SYSTEM

A collective bargaining agreement was reached between managers and the unions in the ELRC (Resolution 8 of 2003) to integrate the existing programmes on quality management in education, into a comprehensive package encompassing the development appraisal system, performance measurement, and the whole school evaluation. This new system was described as a bargained 'compromise' between the state and unions, which combined aspects of previous appraisal systems and was premised on the principle that 'development had to take place before any summative evaluation' (De Clercq, 2013: 44). Appendix A3.1 provides further detail on what was included in the IQMS.

The IQMS relied as a first step on self-evaluation by teachers. As Mosoge and Pilane (2014: 9) point out, the teachers are (understandably) reluctant to expose their weaknesses when they complete the performance improvement plans, for fear of losing out on salary progression. The authors conclude that because of this, IQMS completely loses its developmental power. A DBE review of the IQMS found that 'unreliable and invalid' processes were applied to assessing and rating educators, and that this was linked to the involvement of multiple appraisers (including teachers, departmental heads and principals, peers, and district officials) and their potentially 'different interests and agendas' (De Clercq, 2008: 13, 14).

Even though it was negotiated collectively, the implementation of the IQMS was met with resistance from teachers who considered this new accountability system to be a 'tough-on-schools' policy aimed at apportioning blame on teachers for the ills of education (Smith and Ngoma-Maema, 2003). SADTU rejected the teacher performance appraisal arrangements, stating that learner performance should not be included as part of appraising educators, and called on the delinking of development appraisal from the IQMS. Indeed, De Clercq (2011 in 2013: 44) reports that poor levels of state support for teacher development 'frustrated unions and teachers so much that they decided to manipulate the IQMS scores to qualify for a bonus'. The reliability of the IQMS has been questioned, due to the vast majority of teachers supposedly 'performing well'. A Department of Education commissioned report of the IQMS in 2007 pointed to the unreliable and invalid process through which most educators were assessed and rated, irrespective of the level of learner achievements (Class Act, 2007: 10).

A final serious flaw in the IQMS's whole school approach was the absence of any external testing of learner achievement (Fiske and Ladd, 2004: 196–7). During the negotiation process SADTU and other teacher unions had raised fundamental objections to national learner targets being included in the IQMS, stating that teachers cannot be held accountable for the performance of learners. In the end, the agreements reached in the ELRC watered down the IQMS into a weak form of performance management. There was no reference to learners' outcomes. Teachers were not going to be held accountable for the poor performance of pupils.

3.4 The Continuing Challenge of Incentivising Performance: the Case of the 'Occupation Specific Dispensation'

To better understand why initiatives to strengthen performance management were watered down, this section explores the experience of negotiating the details of one high profile initiative, the occupation specific dispensation (OSD). The OSD originated from a series of agreements following public sector strikes in 2007. In the years following South Africa's transition to democracy there had been several instances in which salary negotiations between public sector unions and the government had resulted in disputes and industrial action. In 1999 an estimated 400,000 public employees in twelve unions engaged in strike action over wages and benefits, and again in 2004 around 700,000 public sector employees went on strike (Banjo and Balkaran, 2009: 120, 121). The 2007 strike was a continuation of a contentious relationship between the state and its employees, which culminated in a twenty-seven-day strike by 700,000 public employees across multiple sectors, supported by seventeen unions across all provinces (Banjo and Balkaran, 2009: 120, 121, 129). The strike had a dramatic effect on the government's ability to deliver public services across the country, disrupting health services, border posts, motor vehicle licensing offices, port authorities, deeds offices, immigration services at airports, the payment of social grants, and schooling (Banjo and Balkaran, 2009: 125).

One of the outcomes of the settlement was an agreement by the state to develop a system of differential pay for different levels of achievement, laying the groundwork for occupation-specific conditions of service in which revised salary structures for specific professional occupations would be introduced in order to incentivise performance by attracting and retaining skilled personnel. The OSD proposed by DBE for the education sector was described as the most comprehensive reform proposals for the educator payment system since the widespread changes that took place in the mid-1990s (Gustafsson and Patel, 2008: 5). However, as this section will detail, the OSD that was eventually promulgated in 2009 was very different in substance from the original proposal. As this section will detail, the OSD process thus serves as a case example of the tactical interplay between the state and unions over the terms of performance management.

3.4.1 *Initial Proposals*

A key purpose of introducing an OSD for public sector teachers was to break through what had emerged as a result of salary compression as a poorly incentivized model of career development. The intention was to enhance the attractiveness of a teaching career and enable salary progression, to reward good performance and introduce incentives for experienced and capable teachers to remain in the classroom (Centre for Education Policy Development, 2011: 4). Recognising that such a proposal would be a hard sell to unions such as SADTU, the initiative also comprised a broad salary increase to all teachers, and raised the starting salary of newly qualified teachers (ELRC, 2008a: 171).

The OSD proposals made by the DBE included:

- A career-pathing model that did not entail automatic increases, but rather systematic increases over pre-determined periods based on specific criteria, such as performance, qualifications, scope of work, and experience (ELRC, 2008b: 3(7)).
- Dual career paths where specialists could progress to salary levels equal to or higher than managerial positions (ELRC, 2008b: 3(8)). This career-pathing model recognised experience and rewarded performance by making provision for accelerated career progression based on performance, and by developing a specialist career path for teachers who wanted to remain in the classroom rather than assume management positions.
- The inclusion of learner performance with due regard to the socio-economic context of the institutions, as a basis for assessing the performance of educators (ELRC, 2008b: 5(1)(3)(7)).
- Performance agreements for principals and deputy principals (ELRC, 2008b: 5(1)(4)(3)).
- A two-yearly pay progression based on performance as measured by the integrated quality management system (IQMS), with 1 per cent for 'satisfactory', 3 per cent for 'good', and 6 per cent for 'outstanding' performance (ELRC, 2008b: 5(5)–5(6)).
- External moderation of assessments in which 'good' or 'outstanding' performance had been awarded (ELRC, 2008b: 5(6)(8)).

3.4.2 *The Negotiations Process*

Negotiations for a collective agreement on the OSD began in the ELRC in September 2007. The proposals comprised a far-reaching departure from the very limited efforts of the IQMS to link pay and performance. Unsurprisingly, despite intense negotiations, in the first phase of negotiations the parties were not able to reach an agreement (ELRC, 2008a: 169).

SADTU strongly opposed the policy in the form initially proposed by the Department of Education. The November 2007 national general council (NGC) meeting resolutions expressed its opposition to the OSD in harsh terms, stating among other concerns that it contained 'empty promises', 'overemphasized performance-related pay', 'rolls back all the gains SADTU achieved heroically since 1990', 'brings back the despised Old Order hierarchy in promotions', and 'attacks Centralized Bargaining' (SADTU, 2007). SADTU was also concerned that the initiative would widen the gap between teachers at the high and low ends of the earnings scale, and that while the proposal spoke about recognising qualifications, it said little about how the DBE would upgrade teachers. The NGC resolved to reject the OSD in its current form and to provide a counter-proposal that preserved the favourable conditions of employment by opposing 'any downward variations'. The counter-proposal comprised a broad minimum 4.5 per cent increase for all educators, the compression of the salary notch structure, the removal of measures to link pay progression to educator performance, accelerating the pay progression of educators, and opposing separate packages for principals and deputy principals (SADTU, 2007).

In January 2008, the director-general of the Department of Education, Duncan Hindle, invited the principals of the trade union parties to explore a resolution on the OSD, and this invitation was accepted by SADTU (ELRC, 2008a: 169). SADTU then met with the deputy director-general and agreed on a process of facilitation, which, during the same month, resulted in trade unions engaging in discussions to formulate a common position on the OSD (ELRC, 2008a: 169).

In February 2008, a facilitation process began, which included four meetings over the course of a month; however, parties could still not reach an agreement. Over the course of March and April, 'special bargaining' meetings were convened and attended to try to reach a consensus. Eventually, near the closing of the deadline, collective agreement 1 of 2008, 'framework for establishment of an occupation-specific dispensation (OSD) for educators in public education', and collective agreement 2 of 2008, 'special task team' was signed by all parties on 3 April 2008 (ELRC, 2008a: 170).

Collective agreements 1 and 2 of 2008 were the first agreements to come out of the ELRC process that dealt with the OSD and took just under nine months of negotiations to reach. However, the agreements were adopted only as a framework in which the negotiations could continue. Collective agreement 1 of 2008 committed parties to the principles that the OSD aimed to achieve, and bound parties to certain procedural agreements. Section 4 of the agreement reflects the core issues which had not yet been resolved and required parties to submit proposals on matters relating to the recognition of experience for salary adjustment purposes, the review of collective agreements affected by the implementation of the OSD, and a number of other technical points. Section 4 also commits the parties to the process of negotiating the OSD under a process manager appointed by the ELRC, and binds the parties to submit themselves to the process manager (ELRC, 2008b).

The second round of OSD negotiations began in 2009, during a period when the public sector was once again gripped by strikes, this time because government had repeatedly postponed the implementation of payments committed to in the 2007 OSD agreements, which had particularly affected the health and correctional services sectors (Banjo and Balkaran, 2009: 128). During this time, SADTU members disrupted classes and went on strike for over a week in a bid to communicate their grievances to the government over OSD and related issues; on 9 June 2009, the Labour Court declared the strike by the SADTU illegal and interdicted members from embarking on protests and work stoppages (ibid.)

On 13 June 2009, the *Mail & Guardian* newspaper reported that, amid tensions around the OSD in the public service, government ministers were 'summoned to a meeting with COSATU at Luthuli House', party headquarters of the ANC, where they agreed to implement the OSD (Rossouw and Letsoalo, 2009). The meeting was reportedly attended by Health Minister Aaron Motsoaledi, Correctional Services Minister Nosiviwe Mapisa-Nqakula, and DBE Minister Angie Motshekga. COSATU is reported to have told ministers that the implementation of the OSD was 'essential to avert further crippling industrial action'. However, this move does not appear to have succeeded in diminishing tensions around the OSD in education, and in July 2009 SADTU threatened 'rolling mass action' if its demands on the OSD were not met (Mbabela, 2009). The pressure to strike appears to have come from members who believed that salaries would increase in April 2009, but had not yet been paid (South African Press Association [SAPA], 2009). At the same time, Chris Klopper, chief executive of Suid-Afrikaanse Onderwysersunie (SAOU), stated that unions had met outside of the bargaining chamber to establish a task team to help end the deadlock between parties (SAPA, 2009).

3.4.3 *The Eventual Agreement*

The OSD impasse finally ended on 14 August 2009, with the signing of ELRC collective agreement 4 of 2009, 'Finalisation of matters linked to the occupational specific dispensation in education'. It must be noted, however, that SADTU was the only party representing unionized teachers to sign this agreement. SADTU General Secretary Mugwena Maluleka hinted at conflict with the other trade unions on this issue by stating that collective agreement 4 was a 'vindication to [*sic*] other opportunistic organisations who tried to claim easy victories on the process that led to the signing of the OSD agreement by spreading lies and didn't append their signatures to the agreement' (SADTU, 2009b). The OSD's proposals on performance assessment was clearly one which divided teacher unions, with NAPTOSA supporting performance evaluation linked to pay progression and lamenting the absence of an appraisal system for educators that rewarded above average or excellent performance (Politicsweb, 2012). This justifies the notion of SADTU as a blocking coalition, namely the OSD process in contrast to other non-signatory unions.

Collective agreement 4 of 2009 notes that the agreement was met under 'an urgent need for parties to conclude discussions and negotiations on matters identified as crucial for the development and provisioning of quality public education' (ELRC 2009). It also confirmed that consensus had not been reached on salary structures for educators, stating that 'there is a need to investigate and research a salary structure applicable to educators in South Africa and to review the remuneration system in education' (ELRC, 2009) and that 'relevant work experience is vital in providing quality teaching' (ELRC, 2009: s.3(6)).

Some of the provisions in the agreement included:

- Further investigation of the salary structure for educators in the ELRC.
- Educators' experience will be recognised on the basis of time served, with one salary notch increment awarded for every three years worked.
- A broad salary increase of 3 per cent will be paid to all educators.
- The accelerated pay progression of 3 per cent for good and 6 per cent for outstanding performance be immediately terminated and the savings from this action will be utilized to fund the broad 3 per cent increase in 2009 and a 1 per cent annual pay progression thereafter (ELRC, 2009).
- The agreement also raised the salaries of educators on the lowest end of the qualifications scale and awarded a one-off cash bonus of 3 per cent of the annual salary notch to senior and master teachers (ELRC, 2009).

Because the provisions for performance-based increases were terminated, as were provisions to stream educators on separate teaching and managerial career paths, the salary structure that was implemented after the 2009 agreement did not allow for teachers to move with reasonable speed through the salary notches (CEPD, 2011: 4). With 3 per cent for 'good' and 6 per cent for 'outstanding' removed, the only way that movement up the notch system could be achieved is through annual notch increases, making the possible maximum salary in a band unachievable in an average working life (CEPD, 2011: 5). This meant that minimum salaries improved, but that teachers with more experience and expertise were not paid significantly more than entry-level teachers, having the overall effect of compressing the salary system (ibid.).

The final agreement of the OSD is consistent with the diluted practice of performance management exemplified in previous instruments, although this time the stakes were much higher for the DBE and recalcitrant unions such as SADTU. The neutering of the original OSD proposals, which were meant to counteract the career disincentive effect of past salary compression, resulted in the introduction of what was meant to be an incentivized carrot-linking salary progression with individualised performance, but dismissed by SADTU as a stick which threatened the union's collective action strength.

3.5 Conclusion

Figure 3.1, introduced at the outset of this chapter, proposed that South Africa's policies for managing performance in basic education could best be explained as the outcome of a strategic interaction among three sets of actors—technocratically oriented public officials in the bureaucracy, teacher labour unions (especially SADTU, as the dominant union), and the ANC in its dual role as the top level of the public sector hierarchy and as the *primus inter pares* within the 'ruling alliance'.

As detailed in section 3.2, almost from the start of the democratic era, South Africa has attempted to introduce robust approaches to performance management in the country's public sector, including in basic education. In practice, the political strength of organized labour resulted in national policies which, beneath their surface, fell well short of the aspiration of robust performance management. Indeed, the result is uncomfortably close to what Pritchett, Woolcock, and Andrews (2010) and Andrews (2013) have described as 'isomorphic mimicry'—a set of outcomes that offer a surface appearance of being consistent with international 'best practices', but in practice do little to advance the (seemingly) intended goals.

Beyond the specifics of the South African case, the results also shed light on the broader issue highlighted in Chapter 1 of how 'good fit' works in practice. As per the analytical approach laid out in that chapter, underlying NPM are some very some strong assumptions about the broader national political context. As laid out in the World Bank's (2004) 'long-route' of accountability, these comprise a set of nested principal–agent relationships governed by tightly specified, impersonal rules of the game in which citizens are principals vis-à-vis politicians; politicians, in turn, are principals vis-à-vis policymakers; policymakers are principals vis-à-vis top levels of the public bureaucracy; and top levels are principals vis-à-vis lower levels.

Practice, of course, inevitably falls short of this ideal type—so NPM will never be implemented as conceived in its 'best practice' blueprint.[2] Here is the conclusion of a landmark review of public administrative reform in ten OECD

[2] It has been argued that performance management in South Africa is less about management reform and more about reasserting new forms of political control over the bureaucracy (Cameron, 2010), hence its inclusion in the hierarchical impersonal cell.

countries—including such noted public management reformers as Australia, New Zealand, Sweden, the United States, and the United Kingdom:[3]

> Reform-watching in public management can be a sobering pastime. The gaps between rhetoric and actions . . . are frequently so wide as to provoke skepticism. The pace of underlying, embedded achievement tends to be much slower than the helter-skelter cascade of new announcements and initiatives. Incremental analysis and partisan mutual adjustment seem to have been very frequent features of public management reform, even if more-than-incremental changes were frequently hoped for . . . To launch, sustain and implement a comprehensive strategy for reform requires . . . a high degree of consensus over what needs to be done, sustained over five-years-plus . . . informed leadership, both from politicians and top public civil servants . . . considerable organizational capacity . . . and a degree of public acceptance. These are seldom all satisfied in the real world of public management reform. (Pollitt and Bouckaert, 2000: 88–9)

In the case of performance management of basic education in South Africa, the disconnect between the 'political settlement' presumptions of NPM and the realities of what we observed at the national level are especially stark. Table 3.3 is our heuristic summary of South Africa's prevailing governance arrangements for national-level policymaking in basic education, using the framework (and 100-point scale) laid out in Chapter 1:

- As per the top-right cell, while the bureaucracy proposed robust performance management measures on the presumption of a 'long route' set of relationships, their de facto influence has been much more modest.[4]
- As per the bottom-right cell, the formal rules of the game required that the eventual rules be negotiated with organized labour in the ELRC.

Table 3.3. National-level policymaking for basic education in South Africa

Hierarchical	15	25
Negotiated	20	40
	Personalized	Impersonal

[3] For a classic discussion of both the opportunities and challenges of reform in the United States context, see Wilson (1989).

[4] As a notable footnote, a presidential commission of inquiry appointed in 2013 to study the remuneration and conditions of service of public servants and educators, which claims it is 'prioritising' the education sector, is effectively revisiting many of the same components negotiated under the OSD. This includes 'sustainable pay progression and performance management', 'skills retention', and 'suitable job classification linked to remuneration' (Presidential Remuneration Review Commission, not dated). At the time of writing, the Commission was still busy with its deliberations. But, it is worth asking whether, post the OSD failure, the Commission represents an attempt by the state to reassert a hierarchical/impersonal posture.

- In practice, at crucial moments, these formal processes stalled. As per the left-hand column of Table 3.3, resolving these impasses required intervention outside the formal channels and within the closed doors of the 'ruling alliance'.

South Africa's intergovernmental system allocates the responsibility for managing the provision of basic education to the provinces (within the constraints of the policies set at the national level). So, it is, of course, possible that a hierarchical approach to provision might work well in some provinces, though not others; the companion chapters on the provision of basic education in the Western and Eastern Cape will shed light on this issue. But, at the very least, the findings of this chapter raise the question as to whether, given South Africa's political realities, top-down approaches to performance management are likely to be implementable.

Grindle's (2004) *Despite the Odds* explores the diverse ways in which a variety of Latin American countries navigated the generally contentious relationship between government and labour in efforts to reform education. As she shows, conflictual, zero-sum approaches all too often resulted in a downward spiral of dysfunctional interactions. Building on both our findings in this chapter and Grindle's insights, perhaps, in the South African context, an approach where negotiation was less about a zero-sum contestation over the robustness of performance management, and more a search for positive-sum, 'win-win' options for engagement between government and labour over education sector reform might yield better results.[5]

Appendix A3.1 The Integrated Quality Management System

The integrated quality management system (IQMS) is a voluminous eighty-four-page document which consists of three programmes, aimed at enhancing and monitoring performance. They are:

- developmental appraisal;
- performance measurement; and
- whole school evaluation.

The purpose of developmental appraisal (DA) is to appraise individual educators in a transparent manner, with a view to determining areas of strength and weakness, and to draw up programmes for individual development.

[5] Elaborating in-depth on win-win options for South Africa's education sector is beyond the scope of this chapter. As an illustrative example of what we have in mind, perhaps the area of training/skills upgrading for teachers is a potential win-win around which government and SADTU could try and build a more collaborative approach.

The purpose of performance measurement (PM) is to evaluate individual teachers for salary progression, grade progression, affirmation of appointments, and rewards and incentives.

The purpose of whole school evaluation (WSE) is to evaluate the overall effectiveness of a school, as well as the quality of teaching and learning.

The IQMS instrument is made up of two parts. One part (made up of four performance standards) is for lesson observation and the other part (made up of eight performance standards) is related to aspects for evaluation that fall outside of the classroom. It needs to be pointed out that these are national performance tools which are binding on teachers in all provinces.

Lesson Observation Performance Standards

This part of the instrument is designed for observation of educators in practice for developmental appraisal, performance measurement, and whole school evaluation (external).

(1) The creation of a positive learning environment.
(2) Knowledge of curriculum and learning programmes.
(3) Lesson planning, preparation, and presentation.
(4) Learner assessment.

Outside the Classroom Performance Standards

The instrument for aspects outside of the classroom:

(1) Professional development in field of work/career and participation in professional bodies.
(2) Human relations and contribution to school development.
(3) Extra-curricular and co-curricular participation.
(4) Administration of resources and records.
(5) Personnel.
(6) Decision-making and accountability.
(7) Leadership, communication, and servicing the governing body.
(8) Strategic planning, financial planning, and Education Management Development (EMD) (pp. 16–17).

There is a four-point rating scale:

- Rating 1: unacceptable.
- Rating 2: satisfies minimum expectations.
- Rating 3: good.
- Rating 4: outstanding.

The rating for educators can be adjusted upwards taking contextual factors into account, such as the lack of opportunities for development, lack of in-service training provided by the district/local departmental office, or lack of support and mentoring within the school (p. 20).

In terms of performance management, you have to be evaluated firstly by your superior, that is, teachers by heads of department, heads of departments by deputy principals, and principals by circuit managers and, secondly, by your peers. The unions are not involved in the evaluations: they only get involved if there are grievances and disputes around the process.

Application of Instrument

For developmental appraisal, no overall ratings or totals are required.

With respect to performance measurement for purposes of pay or grade progression, total scores must be calculated. The final score (total) is used to arrive at an overall rating.

For the purposes of WSE, it is not required to make judgements about the performance of individual educators. It is, however, necessary to evaluate the school's overall performance in respect of each of the performance standards, in order to enable the school to plan for appropriate programmes that will ensure improvement in those areas that are identified (pp. 20–1).

References

Andrews, M. (2013) *The Limits of Institutional Reform. Changing Roles for Realistic Solutions. Changing Rules for Realistic Solutions.* Cambridge: Cambridge University Press.

Armstrong, P. (2009) 'Teacher pay in South Africa: How attractive is the teaching profession?', Stellenbosch Economic Working Papers 04/09. Stellenbosch University, Department of Economics, Bureau for Economic Research.

Banjo, A. and Balkaran, S. (2009) 'A descriptive analysis of the 2007 public sector strike in South Africa', *South African Journal of Labour Relations* 33(2), 120–31.

Cameron, R. (2009) 'New Public Management reforms in the South African public service', *Journal of Public Administration* 44 (4:1), 910–42.

Cameron, R. (2010) 'Redefining Political-Administrative Relationships in South Africa', *International Review of Administrative Sciences* 76(4), 676–701.

Centre for Education Policy Development (CEPD) (2011) *Revised Salary Structure Proposals.* Report prepared for the Education Labour Relations Council by the CEPD, http://db3sqepoi5n3s.cloudfront.net/files/docs/111012cepdreport.pdf.

Class Act (2007) 'IQMS Implementation Review, a DoE commissioned report'. Johannesburg: Class Act.

De Clercq, F. (2008) 'Teacher quality, appraisal and development: The flaws in the IQMS', *Perspectives in Education* 26(1), 7–18.

De Clercq, F. (2009) 'School monitoring and change: A critical examination of whole school evaluation', *Education as Change* 11(2), 97–113.

De Clercq, F. (2011) 'Teacher appraisal reforms in post-1994 South Africa: Conflicts, contestations and mediations'. Unpublished PhD thesis. Johannesburg: University of the Witwatersrand.

De Clercq, F. (2013) 'Professionalism in South African education: The challenges of developing teacher professional knowledge, practice, identity and voice', *Journal of Education* 57, 31–54.

Education Labour Relations Council (ELRC) (2008a) *Annual Report for the Year 2007/2008*, http://www.elrc.org.za/sites/default/files/publications/ELRC%20Annual%20Report%202007-08%20small.pdf.

Education Labour Relations Council (ELRC) (2008b) 'Collective agreement number 1 of 2008: Framework for the establishment of an occupation specific dispensation (OSD) for educators in public education', http://www.elrc.org.za/sites/default/files/documents/CollectiveAgreementNo1of2008.pdf.

Education Labour Relations Council (ELRC) (2009) 'Collective agreement 4 of 2009: Finalisation of matters linked to the occupational specific dispensation in education', http://www.elrc.org.za/sites/default/files/documents/CA%204%20OF%202009.pdf.

Fiske, E. and Ladd, H. F. (2004) *Education Reform in Post-apartheid South Africa*. Washington DC: Brookings Institute Press.

Friedman, S and Kihato, C. (2004) 'South Africa's double reform: Decentralisation and the transition from apartheid'. In P. Oxhorn, J. S. Tulchin, and A. D. Selee (eds), *Decentralization, Democratic Governance and Civil Society in Comparative Perspective*. Washington DC: Woodrow Wilson Center Press, 119–38.

Govender, L. (1996) *When the 'chalks are down': a historical, political and social interpretation of teacher militancy in South Africa*. Pretoria: HSRC Publishers.

Govender, L. (2012) The mediation of teacher unions' participation in policy making: a South African case study. SACHES Conference.

Grindle, M. S. (2004) *Despite the Odds: The Contentious Politics of Education Reform*. Cambridge, MA: Harvard University Press.

Gustafsson, M. and Patel, F. (2008) 'Managing the teacher pay system: What the local and international data are telling us'. Stellenbosch Economic Working Papers 26/06. Stellenbosch University, Department of Economics, Bureau for Economic Research.

Hosking, S. (2000) 'Government-induced teacher failure in South Africa—causes and analysis', *Development Southern Africa* 17(5), 641–65.

Levin, R. (2009) 'Transforming the public service to support the development state', *Journal of Public Administration* 44(4:1), 943–68.

Mbabela, Z. (2009) 'SADTU threatens strike over OSD'. *Sowetan*, 1 July, http://www.sowetanlive.co.za/sowetan/archive/2009/07/01sadtu-threatens-strike-over-osd?service=print.

Miller, K. (2005) *Public Sector Reform Governance in South Africa*. Aldershot: Ashgate.

Mosoge, M. J. and Pilane, M. W. (2014) 'Performance management: the neglected imperative of accountability systems in education', *South African Journal of Education* 34(1), 1–18.

Politicsweb (2012) 'DOE wrong on teacher incentives – NAPTOSA', 14 January 2012, http://www.politicsweb.co.za/news-and-analysis/doe-wrong-on-teacher-incentives–naptosa.

Pollitt, C. and Bouckaert, G. (2000) *Public Management Reform: A Comparative Analysis*. Oxford: Oxford University Press.

Presidential Remuneration Review Commission (Not dated) 'Terms of reference of the Commission of Inquiry into Remuneration and Conditions of Service in Public Service and Schedule 3A and 3C Public Entities (PFMA)'.

Pritchett, L., Woolcock, M., and Andrews, M. (2010) 'Capability traps? The mechanisms of persistent implementation failure', Centre for Global Development. Working Paper 234.

Republic of South Africa (2001) 'Policy on whole school education', *Government Gazette* 433(22512). Pretoria.

Rossouw, M. and Letsoalo, M. (2009) 'Massive injections for state payroll', *Mail & Guardian,* 13 June, http://mg.co.za/article/2009-06-14-massive-injection-for-state-payroll.

Smith, W. J. and Ngoma-Maema, W. Y. (2003) 'Education for all in South Africa: Developing a national system for quality assurance', *Comparative Education* 39(3), 345–65.

South African Democratic Teachers Union (SADTU) (2007) SADTU National General Council 7–9 November 2007, Resolutions, http://www.sadtu.org.za/docs/ngc/2007/ngc.pdf.

South African Democratic Teachers Union (SADTU) (2009a) 'SADTU response to the NEEDU Report, Top heavy on evaluation, light on development', 18 May 2009, http://www.sadtu.org.za/content/sadtu-response-needu-report-top-heavy-evaluation-light-development.

South African Democratic Teachers Union (SADTU) (2009b) 'OSD to be paid in full', 25 November 2009, http://www.sadtu.org.za/content/osd-be-paid-full.

South African Press Association (SAPA) (2009) 'Teacher OSD talks not done', *News24*, 2 July, http://www.news24.com/Africa/News/Teacher-OSD-talks-not-done-20090702.

Swartz, R. (1994) 'South African Democratic Teachers Union: Collective bargaining and education transformation', unpublished Master of Education Research Report, Johannesburg, University of Witwatersrand.

Van der Berg, S. and Burger, R. (2010) 'Teacher pay in South Africa'. Stellenbosch Economic Working Papers 26/10. Stellenbosch University, Department of Economics, Bureau for Economic Research.

Wilson, J. Q. (1989) *Bureaucracy: What Government Agencies Do and Why they Do* It. New York: Basic Books.

World Bank (2004) *World Development Report 2004: Making Services Work for Poor People*. Washington DC: World Bank.

Part II
Provincial Governance and Politics of Education

4

Provincial Governance of Education—The Western Cape Experience

Robert Cameron and Brian Levy

4.1 Introduction

In South Africa's public education system, the national level is assigned responsibility for policymaking, for resourcing the system, and for setting the overall regulatory framework. Responsibility for implementation is delegated to the country's nine provinces. This chapter and the next explore how two provinces—the Western Cape and Eastern Cape—have exercised their implementation responsibilities.

In the years following the democratic elections of 1994, the new South African government enunciated the intention of adopting 'best practice' approaches to policy implementation, at both national and provincial levels. This included a high-profile effort to incorporate into government the principles and practices of results-based 'new public management' (NPM)—both across the public sector as a whole, and within the education sector. The dilemma, though, is that the political and institutional conditions for NPM to be effective are stringent.

As Chapter 3 has shown, efforts at the national level to introduce NPM into South Africa's education sector fell foul of the underlying institutional and political realities. The African National Congress (ANC) governed as an 'alliance'; policies were negotiated among multiple competing factions, with a strong voice for organized labour. In consequence, ambitious-seeming national-level NPM measures ended up being watered down almost to the point of becoming toothless. The majority of provinces mirrored the national level, in the sense that provincial-level institutional and political constraints undercut the potential for effectively introducing NPM.

The Western Cape province emerges as a potential exception. Post-1994, it has seen repeated alternation among competing political parties. At the outset of democracy, it inherited a bureaucracy that was well placed to manage the province's large public education system relatively effectively. Subsequently, irrespective of which political party has been in power, the WCED consistently has sought to implement performance management. The Western Cape thus offers a good opportunity for exploring to what extent determined, top-down efforts, led by the public sector, can turn around a legacy of dismal educational performance.

Our exploration takes the form of an analytically informed historical narrative, following the framework laid out in Chapter 1, and the empirical methodology laid out in Bates, Greif, Levi, Rosenthal, and Weingast (1998). We bring to the research the perspective of scholars in the fields of governance, institutions, politics, and public management. (Neither of us is an education sector specialist.) Our historical narrative is based on interviews with a wide range of current and former senior officials and other stakeholders, and an in-depth review of primary and secondary materials.

Our findings are paradoxical. On the one hand, we find that the WCED is (and long has been) a relatively well run bureaucracy, not only within the South African context, but also (in our experience as specialists in comparative public management, and with reference to comparative indicators of government effectiveness globally[1]) likely so when compared with educational bureaucracies in other middle-income countries; further, we find (and Chapter 6 confirms, using sophisticated econometric techniques) that over the past decade the WCED has been intensifying its commitment to performance management. On the other hand, however, we find that notwithstanding the sustained efforts, educational outcomes, especially among lower socio-economic segments of the population, remain at levels similar to those of countries and regimes with per capita incomes (and public resource availability) that are orders of magnitude below the Western Cape.

This chapter explores this paradox as follows. Sections 4.2 and 4.3 take a long view of the drivers of performance of the WCED. With this history as backdrop, section 4.4 provides an initial comparative assessment (previewing Chapter 7) of education sector performance in the Western Cape relative to other provinces within South Africa and some other African countries; and over time. Section 4.5 extends the review and assessment of performance into the period since 2009, when the Democratic Alliance (DA) put in place a new generation of performance management tools. Section 4.6 reflects more

[1] For a comparative assessment of governance and inequality in South Africa and four other middle-income countries (Brazil, Mexico, Turkey, and Thailand), which draws on governance indicators, see Levy, Hirsch, and Woolard (2015).

broadly on the paradoxical results, on what might be the possible causes of the paradox—and, based on experience in other countries, on what might be some potential entry points for accelerating progress in achieving better educational outcomes.

4.2 The 'Long Route of Accountability' in the Western Cape

Table 4.1 uses the governance typology introduced in Chapter 1 to highlight the contrast between the institutional arrangements for decision-making in education at the national level (as delineated in Chapter 4) and in the Western Cape. (The numbers should be interpreted as indicative of comparative patterns, not precise quantitative estimates.) As per Chapter 4, at the national level the governance of decision-making vis-à-vis education sector policy and regulation is disproportionately negotiated, with a significant personalized dimension. By contrast, for reasons that this section and the next will detail, in the Western Cape governance largely is based on hierarchical and impersonal decision-making.

The World Bank's 2004 *World Development Report* (World Bank, 2004) provides a useful broad framework for thinking about hierarchical decision-making. As illustrated in Figure 4.1, it distinguishes between two sets of hierarchical accountability relationships, which together add up to a 'long route' of public service provision—a 'voice' relationship, through which citizens hold political leaders accountable for delivering results, and a 'compact' relationship, through which top-level policymakers can hold lower-level bureaucrats accountable. On both scores, the Western Cape's legacy is a (relatively) propitious one. This section focuses on the 'voice' link; the next section on the 'compact'.

In the 'long route', the mechanisms through which citizens exercise voice is through political competition—and political competition has played out differently in the Western Cape than in South Africa's other provinces. A key distinction here is between 'programmatic' and 'patronage' political

Table 4.1. Governance of Education—Contrasting Political Settlements

Western Cape education governance			*National-level education policymaking*		
Hierarchical	15–20%	60–65%	Hierarchical	15%	25%
Negotiated	5–10%	5–15%	Negotiated	20%	40%
	Personalized	Impersonal		Personalized	Impersonal

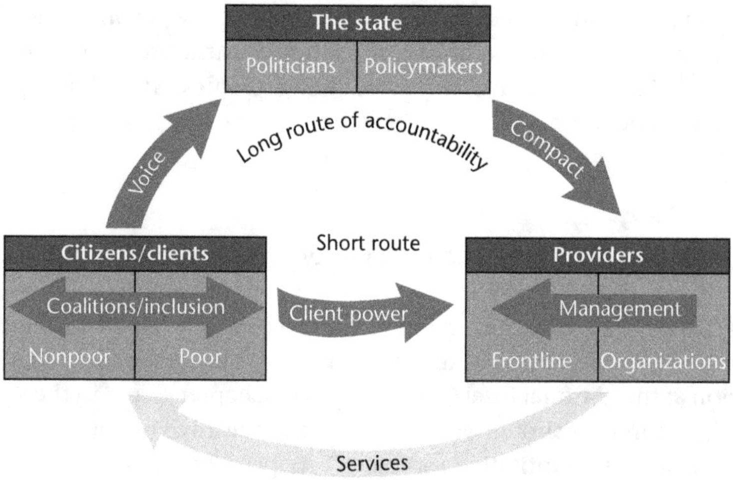

Figure 4.1. The long route of accountability
Source: World Bank (2004).

competition. In programmatic settings, political parties compete around alternative visions of what government should do, with all leading parties equally committed to try and deliver on their promises, should they be elected. In patronage settings, competition is based on the differential abilities of parties to build alliances by offering special, personalized favours to clientelistic networks.

In 1994, South Africa ended centuries of political and economic racial discrimination, and established an electoral democracy. This democracy was organized around a quasi-federal system consisting of a national government, and nine provinces, which were granted some authority (often with shared responsibilities involving both central and provincial government). One of these provinces was the Western Cape, which was previously part of a larger Cape Province; prior to 1994, the Cape Province also included portions of what are now the Eastern Cape and Northern Cape provinces.

Across most of South Africa, electoral politics since 1994 has been dominated by the ANC, which enjoyed large electoral majorities—and which governs through a combination of programmatic commitments and personalized promises (the balance between which varies from province to province). By contrast, the Western Cape has been characterized by robust inter-party-political competition, centred around alternative programmatic agendas. Indeed, as Table 4.2 details, in twenty years there have been seven different political parties/coalitions controlling the province.

To many observers' surprise, the National Party (NP, historically the dominant party of white Afrikaners) won control of the Western Cape province in

Table 4.2. Political Control of the Western Cape Provincial Government: 1994–2014

New NP/African National Congress Government of Provincial Unity	1994–98
New NP	1998–99
New NP/Democratic Party Coalition	1999–2000
Democratic Alliance	2000–01
African National Congress/New NP Coalition	2001–05
African National Congress	2005–09
Democratic Alliance	2009–

Table 4.3. Population Distribution, by Ethnic Background: 1996 Census

	Western Cape		National	
	Numbers	*Percentage*	*Numbers*	*Percentage*
Black/African	826,691	20.9	31,127,631	76.7%
Mixed race ('coloured')	2,146,109	54.2	3,600,446	8.9%
Indian/Asian	40,376	1.0	1,045,596	2.6%
White	821,551	20.8	4,434,697	10.9%
Unspecified/other	122,148	3.1	375,204	0.9%
Total	**3,956,875**	**100%**	**40,583,574**	100%

Source: Republic of South Africa (RSA, Department of Statistics, 1996).

the first democratic elections in 1994. The NP subsequently (unsuccessfully) tried to rebrand itself as the 'New National Party' and then combined with the Democratic Party (DP) to form the DA). In recent years, the Western Cape vote increasingly has shifted to the DA, which in 2009 became the province's majority party, with 51.5 per cent of the vote—and was re-elected in 2014 with a larger majority (59.44 per cent).

Underlying the Western Cape's distinctive form of political competition are its patterns of class composition and ethnic distribution. The role of class composition is explored in Chapter 7; the focus here is on the ethnic distribution. As Table 4.3 shows, as of 1996, over three-quarters of South Africa's populations were black/African. However, this group comprised only 21 per cent of Western Cape residents. The Western Cape majority comprised people of mixed race ('coloureds', in the South African lexicon), for the majority of whom Afrikaans was the home language. Since 1994, country-wide, the overwhelming majority of the black/African vote consistently has gone to the ANC. The coloured vote, by contrast, has been far more contested—not only by competing appeals to ethnic allegiance, but also by programmatic promises to deliver better government.

These differences in ethnic composition and political allegiance have, indirectly, had a further consequence for governance (specifically in education) in the Western Cape—a more constrained South African Democratic Teachers

Union (SADTU). As Chapter 3 has shown, SADTU had a major influence in shaping the content of performance management systems in basic education at the national level. But SADTU has been less influential in the Western Cape.

In part, this is a consequence of SADTU's close alignment with the ANC, which, as we have seen, has been relatively weaker in the Western Cape. In part, it is a consequence of the different trajectories of the anti-apartheid struggle in the Western Cape and elsewhere. SADTU was in important part a focal point of resistance to apartheid's 'Bantu education'. Given the Western Cape's different demographics, the logic of resistance to apartheid took a different turn in the province than elsewhere. This resulted in different patterns of teacher organisation. Even at its peak in 2004, SADTU members never accounted for more than 67 per cent of the Western Cape's teachers. By 2014, SADTU had 54.5 per cent membership and the Amalgamated Teachers Union (ATU),[2] 45.5 per cent. NAPTOSA, the more conservative union, which focuses primarily on professional issues, is the biggest component of ATU. This can be compared with provinces such as Mpumalanga/North West, where SADTU's membership is more than 70 per cent of unionised teachers (Education Labour Relations Council [ELRC], 2005, 2010, 2013).

Labour relations thus played out differently in the Western Cape than elsewhere in the country. For one thing, the relative weakness of SADTU meant that it did not have the de facto veto which it seemingly enjoyed in many other provinces on all management initiatives. For another, the WCED has long had in place a sophisticated Labour Relations Unit with fifty-four staff, which has tried to manage the unions, rather than embarking upon direct confrontation; for example, it has a well-developed process to deal with labour relations disputes, in particular with teachers who are aggrieved that they did not get promotion. Some of the senior WCED management are also SADTU members; broadly, formal WCED-SADTU interactions generally proceed along professional lines, with all bringing the concerns of committed educators to the table.

4.3 The Western Cape's Education Bureaucracy: From 'Good Enough' Weberianism to Performance Management

This section explores the second link in Figure 4.1's long route of accountability chain—the 'compact'. It explores how bureaucratic hierarchy has operated in recent decades within the Western Cape, specifically within the WCED.

[2] ATU consists of a number of independent unions, who combine for the purposes of collective bargaining only.

Historically, South Africa had a centralised form of governance, but the intergovernmental relations system changed substantially as a result of the 1996 constitution, which stipulated the creation of a quasi-federal system, consisting of national, provincial and local spheres of government. Education has been designated as a 'concurrent' function of both national and provincial government. Service conditions for educators and education policy are set nationally. However, the employers of teachers are the respective provincial heads of the education department (the Superintendents-General). The WCED in turn has deconcentrated education to eight districts, which themselves are divided into forty-nine circuits.

Provinces have extremely limited own revenue. In 2008–09, own revenue amounted to 3.7 per cent of provinces' total revenue. The provinces receive most of their revenue from national government via equitable share and conditional grants. In 2008–09, the provinces received 80.1 per cent of their revenue via the equitable share, and 16.2 per cent from conditional grants. Provinces have the discretion to spend their equitable share on their functions as they deem fit. This means national government cannot intervene with the allocation of the respective provincial budgets, although they do have to conform with national norms and standards, which for education are set by the national Department of Education (Jansen and Taylor, 2003: 6–7).

As at November 2014, WCED employed 933 public servants at its Cape Town head office; 1,274 public servants, along with 680 office-based educators, at eight district and circuit offices; and 29,900 teachers at 1,533 government schools. Circuit staff are mainly office-based educators, although they do have a few public servants (administrative support staff) in their team (WCED Data Base, 2014).[3]

Our exploration of how this system has been governed is organized around four sets of themes (and related sub-periods): the bureaucratic inheritance as of 1994; some national-level efforts to restructure the education sector in the initial years of democracy, and their effects within the Western Cape; efforts between 1999 and 2009 to racially 'transform' the bureaucracy; and the introduction at the provincial level of national initiatives to foster performance management (Section 4.5 continues the story beyond 2009, when the DA became the majority party in the Western Cape.) As will become evident, throughout the past two decades, the WCED's platform has been relatively strong.

[3] The data are only for teachers employed directly by the WCED. School governing bodies (SGBs) also have the right to employ teachers directly, but the WCED does not keep data on teachers employed by SGBs, given that the employing authority is individual schools.

4.3.1 *A Platform of Relative Continuity*

As of 1994, the structure, organisation, resource availabilities and quality of South Africa's educational system were overwhelmingly the consequence of a centuries-long legacy of inequality, poverty and apartheid. Democratisation was accompanied by public policies that ended the apartheid organisational structures and, as Chapter 2 details, radically reshaped the flow of public resources in a more pro-poor direction.[4] But the shadow of the past continues to loom large. This continuity is evident (notwithstanding the more progressive fiscal allocations) in the continuing overall advantageous access[5] to resources of public schools that serve elite populations (a topic that is outside the scope of the present chapter). Continuity can also take more subtle forms, for example in the likely persistence over time of divergent organisational cultures within schools and in their proximate bureaucratic sub-systems. Consequently, it is with the organisational legacy at the end of apartheid that our exploration of the evolving operation of the WCED begins.

The state of schools in the Western Cape in the early 1990s just prior to democratisation with respect to performance was as follows.

In terms of historically 'white' (so-called Model-C) schools, there was a well-resourced and performing school system. They were partially funded by the state and had increased autonomy. They were regulated by the Education Department of the Cape Provincial Administration (CPA). There was little evidence of patronage in the appointment/promotion of teachers.

Historically, 'coloured' schools were under the control of the House of Representatives (HoR), the political structures created by the apartheid authorities for the 'self-government' of South Africa's mixed-race population. This was strongly resisted by communities and some teachers (Chisholm et al., 1999; Soudien, 2002; Kallaway, 2002). The system did, however, enable the schools to extract resources from the HoR, which gave them a better education than African schools. As discussed in detail in Appendix A4.1, while there was some evidence of the use of the school system as a source of patronage during the apartheid era, there was no evidence of systematic capture of the system by a predatory elite. The majority of schools had a conservative organisational culture (Fiske and Ladd, 2004: 75–6). In some politically activist schools, there was a strong emphasis on professionalism, which was used as a bulwark

[4] The share of public education expenditure for primary and secondary schools going to schools serving the poorest 20 per cent rose from 19 per cent in 1993, to 22 per cent in 2000 to 26 per cent in 2005; between 1993 and 2005, the corresponding share going to the richest 20 per cent fell from 28 per cent to 13 per cent. Chapter 2 provides additional details.

[5] For example, via the provision of supplementary resources by affluent parents (including for the recruitment of additional teachers); the more favourable inherited physical infrastructure; and the persistence of better-trained and more experienced teachers in elite schools.

against the excesses of apartheid.[6] The HoR did, however, attempt to control the appointment of senior positions, most notably principals.[7]

Black schools were poorly resourced. The Department of Education and Training (DET; the former Department of Bantu Education) which controlled black education was characterized by authoritarian control, poorly trained teachers, personalized patronage (Chisholm et al., 1999), and a lack of performance culture. There was also strong resistance to apartheid education in black schools (Kallaway, 2002; Soudien, 2002). Given the demographics, the DET black school system was disproportionately small in the Western Cape setting.

The new provincial government of the Western Cape, created in the immediate aftermath of the 1994 elections, inherited the education departments that were located within the Western Cape—the CPA, HoR and DeT. Portions of the old CPA hived off and became part of the Eastern Cape and Northern Cape provinces. The Western Cape, unlike many other provinces, did not have any Bantustans[8] to incorporate. This contributed to a more seamless amalgamation than most of the other provinces (where amalgamations with Bantustans had turned out to be time-consuming, disruptive and costly).

Not only was the Western Cape one of two provinces (of a total of nine) which were controlled by the opposition after the 1994 elections,[9] but it was the only province where there was no change of political power. Fiske and Ladd (2004: 75–6) pointed out that during the 1994–95 period, when the power and responsibilities of the provinces were still being established at the national level, the erstwhile CPA bureaucracy that had provided education for white students was still able to exert significant power by providing much of the administrative expertise for the new department. The political forces that had gained control over the education of the coloured students in the 1980s through the HoR continued to be influential and to exert a largely conservative force. In fact, a number of ex-HoR politicians had joined the NP and four of the ministers[10] in Hernus Kriel's 1994 cabinet had come from HoR ranks.

[6] Interview with Crain Soudien, former Professor of Education, University of Cape Town, 27 March 2014.

[7] 'Jobs for Pals', *The South*, 3–9/12/1987; 'Teachers claim Political bias', *The Argus*, 18/6/1987; 'Abuse of Power, Sharp Attack on Hendrickse over teachers', *The Argus*, 7/12/1990.

[8] Territories set aside for black inhabitants of South Africa as part of the policy of apartheid, and governed by so-called independent authorities.

[9] KwaZulu-Natal was then controlled by the Inkatha Freedom Party (IFP), the other opposition-controlled province.

[10] In terms of the Western Cape Constitution, provincial ministers are called ministers. This is the only province which uses this nomenclature.

However, education officials who had previously been employed in the DET were left in a quandary, not knowing whether they were to report to the DET head office in Pretoria that was being shut down, or the new WCED. Despite the uncertainty of the DET, most of the abovementioned factors contributed to the Western Cape department of education being up and functioning quite quickly in comparison with the departments in other provinces.[11]

Table 4.4 provides striking evidence of continuity in government. The bureaucracy largely was insulated from the rapid turnover of the provincial-cabinet-level appointments of political heads (i.e. the provincial ministers of education). As the table shows, over the past two decades, the WCED has effectively been led by three superintendents general—Brian O'Connell, Ron Swartz, and Penny Vinjevold. This degree of stability in bureaucratic leadership is a major asset in underpinning performance.

But continuity also has its costs; old organisational cultures can remain entrenched. Indeed, this is what appears to have happened in the WCED. Interviews with ex-HoR officials and one former minister for education suggested that coloured ex-HoR officials (and not old CPA officials) dominated the new education department. Unlike the CPA, which ran schools on a provincial basis only, the HoR ran education nationally, and had the most staff. As one interviewee said, 'The HoR in effect incorporated the old CPA and DET'.

As noted earlier, and detailed in Appendix A4.1, the HoR's Department of Education brought with it a conservative and rule-bound culture into the WCED. Patronage was present, but it was on the margins of what one might call 'good enough Weberianism'.[12] Interviews suggest that in the immediate aftermath of the 1994 democratic elections, this conservative culture became the dominant strain in the new WCED—'Good enough Weberianism' became the order of the day.

Table 4.4. Superintendents General: WCED 1994–2014

F. Knoetze (acting, 1994–95)
Brian O'Connell (1995–2001)
Johan Fourie (acting, 2001)
Ron Swartz (2002–09)
Brian Schreuder (acting, 2009)
Penny Vinjevold (2009–16)

[11] Interview with senior WCED official, 12 June 2014.

[12] By 'good enough Weberianism', we mean public administration structures that are organized along classically bureaucratic lines, have some significant shortfalls, but are sufficiently strong to support largely programmatic policies (as opposed to patronage). The term builds on Grindle's concept of 'good enough governance'.

4.3.2 *Absorbing Policy Shocks from the National Level*

In the first half-dozen years of democracy, the education sector was characterized by far-reaching structural changes that aimed to decisively leave behind the apartheid legacy. As a companion paper (Hoadley et al., 2016) details, these included: a South African Schools Act, which decentralised very substantial authority to school-level governing bodies; a transformation of the curriculum; a radical shift in how teachers were trained; and a restructuring of the budgetary and personnel policies in an effort to eliminate racial inequities in resources.

From the perspective of the WCED, the most difficult policy change of the first Western Cape legislature (1994–99) was undoubtedly the rationalisation of teachers. In historically white and coloured areas, the pupil–teacher ratio had been almost the same, and substantially higher than in black schools. The new rules on teacher recruitment made provision for schools to use their own sources of revenue; this created an opportunity for schools in relatively privileged areas (the so-called 'former Model C' white schools) to levy relatively high school fees on parents, and thereby cushion the impact of the cuts of government-funded teaching posts by privately providing positions, namely school governing bodies (SGB) posts. The erstwhile coloured schools did not have wealthy parents on whom they could levy high school fees; as a result, they were the group that were most adversely affected by the teacher rationalisation process in the Western Cape. On average, formerly coloured high schools lost more than eleven teacher positions per school between 1996 and 1999. Conversely, former African high schools gained a teacher (Fiske and Ladd, 2004: 108–22, Chisholm et al., 1999: 397–8).

According to Fiske and Ladd (2004: 108–22), about 2,900 teachers opted for voluntary severance packages (VSPs) and almost 2,000 left teaching in 1998 alone. Chisholm et al. (1999: 397–8) pointed out that 25 per cent of principals themselves took the packages; furthermore, the teachers who took severance packages and left the school system had higher average qualifications than those who remained. The average teacher in coloured secondary schools in 1996 had nearly four-and-a-half years of tertiary education, but by 1997 the typical teacher had one-third of a year less training. What was particularly problematic was the impact of the loss of mathematics and science teachers, many of whom were quick to accept the VSP because they had marketable skills which could be utilised in business and other sectors of the economy.

4.3.3 *Transforming Incrementally*

As with all departments across South Africa's public sector, following the 1994 elections, the WCED began to transform its racial composition to mirror

South Africa's democratic realities. Brian O'Connell (1995–2001), then Vice-Rector of Peninsula Technikon, was brought in as the first superintendent general in the democratic Western Cape as a unifying force. He was in charge of the department from 1995 to 2001. It was felt by the ruling NP that choosing someone from outside the three administrations would be less divisive than selecting a leader from within one of the three pre-existing departments.

Some affirmative action began relatively early. The 2000 restructuring of district-level education management and development centres (EMDCs) by O'Connell led to the 'population of districts with more representative appointments'. When the ANC won full control of the Western Cape in 2005, it accelerated this process of affirmative action in the department of education. In some parts of the administration (e.g. the Office of the Premier), organisational restructuring had, according to some interviewees, led to a rapid acceleration of the ANC's 'cadre deployment'[13] strategies, along the lines it had pursued in other parts of the country. So, when ex-SADTU national vice president and then superintendent general of WCED, Ron Swartz, introduced an organisational restructuring of the head office in 2007, this was seen in many quarters as another cadre deployment exercise.

However, interviewees for this research suggested that there was a strong organisational need for this restructuring. The sub-directorate, Branch: Education and Planning, in the WCED was widely viewed as too big and unwieldy; it had curriculum, examinations, specialised education, research, ICT and infrastructure under its control. Ron Swartz split this branch into two. Interviewees suggested that there was logic and sound justification based on this restructuring, which was modelled on earlier reforms in Gauteng province.

The 2007 reorganisation thus involved the creation of a new head office organogram with a number of new positions. About 60 new staff were appointed, with hardly any of the existing staff losing their jobs. In this way, the ANC provincial government responded to pressure from ANC provincial party structures to transform the department. But, according to one long outstanding senior interviewee, it also recognised the need for a dedicated professional approach to the management of teachers, so proceeded with restructuring in a way that did not lead to the exodus of existing expertise.

The placement of staff under the Swartz reorganisation was largely completed when the ANC was voted out of power by the DA in 2009. The

[13] In 1997, the ANC introduced its Cadre Policy and Deployment Strategy, which advocated political appointments to senior positions in the public service. It emphasised recruitment from within the party, and potential deployees were made to understand and accept the basic policies and programmes of the ANC. The strategy made no reference to the need for administrative competence (de Jager, 2009).

DA tweaked the organisation structure in 2011, but there was not a significant change to it (two to three persons were made redundant organizationally). A few staff who were perceived by the DA as incompetent (almost all had been appointed under Swartz), were worked out of the department around 2011.

4.3.4 *Introduction of Performance Management*

Throughout the two decades of democratic government, the WCED has endeavoured to put in place results-oriented approaches to performance management. In the first fifteen years, these efforts took a lead from the systems-building efforts promoted by the national-level department of basic education.

Since the latter 1990s, in an effort to link performance and career-pathing, the national-level department of basic education has come up with an ongoing stream of performance management initiatives—from the development appraisal system (DAS), individual performance management, whole school evaluations (WSE), to the 'integrated quality management system' (the IQMS, which encompasses all of these performance management systems (ELRC, 2003). As Chapter 3 details, these initiatives have often been intensive in bureaucratic processes, but light on results-based follow through. For all the limitations of these initiatives, the Western Cape bureaucracy has consistently taken performance management seriously—both by putting in place systems to implement the national initiatives, and (as we explore later) by taking a series of home-grown initiatives.

First to be introduced (in the late 1990s) were individual performance evaluations. Most interviewees were scathing of the performance management system for individual staff. A former provincial minister for education stated that: 'IQMS is not a proper form of evaluation. It does not add real value. It costs a fortune to administer and is time-consuming.' Other comments ranged from 'a useless form of evaluation', to 'a bit of a joke'. Interviews picked up gaming of performance management.[14] One strategically located interviewee indicated that in some schools, there is a disjuncture between the performance of schools and individual performance of teachers.

[14] The IQMS is made up of four lesson observation performance standards and eight outside the classroom performance standards (see Cameron and Naidoo, 2016). Teachers get evaluated over all twelve performance standards. An example of gaming reported by interviewees is a pattern where school staff whose functions primarily are administrative (e.g. the principal), give three to four lessons just before the IQMS evaluation process, which enables them to be averaged out over twelve rather than eight performance standards.

In some cases, teachers in underperforming schools get high individual performance evaluations.

The whole school evaluation (WSE) was promulgated nationally in 2001 (RSA, 2001), and implemented in the Western Cape in 2006, replacing the old provincial inspectorate system. It involves three steps: pre-evaluation documents prepared by the schools; an external evaluation; and post-evaluation, whereby schools and districts analyse the WSE report and incorporate the recommendations into school improvement plans (SIPs). In the Western Cape, the WSE is carried out by teams, consisting of permanently appointed officials and part-time WCED supervisors appointed by the WCED this purpose. There is a multi-functional team for high schools, which consists of a team leader and three team members. Each school is evaluated according to the nine focus areas specified in the WSE policy. Lesson observation takes place in languages, mathematics, natural/life sciences and an elective (high schools) or foundation phase (primary schools). The length of the visit is three or five days, depending on the size of the school.

There are a number of critiques of WSE. Firstly, from the union perspective, they are described as: 'nice little reports where little is done. WSE is equally useless (in comparison with performance management)'. Another complaint from a couple of interviewees was that, due to SADTU resistance, the external supervisors cannot evaluate teachers in classrooms. However, according to the WCED official in charge of WSE, there are classroom visits but under circumscribed conditions, e.g., the school needs to know in advance. Additional critiques were that WSE is not robust enough, and that it takes too long to implement. The objective is to evaluate high schools once in three years, and primary schools once in five years. There are 1,524 schools in the Western Cape. Since WSE evaluation began, about 757 schools (50 per cent) have been evaluated (WCED Data Base, 2014).

But for all of the criticisms, there was also a sense that WSEs add value. SIPs prepared by schools are monitored online by the districts and are also an early warning system; many WCED staff we interviewed reported this to be a relatively effective measure of monitoring. The WCED follows up with a sample of schools which had been evaluated between 2006 and 2010, and checks on what was already done. Ongoing monitoring and support of schools identified as poorly performing is done by the districts. Interviewees reported that WSE evaluations have led to principals being held to account and, on occasion, disciplined. It has contributed to principals being subtly eased out for non-performance. It was argued by interviewees that good plans backed by competent public administration can add value, even if the tools themselves have substantial built-in limitations.

4.4 Performance of Basic Education in the Western Cape in Comparative Perspective

To what extent did the WCED's bureaucratic assets and commitment to performance management contribute to superior school performance? This section benchmarks Western Cape performance using three sets of measures: a comparative measure of management performance; measures which contrast the Western Cape's educational performance with that of South Africa's other provinces; and a comparative measure of Western Cape performance relative to selected other African countries (Section 4.5 looks in depth at recent changes over time within the Western Cape).

4.4.1 *Comparative Managerial Performance*

Management performance assessment tests (MPATs) have been undertaken across multiple departments across multiple provinces by the department of performance monitoring and evaluation located in the national presidency. The MPAT rates performance according to four levels:

- Level 1—non-compliance with legal/regulatory requirements.
- Level 2—partial compliance with legal/regulatory requirements.
- Level 3—full compliance with legal/regulatory requirement.
- Level 4—full compliance, and doing this smartly.

The MPATs include a comparative assessment of the relative quality of the education bureaucracies across South Africa's nine provinces. Appendix A4.2 describes the MPAT and the detailed results for education departments. Table 4.5 provides a summary overview of the relative performance of the WCED. Given the provenance of the MPAT—and the expectation that the national presidency would not be biased towards showing the only province not governed by the ruling ANC in an undeserved good light, the results are striking. As Table 4.5 signals, the WCED emerges as far and away the best managed of the provincial

Table 4.5. MPAT Assessments of Overall Performance for South Africa's Education Departments

	Level 1	Level 2	Level 3	Level 4
Western Cape	0	21	34	45
Gauteng	14	21	31	34
National average, all provinces	24	31	31	15
Northern Cape	28	41	28	3
Eastern Cape	59	17	17	7

Source: The Presidency, Department of Performance Monitoring and Evaluation (DPME, 2013).

education departments: as of 2012–13, it was fully in compliance (or better) with 79 per cent of the key performance indicators which were assessed. The next best provincial education department (Gauteng) was in compliance (or better) with 65 per cent.

4.4.2 *Comparative Educational Outcomes, 2007/08*

Necessarily, an assessment of the quality of an education system must benchmark the educational outcomes achieved by that system—over time, and relative to other systems. We do so in this subsection and, again, later in the chapter.

Comparative benchmarking is challenging. Educational outcomes depend in important part on the socio-economic profile of a system's learners. Consequently, if one is to rigorously benchmark the quality of an education system's management, using outcome-based indicators, it is necessary to control for demographic variations in the student population. In a South African context, the Western Cape's relatively favourable socio-economic profile is likely to produce relatively strong educational outcomes even if (contra Table 4.5) education in the Western Cape was no better managed than elsewhere in the country. A further complication is that, perhaps even more than elsewhere in South Africa, the Western Cape is extraordinarily dualistic—so average outcomes disguise huge within-system variation, making it difficult to make judgements about quality at different points along the socio-economic spectrum. Yet another challenge has to do with the measurement of outcomes. Tests of learning outcomes are often unreliable, with very large standard error of estimates, even for the same test. Further, changes in test design can undermine year-on-year comparability, even if the intention had been to make seemingly modest tweaks. Finally, in order to show positive outcomes, education systems have come up with many ways to 'game' tests—from 'teaching to the test', to constraining who actually gets to write the test.

Chapter 6 addresses the above issues with a comprehensive, multivariate econometric analysis of education outcomes in the Western Cape relative to other locales, including systematic disaggregation of performance across the socio-economic spectrum. This chapter uses a variety of standardized outcome measures to provide an initial set of descriptive statistical benchmarks of the Western Cape's performance relative to other locales, as of 2007/08. (2007/08 is the time immediately preceding the DA's 2009 provincial electoral victory; the data here thus serve as a useful baseline for the trends under DA governance, presented in Section 4.5.)

We begin with the results of standardised tests administered in 2007 to a large sample of sixth graders in fifteen countries by the independent Southern

Table 4.6. SACMEQ Benchmark I: Western Cape Achievement in Grade 6 Mathematics, Relative to Other South African Provinces, 2007

	50th percentile (median)	25th percentile	75th percentile
Western Cape	560	496	636
Gauteng	548	483	610
Northwest/Northern Cape	483	439	548
Free State	483	439	535
Kwazulu-Natal	469	424	535
Mpumalanga	469	425	522
Eastern Cape	454	408	509
Limpopo	439	408	483

[1] Achievement in grade 6 mathematics by province, 2007.

Source: SACMEQ data files (2007), RSA, DBE (2010a).

and East African Consortium for Monitoring Educational Quality (SACMEQ). (The South African SACMEQ sample comprised 9,083 students drawn from 392 schools; sample size per province ranged from 900 to 1,500 observations.) Table 4.6 reports the SACMEQ scores for the Western Cape relative to South Africa's other provinces. The Western Cape emerges as the best-performing of South Africa's nine provinces, with Gauteng a close second—and the remaining seven lagging significantly behind. The relative ranking of provinces is broadly similar whether one takes the median score, the score for learners at the seventy-fifth percentile of socio-economic distribution, or the score for learners at the lower, twenty-fifth percentile, socio-economic tier. As Chapter 6 shows, for the most part these relative rankings persist even once a wide variety of other, exogenous influences are controlled for.[15]

Table 4.7 reports 'matric' results (the end-of-high-school National Senior Certificate examination) by province for 2008. As of 2008, the Western Cape's performance vis-à-vis matric results was mixed. Using the pass rate as a benchmark, the Western Cape emerges as the top-performing province. However, when the benchmark used is not the percentage of exam-takers who pass, but rather the percentage of eighteen-year-olds who both take and pass the exam, the Western Cape ranks only fourth among nine provinces.[16] As of 2008, Gauteng, Kwazulu Natal and Limpopo were able to successfully

[15] The principal control variables are: the home background of test-takers; their socio-economic status; the scores of teachers on the SACMEQ tests; teacher age, qualification and experience; and classroom factors (teaching time, homework, assessment, and textbook availability).

[16] RSA (2016: Table 22). Western Cape dropout rates are especially high after Grade 9. Why is the Western Cape's performance (relatively) matric pass rate poor, relative to the full age cohort? One possibility, noted in the text, is that provinces 'game' results by adopting a policy of holding back candidates. Another possible explanation is that the Western Cape (especially metropolitan Cape Town) is notorious for its gang culture plus other, related social dysfunctions. One of the consequences of these dysfunctions could be to fuel a counter-norm, at adolescence, one which legitimizes prematurely leaving school.

take a higher proportion of the age cohort through a full twelve years of education than the Western Cape. If, however, the benchmark of success is made more robust—preparation of pupils for university entrance—the Western Cape's strengths re-emerge. As Table 4.7 shows, the Western Cape and Gauteng were by a large margin the two most successful provinces in preparing their pupils for university. Considering together the pass rate, and performance vis-à-vis university entrance, one can reasonably conclude that, relative to other provinces, the WCED served (relatively) well those who persisted within the system.

As a further benchmark, Table 4.8 uses SACMEQ data to compare education performance in the Western Cape with that of Mauritius, Kenya, Tanzania and Botswana. As the data show, the Western Cape's median sixth grader scored below the equivalent learner in Mauritius, and similarly to learners in Kenya and the Tanzanian mainland. At the twenty-fifth percentile (i.e., the lower SES

Table 4.7. National Senior Certificate Results, Full-Time Students (2008)

	As % of exam-takers		As % of 18 year olds		Total number of 18 year olds ('000s)
	% pass	% Bachelors	% pass	% Bachelors	
Western Cape	78.4%	33.0%	35.8%	14.6%	99.1
Gauteng	76.4	30.5	40.0	15.0	187.4
North West	68.0	19.4	34.0	9.1	68.8
Free State	71.8	21.0	34.5	11.8	59.2
Mpumalanga	51.8	13.1	33.4	7.1	88.3
Northern Cape	72.7	20.1	32.3	10.0	23.2
Limpopo	54.3	12.6	38.1	7.9	133.5
Kwazulu Natal	57.6	18.2	38.5	12.9	222.9
Eastern Cape	50.6	14.4	19.6	5.4	161.
National	62.6%	20.1%	34.6%	10.2%	1,044

Note: A 'pass' requires a grade of at least 40 per cent in three subjects; and of 30 per cent in an additional three subjects. A 'bachelors pass' (university eligibility) requires a grade of 50 per cent or better in at least four subjects, and a passing grade for the remaining subjects.

Sources: RSA, DBE (2010b, 2014).

Table 4.8. SACMEQ Benchmark II: Western Cape Mathematics Scores Relative to Other African Countries, 2007

	50th percentile (median)	25th percentile	75th percentile
Western Cape	560	496	636
South Africa (overall)	483	424	548
Mauritius	610	522	718
Kenya	548	509	610
Tanzania	555	500	604
Botswana	521	468	573

Source: SACMEQ data files (2007).

tier), the Western Cape scored marginally below all the comparator countries, other than Botswana. Chapter 6 confirms that these results are statistically robust once other exogenous influences on performance are controlled for.

It is plausible that the Western Cape's relatively low scores reflect the province's many centuries of traumatic history (including servitude, racial oppression and social dislocation, on farms and elsewhere) that are not adequately captured in the socio-economic control measures used in Chapter 6. But set against this is the reality that the per learner expenditure in the Western Cape is five-fold (to cite one comparator country) that of Kenya. As of 2008, relative to some other sub-Saharan African countries, the bureaucratic strengths of the WCED had not translated into superior performance.

4.5 Pragmatic Managerialism—the DA-Governed WCED

This section brings our review of WCED performance and its bureaucratic underpinnings forward to the present—focusing on how the WCED has been managed in the five years since the DA took power. When the DA took the reins of provincial power in the Western Cape in 2009, it did not lack ambition:

> For us, success means becoming the best-run regional government in the world, so that we can realise our vision of an open opportunity society for all in the Western Cape. (Provincial Government of the Western Cape, 2010)

Basic education is a core function of the provincial government—and also a function where better performance is central to the 'vision of an open opportunity society for all'. To what extent has the DA administration made gains vis-à-vis its far-reaching ambitions? Insofar as it has made gains, what have been the key reforms?

4.5.1 *Recent Trends in Performance*

As was evident from Section 4.4, when the DA came to power in the Western Cape in 2009, both bureaucratic quality and performance in basic education were already generally better than elsewhere in South Africa. Subsequent to 2009, as Tables 4.9 and 4.10 will show, there is evidence of continuing gains in performance.[17] But for all of the incremental gains, the gains are within the

[17] A further relevant set of evidence comprises the results for 2002 and 2011 of the international mathematics and science (TIMSS) tests, analysed for South Africa by Reddy, Prinsloo, Arends, and Visser (2012). Among South Africa's provinces, the Western Cape scored highest in both years. However, between 2002 and 2011 its scores declined modestly (from 414 to 404). All other provinces saw an increase, with the overall South African score rising from 285 to 348.

Table 4.9. National Senior Certificate Results, Full-Time Students (2015)

	Total number of 18 year olds ('000s)	As % of 18 year olds	
		% pass	% Bachelors
Western Cape	106.3	43.8%	21.4%
Gauteng	209.4	44.0	18.7
North West	68.2	40.5	13.1
Free State	56.2	46.3	16.5
Mpumalanga	89.3	49.2	16.4
Northern Cape	23.9	34.7	10.5
Limpopo	125.7	54.9	16.8
Kwazulu Natal	214.5	47.8	16.4
Eastern Cape	135.7	36.7	11.3
National	1,029	45.2%	16.3%

Note: A 'pass' requires a grade of at least 40 per cent in three subjects; and of 30 per cent in an additional three subjects. A 'bachelors pass' (university eligibility) requires a grade of 50 per cent or better in at least four subjects, and a passing grade for the remaining subjects.

Sources: RSA, DBE (2010b, 2014).

Table 4.10. Grade 3, 6 and 9 systemic tests—numeracy pass rates (pass set at 50%)

	Grade 3		Grade 6		Grade 9	
Year	Pass rate	Tested	Pass rate	Tested	Pass rate	Tested
2006	31%	82,879				
2007			14%	71,874		
2008	35%	74,119				
2009			17.40%	83,921		
2010	48.30%	78,495	24.40%	81,402	10.40%	83,605
2011	47.60%	79,109	23.40%	78,288	10.90%	81,936
2012	51.50%	83,030	26.40%	79,301	13.90%	89,674
2013	55%	97,375	28,30%	78,723	14.30%	85,320
2014	54%	85,623	30,4%	72,214	14,9%	71,345

Source: WCED (2013, 2014, 2015).

range of what was achieved by other South African provinces—and the results remain below what has been achieved in Kenya and Mauritius, despite the fact that Kenya, for one, had far fewer resources at their disposal than the Western Cape.

Table 4.9 updates for 2015 the 2008 'matric' results that were presented in Table 4.7. A comparison of the two tables reveals that:

- The Western Cape indeed made substantial gains over the seven-year period, increasing the number of graduates by over 11,000 (a 31 per cent increase over the number who passed matric in 2008), and the number reaching a university entrance standard by over 8,000 (a 55 per cent increase over the 2008 number).

- These gains were achieved even as the Western Cape saw some (modest) increase in the total number of eighteen-year-olds. (Gauteng was the only other province where the number of eighteen-year-olds increased.)
- Relative to other provinces, the Western Cape's gains were greater than those achieved by Gauteng over the same period, but about the same as for the other provinces.

As of 2015, the Western Cape system continued to outperform the others in the proportion of pupils who achieved a university entrance standard, but remained below the national average in the proportion of the age cohort which successfully completed high school.

Table 4.10 reports on recent trends in performance of grade 3, 6, and 9 students in 'systemic tests', introduced by the WCED in 2002.[18] As noted earlier, year-on-year comparisons of test results generally are fraught with difficulties. In the case of the Western Cape's systemic tests, comparable test results are available only since 2010. Table 4.10 points to some recent trend improvement but the results also underscore a stark reality. As of 2013, fewer than 30 per cent of grade 6s—and fewer than 15 per cent of Grade 9s—met a minimum passing standard for numeracy. Given these overall pass rates, the results at the lower end of the socio-economic spectrum almost surely continue to be startlingly low.[19]

4.5.2 *Fine-Tuning Performance Monitoring*

In this subsection and the next we turn to the management initiatives that underpinned WCED performance over the 2009–15 period. When we began this study, we expected to find a post-2008 'doubling-down' on the part of the DA administration in NPM-style performance-driven management practices. What we actually found was something more complex—an intriguing combination of heightened attention to performance monitoring, combined with a shift to a more pragmatic managerialism, responding to challenges as they arose with ad hoc, and sometimes discretionary, solutions. Throughout, the

[18] At the national level, a country-wide Annual National Assessment (ANA) was introduced in 2011 to assess literacy and numeracy for grades 3, 6, and 9. However, as of the time of writing this chapter, the ANAs did not yet appear adequate to serve as a basis for comparison across provinces (Spaull, 2013). Published ANA results have raised eyebrows in the academic community, due to the differences between self-reported school performance and independently moderated school performance. For example, for the Eastern Cape, in 2013 the percentage of grade 3 students with a score of 50 per cent or more was self-reported for numeracy as 54.9 per cent, but adjusted downwards after external verification to 42.2 per cent; for literacy, the self-reported score was 50.2 per cent, and the adjusted score 27.0 per cent.

[19] In 2004, only 0.1 per cent (to underscore: one-tenth of 1 per cent!!) of grade 6 learners in schools that were formerly under control of DET met the passing level (50 per cent) proficiency standard for numeracy.

WCED has largely remained committed to a top-down, hierarchical approach to governing the sector, with only a very nascent exploration of more facilitative, horizontal approaches to education sector governance.

In general, the NPM doctrine combines two seemingly disparate, but potentially complementary, departures from classic bureaucratic Weberianism—an intensified focus on the monitoring of performance, combined with greater flexibility (and accountability for results) for front-line service provision units. This subsection focuses on the first of these two areas (performance monitoring)—one where the WCED has progressively strengthened its tools, with the gains continuing into the DA administration.

As of 2015, the centrepiece of the performance monitoring effort is the directorate of business, strategy and stakeholder management which is located in the office of the head of the WCED, the superintendent general. Established in 2007 (i.e. predating DA rule), its formal functions initially comprised 'providing a secretarial and administrative support service to the office of Head of Education'. Since then its powers have expanded. The directorate originally faced resistance from existing directorates, who thought it was an attempt to bypass them. It took three years of effort and sustained support from the highest levels of the WCED to put its performance-monitoring systems in place.

The directorate benefits from a sophisticated online tracking system, which includes the following:

- An 'individual learner tracking system'—which tracks the progress and performance of individual learners throughout their time within the WCED.[20]
- Online SIPs for each of the 1,500 schools in the systems. The SIPs incorporate in an integrated, streamlined fashion, that is accessible to each school:
  - aggregated school-level summaries of the result of the individual learner tracking exercises;
  - the results of whole school evaluations (which, as noted earlier, have been completed for about half the WCED's schools, with 120 additional schools evaluated each year);
  - the school-level results of systemic tests;
  - academic performance plans, completed for each school;
  - a rolling, three-year planning cycle, incorporated into each SIP, progress in the implementation of which can be monitored systematically.

[20] The directorate uses data that are derived from the central education management information system (CEMIS) that are managed by the directorate of knowledge management.

- School-level budget and staffing planning and execution tools—capable of monitoring for each school across the system whether and how budgets are being spent, and including tools for ordering supplies (notably including textbooks, where problems of availability have bedevilled schools throughout South Africa) online, and tracking whether orders have been placed in a timely manner.[21]
- School improvement monitoring—undertaken quarterly, with a specific focus on underperforming schools.
- District improvement plans, which track trends in performance at higher levels of system aggregation than the schools themselves.

The superintendent general is thus supported by a strategically located planning and monitoring unit which appears to be the hub of performance in the WCED. This ensures that there is an 'early warning' system, whereby problems of school performance are brought directly to the attention of the head of department.

According to WCED interviewees, the online tracking system has been highly effective. It has led to a reduction in time for the filling of teachers and principal posts. It can monitor how schools have spent their budgets—and, indeed, whether they have spent their budgets. In recent years, the tool has been used to track teacher absenteeism. Leave forms have been used to calculate the total number of absent days as a percentage of the total number of days people could have been present. Teacher absenteeism has fallen from 19 days annually down to six and then four days per annum. The WCED had anticipated a 4 per cent absenteeism figure, but in practice it has averaged out at a consistent 3 per cent from 2011 to 2013.

In sum, top-down planning and monitoring systems have helped ensure that the vast majority of schools in the WCED are relatively well-managed, at least from a logistical perspective. Teacher posts are filled relatively rapidly, and teachers show up to work; school infrastructure is adequately maintained; supplies, including textbooks, are available; the system adapts reasonably effectively to changes in the numbers of learners within schools, and to the ongoing increase (as a result of migration) in the number of learners in the system as a whole.

4.5.3 *A Turn to Pragmatic Managerialism*

For all that our research found the WCED to be a well-managed and relatively well-resourced hierarchy with robust tools of top-down performance

[21] This is also run by the WCED directorate for knowledge management/centre for e-innovation (Department of the Premier) on behalf of the WCED directorate: resources.

management, as the test scores detailed earlier signal, this has not been sufficient to achieve major gains in educational outcomes. What might be the gap? At the outset of our study we expected that part of the answer lay in the rigid ways in which the top-down systems were implemented. But, intriguingly and unexpectedly, we found that subsequent to 2009, the WCED leadership appears to have become increasingly pragmatic in its application of performance management.

In 2002, seemingly consistent with the two-fold logic of performance management—stronger performance monitoring plus greater facility-level autonomy—the WCED moved towards a formally more decentralised structure, via the re-organisation of much of the department into eight district-level offices. In 2007, it deepened this seeming decentralisation by creating sixty-eight 'circuit' management units within the districts, each responsible for approximately twenty to thirty schools. In practice, as numerous interviewees confirmed, between 2002 and 2009 the decentralisation was largely on paper. Interviewees repeatedly used the same phrase to describe the formalistic (IQMS, WSE etc.) way in which the WCED operated during that period—'management by circular'.

But the new DA team adopted a different (though still largely hierarchical) approach. In 2009, the DA appointed Penny Vinjevold as Superintendent General.[22] (She continued in that role until mid-2016.) From the start of her tenure, Vinjevold identified the districts as the nodes of service delivery that would drive performance, with district directors to be given more autonomy to run their areas of jurisdiction. Districts (and the circuit management teams within each district) are the front-line of promoting performance, the 'eyes and ears' of the WCED. Their functions include ensuring that all teaching posts are filled; that teachers are teaching; that governing bodies are working properly; that schools receive adequate support; that relevant training is provided; and that performance information is used to inform efforts to improve school performance (although a continuing constraint is that many front-line staff lack the statistical skills to use this information effectively).

Along with improving the district-level structures, Vinjevold identified (in an interview for this study) the following as her top four priorities post-2009:

[22] Vinjevold had a long career in education prior to becoming the WCED's superintendent general in 2009. She worked as an educator for many years; returned to complete an MA in Education at the University of the Witwatersrand in 1994; worked as an education researcher from 1994 to 2001; was appointed as a chief director in the WCED by the then ANC government in 2001; and from 2005 to 2009 served as deputy director general in the national department of education.

- As her 'biggest priority' (articulated from 2010 onwards), assuring that all 1,500 schools had a 'good principal'. (Given natural attrition and the age profile of the principal cadre, the opportunity exists to replace almost the entire principal cadre over an eight-year period. Indeed, between 2009 and 2013, 509 out of 1,542 principals were replaced.)
- Assuring that every child had a textbook for every subject—something where the Western Cape, though better than many other provinces, had fallen short in the transition to a new curriculum.
- Managing the budget to ensure that teacher salaries did not exceed 75 per cent of total available budgetary resources, thereby assuring budgetary flexibility for the system as a whole to function.
- Explicitly challenging employees throughout the WCED (including the many administrative positions) with the question: 'how does your job help learning improve?'

Vinjevold's identification of principal quality as her biggest priority is consistent with a central finding of a large body of empirical research that the quality of school-level leadership is an important proximate explanation of school performance (Bush, 2007; Bush, Kiggundu, and Moorosi, 2011; Prew, 2007; Wills, 2016). Consistent with that finding, our companion school-level study (in Chapter 8) also found that the performance over time of its four sample schools was strongly associated with the quality of school-level leadership. We thus use the changing approach of the WCED in recent years to the selection of school principals to illustrate how its post-2009 turn to 'pragmatic managerialism' has played out in practice.

As the school-level study explored in depth, the formal responsibility for selecting principals rests largely with SGBs, with the WCED hierarchy (primarily via the district offices) playing a bureaucratic support role. Where SGBs are committed to the achievement of strong educational outcomes, these arrangements can work well. But where, as was evident in three of the four schools examined in our companion case study of four Western Cape schools (Hoadley et al., 2016), they are prone to manipulation, the result can be a 'low-level equilibrium of mediocrity'.

Since 2009, the WCED has used a variety of managerial tools in an effort to influence principal selection in ways that could shake loose these low-level equilibria. These have included:

- A de facto policy that when vacancies for principal arose in poorly performing schools, the winning candidate should not be a deputy principal from the same school. (The school-level study showed vividly how the prospect of in-house promotion could undermine the competitiveness of the principal selection process.)

- The use of early retirement options and other inducements (e.g. lateral transfers) to encourage principals in poorly performing school to vacate their positions.
- The introduction of written psychometric competency assessment tests for candidates for principal, with the costs of testing borne by the WCED. While, given the rules governing labour relations, these could not formally be required, since these tests (and their financing) have been made available, all SGBs have made use of them.
- A review of the selection process in poorly performing schools—and interventions (including from the highest levels of the WCED) where questions arose as to the likely performance of the selected candidate.

The newly empowered districts are central to these efforts to improve the quality of the principal selection process. Circuit managers sit on selection panels of principals and deputy principals as observers. District directors are expected to form their own views of the candidate for principal, and forward them up the hierarchy—and then be accountable for the quality of principal appointments in their districts. It is too soon to assess systematically to what extent these policies have resulted in a strengthening of school-level leadership. But, in our view, using managerial tools along the lines described above to improve principal selection has the potential to yield significant gains in educational outcomes.

More broadly, looking beyond principal selection, since 2009 the WCED has systematically sought to alter the profile of its bureaucracy. A 2009 staffing scan revealed that fewer than 30 per cent of circuit team managers (circuit teams comprise the direct interface between schools and the WCED bureaucracy) had previously served as school principals; post-2009, in filling line positions in the bureaucracy, preference was given to employees with prior experience at school level, especially as principals. Further, district and circuit offices began to be given greater flexibility in how they went about their business.

But the predominant focus remained hierarchical. Teacher training remained strongly supply-driven. No systematic mentoring arrangements were in place for newly appointed principals and other new senior staff working to turn around hitherto dysfunctional schools (beyond the hierarchical quasi-inspection functions of circuit offices). Until 2009 elected SGBs[23] were viewed more as an obstacle than as a potential asset for school-level governance. Further, the increased focus on direct contribution to learning resulted in a de

[23] SGB elections are held on a three-year cycle. In 2014, funding was provided to two non-governmental organisations to help train new SGBs on their roles, immediately following the 2015 round of SGB elections.

facto reduction of opportunities for engagement on the part of many non-governmental organisations who had been working with schools.

4.6 Is More Performance Management the Answer?

At the outset of this chapter, we noted the paradox of basic education in the Western Cape. On the one hand, as the detailed analytic narrative presented in this chapter underscores, the WCED is (and long has been) a relatively well-run public bureaucracy—not only within the South African context, but also likely so when compared with educational bureaucracies in other middle-income countries; further, the WCED's performance-orientation appears to have increased over time. On the other hand, both the data presented in this chapter and the careful econometric analysis in Chapter 6 show that educational outcomes in the Western Cape are mediocre—with performance no better than, say, Kenya, notwithstanding much greater availability of resources. Sustained, determined efforts to strengthen the operation of the Western Cape's education bureaucracy have not translated into the large, hoped-for gains. Why?

There are multiple possible explanations for the disappointing outcomes. These include:

- The hugely difficult socio-economic setting faced by many children that come into the WCED (broken families; gang-ridden communities; drug addiction and endemic foetal alcohol syndrome; recently established informal settlements as waves of new migrants come into the Western Cape).
- Continuing fallout from the disruptive educational policy shocks from the national level during South Africa's first decade of democracy—the large-scale rationalisation of teachers; the introduction (and subsequent retreat from) a poorly thought-through 'outcomes-based education'.
- Weaknesses in teacher skills, not (yet) offset by sustained and effective efforts to strengthen in-house teacher training.
- The fact that only since 2009 has 'management by circular' been superseded by effective performance management, so gains which might become visible in the future are not yet evident.

Though we certainly do not rule out any of the above, based on our observations of the Western Cape, our comparative experience of public sector governance, and experience of education systems elsewhere (plus the comparative econometric results reported in Chapter 6 below), we believe it is helpful to highlight a further possible explanation—namely, that efforts to improve educational outcomes have been too narrowly pre-occupied with hierarchical approaches, and might usefully be complemented (more than has been the case) with additional effort to support more horizontal, peer-to-peer governance.

As this chapter has shown, over the past two decades the WCED has focused largely on improving its hierarchical management systems. In this, it has been successful. Getting textbooks delivered; ensuring that teaching posts are filled with teachers who meet a minimum set of criteria; tracking how schools use resources (including trends in performance); getting funding to the right places at the right times; pro-actively trying to fill leadership positions with the right people for the job—in contrast to many other departments of education in South Africa and elsewhere, the WCED does all of these things relatively well. These are important strengths.

But is hierarchy sufficient? As Chapter 1 detailed, the literature on public management distinguishes between relatively homogenous 'production' activities and more heterogeneous 'craft' activities. While hierarchy can effectively govern the former, numerous scholars (e.g. Israel, 1987; Wilson, 1989; Lipsky, 2010) have argued that 'craft' activities require more flexible and localised governance arrangements. The global literature on education also includes much evidence and advocacy (and some controversy) as to the potential for horizontal governance to add value. And the case studies of Western and Eastern Cape schools in Chapters 8 and 9 of this volume underscore the centrality of school-level governance dynamics in explaining school performance—for ill as well as good.

In concluding, we feel it important to underscore that we are not advocating for radical, rapid change in the WCED's management of education. For all of the magnitude of the continuing challenges, having a system in place that can deliver on the 'basics' is a valuable asset. Rather, what we propose is complementing the current approaches with greater support for enhancing the effectiveness of those more horizontal initiatives for which formal institutional arrangements already are in place, but (except for schools in higher-income areas) have so far received at best limited support for playing their formally designated roles more effectively—combined with opportunities for learning about which initiatives work (and which do not), and for adaptation to the emerging lessons at the level of school-related communities and networks.

In the short run, the gains from these more bottom-up initiatives might seem localised, and thus modest. But, given that the requisite SGB enabling environment is already in place, the risks also are low; the benefits may or may not turn out to be large. (When network effects take hold, their cumulative consequences can be profound.) Based on our broader experience (outside the education sector) of the drivers of success among public organisations, and also the findings reported elsewhere in this volume, we believe that the case is strong for the WCED to deepen its exploration, via learning-by-doing, of what might be achieved through finally working to bring to life, across the socio-economic spectrum, the arrangements for more horizontal governance, which, for almost two decades, have been part of the formal landscape of school-level governance.

Appendix A4.1: How the House of Representatives Governed Education

Patronage in the House of Representatives

In the early 1980s, the government established separate ethnic administrations (known as the tricameral system) within the public service for whites, 'coloureds', and 'Asians', called the House of Assembly (HoA), House of Representatives (HoR) and House of Delegates (HoD), respectively.

The HoR operated on the margins of a Weberian framework. Formally it operated within a merit-based system, but one which incorporated strong elements of patronage. The Labour Party (LP) had become the dominant party in the HoR elections which had been characterized by voters' boycott and low polls. This meant the HOR had a crisis of legitimacy from day one, which the LP set out to rectify by increasing its support.

The HoR was accused of using the Department of Education and Culture for the purposes of 'jobs for pals', appointing LP supporters to principals' positions ahead of better-qualified appointments. Franklin Sonn, then president of the Cape Teachers Professional Association (CTPA), accused the LP of interfering in professional matters. He went on to say that since the introduction of the tricameral system, the LP was clearly seeking patronage by making party political selections for promotion posts (*The South*, 3–9/12/1987). There were accusations that the minister in charge of the Department of Education and Culture, Carter Ebrahim, failed to produce professional reasons for turning down suitably qualified candidates, despite recommendations from school and selection committees (*The Argus*, 18/6/1987; 7/12/1990).

This was corroborated by interviews with researchers and activists of the 1980s, although these interviewees did suggest that the HoR was more focused on controlling the appointments of promotion posts, most notably principals; they had less interest in influencing entry-level appointments. One interviewee argued that: 'collaborators were appointed to be principals by the government'. In fact, many teachers opposed to the system refused to accept promotion.

In summary, the HoR appears to have adopted a relatively mild form of patronage for the purposes of building a political machine, but little evidence of explicit corruption. Patronage was on the margins within what can be termed 'good enough Weberianism'.

Organisation Culture in Coloured Schools

There have been a number of studies of the organisational culture of the white public service which suggested that the South African public service was steeped in traditional public administration, albeit with an apartheid bent. This home-grown version of traditional public administration contributed to a bureaucratic, hierarchical and unresponsive public service, aimed at controlling rather than developing the citizens of the country (Schwella, 2000; McLennan and Fitzgerald, 1992).

The HoR and its predecessor, the Department of Coloured Affairs, adopted this rule-bound compliance culture of the white public service. The HoR was part of the public service; some senior managers in the Department of Education and Culture (of both white and mixed race ethnic background) had transferred from the mainstream public service. There was also a common language (Afrikaans) and culture among white and coloured staff.

Chisholm et al. (1999) argued that control over teachers' work in black and coloured schools was bureaucratic, hierarchical and authoritarian. The strict control of school boards over teachers' work created a bureaucratic system which was monitored through the use of school inspectors. This included all aspects of school governance, administration and the curriculum of coloured schools. Crain Soudien (2002: 217) argued that 'from oral history testimony of educators at the time, it was inspectors who played a central role in subduing teachers and holding them to account'. This was not to suggest that there were watertight mechanisms of surveillance—in fact there is much evidence of 'alternative education' being offered within and around the official confines of the curriculum (Wieder, 2001: 48).

There was, however, a more complex relationship than simply state control. Chisholm (1991: 15–25) details the marriage of academic excellence and political awareness in Teachers League South Africa (TLSA) schools through 1976. Schools that were considered TLSA strongholds (e.g. Harold Cressy, Livingstone, Trafalgar, and South Peninsula) were known for high standards and political teachings. An interview with seasoned educationalist, Crain Soudien, confirmed that the coloured Department of Education, and subsequently the HoR, were not merely tools of state control; they included committed educational professionals. Further, inspectors were not just there to check on teachers: they were sometimes ambivalent towards activist anti-apartheid teachers. Also, school committees (consisting of parents) were appointed by the state as instruments of control; they sometimes consisted of articulate activists who were able to push back state control.

Chisholm et al. (1999: 114) point out that older, more conservative teacher organisations, which had participated in racially divided departments of education, described themselves as 'professionals'. Soudien argues that in the Western Cape, strong professionalism was a driving force of both the system-orientated Cape Teachers Professional Association (CTPA), and the more radical TLSA (Teachers League of South Africa). This in turn was also a safeguard against the worst excesses of patronage.

Appendix A4.2: Management Performance Assessment Tests

The Management Performance Assessment Tests (MPAT) are a national assessment for public servants (although not for teachers). They are conducted by the Department of Performance, Monitoring and Evaluation (DPME) which is located in the Presidency. The DPME released a report discussing the combined results of the 103 national and provincial departments that submitted self-assessments to DPME (The Presidency, 2012). Here we focus specifically on the results of MPATs of education departments.

The 2013 Assessment was based against thirty-one management standards, in seventeen management areas (developed collaboratively with the Department of Public Service and Administration (DPSA) and National Treasury (NT). Standards were developed collaboratively (with NT, DPSA and Office of the Public Service Commission [PSC], Office of the Auditor General and Offices of the Premier) (The Presidency, 2013).

The assessment process is shown in Figure A4.1.

As per the text, a four-level scale was used to assess each department across each of four dimensions. The results are reported in Tables A4.1–4.5.

It can be seen that the WCED scored 100 per cent at Level 4 for strategic management; 56 per cent at Level 4, 22 per cent at Level 3 and 22 per cent at Level 2 for governance and accountability; 20 per cent at Level 4, 40 per cent at Level 3 and 40 per cent at Level 2 for human resources management; and 43 per cent at Level 4 and 57 per cent Level 3 for financial management. If these scores are averaged out, Western Cape received 45 per cent at Level 4, 34 per cent at Level 3 and 21 per cent at Level 2.

The DPME concluded that the overall performance of education departments varied greatly, mainly due to varying performance on governance and accountability, as well as financial management. It stated that within the education sector, the departments that performed best were the Western Cape, whose performance was underlined by generally good provincial support and co-ordination, along with the Gauteng and Free State (The Presidency, 2013).

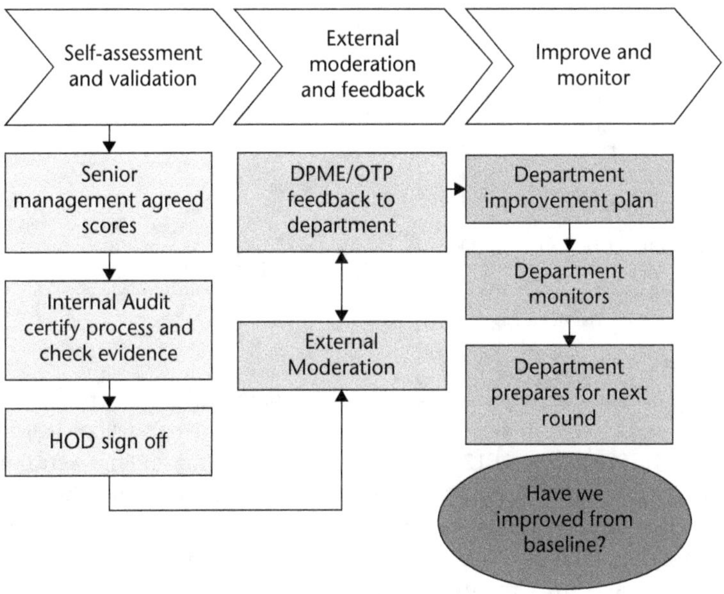

Figure A4.1. MPAT assessment process
The Presidency, DPME (2013).

Table A4.1. MPAT Assessment of Education: Strategic Management

MPAT 2012/13 final scores % of education department scores for strategic management

	Level 1	Level 2	Level 3	Level 4
EC EDU			67	33
FS EDU		33	33	33
GP EDU				100
KZN EDU			67	33
LP EDU		67	33	
MP EDU			67	33
NC EDU			67	33
ND BE			67	33
NW BE&T			67	33
WC EDU				100
ALL EDU	3	12	45	40
ALL RSA	33	44	13	11

Source: The Presidency, DPME (2013).

Table A4.2. MPAT Assessment of Education: Governance and Accountability

MPAT 2012/13 final scores % of education department scores for governance and accountability

	Level 1	Level 2	Level 3	Level 4
EC EDU	67	11	11	11
FS EDU		33	67	
GP EDU	11	22	33	33
KZN EDU	22	67	11	
LP EDU	11	22	22	44
MP EDU		22	33	44
NC EDU	56	22	33	
ND BE	44	22	33	
NW BE&T	44	11	22	22
WC EDU		22	22	56
ALL EDU	30	25	25	20
ALL RSA	38	23	24	15

Source: The Presidency, DPME (2013).

There have been concerns raised about the MPAT approach. The first critique is that the methodology is subjective in that it relies on self-assessment. This is acknowledged by the DPME itself (The Presidency, 2012, 2013), which states that the findings were limited by the availability of evidence to substantiate self-assessment scores from all departments.

The WCED countered this by arguing that they did use external moderation in a systematic way. An examination of the Western Cape raw data (WCED, 2014) suggests, at least at face value, that the external moderation criteria are quite thorough and linked to performance in many ways. For example, if one looks at strategic management, where the WCED received 100 per cent, there were a number of robust criteria

Table A4.3. MPAT Assessment of WCED: Human Resources Management

MPAT 2012/13 final scores % of education department scores for human resource management

	Level 1	Level 2	Level 3	Level 4
EC EDU	70	10	20	
FS EDU	20	30	40	10
GP EDU	10	40	30	20
KZN EDU	30	40	30	
LP EDU	10	50	40	
MP EDU	20	50	30	
NC EDU	30	50	20	
ND BE	20	40	30	10
NW BE&T	20	70	10	
WC EDU		40	40	20
ALL EDU	25	41	29	5
ALL RSA	32	41	21	6

Source: The Presidency, DPME (2013).

Table A4.4. MPAT Assessment of WCED: Financial Management

MPAT 2012/13 final scores % of education department scores for financial management

	Level 1	Level 2	Level 3	Level 4
EC EDU	57	43		
FS EDU	14	29	57	
GP EDU	29		43	29
KZN EDU		14	57	29
LP EDU	14	57	29	
MP EDU	29	43	29	
NC EDU		71	29	
ND BE	14	14	71	
NW BE&T	14	71	14	
WC EDU			57	43
ALL EDU	18	38	35	9
ALL RSA	19	27	45	9

Source: The Presidency, DPME (2013).

that the department had to conform with to achieve this high rating. External moderators had to verify, *inter alia*, that the annual performance plans (APPs) are logically and explicitly linked to delivery agreements and/or programmes of action, as well as the departmental strategic objectives contained in the strategic plan; that the relevance, reliability and verifiability of the information contained in the situational analysis of the APP is according to the framework for managing programme performance information; and whether the APP contains evidence of reconsideration of the situational analysis in the strategic plan, irrespective of whether it resulted in confirming the continued validity of the situational analysis or the amendment of the APP.

Table A4.5. MPAT Assessment of WCED: Overall Score of the Education Department

MPAT 2012/13 final scores % of all KPA scores per education department				
	Level 1	Level 2	Level 3	Level 4
EC EDU	59	17	17	7
FS EDU	10	31	52	7
GP EDU	14	21	31	34
KZN EDU	17	38	34	10
LP EDU	10	45	31	14
MP EDU	14	34	34	17
NC EDU	28	41	28	3
ND BE	24	24	45	7
NW BE&T	24	45	21	10
WC EDU		21	34	45
ALL EDU	24	31	31	15

Source: The Presidency, DPME (2013).

Furthermore, the external moderators must check whether targets in the APP are listed over budget year and MTEF period for each budget programme identified; whether annual targets are broken down in quarterly targets; whether the expression/quantification of strategic objectives and annual and quarterly targets in terms of 'SMART' principle in the APP; whether there is a logical and explicit link between the strategic objectives and targets in the APP and the departmental strategic objectives, as contained in the strategic plan, delivery agreements and/or programmes of action, and whether there is a logical and explicit link between the strategic objectives and targets to budget programmes contained in the APP.

Finally, moderators had to check whether minutes of management meetings reflect use of quarterly performance assessments to inform improvements and whether indicators in annual report and APP are the same and reflect actual annual performance.

The second criticism of the MPAT is that it focuses on compliance rather than performance. DPME (The Presidency, 2013) state in their presentation that the review of compliance does create an awareness of performance. This may be the case, but an awareness of performance does not necessarily translate into performance improvement.

References

Bates, R. H., Greif, A., Levi, M., Rosenthal, J.-L., and Weingast, B. R. (1998) *Analytic Narratives*. Princeton, NJ: Princeton University Press.

Bruns, B., Filmer, D., and Patrinos, H. (2011) *Making Schools Work: New Evidence on Accountability Reforms*. Washington DC: World Bank.

Bush, T. (2007) 'Educational leadership and management: Theory, policy and practice', *South African Journal of Education* 27(3), 391–406.

Bush, T., Kiggundu, E., and Moorosi, P. (2011) 'Preparing new principals in South Africa: The ACE: School Leadership Programme', *South African Journal of Education* 31, 31–43.

Cameron, R. and Naidoo, V. (2016) 'When a "ruling alliance" and public sector governance meet: Managing for performance in South African basic education', ESID Working Paper, No. 62. Manchester: The University of Manchester.

Chisholm, L. (1991) 'Education, politics and organisation: The education traditions and legacies of the Non-European Movement', *Transformation* 15, 1–25.

Chisholm, L., Soudien, Vally, S., and Gilmour, D. (1999) 'Teachers and Structural Adjustment in South Africa', *Education Policy* 13, 386–401.

De Jager, N. (2009) 'No "New" ANC?', *Politikon* 36(2): 275–88.

Education Labour Relations (ELRC) (2003) *Collective Agreement Number 8 of 2003. Integrated Quality Management System,* Pretoria.

ELRC (2005) *Collective Agreement No. 1 of 2005*. Pretoria.

ELRC (2010) *Collective Agreement No. 1 of 2010*. Pretoria.

ELRC (2013) *Collective Agreement No. 1 of 2013*. Pretoria.

Fiske, E. and Ladd, H. F. (2004) *Education Reform in Post-Apartheid South Africa*. Washington DC: Brookings Institute Press.

Grindle, M. S. (2004) '"Good enough" governance: Poverty reduction and reform in developing countries', *Governance* 17(4), 525–48.

Hoadley, U., Levy, B., Shumane, U., and Wilburn, S. (2016) 'The political economy determinants of school performance in four Western Cape Schools', ESID Working Paper No. 84. Manchester: The University of Manchester.

Israel, A. (1987) *Institutional Development: Incentives to Performance*. Washington DC: Published for the World Bank by Oxford University Press.

Jansen, J. and Taylor, N. (2003) *Educational Change in South Africa 1994–2003: Case Studies in Large-scale Education Reform*. World Bank, Education Reform and Management Publication Series, II(I).

Kallaway, P. (ed.) (2002) *The History of Education under Apartheid, 1948–1994: The Doors of Learning and Culture Shall be Opened*. Cape Town: Pearson South Africa.

Levy, B., Hirsch, A., and Woolard, I. (2015) 'Governance and inequality: Benchmarking and interpeting South Africa's evolving political settlement', ESID Working Paper No. 51. Manchester: The University of Manchester.

Lipsky, M. (2010) *Street-level Bureaucracy: Dilemmas of the Individual in Public Service*. New York: Russell Sage Foundation.

McLennan, A. and Fitzgerald, P. (eds) (1992) *The Mount Grace papers. The New Public Administration Initiative and the Mount Grace Consultation*. Johannesburg: Public and Development Management Programme, University of Witwatersrand.

Prew, M. (2007) 'Successful principals: Why some principals succeed and others struggle when faced with innovation and transformation', *South African Journal of Education* 27(3), 447–62.

Provincial Government of the Western Cape (2010) *Delivering the Open Opportunity for All, the Western Cape's draft Strategic Plan*. Cape Town.

Reddy, V., Prinsloo, C., Arends, F., and Visser, M. (2012) *Highlights from TIMSS 2011: The South African Perspective*. Pretoria, Human Sciences Research Council, www.hsrc.ac.za.

Republic of South Africa (RSA) (1996) *Population Census 1996*. Pretoria: Department of Statistics.

RSA (2001) *Government Gazette* 433(22512), *Policy on Whole School Education*. Pretoria: Department of Education.

RSA (2010a) *The SACMEQ III Project in South Africa: A Study of the Conditions of Schooling and the Quality of Education*. Pretoria.

RSA (2010b) *Report on the NSC Examination, 2010*. Pretoria: Department of Basic Education (DBE), Educational Measurement, Assessment and Public Examinations.

RSA (2014) *National Senior Certificate Examination: Technical Report*. Pretoria: Department of Basic Education.

RSA (2016) *Report on progress in the schooling sector against key learner performance and attainment indicators*. Pretoria. Department of Basic Education.

Schwella, E. (2000) 'Paradigms: Context and competencie'. In F. Theron and E. Schwella (eds), *The State of Public and Development Management in South Africa. The Mount Grace II Papers*. Stellenbosch: University of Stellenbosch, 33–43.

Soudien, C. (2002) 'Teachers' responses to the introduction of apartheid education'. In P. Kallaway (ed.), *The History of Education under Apartheid, 1948–1994: The Doors of Learning and Culture Shall Be Opened*. Cape Town: Pearson South Africa.

Southern and East Africa Consortium for Monitoring Educational Quality (SACMEQ) (2007) http://www.sacmeq.org/.

Spaull, N. (2013) 'South Africa's education crisis: The quality of education in South Africa. 1994-2011'. Johannesburg: Centre for Development and Enterprise (CDE).

The Argus, 18/6/1987 'Teachers claim Political bias'.

The Argus, 7/12/1990 'Abuse of Power, Sharp Attack on Hendrickse over teachers'.

The Presidency, Department of Performance Monitoring and Evaluation (2012) *Management Performance Assessment Tool (MPAT) Report on results of assessment process for 2011/2012*. Pretoria.

The Presidency, Department of Performance Monitoring and Evaluation (2013) MPAT. *Management Performance Assessment 2012/13 Final scores Education Sector Feedback*. Pretoria.

The South, 3–9/12/1987 'Jobs for Pals'.

WCED (Western Cape Education Department) (2013) *Annual Report, 2012–13*. Cape Town.

WCED (2014a) *Education Data Base*. Cape Town.

WCED (2014b) *Annual Report, 2013–14*. Cape Town.

WCED (2015) *Annual Report, 2014–15*. Cape Town.

Wieder, A. (2001) 'They can't take our souls: Teachers' League of South Africa reflections of apartheid', *Race, Ethnicity and Education* 4(2), 145–66.

Wills, G. (2016) 'Principal leadership changes in South Africa: Investigating their consequences for school performance', Stellenbosch Economic Working Papers: 01/16.

Wilson, J. Q. (1989) *Bureaucracy: What Government Agencies Do and Why They Do It*. New York: Basic Books.

World Bank (2004) *World Development Report 2004: Making Services Work for Poor People*. Washington DC: World Bank, https://openknowledge.worldbank.org/handle/10986/5986 License: CC BY 3.0 IGO.

5

Provincial Governance of Education—The Eastern Cape Experience

Zukiswa Kota, Monica Hendricks, Eric Matambo, and Vinothan Naidoo

5.1 Introduction

The Eastern Cape province experienced extensive government re-organization following South Africa's 1994 democratic transition. This entailed significant structural consolidation in the provincial government, and the integration of a disparate set of political and administrative actors (including two so-called 'independent' Bantustans, the Transkei and the Ciskei) under the umbrella of the African National Congress (ANC).

Over the subsequent two decades, governance of the province has been fraught with conflict within and amongst a single-party dominant coalition of interests that has severely hampered the delivery of key public services such as education.

This chapter uses the multi-level analytical framework laid out in Chapter 1 to characterize the province's governance transformation, and analyses its effect on the province's capacity to shape and implement policy. As we will show, historical patterns of clientelism were transplanted into a post-apartheid political and administrative settlement. This resulted in considerable intra-party cleavages amongst the political elite, which impeded the growth of a rule-compliant, insulated and performance-driven bureaucracy in large part due to the blurred lines and collusive relationship that developed between factionalized party politics, the senior ranks of the administration, and influential stakeholder groups.

The fragmentation that ensued has been especially acute in the province's education sector, overseen by the Eastern Cape Department of Education (ECDoE). The sector has seen chronic leadership instability, politicization and financial mismanagement, which has compromised the cohesion and integrity of provincial school oversight and policy management. A consequence has been sustained instability in key policy areas such as post provisioning/allocation, which has been most acutely expressed in a contestation over posts at the school level.

Applying the governance typology laid out in Chapter 1 to the provision of basic education in the Eastern Cape, we argue that the primary mode of governance in the province comprises a personalized/negotiated type, displaying a clientelistic orientation and increasing levels of fragmentation (Table 5.1).

We find that the institutional arrangements which shape the governance of basic education resembles a segmented pyramid, illustrated in Figure 5.1—one which flows from the pinnacle (represented by the provincial government level), where hierarchical steering ought to be concentrated, to the education sector bureaucracy (centred in the ECDoE), and down to the school level. We further find that governance becomes less contained and increasingly fragmented as it spreads out from the pinnacle to the base, resulting in a breakdown of hierarchical steering from the provincial cabinet through to the ECDoE and down to the school level, where institutional complexity is most pronounced, and where the space for negotiated outcomes is at its widest.

This chapter describes the governance relationship between these three institutional layers affecting basic education provision in the Eastern Cape.

Table 5.1. Governance of Education in the Eastern Cape

Hierarchical	20	10
Negotiated	*60*	10
	Personalized	Impersonal

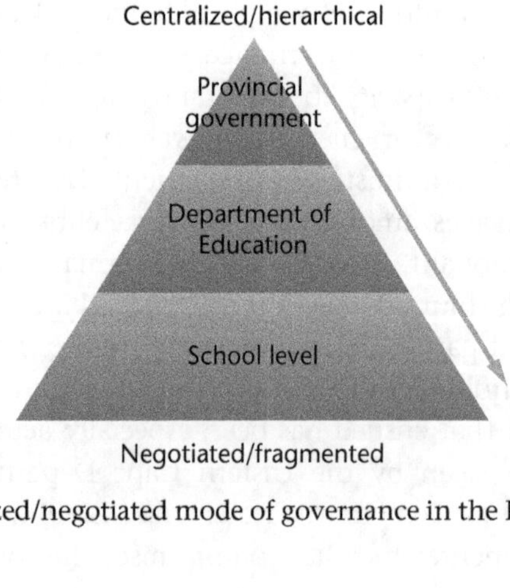

Figure 5.1. Personalized/negotiated mode of governance in the Eastern Cape education sector

In section 5.2, we show that executive politics at a provincial level has shown patterns of centralized clientelism marked by factional contestation within the governing ANC, which has been hierarchically mediated through the provincial premier and cabinet. In section 5.3, we begin to see an erosion of hierarchically mediated clientelism upon entering the education bureaucracy (i.e., the ECDoE), which has experienced considerable leadership instability and a flouting of accountability—including down to the district level, and which has also contributed to policy uncertainty in key areas such as teacher supply/post allocation (the subject of section 5.4). Finally, in section 5.5, we show more pronounced fragmentation and negotiated arrangements over teacher appointments and governance at a school level, where the source of contestation varies and encompasses union influence as well as more interpersonal modes of conflict. Section 5.6 concludes.

Because of the increasingly fragmented nature of education governance in the province, moving from the apex of the pyramid down to its base, the evidence that we present in this chapter cannot show a seamless relationship between the three levels of the pyramid, prompting our segmented portrayal. What this means is that there are multiple plains of contestation, which, in the absence of more extensive empirical data to substantiate the links between these plains, need to be more cautiously assessed on their own merits.

This chapter comprises a mix of secondary and primary sources. The secondary sources consist of academic articles, media reportage, government sources, and research and submissions made by the Eastern Cape-based Public Service Accountability Monitor, a non-governmental provincial watchdog. Section 5.5 also includes data from key informant interviews in the province's education sector.

5.2 The Eastern Cape's Political Context

The seeds of the Eastern Cape's political dynamics can be traced to the circumstances of its birth, in which various regional and ethno-linguistic administrations were merged to form a new Eastern Cape Provincial Government (ECPG). Politico-administrative amalgamation was hamstrung by attempts to integrate the bureaucracies of the Transkei and Ciskei, which were known to be poorly run and prone to corruption (Streek and Wicksteed, 1981; Lodge, 2002; Hyslop, 2005; Picard, 2005). Picard (2005: 297) also observed the particularistic make-up of the constituencies which made up the administration of the former homelands: '[a]t the core of the public service in the homelands was a cadre of traditional leaders, chiefs and headmen who had been transformed into bureaucrats in the 1960s. They represented what passed for collective interests in the homelands.' This traditional leader-cum-bureaucratic constituency had grown accustomed to the patronage and rent-seeking which their access to administrative power had afforded them. This would mark a crucial point of tension between the incoming ANC government in the province and its attempts to unify the bureaucracy, in which the sectional interests of the latter would resist any administrative reform that would substantially weaken their privileges.

The ANC was also constrained by the incorporation of different groupings within the organization with sectional interests to promote. The ECPG's first premier, Raymond Mhlaba, was appointed as a result of a compromise amongst distinct ANC regional interests in the former Eastern Cape, Border and Transkei, each fervently promoting their status as the birthplace of the liberation movement. Mhlaba (2001) acknowledged the opposition he faced in attempting to downsize the province's civil service. As a result, the ANC government had only managed to institute a soft form of downsizing due to the level of opposition to administrative retrenchments, which took the form of not replacing officials exiting the service (Southall, 1999: 159; Lodge, 2005: 741). This was also reflected in reports of thousands of supernumeraries remaining on the provincial payroll as the 1999 elections approached (Southall, 1999: 161). Public finance probity was an early casualty of the political transition and bureaucratic hostility in the ECPG. Gevisser (1996) paints a picture of a province in financial crisis in its early years, blighted by corruption, including theft and rent-seeking in some of the province's largest departments, such as salary embezzlement in the Department of Health, and the phenomenon of 'ghost' or 'phantom' teachers receiving compensation via the government payroll.

The executive politics of the province continued to be afflicted by factional and clientelistic practices, which has permeated the relationship between politics and administration and enabled a continuation of bureaucratic misconduct dating from the province's transition. This became more visible as the province's political institutions began to consolidate. Efforts to entrench political power amongst the Eastern Cape's governing elite intensified as factional battles became more prominent, which was partly reflected in the ideological clashes that erupted within the ANC between 2000 and 2004 (Hoeane, 2011; Lodge, 2004). This also coincided with a change in the ANC's national leadership, under the more centralized stewardship of Thabo Mbeki. Mbeki's scathing attack on critics of the controversial Growth, Employment and Redistribution (GEAR) programme at the SACP's tenth congress in July 1998, in which he lectured delegates on 'the dangers of fake revolutionary posturing, accusing party leaders of trying to boost their following on the basis of scavenging on the carcass of a savaged ANC', showed that battle lines had been drawn between him and 'ultra-leftists' in the alliance (Lodge, 2002: 246). This had repercussions in the Eastern Cape's apparent Mbeki-driven dismissals in the provincial cabinet. Phumulo Masualle was targeted, as a senior SACP member. Masualle, a former provincial minister of public works, was reportedly dismissed in 2002 by Premier Makhenkesi Stofile, who was allegedly ordered by President Thabo Mbeki to purge his cabinet of 'ultra-leftists' (Dawes and Rossouw, 2008).

Intra-provincial factionalism also generated more pernicious clientelistic effects in the Eastern Cape, including the controversial tenure of Raymond Mhlaba's successor, Makhenkesi Stofile. It was under Stofile that the Eastern Cape was subject to multiple Section 100 constitutional interventions, the most serious taking place in 2003, which involved an interim management team (IMT) to assume control of over 80 per cent of the Eastern Cape's budget and a joint anti-corruption task team (JACTT) to investigate and prosecute cases of corruption and fraud (PSAM, 2006). Premier Stofile's response to the report of the IMT, as cited by Hyslop (2005: 786), is particularly illuminating in politically disassociating the cabinet's role in malfeasance:

> Our responsibility is simply to make sure that our policies are in line with national policies, development policies, and the delivery of services. The actual operations are not our responsibility; they're the responsibility of the administration.

Stofile did, however, go further than turning a blind eye to corruption, by actively protecting officials found guilty of corrupt activity. In one case, Stofile intervened to protect the roads and public works head, Dumisani Mafu, as recounted by Zuzile (2004):

> Stofile overruled the decision of an internal disciplinary hearing which found Mr Mafu guilty of financial misconduct, it was learnt this week. Mr Mafu was charged last year with five counts of financial misconduct.... Mr Stofile reported that he had found no wilfulness or negligence on Mr Mafu's part in committing the offences... officials at the premier's office could not say why Mr Stofile had overruled the decision of the hearing. Mxolisi Spondo, one of the premier's spokesmen, said the correspondence between Mr Stofile and Mr Mafu, in which he explains his decision 'is very technical'.

In another case, this time involving a cabinet member, Stofile failed to take action, despite being pressured to do so. The Member of the Executive Council (MEC) for health, Bevan Goqwana, breached the Executive Ethics Act. Goqwana was operating an ambulance company and submitting patients' medical aid claims, despite the fact that the Act required cabinet members and MECs to avoid such conflicts (Lodge, 2002). Ultimately, factional considerations also spelled the end of Stofile's premiership, with Nosimo Balindlela, a Mbeki loyalist, replacing him following the 2004 elections, despite his popular support within provincial structures (Hoeane, 2011: 96).

The efforts of Nosimo Balindlela to consolidate her political grip on the provincial executive displayed a continuation of centrally orchestrated patronage. This was evident in Balindlela's purging of left-leaning members of her cabinet (Cull, 2004; and Naki, 2004, cited in Hoeane, 2011: 96); along with her efforts to rid the Eastern Cape Development Corporation, a provincial public entity, of supporters of her predecessor, Makhenkhesi Stofile (Van der Merwe, 2005, cited in Hoeane, 2011: 98–9). Another example was Balindlela's reversal of the suspension of Department of Health head, Lawrence Boya, by the then MEC Bevan Goqwana, in April 2006, pending an investigation into alleged maladministration and insubordination; only for her to terminate Goqwana a week later (Mail & Guardian, 2009a). It is likely that she had been looking for an opportunity to fire Goqwana, because he was a Stofile loyalist who had enjoyed the former premier's protection.

It was also at the behest of Balindlela that an official, but ultimately discredited, inquiry to highlight persistent financial mismanagement in the Eastern Cape fell prey to factional politics. The judicial commission of inquiry into the finances of the Eastern Cape provincial government ('Pillay Commission of Inquiry') was established by Balindlela in April 2005. The commission had a mandate to evaluate public expenditure management and investigate alleged incidents of procurement-related maladministration, fraud and corruption within the Eastern Cape provincial administration since 1994 (PSAM, 2006). The report, however, sat idly on Premier Balindlela's desk for more than two years, until she decided to have extracts of it leaked to the media to try and ensure her political survival two days before the ANC's national executive committee was to decide her fate as premier (Letsoalo et al., 2008). Balindlela was accused by a rival faction of using the inquiry as a means to discredit her political opponents, some of whom initiated an unopposed High Court challenge against the report, including former premier Makhenkesi Stofile, Enoch Godongwana, Stone Sizani and Mcebisi Jonas. The report was ultimately quashed on a legal technicality in 2009 (Fölscher and Kruger, 2013; Mail & Guardian, 2009b).

The removal of Balindlela following the passage of the ANC presidency from Thabo Mbeki to Jacob Zuma at the ANC's Polokwane elective conference in 2007 signalled a gradual shift of factional power in the province. Her successor, Mbulelo Sogoni, remained within the still influential Mbeki-aligned faction in the province, although appeared to be another compromise candidate at a delicate point in the transition of power from Mbeki to Zuma, given his leftist roots (Rossouw, 2008). The results of the 2009 elections sealed victory for the Jacob Zuma camp in the Eastern Cape's factional politics. The ANC's alliance partner, COSATU, was appeased with the selection of Noxolo Kiviet as premier, with her pedigree in trade union politics in the Eastern Cape, having formerly performed the role of COSATU treasurer in what was then the

Border-Kei region. Mbulelo Sogoni would later be redeployed as the Eastern Cape's top civil servant, or provincial director-general, signalling the blurred lines and revolving door between party politics and the provincial bureaucracy. His appointment was possibly a compromise with members of the Mbeki faction, in a province where the former president remained relatively popular. Sogoni was subsequently redeployed back into a political office, as MEC for economic affairs, environment and tourism.

5.3 Revolving Doors: Unstable Leadership in the ECDoE

The centrally orchestrated character of the Eastern Cape's personalized politics becomes more fragmented when we enter the education bureaucracy, centred in the ECDoE. The department has experienced inordinate leadership turnover and a general flouting of centralized authority. A former national minister of education, Naledi Pandor, decried the 'revolving door syndrome' that had come to define the ECDoE's internal governance. This is depicted in the turnover of incumbents in the posts of MEC and superintendent general since 1994 (see Table 5.2). Between 2002 and 2011 there were at least five MECs in the ECDoE. Of particular concern has been the position of accounting officer (or superintendent general). This post saw eight incumbents in as many years in various acting and permanent appointments since 2008. Leadership instability in the ECDoE, we will show, has not only contributed to sustained problems in resource provisioning, but has also been bound up with clientelistic politics.

The theme of a centrally orchestrated form of patronage giving way to a more fragmented variant in the Eastern Cape's education sector is consistent with Ngoma's (2009) biographical account of the organizational culture of the ECDoE. This includes several illuminating interviews with the department's former political and administrative leadership. Ngoma (2009: 192) describes the post-apartheid transition and subsequent consolidation of the department as characterized by 'fragmented leadership and fragmented spaces of influence', in which the ECDoE represented at its birth an uneasy cohabitation of incumbents who had previously served in the province's various apartheid-Bantustan bureaucracies. These origins left the ECDoE particularly vulnerable to the transplantation of what Ngoma refers to as 'coalitional networks', marked by divergent and competing regional interests, organizational cultures, and patronage ties, which seems to have consistently defied centralized control.

The consequences of the ECDoE's fragmented origins have disabled attempts to entrench organizational stability and counter malfeasance. Obiyo (2013) and Lodge (2005) have highlighted the obstacles faced by the department's leadership. In a particularly revealing empirical study of

Table 5.2. Leadership Chronology in the ECDoE[1]

PERIOD	MEC	Superintendent general
1994 to 1997	Nosimo Balindlela	(appointment date unknown) Dr Ronnie van Wyk (resigned 1997, left 1998)
1998 to 1999	Professor Shepherd Mayatula	Jonathan Godden (acting) (February/March 1998–Sept 2000) Mabandla Tsengiwe
1999/2000 to 2002	Stone Sizani	(Oct 2000–mid 2001) Modidima Mannya Phlip Qokweni (Acting) (Mid 2001–Feb 2003)
2002/2003	(November 2002) Nomsa Jajula	Reverend Lulamile Mbete (March–Dec 2003)
2004 to 2006	Mkhangeli Matomela	Bea Hackula (acting) (Jan–March 2004) (2005/2006 unclear)
2006 to 2007	Johnny Makgato (dates of appointment and resignation unclear)	
2007		Nomlamli Mahanjana
2008	Mahlubandile Qwase	Nomlamli Mahanjana (ousted after union protest)
2009	Mahlubandile Qwase (redeployed to OTP)	Ronnie Swartz (acting; ousted after union protest); Harry Nengwekhulu
2010	Mandla Makupula (2010 till present)	Harry Nengwekhulu (ousted after union protest) (8 November 2010): Modidima Mannya
2011		Advocate Modidima Mannya (ousted in 2011 after union protest and cabinet-led intervention)
2012		Mathanzima Mweli (acting; secondment from DBE)
2013		(March) Mthunywa Ngonzo
2014/2015		(January 2014) Mthunywa Ngonzo (suspended after allegations of maladministration) (July 2015) Ray Tywakadi (acting) (November 2015) Sizakele Netshilaphala (acting)

legislative oversight over the ECDoE, Obiyo (2013: 105) found that 'political deployment' was cited by current and former members of the Eastern Cape provincial legislature's committee for education as contributing to a 'lack of teeth' in performing oversight over the department. He added that MECs for education and their senior officials, with 'some officials outrank[ing] the MECs within the ANC', were deployees of the party who belonged to different divisions, and this had made vertical accountability difficult (Obiyo, 2013: 107). This also raises the prospect of muddied and contested principal forms of accountability. A variant of this problem which has also been observed in the ECDoE indicated that even when a vertical patronage relationship exists between

[1] Sources: PSAM (2006, 2004); Esbend (2005); ECDoE (2012); GCIS (2015) SAPA (2012) *Daily Dispatch* (2012).

the MEC, as political head, and senior officials, this can thwart the authority of other key departmental principals: the superintendent-general or head of department, and their deputies. For instance, a more damning accusation raised by Obiyo (2013) was that senior officials in the ECDoE were running businesses associated with the work of the department and being protected by political heads. Lodge (2005: 747) cites the efforts of former ECDoE superintendent-general, Modidima Mannya, to turn around the department in 2000. Mannya was said to have received death threats following his suspension of ten departmental managers, including some with close political connections. Ngoma (2009: 213) similarly recounts how turnover of MECs in the ECDoE at times 'perpetuated internal battles for power and control', prompting officials to re-assert clientelistic ties to incoming political principals that displaced more senior officials. One episode involved a deputy director-general who, in an interview, described how he was essentially outmanoeuvred and displaced ('expelled') by lower-level officials who re-asserted their regional ties with a new MEC, seemingly re-igniting the coalitional networks described earlier by Ngoma.

The tenure of Modidima Mannya as ECDoE superintendent general starkly illustrates the impact of clientelistic interests. Mannya's first appointment in 2000 under the premiership of Makhenkesi Stofile and MEC Stone Sizani saw him take decisive action against corrupt officials, including suspending ten senior managers (Macfarlane, 2002). In 2001, Mannya insisted that three chief directors sign letters publicly acknowledging their responsibility for the problems in the embattled department. This included the suspension of three directors for providing incorrect teacher deployment information (Esbend, 2001). Several senior officials were targeted by Mannya's anti-corruption activities, some of whom appealed to Premier Stofile's wife. Following Mannya's reports of receiving death threats, the provincial government appointed bodyguards to ensure his personal protection (Macfarlane, 2002). When the bodyguards were later withdrawn, Mannya resigned. According to Macfarlane (2002), Mannya claimed that those that had sought him out to rid the ECDoE of corruption (i.e. Sizani and Stofile), subsequently became hostile towards him. Mannya is reported to have stated that scams appeared to govern staff appointments, with widespread management irregularities involving 'non-compliance with procurement procedures'. 'In almost all the actions I took, there were political representations and responses. Administrative decisions are constantly interfered with by politicians... almost everyone you touch is connected,' Mannya said, citing the example of a chief director he suspended whose wife was close to the premier's wife. 'People are afraid to talk. I touched a raw nerve—but what exactly I'm not sure' (Macfarlane, 2002).

The obstacles to enforcing management control and sustaining leadership continuity in the ECDoE have contributed to chronic financial impropriety.

In October 2009, the Eastern Cape-based Public Service Accountability Monitor (PSAM) called on MEC Mahlubandile Qwase to institute disciplinary action against senior officials in the ECDoE, against whom the auditor-general (AG) cited breaches of the Public Finance Management Act (PFMA) (Luyt, 2009). It was found that the ECDoE had failed to disclose irregular expenditure of at least R1.5 billion in contravention of section 40(3)(b) of the PFMA, and understated fruitless and wasteful expenditure by at least R46 million. The AG further noted that senior management in the ECDoE did not implement plans recommended by his office to address financial management problems. Issues included an inability to maintain effective and efficient systems of financial management and internal control, resulting in irregular expenditure of at least R730 million. According to the AG's report, 'top management has not set the example and acted upon officials found guilty of non-compliance with the required internal control policies and procedures' (Luyt, 2009). In addition, over several years, Luyt (2009) noted a recurring laissez-faire attitude towards disciplinary action against officials contravening the provisions of the PFMA and the Division of Revenue Act, despite calls by the Eastern Cape legislature and MEC Masualle.

Figure 5.2 shows the total number of financial misconduct[2] cases recorded for the ECPG published by the PSC, which in some cases displays dramatic differences between the province's totals and the provincial average (2003, 2005, 2009). The overwhelming majority of cases reported for 2005 were attributed to the ECDoE (127 cases). Education also accounted for the vast majority of cases in 2006 (fifty-eight) and in 2007 (thirty-two cases).

The ECDoE's unstable leadership and clientelistic pressures have also produced a lacklustre and cosmetic commitment to performance management, which at a minimum appears to correspond with the notion of 'isomorphic mimicry'. This suggests that individually oriented performance assessment might be sacrificed in order to preserve collusive ties and interests. According to the South African government's management performance assessment tool (MPAT), which evaluates the compliance of departmental management processes and practices against several key performance indicators, the ECDoE displayed the lowest level of compliance amongst all provincial education departments, and was below the national average (Cameron and Levy, 2016: 10). In a damning self-appraisal of performance management, the ECDoE conceded that there is 'an almost complete lack of accountability and performance management' (ECDoE, 2014: 42; ECDoE, 2015: 40). Ngoma (2009: 222–3) also published enlightening extracts from a former director-general and deputy director-general in the ECDoE, who described performance

[2] Financial misconduct is an umbrella term that incorporates a range of criminal and ethical misconduct, including corruption, fraud, theft and financial mismanagement.

management as 'synthetic', 'artificial', compliance-driven, and oriented towards 'keeping up appearances'.

A weak commitment to performance management in the ECDoE is not otherwise exceptional in the Eastern Cape provincial administration. A report by the PSAM (Overy, 2005: 20) cited a poor performance management compliance culture in other key departments, such as Health and Public Works, along with Education. In another report assessing compliance by senior managers with performance agreements in the Eastern Cape, the PSC (2008) presented similar worrying findings on provincial officials' attitudes towards performance management. This consisted of a very low response rate of senior managers willing to participate in the study, which totalled 32 per cent; a further low number of signed performance agreements submitted relative to the total number of senior managers in the provincial bureaucracy: 49 per cent; and even lower submissions by the largest departments: Health at 35 per cent and Education at just over 40 per cent. The Eastern Cape was also found to have had a poor track record of evaluating heads of department, especially in the period 2003–05 (PSC, 2008: 13, 16, 25). This coincidentally corresponds with a period in which a large number of financial misconduct cases were recorded in provincial departments, and in the ECDoE in particular (see Figure 5.2).

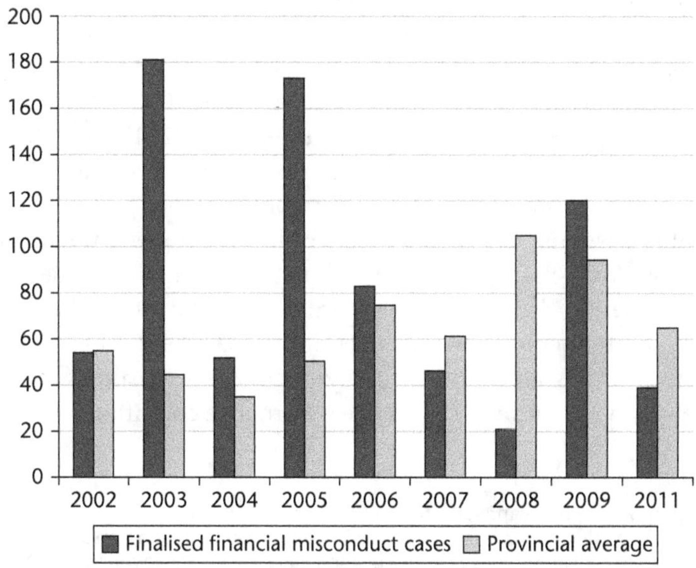

Figure 5.2. Reported cases of financial misconduct in the ECPG

Source: Financial misconduct reports published by the Public Service Commission, various years, see http://www.psc.gov.za

5.4 Instability of Teacher Supply and Demand in the Eastern Cape

Leadership instability and fractured internal governance in the ECDoE has compromised the policy management of education delivery in the Eastern Cape. This has been evident in the problematic management of teacher supply and demand, or post allocation, which has contributed to the department experiencing chronic financial constraints. The picture that emerges is twofold: on the one hand, the ECDoE is a victim of the inordinately complex conditions attending teacher rationalization in the province; on the other hand, poor internal governance coupled with heavy contestation of teacher distribution by unions such as SADTU in the province has effectively scuppered the department's ability to efficiently and equitably distribute teachers, especially in rural areas.

The ECDoE caters for the second largest number of learners in South Africa after KwaZulu-Natal. An intractable challenge facing the province's education sector has been the uneven distribution of qualified educators.[3] The ECDoE, which services a geographically diverse province, is currently divided into twenty-three education districts, covering a complex mix of schools in widely differing communities. The 2014 Education Management Information System (EMIS) revealed that there are 6,227 educational institutions under the ECDoE. This number is comprised of 873 secondary schools, 2,243 primary schools, 42 special schools, 187 ECD centres, 2,428 combined/junior secondary schools, 294 adult centres and 160 independent schools (ECDoE, 2015). Of the 66,138 educators registered in the ECDoE's system in 2013/14, the majority (61,407) were government funded, while 4,731 were funded by school governing bodies (SGBs). In 2014, the ECDoE (2014) reported that 60 per cent of provincial schools had vacant posts for more than 12 months, although this probably includes non-educator personnel.[4]

In addition, Ngoma (2009: 202) observed that the department has been significantly under-managed compared to other provincial departments, exhibiting a senior manager to total employee ratio of 1:1,545, with the next highest ratio being 1:394 in the Health Department. This severely constrains the ECDoE's ability to centrally oversee a vast supply of teaching personnel, even under more favourable governance conditions.

[3] For the purposes of this chapter, the terms 'educator' and 'teacher' will be used interchangeably to define one who educates or imparts knowledge within the schooling system. This may also signify office-based educators, where the discussion relates to staff deployment patterns.

[4] The section containing these statistics is contained in the Department's Annual Performance Plan 'Organisational Environment' section for 2012/13 on pp. 44–5 and also appears verbatim within the 'Organisational Environment' section in the 2014/15 Annual Performance Plan (ECDoE, 2014: 41–2).

Owing to this general situation, the Eastern Cape has over a four-year period (2009–12) seen a reduction in the total number of schools, learners and teachers, with the biggest decline being in learner numbers. Thus, the number of schools fell from 5,809 to 5,754, learners from 2,076,400 to 1,951,523, and teachers from 69,620 to 67,936. The net effect of this decline is that the Eastern Cape has 22.3 per cent of the nation's schools, serving 16 per cent of South Africa's learners. This imbalance has led to the province having the lowest learner–school ratio, of 339, and the lowest teacher–school ratio of 11.8, as compared to national ratios of 481 and 16.5, respectively (DBE, 2014: 4). Contributing to the decline in learner numbers is the fact that the province has consistently had a matric pass rate below the national average—and often the lowest in the country. The comparison, in Chapter 6, of national senior certificate results by province indicated that the Eastern Cape's percentage pass rate was the lowest of all provinces in 2008 (50.6) and again in 2014 (65.4), and was also well below the national average. Feeding into this result is the Eastern Cape's relatively low level of pupil performance on standardized tests (SACMEQ data).

Another factor has been a persistent infrastructure backlog, which has seen a high proportion of 'mud' and structurally unsafe schools. More than five years ago, the ECDoE stated that there were 5,788 schools in the province, of which a staggering 2,650, or 46 per cent, were in a weak or very weak condition. The ECDoE (2009: 8) justified its resistance to addressing this backlog, claiming that many were small rural schools that needed to be 'rationalised . . . to avoid the provision of infrastructure that will soon become under-utilised'. This attitude exacerbated

> the effects of urbanisation and rural depopulation as the slow pace of providing decent infrastructure and resources in rural areas means that they remain poorly-resourced backwaters, while well-resourced cities continue to exert a powerful 'pull'. (Hendricks and Wright, 2012: 20)

One of the consequences of the imbalance between the learner–school ratio and the teacher–school ratio is that schools are being closed, temporary teaching posts are ballooning, while permanent, excess staff are faced with redeployment. To develop appropriate responses to these changing numbers and demographics in schools and meet demand-side pressures, accurate information on the number of schools and teaching posts in the province is indispensable. Yet, it is surprisingly difficult to establish with any certainty the number of schools, posts or the level of posts in the Eastern Cape. It is even more difficult to be certain of teachers' exact field(s) of specialization within a professional qualification, or whether a school has staff with the appropriate subject knowledge mix to teach what the school curriculum offers (Reeves and Robinson, 2010). PERSAL (the government's electronic personnel and salary information system), may not be a reliable source of information to address this problem, since as recently as 2010 there were reports not only of ghost teachers, but of ghost schools in the province. Blaine (2010) reported that the Hawks[5] were tracking R6 million that had been drained out of the ECDoE budget. A manifestation of this concerns the alleged fraudulent appointment and payment of teachers in various primary schools in the Port Elizabeth area by Portia Sizani, who at the time served as the ECDoE's district co-ordinator for early childhood development (Kimberley, 2014).

The problem of teacher shortages in the Eastern Cape is not, strictly speaking, one of absolute shortages, but is complicated by systemic distributional failures. A shortage of teachers in specific subject areas is widespread and of long standing. The fact that public education is a 'vast enterprise of enormous complexity, depending on . . . the work of hundreds of thousands of individuals situated in thousands of institutions' (Jansen and Taylor, 2003: 34) is acutely evident in the Eastern Cape. In April 2005, in an article entitled 'Please give us teachers', it was reported that learners across the province had been without teachers since the start of the academic year, with the schooling of some 9,000 learners' being severely disrupted, as the province was reportedly short of as many as 3,000 teachers (Esbend, 2005).

National norms governing post distribution were first issued in 1998, and subsequently revised in 2002 and 2008.[6] These policies, judging from the 2012 ANC national conference resolution and confirmed by a Deloitte (undated) report, have not been implemented. Through the current model, posts are distributed at schools according to the number of 'weighted' learners. The weighting of learners, as opposed to the use of absolute numbers, is intended to allow for a more equitable distribution of educators in key curriculum areas and to remote rural schools. This model of establishing the staffing needs of a school is a complex one, determined by using a distribution equation which also takes into account the size of a school, maximum class sizes per learning area, learner disability and language/s of instruction and the remoteness of a school (DBE, undated). This last factor is complicated by the rurality of a province and, in the Eastern Cape in particular, historical and spatial arrangements influence the learner-to-school ratio, as previously discussed.

Despite the introduction of the current post allocation model, not all provinces are following this—or the same—model. The findings of the National Education Evaluation and Development Unit (NEEDU) of 2013 reveal that,

[5] Refers to the Directorate for Priority Crime Investigations—a division of the South African Police Service (SAPS).

[6] Government Notice 1676 of 1998; Government Notice 1451 of 2002; Post Distribution Model for the Allocation of Posts to Schools (2008).

across all nine provinces, the model is applied differently and to varying degrees. Creating further confusion, another report (Deloitte, undated) states that it is apparent that the DBE itself is not consistent about the details of the model that it instructs provincial departments to use. Furthermore, it appears that there are at least five different versions of the post allocation policy being used in the country (Deloitte, UNICEF, DBE, undated), thereby compromising oversight over provincial practices. The decentralized and discretionary application of post allocation also risks subjecting the process to variable management capacity and potentially unscrupulous actions. The recently appointed ECDoE superintendent general (see Figure 5.2) released a circular in November 2015 alerting education stakeholders about various shortcomings within the sector. The circular (23 of 2015) outlines problems in the Department, such as teacher shortages and the 'eroding of (the) culture of teaching and learning, non-compliance on a number of policy imperative(s), low staff morale, and dysfunctionality of schools'.

Zokufa (2007) and Jansen and Taylor (2003) provide detailed accounts of the initial process of redeployment in the Eastern Cape, beginning with an initial five-year plan in April 1995. However, this was never implemented adequately, nor was the magnitude of the problem fully exposed. In an attempt to shift approximately 20 per cent of national education expenditure to previously neglected provinces like the Eastern Cape, the teacher rationalization policy was introduced (Jansen and Taylor, 2003). This included equalization of teacher: pupil ratios. In 1996, for example, the Eastern Cape ratio at primary school level was 48.7:1, while the Western Cape's was 26.4:1 (Jansen and Taylor, 2003). The policy prescribed the national norm at 40:1 for primary schools (Jansen and Taylor, 2003). The declaration of the post basket for schools in the ECDoE via circular no. 7 of 2003/04 subsequently revealed significant disparities between learner and educator numbers, highlighting the need to redeploy thousands of educators. According to Zokufa (2007), this affected an estimated 10,289 teachers in addition; 6,900 of them in Port Elizabeth (district) alone—with only 3, 161 vacant posts in the province. Voluntary severance packages were offered to encourage excess educators who could not be placed to exit the system (Jansen and Taylor, 2003).

While the need for redeployment had been acknowledged as early as 1996, opposition to the process was considerable. Teachers were unhappy at the prospect of being moved from their existing schools and communities, and refused to do so. Understaffed schools thus remained understaffed. This led to the filling of vacancies with temporary educators, as guided by Education and Labour Relations Council (ELRC) collective agreement no. 2 of 2003 (Zokufa, 2007). This was arguably the beginning of the phenomenon of 'double-parking' in the Eastern Cape. Earlier attempts at forced redeployment by the ECDoE resulted in a court case, in which the Department was forced to concede defeat and allow teachers to return to their original posts (Zokufa, 2007). This, of course, did not resolve the problem of overstaffed and understaffed schools. Instead it effectively institutionalized 'double-parking'—a problem that still existed in 2016.

On 7 August 2008, an ELRC agreement between the ECDoE and SADTU representatives was signed, agreeing to the permanent appointment of all temporary educators occupying vacant substantive level 1 posts (ELRC, 2008). Several collective agreements since then between the same parties have been unsuccessful at resolving key aspects of educator post allocation in the province (ELRC, 2012). One reason that teacher shortages have not been resolved is the Department's outright failure to respond to court orders. A case in point was *FEDSAS and three Others v. MEC for Department of Basic Education, Eastern Cape and Another*, in which the ECDoE failed to appoint and pay an estimated 4,000 temporary teachers (Beckman and Prinsloo, 2015). Despite the court order directing the Department, the plight of teachers was not mitigated nor was the situation of schools experiencing teacher shortages. The Department effectively ignored the court order, allowing the detrimental consequences for schooling to persist. On a national scale, Jansen and Taylor (2003) note that the rationalization policy (at the core of which sits redeployment) had a number of unintended consequences. Not least of these was the creation of a 'hiatus in the normal patterns of supply and demand' of educators (Jansen and Taylor, 2003: 35). This meant that instead of filling teacher posts as and when vacancies occurred, the Department initially placed a moratorium on the filling of such posts until such a time as the teachers in excess were either redeployed or exited the system—effectively (unintentionally) entrenching unequal resourcing at schools.

This situation has imposed severe financial constraints on the ECDoE, resulting in a ballooning salary budget. Continued over-expenditure in the personnel line item –partly due to educators in excess—illustrates the extent to which the ECDoE has lost control of provincial post allocation. Expenditure has tended to exceed the 80:20 ratio of personnel to non-personnel prescribed nationally for several years. This over-expenditure on personnel has squeezed other line items, such as goods and services, and learner and teacher support materials (ELRC, 2012). In 2012–13, for example, an additional allocation of R65 million was approved to mitigate the extreme pressure on the goods and services budget in light of the burgeoning costs of employee compensation (Kota, 2013b). Between 2010–11 and 2012–13, this ratio worsened from 84:16 to 89:11 and finally to 90:10, respectively (NEEDU, 2013; ECDoE, 2014).

Despite an acknowledgement by the then MEC of the centrality of post allocation to the ECDoE's challenges, the five-year strategic plan (2010/11–2014/15) made no mention of explicit plans to address this significant cost-driver (Kota, 2012). Further investigation by the PSAM of the ECDoE's strategic planning in 2012 also uncovered serious gaps and deficiencies in district-level resource needs assessments, which would explain the lack of detail in the ECDoE's strategic planning. In order to understand the situational needs of districts, an examination of their individual operational plans was conducted. These plans, submitted to the provincial office on an annual basis, inform the ECDoE's resourcing needs, including personnel. Of the twenty-three districts contacted, the PSAM was only able to confirm the existence of eight district operational plans. Of the eight available plans, only four were complete and adequately prepared for inclusion in provincial needs assessment and planning (Kota, 2012). This suggests a clear lack of district-level engagement in school-level resourcing needs and a concomitant lack of centralized co-ordination and oversight of districts by the ECDoE.

A lack of ECDoE-district co-ordination and oversight has also been evident at a sub-district level, as recounted in an interview with a district director.[7] In an effort to improve the district pass rate, the district director focused on particular schools, honing in on key aspects, such as educator timeliness and learner attendance over the 2015 academic year. In an attempt to elicit this information, the director expressed frustration at a complete lack of accountability on the part of the circuit manager from whom such information should be readily available. Over several months, the circuit manager[8] was unable or unwilling to provide the required reports for individual schools within their circuit, resulting in the district director being unable to obtain this information. He stated that he was 'hamstrung' in taking any disciplinary measures against the circuit manager. Notwithstanding the line of accountability of the manager to the director, the powers of the director were, in effect, neutralized as the circuit manager had reportedly been politically deployed into their post, with questionable qualifications and in an untransparent manner. Moreover, the circuit manager was in a position of higher seniority, as a SADTU member, than the district director.

A consequence of the ECDoE's strategic planning resulted in a chaotic start to the 2011 school year, when officials realized that the education budget was overspent by R1.8 billion (Gernetzky, 2011). In response, various cost-cutting measures were implemented, such as the suspension of the scholar transport programme, which adversely affected rural learners; halting the delivery of learner and teacher support material to schools because of tender irregularities and the termination of the school nutrition programme, which again disproportionately affected poor and rural learners. Additionally, the ECDoE decided not to re-appoint over 4,000 temporary teachers, which led to

[7] Interview 2: Thursday 10 July 2015, Grahamstown.

[8] A district director's powers and responsibilities are conveyed by the provincial head of department, while a circuit manager is accountable to the district director.

serious staff shortages at many schools (Plaatjie, 2011). In response, teacher, learner and parent protest marches were organized for several district offices across the province (Plaatjie, 2011) and the most populous teacher union, SADTU, was openly critical of Modidima Mannya, making his second appearance as department head, calling for his dismissal. On 16 March 2011, in a historic move, the cabinet invoked Section 100 (1) b of the Constitution, which allows for the administrative take-over of a dysfunctional provincial department by the national government (Motshekga, 2011).

The section 100(1)b intervention proposed human resource management as a core challenge, reflecting the aforementioned post allocation problems as a key source of the department's financial crisis. The following problems were identified:

a. Lack of utilization of existing systems and processes to ensure that the necessary human resources are in place.
b. Inadequate quantity and quality of teachers.
c. Inability to use teachers to their optimum capacity.
d. Inability to anticipate and manage surpluses and shortages of teachers (ECDoE, 2012).

SADTU was joined by COSATU in calling for the dismissal of Mannya; however, the axis of SADTU-ECDoE-ANC, the latter being part of a political alliance with SADTU, appeared more complex and fragmentary. For instance, despite SADTU's call for the dismissal of Mannya, a position which, according to Figure 5.2, precipitated the removal of previous SGs, the ANC and SACP were more cautious about the consequences of this action. The ANC provincial secretary reportedly said:

> It cannot be that the whole education system in the Eastern Cape collapses just because SADTU doesn't want the HoD (Mannya)... We will be creating a suicidal precedent of reversing the strides that labour together with government have progressively achieved, where you could just simply hire and fire without following the laws of the country. (Mgaqelwa et al., 2012)

The refusal of unions to support redeployment from over-staffed to under-staffed (often rural) schools was at the centre of disputes with Advocate Mannya. A member of the Eastern Cape legislature, Edmund van Vuuren, was quoted in local media attributing Mannya's departure to the actions of SADTU in particular: 'SADTU defied Mannya on many occasions, and absolutely resisted the carrying out of post provisioning for 2012, in other words, the movement of excess educators to substantive vacant posts' (SAPA, 2012). Despite this, Mannya's political head, MEC Mandla Makupula, appeared to support the embattled superintendent-general when citing his performance (Mgaqelwa et al., 2012).

In 2012, NEEDU highlighted the dire budgetary constraints in 2011 that resulted from the appointment of additional teachers after a failure to distribute teachers in response to learner migration patterns (NEEDU, 2013). The report emphasized that population migration is a significant factor that further complicates post allocation in the Eastern Cape, particularly in relation to the outflow from rural areas. In April 2003, this had already been identified as a problem, leading to collective agreement 2 of 2003 in which relevant parties agreed not only on procedures to make permanent appointments, but, more importantly, to identify and transfer teachers in excess (ELRC, 2003). Despite the identification of this as both a hindrance to education in the province as well as a constraint on the ECDoE's budget, the Department has found it close to impossible to address educator distribution.

> This is why this double-parking of teachers will happen. Instead of moving people, they hire temporary teachers...and then the mess gets bigger because those temporary ones must be [made] permanent...now you are paying two people for one job basically. (Interview 2, 2015)

Following the failure of the ECDoE to appoint teachers and reduce vacancies since 2005, the PSAM, in a report shared with members of the Eastern Cape provincial executive, noted that it was 'patently evident that key stakeholder relations in the Eastern Cape Department of Education, primarily between the Department and teacher unions, are dysfunctional' (Kota, 2013a: 6). Amongst the recommendations was the need to foster co-operative relations and for decisive action by teacher unions at the national level 'to ensure that their respective provincial subordinates are working towards resolving obstacles to the implementation of teacher redeployment and distribution plans at the beginning of each academic year'. This was despite collective agreement 1 of 2012 of the Education Labour Relations Council (ELRC, 2012) signed on 13 June 2012, declaring, amongst other things, that all substantive vacant posts would be filled, and affected temporary teachers reinstated with immediate effect. This appeared to single out SADTU structures in the Eastern Cape as an obstacle to resolving the teacher redeployment stalemate, and the responsibility of the union's national leadership to enforce collective agreements. It also signalled a potentially fragmented relationship between SADTU national and provincial structures, which subsequently materialized in the acrimonious disbandment of SADTU's provincial leadership by the union's national executive committee in 2015, citing irregularities in the governance of the provincial structure.

5.5 Contestation at a School Level: Widening Fragmentation

The problematic planning and distribution of teaching posts at a provincial and district level gives way to an even more fragmented and contested distribution of posts at a school level. School-level governance can be shaped by conflicting interests pitting school management—embodied mainly by principals—against unionized teachers, with school governing bodies sometimes caught in the middle. The source of conflict may be linked to contestation over the filling of posts, which appears prone to patronage pressures, as revealed in some media reportage.[9] Although this cannot be directly and systematically attributed to provincial-level post allocation and teacher distribution, we suggest that it could represent a micro-level consequence of dysfunctional distribution patterns higher up, by encouraging a kind of 'up for grabs' mentality amongst actors at the school level. Intriguingly, Levy and Shumane's companion four-school district-level study in the Butterworth area (Chapter 9 of this volume) confirms intra-school stakeholder contestation, but also shows that fraught relations between principals, teachers and SGB actors are more complex and multi-directional, and indeed can recover through the co-operative will of new incumbents intent on reversing what the authors describe as 'toxic' governance cultures. Moreover, they also showed that union interests in general, and SADTU in particular, are not always the source of contestation, which can take on a more inter-personal character.

For this component of the chapter, we undertook a series of interviews with key informants representing various school-level stakeholders. Interview selection was limited to the Grahamstown, King Williamstown and Port Elizabeth districts, given their immediate proximity to the authors' place of residence. We made contact with district directors, principals and officials with whom work relations had already been established and through whom further contact with other officials, educators and union officials could be made.

Interviews were conducted with education stakeholders within the Eastern Cape who were identified by the researchers for their experience either as decision-makers, policy-makers or as educators within the sector. All interviews were semi-structured discussions, with the central, open-ended question being: 'What are your thoughts on the manner in which teacher allocation, appointment and deployment is undertaken in the Eastern Cape?' Additional discussion questions were formulated according to the interviewees' roles within the sector and sought to elicit interviewees' perceptions about the

[9] Masondo (2015) reported on an investigation commissioned by the national Department of Basic Education, which found that senior members of SADTU in the Eastern Cape received gratification in return for allocating several principal positions in the province.

impact of provincial post allocation practices. The district director was explicitly selected, given recurring post provisioning problems and overall underperformance within his district. The aim of the district interviews was not to generate overarching provincial conclusions, but to tease out the implications at a district and school level of systemic failures in the allocation of educators.

Interview requests were also made to SADTU representatives in the Eastern Cape, although we experienced considerable difficulties obtaining commitments. We expect that this was due to the organizational turmoil within SADTU structures in the Eastern Cape, which was disbanded in February 2015. While interim measures were put in place to accommodate daily administration of SADTU's provincial offices, no official representatives were available for comment.

Interviews were conducted with the following individuals:

Interview 1: The provincial chairperson of the National Association of School Governing Bodies (NASGB).

Interview 2: A district director (a district in which post allocation challenges are a reality and in which a working relationship with the district director exists).

Interview 3: A school principal in a school within the same district.

Interview 4: An educator and member of SADTU within the same district.

Interviewees were identified using existing contacts amongst education practitioners with some knowledge or direct engagement with educator post allocation matters. All interviewees were asked two primary, open-ended questions;

1. *Please describe your experience of teacher appointments and the post allocation model in the Eastern Cape.*
2. *Why do you think the current problems with teacher shortages and teachers in addition have persisted for so long in the Eastern Cape?*

In an interview with the SADTU-affiliated educator, it was evident that, despite the problematic post-allocation planning at the provincial level, the process appeared particularly susceptible to negotiated outcomes at the district and school levels:

> the problem [with the process of teacher appointment] is not really at the provincial level or higher up . . . you have to look at districts and schools. That's really where no one even knows what really happens. And it's very bad in the more remote places—not in town [e.g. urban schools and districts].[10]

[10] Interview 4, Monday, 22 June 2015, Grahamstown.

In an effort to explain the possible motive and source of influence over post allocation in more rural school districts, the educator cited a greater reverence for teachers and SADTU members by community members. This was corroborated in an interview with the provincial chair of the National Association of School Governing Bodies.[11] A more heightened level of post contestation in rural school districts may be indicative of acute teacher scarcity in these areas, resulting from the ECDoE's failure to enforce equitable teacher rationalization—in the face of union/SADTU opposition in particular—as well as unpredictable learner migration patterns.

Of greater concern, however, has been the findings of a DBE investigation, which uncovered evidence that senior SADTU officials had controlled the allocation of several principal posts in the Eastern Cape, in exchange for payment in cattle (Masondo, 2015). Examples such as these highlight the personalized motives of union-affiliated actors seeking to capture appointment processes, and raise questions about the actions of accountability structures at the district and provincial (ECDoE) levels. Levy and Shumane's Butterworth study describes a general tendency of district offices and the ECDoE to steer clear of becoming embroiled in school-level contestation, along with other instances in which district officials were accused of abetting procedurally unfair appointment processes and school leadership transgressions. This corresponds with earlier references to weak district engagement around school-level resourcing, as well as strained and politicized relations between district and circuit officials, which compromised the former's efforts to conduct school-level monitoring.

Other instances in which unionized teachers have sought to intervene in school-level appointment processes were cited by the chair of the NASGB, describing undue influence by members in the appointment of principals and the deliberate transgression of legislated provisions. The chair emphasized a combination of ignorance amongst parent members of SGBs, coupled with 'lobbying' by union officials who knew but opted to ignore the law in order to appoint and/or promote specific candidates. He added that: 'weak [school] governing bodies can—and are—easily dominated by the teachers and principal of a school... or [can] even be influenced by other mischief [*sic*].'

A similar picture is portrayed in Msila's (2014) study of the relationship dynamics between principals and unionized teachers in ten Eastern Cape schools. The research, which sampled schools in the Port Elizabeth district, carried out interviews with principals, official school-based union representatives, and various other teachers. Although there were variations across the schools, key informants from a majority of sites described school governance

[11] Interview 1, Wednesday, 22 July 2015 Grahamstown.

as being prone to contested and negotiated processes. The extent to which unionized teachers challenged the *de jure* authority of principals played out across a range of activities, including over appointments, meetings of union members during school hours, and disciplinary procedures. Msila's (2014) findings were not, however, without some if limited evidence showing more collaborative relations between unionized teachers and school management (principals), where the hierarchical integrity of the relationship seemed to hold. This appeared to be acutely sensitive to principals being willing and able to assert their authority and responsibility for school governance, which speaks to what this book's conceptual framework (laid out in Chapter 1) describes as the possible virtues of a zone of autonomy being present at the school level, enabling the well-intentioned authority of principals to facilitate successful outcomes.

The perspectives of principals interviewed within the Grahamstown district were, however, consistent with the predominant pattern of hierarchical breakdown and contestation. The principal of one secondary school recounted the difficulty and intimidation she experienced overseeing formal disciplinary processes and the politicization of the process. In addition, she referred to significant pressure being applied in relation to vacancies and/or promotion posts, describing it as 'incredibly stressful—you almost just want to give in because the union will always make everything so hard. It's almost paralysing'.[12] In addition, the district director interviewed[13] relayed the story of alleged financial mismanagement levelled by teachers against a principal in his district, in which the principal was suspended, pending the completion of an investigation by the ECDoE. The findings of the investigation cleared the principal of any wrongdoing. The principal cited several reasons why some of his staff wanted him dismissed. He remarked that he had experienced significant hostility when he attempted to prevent his staff from attending union meetings during school hours. In addition, several teachers in lower-level posts sought promotion to the level of head of department across various subjects for which they were not qualified. He alleged that a conspiracy to have him dismissed was fabricated, in order that a union member could take up the post of principal as a means of paving the way for other promotions.

5.6 Conclusion

The governance of basic education in the Eastern Cape presents a difficult dilemma. Our general characterization of the province reveals a sector that is

[12] Interview 3: Wednesday, 6 May 2015, Grahamstown.
[13] Interview 2: Thursday, 10 July 2015, Grahamstown.

predominately prone to personalized/negotiated outcomes. A more segmented analysis of governance at different levels did, however, highlight a differentiated pattern of progressive fragmentation from the central political level to the school level, resembling a pyramidal shape. This indicated that hierarchical features, where these do appear, have been employed to advance more personal aims, producing intra-party factional and partisan contestation. This has, moreover, severely scuppered the consolidation of stability within the provincial education bureaucracy, which has experienced persistent leadership instability, financial distress and mismanagement, unreliable performance management, and chronic policy failure in teacher distribution.

The dilemma facing the Eastern Cape is determining through what means the detrimental consequences on teaching and learning produced by the province's education governance can be most effectively mitigated. The heuristic matrix presented in Table 5.1 at the outset of this chapter offers some guidance, as well as cautionary signals about the possibilities. We suggest that two scenarios are possible.

One avenue, perhaps the more ideal, is to ramp up efforts that could shift the sector's governance culture and weighting towards hierarchical/impersonal. This, however, seems highly improbable in at least the short term, given prolonged and acute institutional instability in the ECDoE, as well as failed national-level interventions. In any event, does the notion of education as a 'craft' activity, not realistically defined by routinized forms of production, and therefore best governed by allowing school-level actors a necessary 'zone of autonomy', expose the normative limitations of this approach? This is not to suggest that some movement towards hierarchical/impersonal governance is undesirable. This, given that we acquired a suggestive, if not empirically extensive, basis for believing that dysfunctional teacher distribution at the provincial level, together with weak or compromised district-level oversight, can contribute to heightened stakeholder contestation at the school level.

So, if moving the Eastern Cape in the direction of the hierarchical/impersonal is implausible in the near term, is there an alternative course of action that might be more feasible, if not ideal? A second pathway that could be pursued would not necessarily require shifting the governance weighting, but working within the bottom half of the matrix (i.e. the negotiated/personal/impersonal space) by localising a solution within this area to the school level. This is based on the reasoning that, as suggested in Chapter 1, horizontal governance arrangements (i.e. at the school level) can serve as 'partial institutional substitutes' where hierarchical accountability is weak. The bulk of this chapter's focus, on provincial-level political oversight and education governance, has presented evidence that we believe can at least substantively defend this scenario. What we cannot robustly defend, however, based on our limited data, is the likelihood that school-level circumstances in the Eastern Cape can enable horizontal governance arrangements to be effective; that is, for a coalition of 'developmentally-oriented stakeholders' to thwart the predatory impulses of other actors. The companion school-level study in Chapter 9, along with findings from other literature (e.g. Msila, 2014) offer more substantive reasons to be optimistic that stakeholder interactions in Eastern Cape schools can be re-calibrated in ways that reduce predation and increase developmentally-oriented outcomes.

References

Beckman, J. and Prinsloo, J. (2015) 'Some aspects of education litigation since 1994. Of hope, concern and despair', *South African Journal of Education* 35(1), 1–11.

Blaine, S. (2010) 'Ghost schools scam could cost Eastern Cape R 12 million'. *Business Day Live*, 7 May, http://www.bdlive.co.za/articles/2010/05/07/ghost-schools-scam-could-cost-eastern-cape-r12m.

Cameron, R. and Levy, B. (2016) 'The potential and limits of performance management: Improving basic education in the Western Cape'. ESID Working Paper No. 62. Manchester: Effective States and Inclusive Development Research Centre, The University of Manchester.

Cull, P. (2004) 'East Cape mired in controversy throughout year'. *Herald*, 21 December, p. 7.

Daily Dispatch (2012) 'Mannya had to go', 25 April.

Dawes, N. and Rossouw, M. (2008) 'Waiting in the wings'. *Mail & Guardian*, 18 July, http://mg.co.za/article/2008-07-18-waiting-in-the-wings.

Deloitte, UNICEF, DBE (undated) *National Implementation of Post Provisioning: National Report*, http://www.education.gov.za/LinkClick.aspx?fileticket=Ub4vJ%2BeV9ds%3D&.

Department of Basic Education (2014) *Education Statistics in South Africa*, www.education.gov.za.

Department of Basic Education (undated) *Provision of 2014 Teaching Staff Establishments to Ordinary Public Schools*. Pretoria.

Eastern Cape Department of Education (2009) 'Discussion paper on infrastructure', http://www.ecdoe.gov.za/files/documents/Discussion.

Eastern Cape Department of Education (2012) *Annual Performance Plan 2012/13*. Zwelitsha.

Eastern Cape Department of Education (2014) *Annual Report 2013/14: Building Blocks for Growth*. Zwelitsha, http://ecdoe.co.za/files/resources/resource_253.pdf.

Eastern Cape Department of Education (2015) *Annual Performance Plan 2015/16*. Zwelitsha.

Education Labour Relations Council Collective Agreement Number 2 of 2003. *Transfer of Serving Educator in terms of Operational Requirements*, 10 May.

Education Labour Relations Council Collective Agreement Number 1 of 2008. *Permanent Appointment of Temporary Educators in Vacant Substantive Posts*, 7 August.

Education Labour Relations Council Collective Agreement Number 1 of 2012.

Esbend, F. (2001) 'Corruption buster back on track'. *Mail & Guardian*, 26 January, http://mg.co.za/article/2001-01-26-corruption-buster-back-on-track.

Esbend, F. (2005) 'Give us teachers please'. *Mail & Guardian*, 21 April, http://mg.co.za/article/2005-04-21-please-give-us-teachers.

Fölscher, A. and Kruger, J. (2013) 'When opportunity beckons: The impact of the Public Service Accountability Monitor's work on improving health budgets in South Africa'. Partnership Initiative Case Study Series: Study No. 14. Cape Town: International Budget Partnership.

GCIS (2015) Government Communication and Information System: *Listing of MECs of the Provincial Governments*, http://www.gcis.gov.za/content/resource-centre/contact-directory/contact-list/list/6.

Gernetzky, K. (2011) 'Zuma upbeat on Eastern Cape education fix'. *Business Day*. 15 September.

Gevisser, M. (1996) 'Oom Ray in the Wild East'. *Mail & Guardian*, 12 January, http://mg.co.za/article/1996-01-12-oom-ray-in-the-wild-east.

Hendricks, M. and Wright, L. (2012) 'Power bedevils everything: Improving education in the Eastern Cape. An interview with Frank Peters'. In L. Wright (ed.), *South Africa's Education Crisis: Views from the Eastern Cape*. Grahamstown: NISC.

Hoeane, T. (2011) 'Political contestation and the ANC in the Eastern Cape'. In G. Ruiters (ed.), *The Fate of the Eastern Cape: History, Politics and Social Policy*. Scottsville: University of KwaZulu-Natal Press, pp. 93–101.

Hyslop, J. (2005) 'Political corruption: Before and after apartheid', *Journal of Southern African Studies* 31(4), 774–89.

Jansen, J. and Taylor, N. (2003) 'Education change in South Africa: 1994–2003: Case studies in large-scale education reform', *Country Studies and Management Publication* Series 2(1), October.

Kimberley, K. (2014) 'Principals tell of ghost teachers, appointed with falsified details'. *Business Day BDLive*. 20 August, http://www.bdlive.co.za/national/2014/08/20/principals-tell-of-ghost-teachers-appointed-with-falsified-details.

Kota, Z. (2012) *Strategic Plan Evaluation: Eastern Cape Department of Education, Annual Performance Plan 2012/13*. Grahamstown: Public Service Accountability Monitor.

Kota, Z. (2013a) *Strategic Plan Evaluation: Eastern Cape Department of Education 2013/14*. Grahamstown: Public Service Accountability Monitor.

Kota, Z. (2013b) *Budget Analysis Eastern Cape Department of Education 2013/14*. Grahamstown: Public Service Accountability Monitor.

Letsoalo, M., Rossouw, M., and Mhlana, Z. (2008) 'No one in the ANC is permanent'. *Mail & Guardian*, http://mg.co.za/article/2008-07-16-no-one-in-the-anc-is-permanent.

Lodge, T. (2002) *Politics in South Africa: From Mandela to Mbeki*. Cape Town: David Philip.

Lodge, T. (2004) 'The ANC and the development of party politics in modern South Africa', *The Journal of Modern African Studies* 42(2), 189–219.

Lodge, T. (2005) 'Provincial government and state authority in South Africa', *Journal of Southern African Studies*, 31(4), 737–53.

Luyt, D. (2009) 'Financial mismanagement in the provincial departments of Education and Health continues to thwart the Eastern Cape government's drive towards improved financial control and clean audits'. *Daily Dispatch*, 21 October.

Macfarlane, D. (2002) 'Controversy haunts Eastern Cape Premier'. *Mail & Guardian*, 4 November, http://mg.co.za/article/2002-11-04-controversy-haunts-eastern-cape-premier.

Mail & Guardian (2009a) 'Eastern Cape health chief shown the door', http://mg.co.za/article/2009-05-04-east-cape-health-chief-shown-the-door.

Mail & Guardian (2009b) 'Judge rules Pillay Report be scrapped', http://mg.co.za/article/2009-05-18-judge-rules-pillay-report-be-scrapped.

Masondo, S. (2015) 'SADTU selling principals' posts in exchange for cows, sheep and goats'. *City Press*, 17 May, http://www.news24.com/SouthAfrica/News/Sadtu-selling-principals-posts-in-exchange-for-cows-sheep-and-goats-20150517.

Mgaqelwa, A., Plaatjie, P., and Feni, L. (2012) 'Mannya strains ANC alliance'. *Daily Dispatch*, 27 January.

Mhlaba, R. (2001) *Raymond Mhlaba's Personal Memoirs: Reminiscing from Rwanda and Uganda*. Benoni: HSRC and Shereno Printers.

Motshekga, A. (2011) 'Statement to the National Assembly on the Eastern Cape Education Department intervention by Mrs Angie Motshekga, Minister of Basic Education', 16 March, http://www.gov.za/statement-national-assembly-eastern-cape-education-department-intervention-mrs-angie-motshekga.

Msila, V. (2014) 'Teacher unionism and school management: A study of (Eastern Cape) schools in South Africa', *Educational Management Administration & Leadership* 42(2), 259–74.

Naki, E. (2004) 'Balindlela defies EC ANC executive'. *Daily Dispatch*, 30 April, p. 1.

NEEDU (National Education Evaluation and Development Unit) (2013) *National Report 2013: Teaching and Learning in Rural Primary Schools*. Pretoria.

Ngoma, W. (2009) 'The potholes of service delivery: Reflections on the Eastern Cape Department of Education'. In A. McLennanand and B. Munslow (eds), *The Politics of Service Delivery*. Johannesburg: Wits University Press.

Obiyo, R. (2013) 'Oversight of the Executive in the Eastern Cape Province, South Africa', *Journal of Contemporary African Studies* 31(1), 95–116.

Overy, N. (2005) *Staff Shortages, Incapacity and the Excessive Use of Consultants by the Eastern Cape Provincial Government*. Grahamstown: Public Service Accountability Monitor.

Picard, L. A. (2005) *The State of the State: Institutional Transformation, Capacity and Political Change in South Africa*. Johannesburg: Wits University Press.

Plaatjie, T. (2011) 'Education officials failed community, says MEC'. *Grocott's Mail*, 17 February.

Public Service Accountability Monitor (PSAM) (2004) Press release: 'Financial mismanagement and other organisational problems mitigate against improved education for learners', 12 January.

Public Service Accountability Monitor (PSAM) (2006) *Submission to the Commission of Inquiry into the Finances of the Eastern Cape Provincial Administration*. Grahamstown.

Public Service Commission (2008) *Report on Senior Management Service Compliance with Performance Agreements in the Eastern Cape Provincial Administration*. Pretoria.

Reeves, C. and Robinson, M. (2010) 'Am I "qualified" to teach? The implications of a changing school system for criteria for teacher qualifications', *Journal of Education* 50, 7–34.

Rossouw, M. (2008) 'Meet Premier Sogoni'. *Mail & Guardian*, http://mg.co.za/article/2008-07-26-meet-premier-sogoni.

SAPA (2012) 'Eastern Cape education head quits', http://www.timeslive.co.za/politics/2012/04/24/eastern-cape-education-head-quits.

Southall, R. (1999) 'The struggle for a place called home: the ANC versus the UDM in the Eastern Cape', *Politikon* 26(2), 155–66.

Streek, B. and Wicksteed, R. (1981) *Render under Kaiser: A Transkei Dossier*. Johannesburg: Ravan Press.

Van der Merwe, D. (2005) 'ANC, COSATU welcome dropping of charges in ECDC trial'. *Daily Dispatch*, 23 September, p. 4.

Zokufa, F. (2007) 'The Impact of Redeployment of Teachers in Port Elizabeth Schools'. Med Management in Education thesis. Nelson Mandela Metropolitan University.

Zuzile, M. (2004) 'Opposition queries Stofile's overruling of Mafu case'. *The Herald*, 21 April.

6

Explaining the Western Cape Performance Paradox

An Econometric Analysis

Gabrielle Wills, Debra Shepherd, and Janeli Kotzé

6.1 Introduction

What accounts for variations across locales in educational outcomes? One common explanation focuses on the availability of resources. However, the correlation in Figure 6.1 confounds any simplistic explanation along these lines.

As the figure shows, Kenya and Tanzania spend less than one-third the amount per learner that is spent by the three South African provinces (and also Botswana). Even so, their outcomes measured by SACMEQ mathematics test score results for Grade 6 students are as good as the Western Cape and Gauteng, and better than the South African average. This is not to say that resources are not important at all, but 'the main message is still not one of broad, resource-based policy initiatives' (Hanushek and Woesmann, 2007: 67).

A rich global literature has explored the impact of a wide variety of causal factors on educational outcomes in developing countries. The overall focus of the book of which this chapter is a part is on the influence on educational progress of some key aspects of how education is governed. As Chapter 1 detailed, one set of questions concerns the benefits of having in place a high-quality bureaucracy and, related, the possible limitations of an exclusive pre-occupation with strengthening bureaucratic capability as a way of improving the governance of education. A second set of questions concerns the potential and limitations of 'horizontal' governance—enhanced governance authority and flexibility at the school-level—as a means of improving educational outcomes. Is good horizontal governance potentially a complement to

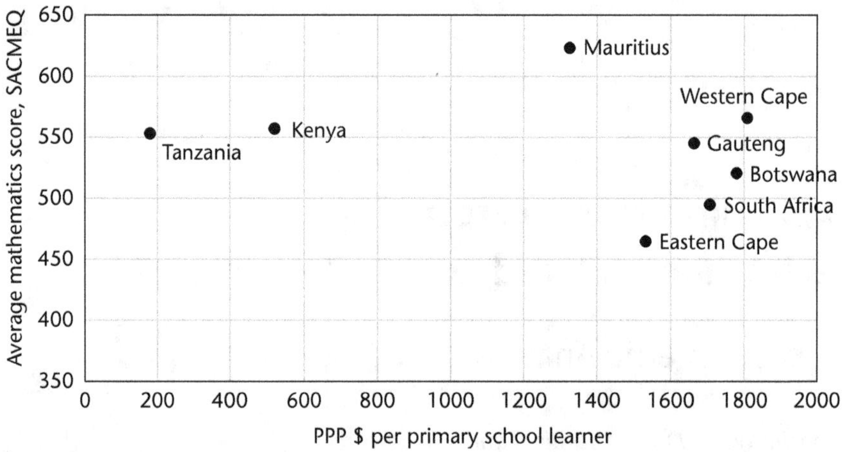

Figure 6.1. Average country and region test performance against spending per primary school learner

Source: Spending data for countries retrieved from UNESCO Institute for Statistics. The expenditure data for South African provinces is obtained from the Provincial Budgets and Expenditure Review 2005/06–2011/12. Average test scores are calculated using SACMEQ III (2007). Expenditure only includes public expenditures and is expressed in Purchasing Power Parity (PPP) dollars. Private expenditures may vary notably across countries but this is not shown here.

hierarchy, improving outcomes even where bureaucracy is highly capable? Might it also be a substitute source of institutional capability, a way of improving outcomes even in settings where hierarchical institutions are weak?

In most of this book the above questions are explored using case study analyses. This chapter complements these qualitative approaches with statistical analysis. We build especially on the analysis of the Western Cape education system in Chapter 4. In that chapter, the Western Cape Education Department emerges as an unusually high-quality bureaucracy.

Using the Western Cape's educational outcomes as a benchmark enables us to explore econometrically a number of 'paradoxes' suggested by Figure 6.1: is the Figure 6.1 pattern, in which the Western Cape achieves better educational outcomes than other South African provinces (notwithstanding similar resources, and a similar policy and regulatory framework), empirically robust once other non-governance-related causal influences are taken into account? To what extent can the Western Cape's performance be accounted for by stronger bureaucratic capabilities? Insofar as the Western Cape bureaucracy is indeed unusually strong, why do Tanzania and, especially, Kenya achieve similar outcomes, notwithstanding their substantially lower levels of resources? We address these questions using a statistical methodology which enables us to identify a distinctive 'Western Cape effect'—the unexplained variation in education outcomes that remains even after controlling for the influence of a comprehensive set of factors which potentially might drive performance.

Our analysis proceeds as follows. Section 6.2 drills down into the 'dependent variable'; it uses a variety of data sources to benchmark educational outcomes in the Western Cape relative to other locales. Section 6.3 reports the results of our multivariate statistical estimation, and assesses the sign and magnitude of a 'Western Cape effect', once other sources of variations in educational outcomes are controlled for. Section 6.4 drills down into some micro-level details of interactions between socio-economic status, bureaucratic capability, and educational outcomes. Section 6.5 concludes.

6.2 Benchmarking the Western Cape Outcomes

The econometric analysis in this chapter uses the SACMEQ III data series, a school survey representative of Grade 6 students, as the principal data source. SACMEQ test scores are used as the dependent variable, and a variety of SACMEQ descriptive statistics as our independent variables. In addition to SACMEQ, other measures are also available for benchmarking the performance of the Western Cape education system relative to other locales. This section first provides some background on the SACMEQ data and then places its performance measures in perspective by contrasting the SACMEQ patterns with some other comparative benchmarks.

The Southern African Consortium for Monitoring Educational Quality (SACMEQ) is a group of education ministries, policy-makers, and researchers which in conjunction with UNESCO's International Institute for Educational Planning (IIEP) has administered four cross-national surveys of Grade 6 learning across fifteen SACMEQ ministries of education since its inception. As of the time of the writing of this study, the most recent SACMEQ IV survey of 2013 has not yet been released in the public domain.[1] We therefore rely on older SACMEQ III data collected during the last quarter of 2007 from 61,396 pupils, 8,026 teachers and 2,779 schools. Across each sample, the data was explicitly stratified by region reflecting that data is representative of Grade 6 students not only at the country level but at the regional or provincial level.

[1] More recent datasets on learning such as PIRLS and pre-PIRLS 2011 are not sampled to be representative at the provincial level and include very few comparator African states. TIMSS (Trends in International Mathematics and Science Study) 2015 has been released, but includes only one other comparator African state at the Grade 8 or 9 level, namely Botswana. TIMSS 2015 testing also takes place at a later Grade 9 level when drop-out is likely to complicate the interpretation of results. Although South Africa participated in TIMSS Numeracy for the first time in 2015, a test of mathematics and science skills at the Grade 5 level, Botswana did not participate at this level.

Students were tested in three subject areas—literacy, mathematics and health—although we only use the first two performance measures in this chapter. Each SACMEQ outcome measure is obtained using a Rasch scaling approach,[2] and is set to have a mean of 500 and standard deviation of 100. In the econometric analysis, we convert the scale to z-scores with a mean of 0 and standard deviation of 1 for ease of interpretation. Table 6.1 summarizes the SACMEQ Grade 6 mathematics outcomes for the Western Cape, for two other South African provinces (Eastern Cape and Gauteng), and some other African states. According to these data, the Western Cape is among the highest performing of the South African provinces but performs substantially below Mauritius, and parts of Kenya using averages and points along a performance distribution.

Along with SACMEQ, the Trends in International Mathematics and Science Study (TIMSS) is another multi-country benchmarking effort in which South Africa participates; comparative global results confirm that South Africa is a startlingly low performer relative to other countries. More interestingly for present purposes, TIMSS generates province-by-province information on education outcomes over time (Reddy et al., 2016; DBE, 2016). Table 6.2 reports average mathematics performance at the Grade 9 level for all South African provinces for 2003, 2011 and 2015. The Western Cape's performance exceeded other provinces in 2003 and 2011, but performance declined in 2015, with Gauteng ranking as the best-performing province in the most

Table 6.1. SACMEQ III: Western Cape Mathematics Scores Relative to Other African Countries

	Mean	25th percentile	50th percentile	75th percentile	N schools in sample
South Africa all provinces	**495**	**424**	**483**	**548**	**392**
South Africa—Western Cape	566	496	560	635	40
South Africa—Gauteng	545	483	548	610	43
Mauritius all regions	**623**	**522**	**610**	**718**	**152**
Kenya all regions	**557**	**509**	**548**	**610**	**193**
Kenya—Central	574	509	560	636	24
Kenya—Nairobi	610	535	585	662	16
Tanzania—Central	549	500	553	604	16
Botswana all regions	**521**	**468**	**522**	**573**	**160**
Botswana—Gaborone	569	509	560	623	20

Source: SACMEQ III, 2007 data (own calculations) and Hungi et al. (2010).

[2] Rasch scaling, which accounts for the difficulty level of each test item, was used to generate the literacy and mathematics scores. Different test levels can be used to ascertain mathematics and literacy competencies providing a concrete analysis of what pupils and teachers can do (Hungi et al., 2010).

Table 6.2. TIMSS Performance—Provincial Comparisons Across Years

	TIMSS 2003 (Gr 9)	TIMSS 2011 (Gr. 9)	TIMSS 2015 (Gr. 9)		TIMSS Numeracy 2015 (Gr. 5)	
	Average math. score	Average math. score	Average math. score	standard error	Average math. Score	standard error
Western Cape	414	404	391^	11	441	10.7
Gauteng	303	389*	408^	11.4	420	10.6
Eastern Cape	250	316*	346^	14.4	343	7.4
Free State	291	359*	367^	7.8	373	9.8
KwaZulu-Natal	278	337*	369^	11.8	367	7.8
Limpopo	244	322*	361^	13.4	344	10.1
Mpumulanga	287	344*	370^	7.8	384	11.3
Northern Cape	341	366	364^	7.2	373	12.7
North West	280	350*	354^	7.9	355	5.8
South Africa	**285**	**348**	**368**	**4.9**	**376**	**3.4**

Notes: In comparing 2003 and 2011 Grade 8/9 TIMSS results in DBE (2016) a difference-in-means test was run for each province. The result was that for seven provinces, specifically those with values close to zero in the final column, differences from 2003 to 2011 are indeed statistically significant as reflected by the * except for the Northern Cape and Western Cape. Reddy et al (2016) indicate whether differences between 2003 and 2012 scores are statistically significantly different. This is indicated here by a ^. All scores are on a scale of 0–1000 with 500 as the international mean and a standard deviation of 100. TIMSS Numeracy scores at the Grade 5 level cannot be compared with the Grade 8/9 results.

Source: Reddy et al. (2012), Reddy et al. (2016), DBE (2016).

recent 2015 results. Statistically significant improvements between 2003 and 2015 were observed in all other eight provinces. For example, Gauteng and the Eastern Cape show improvements of over two years of learning. The Western Cape is the only province that experienced declines in performance over the same period as shown in Table 6.2.

The Western Cape's declines in Grade 9 TIMSS performance however must be qualified in with respect to two factors. First, its results come off a considerably higher base level compared to other provinces. Second, there have been reported changes in the compositional characteristics of students in the province possibly due to in-migration from poorer provinces (Reddy et al., 2016). The data points to a more disadvantaged composition of Western Cape students that attempted the 2015 test, compared with earlier years.[3] Note, though, that in the newly introduced TIMSS Numeracy at the Grade 5 level, the Western Cape continues to outperform all other provinces.

A third measure for comparing learning outcomes is South Africa's National Senior Certificate (NSC) or matriculation outcomes—the NSC is the critical document that provides students with added advantage in accessing further

[3] For example, Reddy et al. (2016) report significant declines across 2003, 2011 and 2015 in the proportion of students in the Western Cape TIMSS sample with more than twenty-five books at home, parents or guardians with an education above Grade 12, and who speak the language of the test at home.

Table 6.3. Matriculants (NSC passes) by Province Relative to the Youth Population According to the General Household Survey

	% of youths who obtain Matric: average 2009–2011	% of youths who obtain Matric: average 2012–2014	Difference
Eastern Cape	39.4	43.2	3.8
Free State	48.2	51.2	3.1
Gauteng	58.5	64.5	5.9
Kwazulu Natal	49	56	6.9
Limpopo	38	45.2	7.2
Mpmualanga	45.4	50.6	5.2
Northern Cape	41.2	48.9	7.7
Northwest	41.3	48.1	6.8
Western Cape	50.9	48.8	−2
All South Africa	48	51.5	3.5

Source: DBE (2016). Youths are individuals aged 20–28.

tuition and higher earnings in the labour market. Although the proportion of those who sit the matriculation examination and pass is high in the Western Cape, other provinces such as Gauteng, KwaZulu-Natal or even Limpopo and Mpumulanga are more effective at producing larger proportions of their provincial population of youths with a NSC pass, as seen in Table 6.3. An analysis of the General Household Survey data for the periods 2012–14 reveals that Gauteng has the highest percentage of youths aged 20–28 with a completed Grade 12.[4] (Note though that, as Chapter 4 details, as of 2015, the Western Cape was the top provincial performer when the more stringent measure of a 'university pass' is used.) The Western Cape, though a relatively good performer at the Grade 12 level, might have been expected to perform a lot better at that level if one considers that standardized test results show it to be the top performing province in the earlier grades (DBE, 2013: 3).

Furthermore, the recent improvements in student matric results that are evident in other provinces are not necessarily observed in the Western Cape. In examining growth rates in the number of high-level mathematics and physical science passes in the matriculation examination between 2008 and 2015, the Western Cape shows some of the lowest rates of growth in the percentage of students achieving 60 per cent or more in mathematics or physical science (DBE, 2016).

Gustafsson, in the Department of Basic Education's 2013 and 2016 education sector reports, compares student achievement across nine provinces using different grade and subject test results from the Annual National

[4] Part of this Gauteng advantage in the NSC could relate to in-migration of educated youth into the province in search of job opportunities. (Gauteng has increasingly become a hub of economic activity in South Africa).

Assessments (2011–14), SACMEQ III mathematics performance, pre- PIRLS 2011, TIMSS 2011 and different measures of Grade 12 performance in the matric examinations (DBE, 2013; DBE, 2016). In total, he identifies thirteen different outcome measures. The Western Cape performs best across nine of the thirteen measures—not all thirteen measures (DBE, 2016).

In sum, considered together, the evidence summarized in this section suggests that while the Western Cape is *a* high-performing provincial department with respect to observed educational outcomes in South Africa, it has not translated into its schools consistently being the best performers in the country. Depending on what educational outcome is considered, the grade level and the position at which performance is measured along the student socio-economic profile, Gauteng or other provinces at times fare better.

6.3 Multivariate Estimation

We turn now to econometric analysis of the consequences (both strengths and limitations) for learning outcomes of the Western Cape Education Department (WCED)'s strong bureaucratic capability.

6.3.1 *The Model and Variables*

Our point of departure is the classic education production function, which at the most general level can be specified as:

$$Y_{is} = f(x_1, x_2 \ldots x_n) \tag{1a}$$

where Y_{is} is the test score of student i in school s, and $x_1 - x_n$ are the many variables which influence educational outcomes. As numerous studies the world over (including in South Africa) have shown, variables which have a significant impact on learning outcomes include: the socio-economic status and other personal/home characteristics of learners; the quality of teachers; the presence of school resources that support learning (infrastructure, other classroom resources and particularly textbooks); and the quality of a variety of hierarchical and horizontal governance, management and accountability relationships (Hanushek, 2007; Gustafsson and Taylor, 2016; Kingdon et al., 2014; McEwan, 2015; Van der Berg et al., 2016; Evans and Popova, 2015; Crouch and Mabogoane, 2001; Fiske and Ladd, 2004).

The specific education production function which we estimate, using the SACMEQ data, has the following specification:

$$Y_{is} = WC + \delta' I_s + \beta' H_{is} + \alpha SES_{is} + \gamma' R_{is} + \epsilon_{is} \tag{1b}$$

Where:

- *WC*, the Western Cape effect, is the variable of most immediate interest for the purposes of the present study. We discuss our estimation strategy, interpretation, and results below.
- I_s is a vector of school/institutional factors; some are directly relevant for our core questions, others function more as control variables.
- H_{is} is a vector of student and home background factors, which serve as control variables in analyses.
- SES_{is} is our measure of the socio-economic status of learners; our measurement and estimation approaches are discussed in detail in Section 6.4.
- R_{is} is a vector of classroom and teacher resources—some of these measures are discussed further below.

Appendix A6.1 provides comprehensive detail on all the independent variables used from the SACMEQ data series.

Evidently, there are significant differences in the country and regional student samples which need to be controlled for when comparisons are being made to the Western Cape relative to other locales. Our econometric analysis does this using a regression framework combined with a propensity score matching approach. Propensity score weights ensure that the estimated WC coefficient is computed using the most suitably comparable groups of students across two country/regional settings.[5] This technique requires that only regions or countries that are sufficiently comparable to the Western Cape in terms of student socio-economic and home background factors are considered; for this reason, in the econometric analyses, only the Nairobi and Central regions of Kenya are selected for comparison. In Section 6.4 we consider performance for the entire Kenyan student sample in a descriptive analysis.[6]

In reporting our results, we focus not on the coefficients of the full set of variables (where our results by-and-large are consistent with the patterns

[5] Following Li, Morgan, and Zaslavsky (2014), students in the Western Cape are assigned propensity score weights equal to 1 – e(x) and learners in the comparison country/region are assigned weights equal to e(x), where e(x) is the propensity score of being a Grade 6 student in the Western Cape estimated from a probit model where student and home background characteristics are regressed onto the WC indicator. This weighting places greater emphasis on units with propensity scores close to 0.5 where overlap between the two student groups is greater. The final model controls for the propensity weights as well the same student and home background variables used in estimating the propensity score on which the weights are computed. This regression-adjustment attempts to resolve any observed imbalances that may remain between groups (Hill and Reiter, 2006; Ho, Imai, King, and Stuart, 2007; Stuart, 2010), increases the precision and efficiency of the estimation and reduces bias (Abadie and Imbens, 2011; Kang and Schafer, 2007; Rubin and Thomas, 2000).

[6] Tanzania is included in the analysis of the working paper version of this chapter, but has been intentionally excluded here due to low levels of overlap in the control variables with the Western Cape. The two samples of students are so different that it is not possible to adequately control for their observed differences in a regression (as this requires some common overlap in their characteristics) or to improve overlap with propensity score matching.

obtained in many analyses of education production functions), but on the Western Cape effect. This is captured by 'WC'—a fixed effect that takes a value of 1 if the student is taught in a Western Cape school, and 0 otherwise. It measures the difference in expected performance between Western Cape students and another country or regions' student group once controlling for contextual poverty, home background and school resourcing variables. We estimate the WC effect by sequentially pooling the data for the Western Cape and each of our comparator locales.

6.3.2 *Econometric Results—Some Overall Patterns*

Tables 6.4 and 6.5 report the sign, magnitude and significance of the WC effect on mathematics and literacy outcomes for each of these pairwise pools—using, as per the lower part of the tables, a range of specifications differing in terms of which control variables are included. Formally, the coefficients on WC measure the direction and magnitude of systematic unexplained differences in performance between the Western Cape and other locales. Insofar as the set of controls is comprehensive—and the control variables do not include measures of the hierarchical and horizontal governance factors which are of interest—we can interpret the WC effect as approximations of these (unmeasured) dimensions of the Western Cape's institutional arrangements for education.[7] From this perspective, a positive coefficient can be interpreted as indicating that the Western Cape's institutions are stronger than those of the comparator locale; a negative coefficient signals relative institutional weakness for the Western Cape.

The first specification in Tables 6.4 and 6.5 controls for a Western Cape fixed effect only (column 1). The subsequent specifications discussed in this subsection expand the range of variables to include socio-economic, home background, classroom and school factors. This process aims to separate that part of the performance gap that might be explained by resourcing and home background factors from the part that may be linked to institutional factors.

Table 6.4, an estimation of mathematics scores, shows the changes on the Western Cape coefficient from progressively expanding the set of controls. The SACMEQ patterns in Table 6.1 turn out to be robust even once the controls are added. With home background and socio-economic status of

[7] We note, though, that some unmeasured determinants of outcomes may be unrelated to governance. For example, the Western Cape's long and difficult social history (which is distinctive from other parts of South Africa) may have resulted in a variety of (unmeasured) social and family deficits—as illustrated by, say, the province's unusually high levels of alcoholism and foetal alcohol syndrome.

Table 6.4. Multivariate regression of SACMEQ III Grade 6 mathematics z-scores using propensity score weights

Comparison country/region:	1	2	3	4	5	6	7	8	9
	Coefficient on Western Cape Dummy								
Kenya (Nairobi & Central)	−0.605***	−0.375***	−0.344***	−0.373**	−0.376**	−0.434**	−0.355*	−0.359*	
	(0.16)	(0.18)	(0.17)	(0.17)	(0.16)	(0.16)	(0.19)	(0.19)	
R-squared	0.085	0.398	0.412	0.453	0.462	0.471	0.473	0.484	
Botswana [a]	0.320***	0.282***	0.222***	0.254***	0.289***	0.413***	0.337***	0.421***	
	(0.14)	(0.06)	(0.06)	(0.07)	(0.07)	(0.07)	(0.07)	(0.07)	
R-squared	0.024	0.454	0.458	0.493	0.499	0.511	0.514	0.517	
Mauritius [a, b]	−0.604***	−0.259***		−0.232**	−0.300**	−0.251	−0.211	−0.236	
	(0.15)	(0.09)		(0.11)	(0.15)	(0.17)	(0.17)	(0.18)	
R-squared	0.052	0.399		0.424	0.436	0.45	0.454	0.454	
Eastern Cape	0.438***	0.490***	0.430***	0.488***	0.492***	0.890***	1.023***	0.861***	0.759***
	(0.18)	(0.13)	(0.13)	(0.11)	(0.11)	(0.16)	(0.19)	(0.19)	(0.20)
R-squared	0.043	0.284	0.291	0.384	0.409	0.457	0.478	0.491	0.493
Gauteng	0.257	0.320***	0.278***	0.296***	0.354***	0.408***	0.454***	0.402***	0.405***
	(0.19)	(0.08)	(0.08)	(0.07)	(0.08)	(0.07)	(0.07)	(0.07)	(0.07)
R-squared	0.013	0.5	0.507	0.555	0.562	0.59	0.591	0.595	0.595
Other controls:									
Home background		X	X	X	X	X	X	X	X
Socio-economic status		X	X	X	X	X	X	X	X
Teacher test scores[c]			X	X	X	X	X	X	X
Teacher/ classroom characteristics				X	X	X	X	X	X
'Governance' indicators					X	X	X	X	X
Parents contribute to school building & teaching materials						X	X	X	X
Parents contribute to salaries							X	X	X
Parents contribute to extra-curricular & teaching activities								X	X
Teacher days lost to strike activity									X

Observations:									
Western Cape	900	900	900	876	876	876	876	876	876
Kenya	920	920	920	899	899	899	899	899	
Botswana	3868	3868	3868	3868	3868	3868	3868	3868	
Mauritius	3524	3524	3524	3524	3524	3524	3524	3524	
Eastern Cape	1066	1066	1066	981	981	981	981	981	981
Gauteng	1020	1020	1020	1020	1020	1020	1020	1020	1020

Notes: Teacher and classroom characteristics include teacher education, teacher age, teacher experience, weekly teaching time (hours), textbook availability, class size, pupil-teacher ratio (PTR), frequency and discussion of homework and frequency of classroom assessment. Due to lack of overlap in teacher characteristics between the Western Cape and Kenya, only textbook availability, class size and frequency of assessment are controlled for. Standard errors are clustered at the school level and shown in parentheses.

*** significance at 1% level; ** significance at 5% level; * significance at 10% level.

[a] In the case of Botswana and Mauritius, SES is measured using a context specific asset index as household consumption data was not publicly available for these countries. In all other analyses, log per capita consumption is used.

[b] No teacher test scores are available for Mauritius.

[c] Test scores are missing for approximately 20% of the South African Grade 6 mathematics teachers sampled. A dummy variable equal to 1 for a missing test score and 0 otherwise is included in the analysis as not to exclude students taught by these teachers from the sample. Students taught by mathematics teachers with missing test scores had significantly higher mathematics test scores, therefore excluding these students from the analysis is likely to bias the estimated coefficients. Teacher strike days only vary in South African provinces and not the other comparator countries.

Table 6.5. Multivariate regression of SACMEQ III Grade 6 literacy z-scores using propensity score weights

Comparison country/region:	1	2	3	4	5	6	7	8	9
	Coefficient on Western Cape Dummy								
Kenya (Nairobi &	−0.424**	−0.269**	−0.208*	−0.261*	−0.133	−0.277*	−0.238	−0.244	
Central)	(0.17)	(0.12)	(0.11)	(0.14)	(0.14)	(0.15)	(0.18)	(0.18)	
R-squared	0.04	0.346	0.37	0.422	0.454	0.466	0.467	0.472	
Botswana [a]	0.282***	0.255***	0.190***	0.229***	0.265***	0.401***	0.395***	0.393***	
	(0.13)	(0.06)	(0.07)	(0.07)	(0.07)	(0.07)	(0.09)	(0.09)	
R-squared	0.018	0.455	0.46	0.496	0.501	0.508	0.508	0.51	
Mauritius [a, b]	0.092	0.376***		0.345***	0.299***	0.380***	0.397***	0.427***	
	(0.12)	(0.07)		(0.10)	(0.11)	(0.13)	(0.14)	(0.15)	
R-squared	0.002	0.39		0.414	0.424	0.437	0.441	0.442	
Eastern Cape	0.662***	0.704***	0.593**	0.619***	0.631***	1.175***	1.153***	1.215***	1.038***
	(0.19)	(0.12)	(0.13)	(0.11)	(0.16)	(0.20)	(0.18)	(0.18)	(0.20)
R-squared	0.093	0.376	0.398	0.444	0.465	0.514	0.532	0.539	0.542
Gauteng	0.136	0.180**	0.137*	0.101	0.045	0.043	0.086	0.08	0.072
	(0.18)	(0.08)	(0.08)	(0.07)	(0.08)	(0.08)	(0.08)	(0.09)	(0.08)
R-squared		0.505	0.513	0.559	0.568	0.582	0.586	0.587	0.59
Other controls:									
Home background		X	X	X	X	X	X	X	X
Socio-economic status		X	X	X	X	X	X	X	X
Teacher test scores [c]			X	X	X	X	X	X	X
Teacher/classroom characteristics				X	X	X	X	X	X
'Governance' indicators					X	X	X	X	X
Parents contribute to school building & teaching materials						X	X	X	X
Parents contribute to salaries							X	X	X
Parents contribute to extra-curricular & teaching activities								X	X
Teacher days lost to strike activity									X

Observations:									
Western Cape	907	907	907	883	883	883	883	883	883
Kenya	922	922	922	901	901	901	901	901	
Botswana	3868	3868	3868	3868	3868	3868	3868	3868	
Mauritius	3524	3524	3524	3524	3524	3524	3524	3524	
Tanzania	4194	4194	4194	4171	4171	4171	4171	4171	
Eastern Cape	1068	1068	1068	982	982	982	982	982	982
Gauteng	1020	1020	1020	1020	1020	1020	1020	1020	1020

Notes: Teacher and classroom characteristics include teacher education, teacher age, teacher experience, weekly teaching time (hours), textbook availability, class size, pupil-teacher ratio (PTR), frequency and discussion of homework and frequency of classroom assessment. Due to the lack of overlap in teacher characteristics between Western Cape and Kenya, only textbook availability, frequency of assessment and class size are controlled for. Standard errors are clustered at the school level and shown in parentheses.

*** significance at 1% level; ** significance at 5% level; * significance at 10% level.

[a] In the case of Botswana and Mauritius, socio-economic status is measured using the context specific asset index. In all other analyses, log per capita consumption is used.

[b] No teacher test scores are available for Mauritius.

[c] Test scores are missing for approximately 17% of the South African Grade 6 literacy teachers sampled. A dummy variable equal to 1 for a missing test score and 0 otherwise is included in the analysis as not to exclude students taught by these teachers from the sample. Students taught by literacy teachers with missing test scores had significantly higher test scores, therefore excluding these students from the analysis is likely to bias the estimated coefficients. Teacher strike days only vary in the South African sample and not in the other comparator countries.

students controlled for, the Western Cape effect in mathematics is positive and significantly different from zero in comparison to Botswana, the Eastern Cape *and* Gauteng. The Western Cape's relative strength in governance is one plausible explanation for this robust pattern. However, the opposite effect holds in relation to Kenya and Mauritius—suggesting (following similar logic) that overall, the latter two countries might have a better governed education sector than the Western Cape with, given the strong hierarchical management of the Western Cape, other 'soft' governance factors plausibly playing a decisive role.[8]

Strikingly, the addition of the teacher content knowledge variable does not affect the results. The further inclusion of teacher and classroom characteristics does not have any significant effect on the size and significance of the Western Cape coefficient in any of the country or region comparisons (an illustrative sample of those variables is provided in Table 6.6; the full set of variables is in Appendix A6.1). Even when one accounts for observed differences in the instructional core—the place where the student and teacher interact around content—the Western Cape effect remains in the initial direction.[9]

Table 6.5 reports the econometric results when literacy scores are used as the dependent variable. The broad effects of controlling for teacher test scores, teacher characteristics and governance indicators on the Western Cape coefficient are largely similar to the results reported in Table 6.4. However, the direction of the effects occasionally differs when literacy rather than mathematics is the outcome variable. Part of these differences may reflect differential exposure to English in these countries, which may not be fully captured by indicators for frequency of speaking English at home. In literacy, Western Cape students *outperform* rather than underperform relative to their peers in Mauritius, but continue to underperform relative to Kenya (although this difference becomes insignificant from regression 7 onwards). They also continue to significantly outperform Botswanan students in literacy, but there is little evidence of an observed advantage over Gauteng students at least after accounting for classroom factors. In particular, the Western Cape learning advantage relative to the Eastern Cape in literacy is more pronounced than in mathematics.

[8] The advantage to Mauritius is also augmented by the reality that its Grade 6 students are on average nearly a year younger than Grade 6 students in the Western Cape. Due to overlap problems, we couldn't adequately control for age differences. The bias however generated would underestimate the Mauritian advantage over the Western Cape.

[9] We do qualify, however, that the model comparing the Western Cape to the two Kenyan regions does not effectively control for teacher characteristics (for reasons of lack of common support). Therefore, it is possible that part of the negative (positive) Western Cape (Kenya) effect is accounted for by teacher factors we are unable to observe.

Table 6.6. Selected SACMEQ measures of mathematics teacher and classroom characteristics

	Western Cape	Kenya	Botswana	Mauritius*	Gauteng	Eastern Cape
Math teacher test score	852.8	898.3	781.0		790.6	726.7
Teacher qualification:						
Secondary education or less	0.19	0.67	0.59	0.33	0.20	0.39
Post-secondary/degree	0.79	0.33	0.41	0.67	0.80	0.53
Teaching experience:						
0–5 years	0.07	0.24	0.19	0.06	0.12	0.16
6–10 years	0.11	0.18	0.20	0.13	0.12	0.07
11–20 years	0.60	0.36	0.45	0.34	0.51	0.48
20+ years	0.20	0.22	0.15	0.46	0.25	0.22

Notes: Teachers in Mauritius did not write the test. Except for test scores, statistics are expressed in proportions.
Source: SACMEQ, see Appendix A6.1.

6.3.3 *The Influence of School-Level Governance*

We turn now to our econometric analysis of the influence on performance of school-level governance. The SACMEQ data include a variety of measures of school-level governance. Table 6.7 shows some of these, distinguishing conceptually between outcomes of governance and indicators which underlie the hierarchical or horizontal governance construct. Appendix A6.1 lists the full set.

As per Table 6.7 and Appendix A6.1, while significant parent contributions in the Eastern Cape are largely related to the building and maintenance of school facilities as well as the purchase of equipment and furniture, parent contributions in the Western Cape (and Gauteng) are characterized more by financial provisions for learning materials and staff salaries. This is not surprising, given wealth differences across these provinces, with historical infrastructural backlogs in more disadvantaged (typically non-fee-paying) Eastern Cape schools. Parents of students in wealthier Western Cape schools, which are more likely to be fee-paying, likely use their contributions through fees towards hiring additional school governing body paid teachers in addition to state paid teacher allocations.

The regression specifications in Tables 6.4 and 6.5 distinguish between the 'parental contribution' or horizontal governance controls, and the other outcome and hierarchical SACMEQ governance indicators. As the tables show, incorporating the outcome and hierarchical governance measures has very little effect on the results. By contrast, incorporating the parental contribution measures (notably contributions to school building and teaching materials) has a major effect. This is evident in some especially striking changes in the Western Cape coefficient in estimations of both literacy and mathematics in regressions 6 to 8.

Table 6.7. Some SACMEQ measures of school-level governance

	Western Cape	Kenya	Botswana	Mauritius	Gauteng	Eastern Cape
Outcome:						
Teacher absenteeism						
sometimes a problem	0.37	0.60	0.55	0.50	0.55	0.65
Often a problem	0.11	0.09	0.08	0.05	0.05	0.12
Hierarchical:						
Number of school visits by inspector in past 2 years	3.32	5.58	1.36	26.02	3.17	3.15
Horizontal:						
Parents assist with building facilities	0.13	0.55	0.19	0.11	0.21	0.57
Parents assist with maintaining facilities	0.18	0.42	0.14	0.32	0.47	0.65
Parents contribute to teacher salaries	0.48	0.50	0.03	0.01	0.63	0.08

Note: statistics are expressed in proportions.
Source: SACMEQ, see Annex 6.A.

When the parental contribution variables are included in the pooled Western Cape-Mauritius regression, the significance of the Western Cape disadvantage (negative WC effect) in mathematics disappears. The pattern is reversed when the controls for parent and community involvement are included in the Western Cape-Eastern Cape comparison. Both the Mauritius and the Eastern Cape results are consistent with the propositions that parent and community involvement adds value to educational performance, and that this 'hands-on' type of participation is relatively low in the Western Cape:[10]

- For the Eastern Cape comparison: relatively high parent and community involvement can be interpreted as being a positive governance influence—offsetting to some extent the weaknesses in that province's education bureaucracy which are detailed in Chapter 5 of this book. Once this involvement is controlled for, the impact of these weaknesses on education performance emerges even more starkly—as evident in an increase in the coefficient of the Western Cape effect by almost a factor of two in both mathematics and literacy. (A similar pattern is evident

[10] As an interesting aside, a one-way analysis of variance (ANOVA) is used to determine whether expected parental involvement in a region differs significantly according to measures of school governance, such as teacher absenteeism. Only in the case of Kenya and the Gauteng and Western Cape provinces of South Africa is teacher absenteeism found to be significantly negatively related to parent involvement; that is, higher levels of parent involvement are related to lower teacher absenteeism problems. Parent involvement is estimated to be significantly and negatively related to teaching days lost due to strike activity in Gauteng only. This suggests that parent involvement and governance appear to play different roles in different regions, and the estimated Western Cape effect may be masked by non-linear relationships between school governance and performance.

vis-à-vis Botswana, though the differences in both the extent of participation and the quality of the bureaucracy are not as stark as for the Eastern Cape.)

- For the comparison with Mauritius: the seemingly statistically significant weakness of Western Cape educational institutions in econometric results where participation is not controlled for could reflect differences in horizontal governance between the two systems.

While the results point to interesting dynamics between horizontal governance in schools and learning it is impossible in this analysis to disentangle how parental involvement indicators influence learning outcomes separately from how they may also reveal wealth differences (where wealth is typically the strongest determinant of learning outcomes in models of academic achievement).

6.4 Unbundling by Socio-Economic Status

Empirical estimation of education production functions consistently shows that learners' socio-economic status (SES) has a powerful impact on learning outcomes. This is, of course, why we include SES as one of the control variables in our econometric analysis. However, as this section explores in depth, there are some special challenges associated with incorporating SES. There also are some distinctive patterns—beyond the sign and significance of its coefficient in an aggregate education production function—in the way in which SES and bureaucratic capability interact.

In South Africa, the relationship between educational outcomes and socio-economic status of students (and particularly the school), is extremely strong and convex by international standards. This partly reflects the stark disparities of the apartheid era, which resulted in substantial inequalities in the provision of quality education along lines of race (which is unfortunately closely predictive of socio-economic status). Using a number of different international tests of student achievement, Stephen Taylor and Derek Yu (2009) highlighted how a considerable degree of the variance in reading and mathematics scores among South African students can be attributed to a students' SES, and particularly to overall school SES. Furthermore, this relationship is considerably stronger when compared to other international contexts; in fact, all other countries that participated in PIRLS 2006 (Taylor and Yu, 2009: 23; Taylor, 2010).[11]

[11] As an example, Taylor and Yu (2009: 23) note that in 'South Africa a student with a given SES has more than twice the chance of achieving a reading score approximately equal to the reading score predicted by the SES gradient, than would be the case in the USA.'

Effectively adjusting for home advantage requires a regionally and nationally comparable measure of student SES. How SES measures are constructed can significantly influence the performance rankings of countries over the student socio-economic profile (Kotze and Van der Berg, 2015; Harttgen and Vollmer, 2011). Following Kotze and Van der Berg (2015), we rely on an internationally calibrated measure of SES to compare test scores across equally poor students in different systems.

This is achieved by constructing a log of per capita consumption SES measure, the outcome of linking an index of student's reported asset ownership in SACMEQ to national income distributions in household survey data. This wealth indicator enables the comparison of equally poor students under different education systems. For example, the literacy level of a child living on less than $1.25 or $2 a day in the Western Cape can be compared to the literacy level of a child who is equally poor in the Eastern Cape or in Kenya. In cases where we were not able to access household data for a country[12] we use a standard asset index of student SES following Filmer and Pritchett (2001). To further increase the accuracy of a comparable SES measure, our analyses (specifically the depictions of social learning gradients) are adjusted to account for out-of-school children.[13] Some countries may perform better than others if only the strongest of candidates are enrolled in the school system. Effective access to education must account for both enrolment patterns and what students learn in school (Taylor and Spaull, 2015). SES scale construction and our methodology for accounting for enrolment patterns is explained in more detail in a related working paper (Wills, Shepherd, and Kotze, 2016).

Using the log of per capita consumption SES measure we can compare how Western Cape Grade 6 students fare at different points along the socio-economic student profile, relative to their peers in other South African provinces. The descriptive statistical patterns (i.e. not controlling for other variables) are graphically depicted in Figures 6.2 and 6.3 using social learning gradients, which are best-fit lines through the available data points to show the typical performance of a province (or country) at a specific level of student wealth.[14]

[12] Mauritian and Botswanan datasets are not open source. An additional barrier to using datasets collected by Central Statistics in Mauritius is that by law they require a representative to collect the data in person.

[13] We calculate the percentage of eleven- to fifteen-year-old children who are currently not in school at each percentile and assume that these students would have performed at the same level as the lowest-performing fifth percentile had they written the SACMEQ tests. For a more detailed discussion on the SES scale construction the reader is referred Kotze and Van der Berg (2015).

[14] This best-fit line, referred to as a locally weighted polynomial regression, is similar to a two-variable ordinary least squares regression line, except that fewer restrictions are placed on the model, allowing for non-linear relationships to be seen by fitting simple models to localized subsets of data.

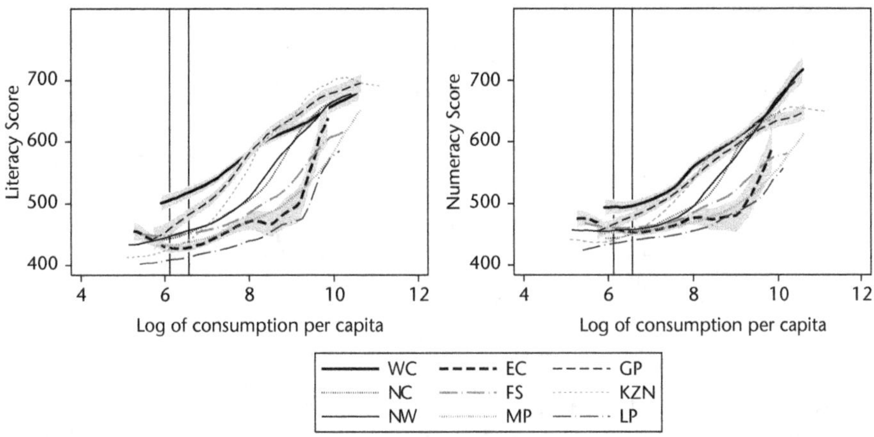

Figure 6.2. Mathematics and literacy scores for Grade 6 students by student socio-economic status (measured in log of consumption per capita) for all South African provinces

Notes: The vertical lines reflect the point at which students live at the poverty line as reflected by \$1.25 per day or \$2 per day. The grey areas reflect 95% confidence intervals about the non-parametric regression lines for key provinces of interest.

Source: SACMEQ III and NIDS household dataset.

The social learning gradients in Figure 6.2 reveal that amongst the poorest Grade 6 students, more learning is taking place in the Western Cape than in any other South African province. Specifically, the performance of students who are living on \$1.25 or \$2 dollars a day, as transformed onto the log of per capita consumption scale and reflected by the two vertical lines, is statistically significantly better in the Western Cape than in other provinces, in both mathematics and literacy. This suggests that the bureaucratic efficiency of the Western Cape Education Department does not just benefit the wealthy; on the contrary, the figure suggests that the benefits are disproportionately large for the poorest students in their system. As will be shown immediately below, this is also confirmed in the econometric results.

Figure 6.3 redraws social gradients for the Western Cape and Gauteng provinces—but now including Kenya as a comparator (using the full range of SACMEQ observations for the country, not only the Nairobi and Central regions). As the figure shows, the Kenyan line consistently is well above that of the two South African provinces—underscoring that Kenyan Grade 6 students outperform South Africa's two best-performing provinces at all levels of socio-economic status, particularly in mathematics.

We turn now to the econometric analysis of whether the inferences suggested by Figures 6.2 and 6.3 are robust. Using the estimation approach described in Section 6.3, and incorporating the full range of control variables,

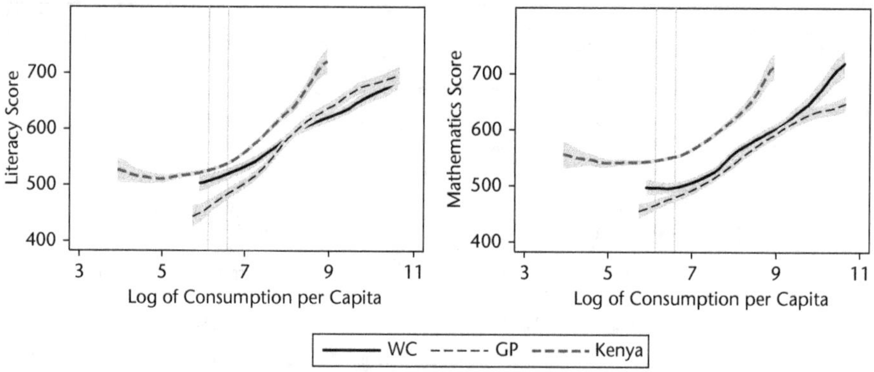

Figure 6.3. Literacy and mathematics scores for Grade 6 students by student socio-economic status (measured in log of consumption per capita) for the Western Cape, Gauteng, and Kenya

Source: SACMEQ III and survey household datasets. See notes to Figure 6.2.

Table 6.8 reports the 'WC effect' for sub-samples of students attending schools that have a relatively similar student wealth composition within the specific country or region. This is achieved through interacting the WC dummy with indicators of four school wealth groupings; that is, each school is assigned to a country or region-specific school wealth quartile constructed using the average of students' per capita log consumption in each school. All models control for propensity reweighting, home background factors, teacher and classroom factors, governance and parent/community indicators.[15] The WC effect is interpreted relative to students taught in schools falling within the first school wealth quartile in the comparator system (whose coefficient is set to zero).

No significant literacy performance advantage is observed in the two Kenyan regions compared with the Western Cape at all school wealth quartiles after we account for differences in teacher and school inputs. However, students attending the wealthiest schools in Kenya perform significantly better than students attending the wealthiest schools in the Western Cape with regards to mathematics. Where wealth is measured in log per capita consumption, Panel B of the table describes average student wealth by school wealth quartiles in each system. Clearly, relative to the comparator regions in Kenya, schools in the Western Cape and Gauteng are wealthier, while schools in the Eastern Cape are of similar wealth. In fact, the wealthiest quartile of schools in the Eastern Cape and in Kenya (Central and Nairobi) are far more comparable to the second quartile of Western Cape schools. This reinforces how much

[15] As with the analysis of Tables 6.4 and 6.5, in the case of Kenya, only textbooks, class size and assessment are used as regression controls because all the other teacher/classroom variables have very little overlap with the Western Cape or are homogenous in Kenya.

Table 6.8. 'Western Cape' effect when comparing students attending schools with similar relative values of school socio-economic status

PANEL A	Western Cape	Kenya	Diff.	Western Cape	Gauteng	Diff.	Western Cape	Eastern Cape	Diff.
Mathematics test scores									
Quartile 1	−0.606	0.000	−0.606*	0.312	0.000	0.312**	−0.415	0.000	−0.415
Quartile 2	−0.228	0.063	−0.291	0.661	0.319	0.342**	0.713	−0.670	1.383***
Quartile 3	−0.175	0.178	−0.353	0.792	0.278	0.314***	0.658	−0.621	1.279***
Quartile 4	−0.087	0.633	−0.710**	0.963	0.838	0.125	1.231	0.333	0.898**
R-squared	0.471			0.584			0.551		
Literacy test scores									
Quartile 1	−0.405	0.000	−0.405	0.326	0.000	0.326**	0.628	0.000	0.628***
Quartile 2	−0.285	0.126	−0.411	0.616	0.334	0.282*	1.001	0.364	0.637**
Quartile 3	−0.083	0.136	−0.219	0.580	0.520	0.060	0.810	0.035	0.775***
Quartile 4	0.043	0.387	−0.344	0.620	0.736	−0.116	0.909	0.478	0.431
R-squared	0.460			0.614			0.593		

PANEL B	Average student log per capita consumption by school log per capita consumption quartile			
	Quartile 1	Quartile 2	Quartile 3	Quartile 4
Kenya (Central and Nairobi)	6.398	6.752	7.149	7.933
Eastern Cape	6.217	6.643	7.035	7.606
Gauteng	6.995	7.513	8.544	9.297
Western Cape	7.187	7.734	8.384	9.292

Notes: Regression models control for home background and student characteristics, teacher and classroom characteristics, governance indicators and parent/community involvement indices (see the notes to Tables 6.4 and 6.5 for further information). Due to lack of overlap in teacher characteristics between the Western Cape and Kenya, only textbook availability, frequency of assessment and class size are controlled for at the teacher/classroom level. Standard errors clustered at the school level are shown in parentheses. Statistically significant at *** 1% level ** significance at 5% level * significance at 10% level. The difference in coefficients (Diff.) is calculated as the Western Cape coefficient less the comparator locale's coefficient.

Source: SACMEQ 2007.

better Kenyan schools are performing in mathematics relative to the Western Cape considering differences in the relative wealth of students.

Students in wealthier Gauteng schools perform similarly to their Western Cape counterparts; the primary differences occur in poorer parts of each system, where Western Cape students perform significantly better in mathematics and literacy. This is consistent with Figure 6.2—although the regression analysis confirms that this finding holds even after controlling for a wide range of other variables. In literacy, we observe similar findings in Eastern and Western Cape comparisons, except the difference is significant even at the top end of the distribution, and the size of the difference is much larger. The gap in mathematics performance comparing Western Cape and Eastern Cape schools is significant and very large for schools in quartiles 2 to 4 but not quartile 1. But if we use absolute wealth quartiles as an alternative measure (not shown here[16]), the significant advantage to the Western Cape in the poorest quartile 1 schools emerges.

6.5 Discussion

This chapter has used the Western Cape as a benchmark for comparative econometric analysis of education outcomes. The goal has been to assess the influence on outcomes of some key aspects of how education is governed—the influence on outcomes of bureaucratic capability, and of school-level governance. Three sets of conclusions emerge from the analysis.

A first set of conclusions concerns the extent to which variations across South Africa's provinces in their bureaucratic capabilities help account for divergent educational outcomes. Descriptive analysis of student learning outcomes across South African provinces suggests that, when multiple performance indicators are considered, the Western Cape is a top-performing bureaucracy, but this has not consistently led to its schools being the top performers. Econometric analysis (using 2007 SACMEQ data) shows a more consistently positive Western Cape effect at the primary school level. Both the econometric and descriptive analyses suggest that Western Cape Grade 6 students perform better at lower ends of the socio-economic distribution than students in other provinces using SACMEQ data. Considered in tandem with the evidence in Chapter 5 that the Western Cape Education Department (WCED) is a well -managed bureaucracy, this suggests that the benefits of a functional WCED extends to the poorest of students in their system. WCED bureaucratic efficiency and their approach to managing the school terrain

[16] See Wills, Shepherd, and Kotze (2016) for a detailed discussion of wealth quartiles as an alternative SES measure.

provides some hope that improving the quality of education institutions can make a difference for the poorest of South Africans and thereby tackling inherent learning inequalities in the system.

It is important to qualify, however, that this 2007 SACMEQ data is now a decade old. Performance changes have taken place across provinces as evidenced for example in Grade 9 TIMSS 2015 scores. It will be useful to repeat the analysis of this chapter using SACMEQ 2013 data as they become available. Furthermore, the results cannot be interpreted as causal, but reflect mere approximations of a Western Cape effect. To accurately measure the impact of an administration on student learning, one would need to relocate a school and its surrounding community in a weakly functioning province or national education system and then assess the level of improvement when reassigned to a better provincial or national education administration (van der Berg et al., 2016). While this seems an impossibility, the re-demarcation of some of South Africa's provincial boundaries created the ideal 'natural experiment'. Gustafsson and Taylor (2016) explored statistically the impact of these boundary shifts on educational outcomes for the affected schools.[17] They found that:

> by 2013, schools moving to better provinces had seen an improvement, over and above that which may have existed in other schools, equivalent to around one year of progress in a rapidly improving country. The conclusion that paying attention to a province's administration is a worthwhile policy priority seems supported. (Gustafsson and Taylor, 2016: 26)

A second set of conclusions from our analysis concerns the performance of the Western Cape relative to some other African countries (notably Kenya). Despite the success of the WCED in providing quality education within the South African context, when considering the WCED's performance relative to other Southern and East African systems, especially Kenya (and its Central and Nairobi regions) and to a lesser extent Mauritius, there is indeed a puzzling result of lower mathematics performance. This is evident both in the comparative descriptive statistics, and in the econometric estimations which incorporate a range of control variables. Especially noteworthy is that teacher content knowledge as measured by teacher scores on the SACMEQ

[17] Between 2005 and 2007, South Africa's provincial boundaries were adjusted to ensure that no municipality straddled two provinces. This 'quasi-experiment' allowed for the identification of a causal relationship between provincial administrations of education and learning outcomes in schools (Gustafsson and Taylor, 2016). The redrawing of provincial boundaries affected seven of nine provinces (though not the Western Cape). The changes in matriculation outcomes of province-switching schools were consistent with the direction of perceived functionality of different provinces. In particular, schools that shifted from the North West to the Gauteng provincial administration experienced improvements in their matriculation examination outcomes.

mathematics test did not account for performance gaps in favour of Kenya. Of course, one can't rule out that teacher test scores fail to capture other teacher pedagogical skills, unobserved abilities and motivations that may be important for learning. As discussed elsewhere in this book, the Western Cape bureaucracy almost surely is more capable (in a 'Weberian' sense) than its Kenyan counterpart. The pairwise comparison between the Western Cape and Kenya raises the possibility that other, 'soft' governance characteristics might also play an important role in shaping educational outcomes.

This brings us to the third set of conclusions, which concern the impact on performance of school-level (horizontal) governance. Econometric analysis revealed that the Western Cape effect was very sensitive to the inclusion of controls for parent involvement in schools and their contributions to the school institution. For example, after inclusions for parental involvement the significant Mauritian advantage to the Western Cape in mathematics falls away; conversely, the Western Cape advantage relative to the Eastern Cape almost doubles in both mathematics and literacy. This occurs even after accounting for school resourcing (including pupil–teacher ratios), student home background and teacher factors. With non-linearity in the relationship between patterns of parental involvement and student performance in some contexts, and very different relationships between parental involvement and student or school wealth, we cannot disentangle here the different pathways by which parent involvement affects learning. But this does point to potentially interesting dynamics between horizontal governance in schools and learning that are worthy of further exploration—with the school-level case studies in Chapters 8 and 9 illustrative of how such work might proceed.

Table A6.1. Control Variables for SACMEQ Countries and South African Provinces

Variable	Western Cape	Kenya		Botswana		Mauritius		Gauteng		Eastern Cape	
Home background characteristics:											
Female	0.52	0.48	**	0.51		0.49	*	0.52		0.51	
Age (in months)	150.6	165.5	***	153.5	***	136.5	***	150.2		159.7	***
Live with parents	0.83	0.80	**	0.73	***	0.94	***	0.83		0.62	***
Learner has used a computer	0.92	0.13	***	0.36	***	0.99	***	0.83	***	0.18	***
Days absent from school in last month	0.92	1.22	***	0.27	***	1.81	***	0.75	**	1.71	***
Mother's education:											
Senior secondary	0.19	0.29	***	0.11	***	0.15	***	0.20		0.20	***
Tertiary	0.28	0.05	***	0.22	***	0.12	***	0.36	***	0.04	***
Father's education:											
Senior secondary	0.17	0.39	***	0.10	***	0.16		0.19		0.21	***
Tertiary	0.29	0.08	***	0.24	***	0.15	***	0.34	***	0.05	***
Lots of books present in the home	0.51	0.22	***	0.39	***	0.72	***	0.50		0.20	***
Attended pre-school:											
for a year or less	0.33	0.50	***	0.17	***	0.08	***	0.25	***	0.42	***
for 2+ years	0.49	0.42	***	0.24	***	0.90	***	0.60	***	0.30	***
Speaks English at home:											
Sometimes	0.58	0.75	***	0.69	***	0.66	***	0.63	**	0.64	***
Most of the time	0.13	0.11		0.08	***	0.03	***	0.15		0.04	***
All the time	0.12	0.05	***	0.03	***	0.01	***	0.12		0.03	***
Siblings:											
1 to 3	0.75	0.30	***	0.55	***	0.81	***	0.69	***	0.44	***
4 to 5	0.13	0.26	***	0.22	***	0.06	***	0.15		0.27	***
More than 5	0.04	0.41	***	0.14	***	0.03	***	0.06	*	0.21	***
Meals:											
Has meal at school	0.77	0.21	***	0.92	***	0.72	***	0.65	***	0.75	
Eats breakfast often	0.84	0.79	***	0.82	*	0.89		0.78	***	0.83	
Receives help with homework:											
Never	0.05	0.13	***	0.05		0.13	***	0.04		0.05	
Sometimes	0.65	0.62	**	0.53	***	0.69	**	0.63		0.60	**
Mostly	0.27	0.21	***	0.41	***	0.17	***	0.29		0.28	

(*continued*)

Table A6.1. Continued

Variable	Western Cape	Kenya		Botswana		Mauritius		Gauteng		Eastern Cape	
Repeated:											
Once	0.18	0.34	***	0.26	***	0.20		0.16		0.28	***
Twice	0.03	0.09	***	0.04		0.02	**	0.02		0.05	***
3+ times	0.03	0.03		0.02	***	0.01	***	0.01	***	0.08	***
Mathematics teacher and classroom characteristics:											
Math teacher test score	852.8	898.3	***	781.0	***	–		790.58	***	726.7	***
Textbook availability:											
Only for teacher	0.18	0.02	***	0.04	***	0.03	***	0.22	**	0.15	
Shared between 2+	0.04	0.56	***	0.12	***	0.04		0.07	***	0.17	***
Shared between 2	0.27	0.22	***	0.21	***	0.04	***	0.28		0.19	***
Textbook per learner	0.47	0.18	***	0.62	***	0.88	***	0.34	***	0.34	***
Teacher age:											
Younger than 30 years	0.03	0.19	***	0.14	***	0.07	***	0.06	***	0.00	***
30–40 years old	0.43	0.36	***	0.47	**	0.33	***	0.35	***	0.39	
41–50 years old	0.39	0.29	***	0.32	***	0.27	***	0.37		0.41	
Older than 50 years	0.13	0.16	***	0.06	***	0.33	***	0.23	***	0.12	
Teacher qualifications:											
Less than secondary education	0.17	0.04	***	0.25	***	0.02	***	0.16		0.28	***
Senior secondary education	0.01	0.63	***	0.33	***	0.32	***	0.04	***	0.11	***
Post-secondary education	0.17	0.29	***	0.18		0.59	***	0.21	**	0.06	***
Degree or higher	0.62	0.04	***	0.23	***	0.08	***	0.59		0.47	***
Teaching experience:											
0–5 years of experience	0.07	0.24	***	0.19	***	0.06		0.12	***	0.16	***
6–10 years of experience	0.11	0.18	***	0.20	***	0.13	*	0.12		0.07	***
11–20 years of experience	0.60	0.36	***	0.45	***	0.34	***	0.51	***	0.48	***
20+ years of experience	0.20	0.22	**	0.15	***	0.46	***	0.25	***	0.22	
Weekly teaching time:											
10–14 hours per week	0.05	0.08	***	0.12	***	0.03	***	0.10	***	0.07	**
15–19 hours per week	0.19	0.31	***	0.10	***	0.15	***	0.08	***	0.10	***
20–25 hours per week	0.56	0.58		0.59	*	0.64	***	0.56		0.32	***
25+ hours per week	0.15	0.01	***	0.02	***	0.10	***	0.19	**	0.22	***

Class assessments:											
1 test per term	0.07	0.00	***	0.01	***	0.17	***	0.05	***	0.02	***
2–3 tests per term	0.49	0.40	***	0.43	***	0.42	***	0.49		0.54	**
2–3 tests per month	0.30	0.35	***	0.36	***	0.24	***	0.25	***	0.23	***
Weekly tests	0.11	0.24	***	0.20	***	0.17	***	0.22	***	0.13	
Literacy teacher and classroom characteristics											
Literacy teacher test score	813.3	791.0	***	770.1	***	–		776.5	***	717.9	***
Textbook availability:											
Only for teacher	0.05	0.02	***	0.03	***	0.03	***	0.07	**	0.08	***
Shared between 2+	0.05	0.54	***	0.12	***	0.04		0.12	***	0.17	***
Shared between 2	0.18	0.23	***	0.21	**	0.04	***	0.34	***	0.26	***
Textbook per learner	0.69	0.21	***	0.64	***	0.87	***	0.44	***	0.43	***
Teacher age:											
Younger than 30 years	0.04	0.26	***	0.14	***	0.07	***	0.10	***	0.00	***
30–40 years old	0.37	0.34	*	0.50	***	0.33	**	0.33	*	0.31	***
41–50 years old	0.34	0.31		0.31	*	0.27	***	0.34		0.42	***
Older than 50 years	0.23	0.09	***	0.05	***	0.33	***	0.24		0.19	**
Teacher qualifications:											
Less than secondary education	0.17	0.02	***	0.26	***	0.02	***	0.27	***	0.26	***
Senior secondary education	0.04	0.65	***	0.33	***	0.32	***	0.09	***	0.10	***
Post-secondary education	0.16	0.28	***	0.19	***	0.59	***	0.12	***	0.14	
Degree or higher	0.60	0.06	***	0.22	**	0.08	***	0.52	***	0.42	***
Teaching experience:											
0–5 years of experience	0.09	0.33	***	0.21	***	0.06	***	0.19	***	0.11	
6–10 years of experience	0.14	0.12		0.19	***	0.13		0.09	***	0.02	***
11–20 years of experience	0.42	0.37	***	0.45		0.34	***	0.33	***	0.56	***
20+ years of experience	0.33	0.18	**	0.15	***	0.46	***	0.40	***	0.23	***
Weekly teaching time:											
10–14 hours per week	0.02	0.09	***	0.11	***	0.03		0.09	***	0.10	***
15–19 hours per week	0.18	0.32	***	0.10	***	0.15	**	0.20		0.19	
20–25 hours per week	0.52	0.56	**	0.61	***	0.64	***	0.50		0.16	***
25+ hours per week	0.21	0.01	***	0.01	***	0.10	***	0.09	***	0.27	***

(continued)

Table A6.1. Continued

Variable	Western Cape	Kenya		Botswana		Mauritius		Gauteng		Eastern Cape	
Class assessments:											
1 test per term	0.14	0.01	***	0.01	***	0.17	**	0.25	***	0.02	***
2–3 tests per term	0.52	0.47	***	0.42	***	0.42	***	0.43	***	0.47	**
2–3 tests per month	0.25	0.26		0.37	***	0.24		0.14	***	0.28	
Weekly tests	0.06	0.26	***	0.20	***	0.17	***	0.18	***	0.14	***
Other classroom characteristics:											
Average class size	38.00	44.00	***	29.00	***	34.00	***	41.00	***	44.00	***
School pupil-teacher ratio	33.80	43.80	***	28.10	***	22.00	***	32.30	***	36.30	***
'Governance' and parent/community involvement:											
Teacher absenteeism:											
Sometimes a problem	0.37	0.60	***	0.55	***	0.50	***	0.55	***	0.65	***
Often a problem	0.11	0.09	*	0.08	**	0.05	***	0.05	***	0.12	
Teachers skipping class:											
Sometimes a problem	0.10	0.52	***	0.25	***	0.10		0.32	***	0.25	***
Often a problem	0.03	0.11	***	0.04	**	0.00	***	0.03		0.12	***
District support:											
School has never been fully inspected	0.12	0.06	***	0.04	***	0.41	***	0.25	***	0.27	***
Number of school visits by an inspector in the past 2 years	3.32	5.58	***	1.36	***	26.02	***	3.17		3.15	
Parental involvement: Parents/community—											
assist with building facilities	0.13	0.55	***	0.19	***	0.11	*	0.21	***	0.57	***
assist with maintaining facilities	0.18	0.42	***	0.14	**	0.32	***	0.47	***	0.65	***
purchase furniture and equipment	0.17	0.38	***	0.12	***	0.41	***	0.36	***	0.43	***
purchase textbooks	0.23	0.11	***	0.11	***	0.23		0.36	***	0.17	***
purchase stationery	0.42	0.09	***	0.22	***	0.35	***	0.52	***	0.25	***
contribute to exam fees	0.00	0.83	***	0.06	***	0.09	***	0.11	***	0.16	***
contribute to teacher salaries	0.48	0.50		0.03	***	0.01	***	0.63	***	0.08	***
contribute to staff salaries	0.36	0.15	***	0.06	***	0.01	***	0.52	***	0.27	***
assist with extra-curricular	0.71	0.57	***	0.94	***	0.86	***	0.75	*	0.85	***
assist with teaching	0.37	0.13	***	0.29	***	0.03	***	0.23	***	0.27	***
assist with school meals	0.32	0.26	***	0.15	***	0.13	***	0.31		0.25	***
Political disruptions: Days absent due to strike action—											
maths teachers	5.11							5.83	**	13.74	***
reading teachers	5.06							6.46	***	13.90	***

References

Abadie, A. and Imbens, G. (2011) 'Bias-corrected matching estimators for average treatment effects', *Journal of Business & Economic Statistics* 29(1), 1–11.

Crouch, L. and Mabogoane, T. (2001) 'No magic bullets, just tracer bullets: The role of learning resources, social advantage, and education management in improving the performance of South African schools', *Social Dynamics* 27(1), 60–78.

DBE (2013) Report on Progress in the Schooling Sector Against Key Indicators. Report prepared by M. Gustafsson. Pretoria: Department of Basic Education, http://www.education.gov.za/Portals/0/Documents/Reports/Report%20on%20Progress%20in%20the%20Schooling%20Sector%20Against%20Key%20Indicators.pdf?ver=2013-11-11-111554-463.

DBE (2016) Report on Progress in the Schooling Sector Against Key Learner Performance and Attainment Indicators. Report prepared by M. Gustafsson. Pretoria: Department of Basic Education, http://www.education.gov.za/Portals/0/Documents/Reports/Education%20Sector%20review%202015%20-%202016.pdf.

Evans, D. and Popova, A. (2015) 'What Really Works to Improve Learning in Developing Countries? An Analysis of Divergent Findings in Systematic Reviews'. Washington DC: World Bank Policy Research Working Paper No. 7203.

Filmer, D. and Pritchett, L. H. (2001) 'Estimating the Wealth Effects without Expenditure Data or Tears: An Application to Educational Enrollments in States of India', *Demography* 38(1), 115–32.

Fiske, E. B. and Ladd, H. F. (2004) *Elusive equity: Education reform in post-apartheid South Africa*. Washington DC: Brookings Institute Press.

Gustafsson, G. and Taylor, S. (2016) 'Treating schools to a new administration: Evidence from South Africa of the impact of better practices in the system-level administration of schools'. Stellenbosch Economic Working Paper Series WP No. 05/16, Stellenbosch University, Department of Economics.

Hanushek, E. (2007) Education Production Functions, Palgrave Encyclopaedia, https://hanushek.stanford.edu/sites/default/files/publications/Hanushek%202008%20PalgraveDict.pdf.

Hanushek, E. and Woesmann, L. (2007) 'The Role of School Improvement in Economic Development'. NBER Working Paper Series No. 12832, Cambridge, MA: National Bureau of Economic Research, http://www.nber.org/papers/w12832.

Harttgen, K. and Vollmer, S. (2011) 'Inequality decomposition without income or expenditure data: Using an asset index to simulate household income', Human Development Research Paper 2011/13. Human Development Reports. United Nations Development Programme.

Hill, J. and Reiter, J. P. (2006) 'Interval estimation for treatment effects using propensity score matching', *Statistics in Medicine* 25(13), 2230–56.

Ho, D., Imai, K., King, G., and Stuart, E. (2007) 'Matching as nonparametric preprocessing for reducing model dependence in parametric causal inference', *Political Analysis* 15(3), 199–236.

Hungi, N., Makuwa, D., Ross, K., Saito, M., Dolata, S., van Cappelle, F., Paviot, L., and Velien, J. (2010) 'SACMEQ III Project Results: Achievement levels in reading and mathematics'. Working Document No. 1.

Kang, J. D. Y. and Schafer, J. L. (2007) 'Demystifying double robustness: A comparison of alternative strategies for estimating a population mean from incomplete data', *Statistical Science* 22(4), 523–39.

Kingdon, G. G., Little, A., Aslam, M., Rawal, S., Moe, T., Patrinos, H., Beteille, T., Banerji, R., Parton, B., and Sharma, S. K. (2014) 'A rigorous review of the political economy of education systems in developing countries'. Final Report. Education Rigorous Literature Review, Department for International Development.

Kotze, J. and Van der Berg, S. (2015) 'Investigating cognitive performance differentials by socio-economic status: Comparing Sub-Saharan Africa and Latin America', Third Lisbon Research Workshop on Economics, Statistics and Econometrics of Education, 23–24 January, Lisbon.

Li, F., Morgan, K. L., and Zaslavsky, A. M. (2014) 'Balancing Covariates via Propensity Score Weighting', http://www2.stat.duke.edu/~fl35/papers/psweight_14.pdf.

McEwan, P. J. (2015) 'Improving learning in primary schools of developing countries: A meta-analysis of randomized experiments', *Review of Educational Research* 85(3), 353–94.

Reddy, V., Prinsloo, C., Arends, F., and Visser, M. (2012) 'Highlights from TIMSS 2011: The South African perspective', http://www.hsrc.ac.za/en/research-data/ktree-doc/12417.

Reddy, V., Visser, M., Winnaar, L., Arends, F., Juan, A., Prinsloo, C., and Isdale, K. (2016) 'TIMSS 2015 Highlights of Mathematics and Science Achievement of Grade 9 South African Learners'. Pretoria: Human Sciences Research Council, http://www.timss-sa.org.za/timss-2015/.

Rubin, D. and Thomas, N. (2000) 'Combining propensity score matching with additional adjustments for prognostic covariates', *Journal of the American Statistical Association* 95(450), 573–85.

Stuart, E. (2010) 'Matching methods for causal inference: A review and a look forward', *Statistical Science: A Review Journal of the Institute of Mathematical Statistics* 25(1), 1.

Taylor, S. (2010) 'The Performance of South African Schools: Implications for Economic Development', PhD thesis, University of Stellenbosch.

Taylor, S. and Spaull, N. (2015) 'Measuring access to learning over a period of incresaed access to schooling: The case of Southern and Eastern Africa since 2000', *International Journal of Educational Development* 41, March, 47–59.

Taylor, S. and Yu, D. (2009) 'The importance of socio-economic status in determining educational achievement in South Africa'. Stellenbosch Economic Working Paper Series No. 01/09, University of Stellenbosch, https://www.ekon.sun.ac.za/wpapers/2009/wp012009/wp-01-2009.pdf.

Van der Berg, S., Spaull, N., Wills, G., Gustafsson, M., and Kotze, J. (2016) 'Identifying Binding Constraints to Educational Improvement. Synthesis Report for the Programme to Support Pro-poor Policy Development (PSPPD)'. Stellenbosch University: Research on Socio-Economic Policy.

Wills, G., Shepherd, D., and Kotze, J. (2016) 'Interrogating a Paradox of Performance in the WCED: A Provincial and Regional Comparison of Student Learning'. Stellenbosch Economic Working Papers No. 14/16, Stellenbosch, http://www.ekon.sun.ac.za/wpapers/2016/wp142016/wp-14-2016.pdf.

7

Context and Capability

A Tale of Two Bureaucracies

Brian Levy, Robert Cameron, and Vinothan Naidoo

7.1 Introduction

Chapters 4 and 5 examined in depth the workings of the Western Cape and Eastern Cape education bureaucracies. Even though the two provinces operate within an identical inter-governmental framework, they differ starkly from one another in their socio-economic, political and institutional contexts. They thus provide an ideal platform for exploring comparatively some fundamental questions concerning the relationship between context and bureaucracy.

In what ways does context shape how bureaucracies operate? Where bureaucracy is relatively weak, to what extent does context constrain the prospects for improving performance? Where bureaucratic capability is relatively strong but politics turns toxic, to what extent can bureaucracy serve as a brake on a downward spiral? Can participatory 'horizontal' governance help improve public service provision—both as a complement to a relatively strong bureaucracy, and as a substitute in settings where capability is weak? Building on the empirical platform provided by the earlier chapters, this chapter explores these questions.

7.2 Two Divergent Bureaucracies

We begin by summarizing some of the findings from earlier chapters as to the quality of the education bureaucracy in the two provinces. Table 7.1 reports the results for 2012/13 of Management Performance Assessment Tests (MPATs) for the Departments of education in the Western Cape, the Eastern

Table 7.1. MPAT Assessments of South Africa's Education Departments (selected provinces 2012/13; distribution of scores, by level for assessed key performance areas)

	Level 1	Level 2	Level 3	Level 4
Western Cape	0	21	34	45
Gauteng	14	21	31	34
National average, all provinces	24	31	31	15
Northern Cape	28	41	28	3
Eastern Cape	59	17	17	7

Notes: Level 1—non-compliance with legal/regulatory requirements; Level 2—partial compliance with legal/regulatory requirements; Level 3—full compliance with legal/regulatory requirement; Level 4—full compliance, and doing this smartly.
Source: The Presidency, 2013.

Cape and two other provinces. The MPATs, sponsored by South Africa's Department of Policy Monitoring and Evaluation, located in the office of the Presidency, benchmark over a hundred national and provincial government departments against a variety of key performance indicators. As the table suggests, the Western Cape Education Department (WCED) was rated as the best managed of the country's nine provinces (Gauteng rated second). The Eastern Cape Department of Education (ECDoE) rated the weakest (the Northern Cape rated second weakest (The Presidency, 2013).

Good bureaucratic processes need not, however, translate into good results. Along with managerial quality, educational outcomes comprise another relevant benchmark for assessing the performance of departments of education. Here, too, as Table 7.2 shows, the Western Cape benchmarks well against other South African provinces.

Table 7.2 summarizes some scores from standardized tests administered in 2007 to a large sample of sixth graders in fifteen countries by the independent Southern and East African Consortium for Monitoring Educational Quality (SACMEQ).[1] As the table suggests, the Western Cape was the top performer among South Africa's nine provinces, with Gauteng a close second; the Eastern Cape was the weakest performer. The ranking of provinces is similar whether one takes the median score, the score for learners at the seventy-fifth percentile of socio-economic distribution, or the score for learners at the lower, twenty-fifth percentile, socio-economic tier. As Chapter 6 explored econometrically, the Western Cape remained the strongest SACMEQ performer among South Africa's nine provinces even after controlling for a variety of exogenous influences on performance. (Note that scores for Kenya also are included in the table and that relative to Kenya the Western Cape does not benchmark as well. Possible reasons for this, and its implications, are considered further in the final section of this chapter.)

[1] The South African SACMEQ sample comprised 9,083 students drawn from 392 schools; sample size per province ranged from 900 to 1,500 observations (RSA, 2010).

Table 7.2. The Western Cape's SACMEQ Scores in Comparative Perspective

	50th percentile (median)	25th percentile	75th percentile
Western Cape	560	496	636
Gauteng	548	483	610
Eastern Cape	454	408	509
South Africa (overall)	483	424	548
Kenya	548	509	610
Kenya (Nairobi)	585	535	662

Note: *achievement* in Grade 6 mathematics and home language by province, 2007.

Source: SACMEQ data files (2007) RSA, DBE (2010).

Corresponding to the differences between the two provinces in performance, the modes of operation of the two bureaucracies also were starkly different. We characterize these differences using the 2×2 governance framework introduced in Chapter 1 and applied in Table 7.3 below. One dimension of the framework comprises whether governance arrangements are hierarchical (that is, organized around vertical relationships between 'principals' and 'agents'), or whether they are negotiated (that is, organized around horizontal 'principal–principal'/peer-to-peer arrangements). The second dimension distinguishes among governance arrangements according to whether they are based on impersonal rules of the game, which are applied impartially to all who have standing, or whether they are organized around personalized 'deals' among influential actors. This gives us four distinct (and familiar) patterns of bureaucratic operation.

The first two patterns build on a foundation of impersonal rules. The first of these, *hierarchical-impersonal bureaucracy*, captured in the top-right cells of Table 7.3, is the classic mode of rule-governed bureaucracy delineated by Max Weber (1922) as the mechanism through which government pursues public purposes and partially 'modernized' in recent decades under the rubric of New Public Management (NPM).[2] The second (though not strictly speaking an example of bureaucracy), captured in the bottom-right cells of the table, comprises a form of 'corporatism'—formal processes through which multiple principals agree collectively on codified rules of the game for policymaking and implementation.

[2] There is a strand of NPM which advocates giving managers greater autonomy in order to achieve results (Hughes, 2003). This version of management would perhaps fall in the *hierarchical-personalized* cell. It has also been argued that NPM in South Africa, particularly performance management, is less about management reform and more about asserting new forms of political control over the bureaucracy, (Cameron, 2009, 2010).

For an in-depth comparative analysis on public management NPM in high-income, OECD countries, and its limitations, see Pollitt and Bouckaert (2011). For similar studies in developing countries see Schick (1998) and Manning (2001).

The third and fourth patterns operate on the basis of informal, de facto rules of the game. *Hierarchical-personalized bureaucracy*, the top-left cell, is similar in part to Weberian bureaucracy insofar as the mode of organization is hierarchical, and thus governed via nested principal–agent relationships—but here compliance on the part of agents follows from the personalized authority of the leadership, rather than a system of rules; the system is one of patronage. Merilee Grindle, in her 2012 book *Jobs for the Boys,* underscores 'the fatal weakness of patronage systems is not that they are inevitably incompetent, but that they are capricious'[3]—unconstrained by rules, and thus subject to the preferences of the hierarchical leadership.

In the final pattern, *fragmented-personalized bureaucracy* (in the bottom-left cells), neither formal rules nor a well-defined hierarchy of authority are in place. Appointments into public positions are politicized, with the right to appoint distributed across political factions; appointees generally focus their efforts on serving the interests of their various patrons. Where intermediate- and lower-level officials are committed to developmental goals and are skilful in nurturing alliances among internal and external stakeholders, they may be able to create 'islands of effectiveness'. But in this pattern, overall effectiveness is low.

As Chapter 4 explored in depth, viewed through the lens of the above framework the Western Cape Education Department (WCED) emerges as disproportionately 'hierarchical-impersonal'. It has a strong professional orientation among both the administrative bureaucracy and teaching staff. Turnover among the senior bureaucratic officials has been low, insulating the bureaucracy in significant part from the cycles of political change, including the rapid turnover of the provincial-cabinet-level appointments of political heads (i.e. the provincial ministers of education). Throughout two decades of democratic government, the WCED has endeavoured to put in place results-oriented approaches to performance management. It consistently worked to implement the ongoing stream of results-oriented systems reform initiatives which emanated from the national level, and complemented them with a variety of more home-grown initiatives (implemented especially vigorously under the Democratic Alliance (DA) administration which has governed the province since 2009). These include sophisticated computerized tools for managing budgets, staffing and procurement, school improvement plans (SIPs) for each of the provinces 1,500 schools, and online tracking systems for monitoring the progress of individual learners through the WCED system, and (on a quarterly basis), the progress of schools in implementing their SIPs.

[3] Grindle (2012: 32).

Table 7.3. Characterizing Education Bureaucracies—Two Contrasting Patterns

A: Western Cape			*Eastern Cape*		
Hierarchical	15–20%	60–65%	Hierarchical	20–25%	5–15%
Negotiated	5–10%	5–15%	Negotiated	40–50%	20–25%
	Personalized	Impersonal		Personalized	Impersonal

Source: chapters 4 and 5.

The left-hand side of Table 7.3 provides an heuristic summary of the Western Cape bureaucracy in terms of the two governance dimensions highlighted above, allocating 100 points across the four cells.[4] For reasons delineated in Chapter 4, the Western Cape bureaucracy is depicted in the table as predominantly, but not exclusively, impersonal and hierarchical: the top leadership of the bureaucracy exerts discretionary authority over some decisions; other decisions are painstakingly negotiated between the bureaucracy and other stakeholders (including teachers' trade unions) through tightly formalized processes. Yet overall, the Western Cape is an exemplar of a well-managed, hierarchically oriented and rule-bound bureaucracy.

By contrast, the Eastern Cape Department of Education (ECDoE) resembles more closely the 'fragmented personalized' pattern of bureaucratic operation. As Chapter 5 detailed, it has been bedevilled by divergent and competing regional interests, organizational cultures, and patronage ties which consistently defied centralized control. Since 1994 the ECDoE has experienced repeated leadership turnover, and a general flouting of centralized authority. Obstacles to enforcing management control and sustaining leadership continuity have contributed to chronic weaknesses in both financial and personnel management. In March 2011 national government intervened, and temporarily took over administration of the ECDoE. But this did not stem the crisis. Provincial politics proved too powerful. After a few years, intervention was scaled back, having had only a limited impact.

The right-hand side of Table 7.3 characterizes the Eastern Cape pattern heuristically by allocating about two-thirds of the percentage points to the personalized column. Mirroring the fragmentation of the bureaucracy, the bulk (but, again, not all[5]) of these are in the negotiated rather than hierarchical cell.

[4] Ranges are used to signal the heuristic nature of the allocation across cells.

[5] The ECDoE does more-or-less deliver on some core bureaucratic functions. Teachers are paid; some (but not all) schools receive textbooks; most (but not all) school buildings are maintained.

7.3 Accounting for the Divergent Bureaucratic Patterns

This section explores how context influences bureaucracy. Bureaucratic behaviour and performance are interpreted as endogenous, shaped by decisions of political elites as to whether to direct their efforts towards providing public services or for more narrowly political or private purposes—with the incentives and decisions of political elites shaped in turn by 'exogenous' variables. Viewed from this perspective, the divergences in behaviour of the Western Cape and Eastern Cape education bureaucracies laid out in section 7.2 can be attributed to differences in context across the two provinces.

Applying the analytical framework laid out in Chapter 1, Table 7.4 groups the relevant contextual differences between the Western Cape and Eastern Cape provinces into three categories—socio-economic, political and institutional. The discussion which follows provides detail on each of these, and identifies four causal mechanisms which link the contextual variables identified in the table to bureaucratic behaviour and performance, distinguishing between demand-side and supply-side influences.

7.3.1 *Demand-Side Pressures for Performance*

The first two causal mechanisms highlight the influence of exogenous socio-economic and political variables on the *effectiveness* of citizens' demands on bureaucrats and politicians for decent public services. The first mechanism comprises the well-recognized[6] relationship between social class and effective demand—with middle-class citizens generally better positioned than their low-income counterparts to exercise voice effectively in response to poor-quality services (and mismanagement and corruption more broadly), and thus more likely to exercise voice to pressure for better public performance.

Economically, the Western Cape was (and remains) among the wealthiest of South Africa's nine provinces; as of 1996, its per capita income was 50 per cent higher than for the country as a whole. The Eastern Cape, by contrast, was the poorest province in the country; its per capita income has hovered at around 50–60 per cent of the national average. These differences in average income

[6] For some analyses of the role of a rising middle class in pressing for greater public sector accountability, see Lipset (1959), Moore (1966), Huntington (1991), Acemoglu and Robinson, (2006), Fukuyama (2014). In recent work Tim Kelsall and Matthias vom Hau (2017) refine and extend the 'middle-class' hypothesis by introducing the concept of a 'social configuration' of power, comprising those groups that can threaten the hold on power of political leadership. They hypothesize that the broader the social foundation the more inclusive will be development outcomes.

Table 7.4. Two Divergent Contexts

	1. Socio-economic	2. Political	3. Inherited institutions
Western Cape	Diverse social composition—both ethnically and by economic class	- elites dispersed across multiple political parties, with two broad groupings - competitive elections	Inheritance of 'impersonal' bureaucracy
Eastern Cape	Homogenous social composition—disproportionately poor & Xhosa-speaking	- ANC electorally dominant; - deep intra-party fragmentation	Inheritance of patronage bantustan bureaucracies

Table 7.5. Distribution of Social Classes in South Africa, 2014

	South Africa (all)	Western Cape	Eastern Cape
Elite	4%	5%	2%
'Middle' class	20	35	13
Vulnerable	14	15	10
Transient poor	13	20	5
Chronic poor	49	25	70
TOTAL	100%	100%	100%

Note: The distribution is based on an empirical analysis of four waves of panel data collected between 2008 and 2014 by South Africa's National Income Dynamics Study.

Source: Schotte, Zizzamia, and Leibbrandt (2017)

between the two provinces translate into far-reaching differences in class composition.[7]

Table 7.5 reports some findings from Schotte, Zizzamia, and Leibbrandt's (2017) disaggregation of South Africa's income distribution into five distinct social classes. Based on this disaggregation, 49 per cent of South Africa's total population is classified as 'chronically poor'.[8] In the Eastern Cape, the share of the population which is 'chronically poor' rises to 70 per cent. In the Western Cape, it is 25 per cent. The 'modal' social class in the Western Cape is the middle class (35 per cent of the total population), with the 'vulnerable' and

[7] These differences in social class composition would, of course, be magnified (or diminished) if the provinces also differed in their (intra-province) patterns of relative inequality. But the limited available evidence on provincial-level Gini coefficients suggests that these differences are relatively small.

[8] The high proportion of the population that is 'chronically poor' is not an artifact of where the benchmark is set. For one thing, over half of the income of this group comes from social grants (pensions, child support and disability), set at less than $100 per month. For another, South Africa's 'chronically poor' are notably poor when benchmarked against other middle-income countries. As Levy, Hirsch, and Woolard (2015) detail, in 2000 the poorest 40 per cent of South Africans accounted for only 5.5 per cent of expenditure, a starkly lower share than for the comparator countries (all of which have similar per capita incomes): Brazil (8.1 per cent), Mexico (11.4 per cent), Turkey (15.1 per cent) and Thailand (17.1 per cent). As of 2010, the South African share had risen to 6.9 per cent, still below the comparators.

'transient poor' accounting for a further 35 per cent. Insofar as there is a positive correlation between economic status and voice, then solely on the basis of these differences in class composition, non-elite citizens in the Western Cape generally are likely to be better positioned to demand better public services than are their Eastern Cape counterparts.

The second demand-side mechanism works via the electoral process. Here, the key proposition is that citizens will be better positioned to exert demand-side pressure for decent public services in settings where elections are competitive than in those where politicians can take the support (or acquiescence) of citizens for granted, independent of how well they govern.[9] The differences between the two provinces in electoral competitiveness are stark—for reasons which are rooted partly in demography, and partly in history.

In the Eastern Cape, 86 per cent of the 1996 population of 6.1 million was black African, almost all Xhosa-speaking. (For South Africa as a whole, the 1996 black African share of the total was 77 per cent.) In the Western Cape, by contrast, the largest ethnic subgroup of the population was (in the South African lexicon) coloured. In 1996, this group comprised 54 per cent of the 4.1 million people in the province; black Africans comprised only 21 per cent. By 2011, population in the Western Cape had risen to 5.8 million (with the increase driven in significant part by migration from the Eastern Cape), with the black African and coloured shares now comprising 33 per cent and 49 per cent, respectively.

The Western Cape's relatively high ethnic diversity provided a platform for closely contested elections. To be sure, the province had been a major locus of opposition to apartheid and, as elsewhere in the country, most non-white anti-apartheid activists identified strongly with the African National Congress (ANC). But the distinctive ethnic characteristics of the Western Cape implied that among at least part of the population, loyalty to the ANC was not necessarily unequivocal—and insofar as the ANC framed the basis for its allegiance in narrowly 'African nationalist' terms, rather than an inclusive non-racialism, there was ample scope for shifting allegiances, and thus voting patterns, away from the ANC and towards the opposition DA, and other political parties.[10]

The result was a highly competitive provincial politics, with multiple competing political parties, and hotly contested elections. Over the course of the first two decades of democracy, seven different political parties/coalitions

[9] Acemoglu and Robinson (2006). Khemani (2016: chapter 5) reviews the literature on the impact of democratic political engagement on development outcomes.

[10] The DA elite comprised those in the upper tiers of business, the professions and the bureaucracy within the province. Cohesion did not come naturally among these elite sub-groups. At the dawn of democracy, there was a clear split between those with historical allegiance to the apartheid National Party, and those aligned with more liberal (but not revolutionary) white opposition parties. Over subsequent decades, these two factions largely merged—and were joined by smaller, independent (non-ANC) parties, whose allegiance was generally not 'white', and who historically had been very active in the struggle against apartheid.

have controlled the province. In these contested elections, non-elite swing voters (in the 'middle', 'vulnerable' and 'transient poor' classes) became politically central. Indeed, contestation among rival political parties for the allegiance of this demographic and economic middle has been heated.

In sum, consistent with the second causal mechanism, in the Western Cape, how a party governed while in power—whether it was perceived to use public resources well, or for more narrowly personal and political purposes—mattered for its future electoral prospects.

In the Eastern Cape, by contrast, the ANC dominated electorally. In 1994 it won 84 per cent of the vote in the province; this percentage declined subsequently, but as of 2015 had not fallen below 70 per cent. The electoral dominance of the ANC can be explained in part by the interaction between the province's ethnic homogeneity and its distinctive historical legacy. A disproportionate number of the leaders of the struggle for liberation from apartheid—including Nelson Mandela, Oliver Tambo, Thabo Mbeki, Winnie Madikizela Mandela, Chris Hani and Walter Sisulu—were Xhosa-speaking sons and daughters of the province. This proud history translated into strong electoral loyalty to the ANC on the part of the numerically preponderant Xhosa-speaking voters.

To be sure, demand-side pressures are not the only determinants of a political party's commitment to provide decent services. Even if middle class voices are weak, and elections uncompetitive, a commitment to better services might nonetheless derive from solidarity between a political party and its non-elite supporters. Further, it is plausible that electoral dominance could provide a ruling political party with the authority and long time horizon supportive of better service provision.[11] However, for reasons which will become apparent in the next subsection, this is not what happened in the Eastern Cape.

7.3.2 *Politics, Institutional Inheritances, and the Supply of Services*

We turn now to the two 'supply-side' causal mechanisms through which politics and institutions influence bureaucratic behaviour: the role of inherited institutional legacies; and patterns of intra-elite contestation within a governing political party.

As Keefer and Khemani (2005) explore, in choosing how to seek the allegiance of non-elites, political leaders confront a fundamental choice. One option is 'programmatic'—leaders might try to win legitimacy by promising

[11] Here, again, Kelsall and vom Hau's (2017) categories are useful. They distinguish between unipolar (hierarchically organized) and multipolar configurations of political power, and argue that a combination of unipolarity and a broad social foundation potentially can provide a strong platform for service provision. Khan (2010) makes a similar argument.

a specific programme of public action, and then utilize the public bureaucracy to deliver on these promises. Alternatively, they could seek to win support through personalized patronage and clientelistic vertical networks that link elite and 'intermediate class'[12] power-brokers with local communities. A key determinant of how political leaders choose between these two mechanisms is whether their promises to provide broad-based services (rather than targeted patronage) are perceived to be credible by voters. This is where inherited institutional legacies come into play.

The Western Cape inherited a bureaucracy which could straightforwardly respond to the relatively strong effective demand of citizens for services. During the apartheid era, alongside the white political and bureaucratic structures, the apartheid government had established a parallel 'parliament' and bureaucracy, the (coloured) House of Representatives (HoR). The white civil service and the HoR bureaucracy together were responsible for the provision of services (including education services) to the large majority of the Western Cape population.[13] As numerous studies of organizational culture have shown,[14] both South Africa's white public service and the HoR bureaucracy were steeped in traditional public administration, albeit with an apartheid bent. This culture has been described as bureaucratic, hierarchical and unresponsive, aimed more at controlling rather than developing the citizens of the country—but it generally operated on impersonal and hierarchical (that is, 'Weberian') lines. This inherited legacy of a relatively capable bureaucracy meant that voters were likely to perceive politicians' promises to provide public services as credible, adding to the impetus for political competition to be oriented around competing programmatic platforms, rather than patronage.

In the Eastern Cape, by contrast, the so-called 'Bantustans' comprised the crucial institutional legacy from the apartheid era. Two-thirds of the Eastern Cape's total 2015 population of 6.9 million people reside in areas which formerly had been part of either the Transkei or Ciskei Bantustans. Both the Transkei and Ciskei had nominally been independent (recognized as such only by the apartheid South African government). Both had large-scale bureaucratic apparatuses which were moulded together to comprise the major[15] part of the post-apartheid provincial bureaucracy.

[12] The term is used in this way in Khan and Jomo's (2000) analysis of rent networks in South Asia.

[13] Africans living in urban townships were under the control of the Department of Education and Training (DET). In the Western Cape, Africans were a minority and the number of DeT schools in the province were relatively small. There were also no Bantustans in the province. This meant that the province had to deal with only a modestly sized 'deadweight' of the most dysfunctional, control-oriented part of the apartheid state (Fiske and Ladd, 2004).

[14] McLennan and Fitzgerald (1992); Schwella (2000).

[15] Along with the two Bantustan bureaucracies, the third part of the Eastern Cape bureaucracy comprised some portions of the apartheid era Cape provincial bureaucracy—though the head

The two Bantustans had been organized along personalized, patronage lines.[16] These patronage patterns carried forward into the workings of the Eastern Cape province via two distinct mechanisms. As per Keefer and Khemani (2005), one mechanism worked through the credibility of political promises: weakness of the bureaucracy at the outset of the democratic era meant that, even under the best of circumstances, persuading citizens that promises to provide decent services would be credible would be an uphill challenge. But the circumstances prevailing in the province were especially unpropitious. This brings us to the second supply-side influence on bureaucratic behaviour—the role of intra-elite contestation within a governing political party.

The propensity for patronage in the Eastern Cape was compounded by the way in which Bantustan political elites were incorporated politically. In the wake of the dissolution of the Transkei and Ciskei Bantustans, a large majority of their political and bureaucratic elites (and also many ordinary citizens) joined the ANC—not out of conviction, but as members of convenience. Further, the (non-Bantustan) Eastern Cape ANC was itself hardly an ideologically unified party. In its early years, the ANC (both within the Eastern Cape and nationally) reflected the aspirations of a mission-educated aspirant African middle class which increasingly was being constrained by racially discriminatory policies.[17] In the decades prior to democracy, parts of the party had become increasingly militant; both Govan Mbeki (Thabo Mbeki's father) and Chris Hani were stalwarts of the South African Communist Party. The result was that the Eastern Cape ANC was less a disciplined, programmatically oriented political organization than an overall umbrella beneath which inter-elite contestation was endemic. This continuing contestation afforded the ANC's provincial leadership neither the authority nor the longer-term time horizon needed to translate electoral dominance into a commitment to better service provision.[18]

In sum, the Eastern Cape was especially poorly positioned vis-à-vis each of the causal mechanisms linking context to bureaucratic operation and performance. The middle class was weak. Elections were uncompetitive. The bureaucratic legacy was dismal. The wide diversity of ideologies and motivations resulted in ongoing internecine struggles within the Eastern Cape ANC's leadership. Patronage, not programmatic commitments to improve services, became the default mechanism for maintaining the political allegiance of non-elites.

office, and senior staff, had been located in Cape Town, and most transferred into the Western Cape's bureaucracy.

[16] Streek and Wickstead (1981). [17] Lodge (2014); Southall (2004).

[18] In the terminology of Kelsall and vom Hau, the Eastern Cape ANC was a multipolar rather than unipolar political party.

7.4 From Context to Action

What does the evidence that 'context matters' imply as to the prospects for improving bureaucratic performance?[19] Does better bureaucratic performance translate into better service provision? Insofar as the bureaucracy is weak, what are the prospects for improvement? This final section explores these questions.

7.4.1 *Cumulative Causation—Virtuous and Vicious Circles*

A central goal of this chapter is to clarify and illustrate how political drivers shape and constrain the performance of bureaucracies. The interactions between the political and bureaucratic realms turn out to be more complex, with more potential for two-way causality, than is implied by simple nostrums along the lines of, say, 'politics is trumps'.

Chapter 1 identified four distinct 'ideal types' of political settlement, each cascading down through multiple institutional, political, and organizational levels. While specific contexts often can be hybrid combinations of the four patterns, in practice the Western Cape and Eastern Cape turned out to be paradigmatic provincial-level examples of two distinct types:

- The Western Cape emerged as a classic example of a 'competitive with rule-of-law' provincial-level political settlement; as section 7.3 has detailed, all of the exogenous variables mutually reinforced one another in a way which fostered a high-level equilibrium of a capable bureaucracy.
- The Eastern Cape, by contrast, was a paradigmatic example of a personalized competitive (or competitive clientelist) settlement; the exogenous variables reinforced each other in the opposite direction from the Western Cape, locking in a low-level equilibrium.

The two case study provinces provide an opportunity for considering the dynamics of each of the two polar opposite 'ideal types'. Consider, first, an Eastern Cape type starting point of an initially weak socio-economic, political and institutional setting. As the Eastern Cape case suggests, the result of this mutually reinforcing pattern is a low-level equilibrium trap. From that starting point, whether a virtuous spiral of improvement takes hold—or whether a

[19] For an in-depth analysis of how context shapes development policymaking and practice, including vis-à -vis public bureaucracies, see Levy (2014).

vicious circle of a continuing low-level equilibrium of patronage and poor service provision persists—follows directly from actions which emanate from the political realm.

A vicious circle will persist if an initially weak political context remains unsupportive (with, say, continuing inter-elite competition and continuing neglect of the development challenges confronting non-elites). In such circumstances, the incentives transmitted from the political to the bureaucratic levels reinforce factionalized loyalty within multiple patronage networks, with little incentive to improve the provision of public services.

In a context such as this, technocratic tinkering to improve bureaucratic performance is unlikely to gain traction. Rather, a necessary condition for change would be a transformation of the political context in a way which altered the incentives emanating from the political level in directions more supportive of development. Thus, a virtuous spiral might become possible if, say, the governing party were to become more developmental (perhaps as a result of internal changes within the party, perhaps the result of electoral success on the part of a newly emergent opposition). But even then, the continuing 'stickiness' of the other exogenous variables (weak effective demand; weak institutions), the journey of public sector transformation would be long and difficult, and risks of reversal would abound. In such contexts, policymakers and others might usefully focus on trying to improve service within 'islands of effectiveness' which are not dependent on broader socio-economic, political, and institutional change.

Now consider an alternative, Western Cape type, starting point where both the demand side and supply sides support the provision of decent services. This high-level equilibrium provides something of a buttress against a politically driven downward spiral: If the political leadership remains pro-developmental (with or without an actual alternation of the governing party) then good quality service provision can be sustained.

If, notwithstanding the initially strong capabilities, a new set of elites won power and sought to pursue private interests, they would be constrained (at least for a while) by the prevailing system—both the strong 'Weberian' culture of adherence to impersonal rules, and by the fact that within a few years they would need to defend their record in what almost certainly would be a highly contested election. Eventually, sustained predatory pressures from political leaders could breach the buttresses. However, the conflicts between predatory politics and a rule-governed bureaucracy would, at a minimum, provide time and opportunity for the political realm to self-correct, before a downward spiral could take hold.

Note that the robustness of the above two equilibria is derived from the mutually reinforcing configuration of the 'exogenous' contextual variables.

Had the research been undertaken in other provinces, it is likely that in at least some of them, the exogenous variables would have aligned in a more mixed way:

- Relative to the Eastern Cape, some provinces potentially could have a stronger institutional inheritance, or a more internally coherent provincial wing of the ANC. In such settings, the challenge of turnaround might not be as daunting as it is for the Eastern Cape.
- Relative to the Western Cape, some provinces (Gauteng is an obvious example, at least until 2016) might have had a similarly strong institutional inheritance and middle class, but less closely contested elections.

In these more mixed cases, the quality of public bureaucracy would be more of a knife edge. In the former group, were a developmentally oriented political leadership to win control of the province, the path to improving bureaucratic performance could be easier than in the Eastern Cape. Conversely, in provinces which were partial approximations of the Western Cape, because the 'guardrails' are relatively weaker, were control to pass into the hands of a predatory leadership, the bureaucracy could more readily slide into a downward spiral.

To make the point differently, our analysis is not intended to imply that there is no scope for provincial-level leaders (both political and technocratic) to make a difference, for good or ill. But it does imply that the broader socioeconomic, political, and institutional context has a powerful influence on how much change is feasible.

7.4.2 *Improving Educational Outcomes—Bureaucracy and its Limits*

While context may shape bureaucratic quality, how well bureaucracy functions is not the only governance determinant of educational outcomes. To be sure, a well-functioning hierarchy can undertake efficiently many of the logistical tasks (e.g. teacher post provisioning; payroll; infrastructure provisioning and maintenance; textbook and supplies management) associated with a large public educational system. Further, a well-functioning bureaucracy potentially might function as a sort of transmission belt, communicating emerging evidence as to pedagogical approaches which improve educational outcomes throughout the school system.

Yet for all of these potential benefits, the research reported in Chapters 4–6 also underscores some of the limits of hierarchical approaches to improving outcomes. One limitation is political. As the study of the Eastern Cape bureaucracy in Chapter 5 underscores (as does, to a lesser degree, the Chapter 3 analysis of efforts to introduce performance management nationally), the explanations for weak bureaucratic performance often are to be found, not in shortfalls of management, but in constraints which derive from the ways in which political actors interact with one another. In such settings, insofar as these constraints are decisive, it follows that efforts to improve educational outcomes might more usefully focus on approaches whose efficacy is not dependent on unachievable gains in bureaucratic functioning. To make the point differently, in such settings, horizontal governance potentially might function as a potential institutional *substitute,* providing a platform for school-level 'islands of effectiveness' to take on, reasonably effectively, some tasks which in bureaucratically better-endowed settings might be better done hierarchically.

Now consider the contrasting Western Cape setting where bureaucracy functions relatively well. In such settings, are hierarchical approaches to improving educational outcomes sufficient—or might there be case for *complementing* them with more horizontal initiatives? Both theory and evidence suggest that there may indeed be a case for the latter. Theoretically, as Chapter 1 details, the case revolves around the ways in which locating authority close to the service provision front-line can create opportunities for customization, for improving local-level motivation, and for utilizing local-level information.[20] Empirically, the evidence from Chapters 4 and 6 on the performance of the Western Cape bureaucracy underscores the limits of hierarchy.

Consider first evidence on the contrasting educational performance of the Western Cape and Kenya. As Table 7.2 showed, even though Kenya has a per capita income less than a quarter that of South Africa's, and thus substantially fewer resources per pupil (with not all of these differences captured in the explanatory variables), its education system systematically outperforms the Western Cape. Of course, outcomes depend on multiple influences—so focusing only on outcome measures as a basis for assessing performance is misleading.

Chapter 6 of this volume reports the results of a careful econometric effort to control for these other influences. The econometric strategy was to isolate a 'Western Cape effect' on educational outcomes (in the form of the coefficient of a dummy variable for the province) once other influences were controlled for—home background, socio-economic status, teacher qualifications, other teacher/classroom characteristics, plus a subset of governance indicators.[21] With these controls, the coefficient of the Western Cape

[20] Key contributions to literature on the value added of front-line autonomy include Sah and Stiglitz (1986), Aghion and Tirole (1997), Wilson (1989), Lipsky (2010) and Scott (1998).

[21] Each of these are composite measures, built on very detailed student, parent and school-specific information collected in the SACMEQ survey. Chapter 6 provides additional information on each of the underlying data points, including average scores for each in each of the locales they analyse.

dummy variable can be interpreted as being, in significant part an (unmeasured) 'governance effect'.

Table 7.6 reports on a few of the results from the Chapter 6 effort. As the table shows, relative to Kenya[22] the Western Cape effect is negative; even after controlling for a wide variety of influences. Given the evident robustness of the Western Cape bureaucracy, and the well-known unevenness of Kenya's public management systems, it is highly unlikely that the performance gap can be explained by superior hierarchical management on the part of Kenya. Rather, the results could be interpreted as pointing to the possibility that it is in the 'softer' side of the governance of education—perhaps motivation on the part of teachers and other stakeholders, perhaps the patterns of participatory, horizontal governance—that Kenya has an advantage. The comparison with Kenya is explored further in Chapter 10.

The econometric comparison of the Western and Eastern Cape offers an intriguing added pointer as to the relevance of the softer side of governance, in this case as a partial substitute for weak bureaucratic capability. Unsurprisingly, as Table 7.6 shows, relative to the Eastern Cape, the Western Cape effect is significant and positive. However, the inclusion of 'parental contribution to school building and teaching materials' as an explanatory variable increases substantially the absolute value of the effect. Why? In the SACMEQ data series, 57 per cent of Eastern Cape parents (but only 13 per cent of Western Cape parents) assist with school building—and 65 per cent (but only

Table 7.6. Grade 6 Mathematics SACMEQ Scores—The 'Western Cape' Effect (coefficient on Western Cape dummy variable)

Comparison country/region:	1	2
Kenya (Nairobi and Central)	−0.373**	−0.434**
Eastern Cape	+0.488***	+0.890***
controls:		
Home background	X	X
Socio-economic status	X	X
Teacher test scores	X	X
Teacher/classroom characteristics	X	X
Parents contribute to school building and teaching materials		X

***significance at 1% level **significance at 5% level *significance at 10% level.

Source: Wills, Shepherd and Kotze (chapter 6)

[22] The comparison is specifically with results for Kenya's Nairobi and Central provinces. As Wills et al. detail in Chapter 6, these provinces are reasonably similar in their SES demographic to the Western Cape. The statistical procedures break down when SES differences across the populations are too large.

18 per cent in the Western Cape) with school maintenance.[23] Plausibly, parental participation serves as a partial institutional substitute for weaknesses in the Eastern Cape bureaucracy—with the true magnitude of the costs imposed on Eastern Cape children by weaknesses in the ECDoE only evident once the parental role is accounted for.

In sum, the econometric results suggest that bureaucracy need not be destiny—that there are other dimensions of the governance of education systems which can, as in the Eastern Cape, be partial institutional substitutes for relatively weak hierarchical bureaucratic capability, or (as seems likely in Kenya) can be complements, adding to the overall efficacy of the system. Chapters 8–10 explore the potential role of more horizontal, participatory mechanisms via an in-depth look at school-level governance dynamics, and their relation to educational outcomes.

References

Acemoglu, D. and Robinson, J. A. (2006) *The Economic Origins of Dictatorship and Democracy*. New York: Cambridge University Press.

Aghion, P. and Tirole, J. (1997) 'Formal and real authority in organizations', *Journal of Political Economy* 105, 1–29.

Cameron, R. (2009) 'New Public Management reforms in the South African public service: 1999–2009, *Journal of Public Administration* 44(4.1), 910–42.

Cameron, R. (2010) 'Redefining political-administrative relationships in South Africa', *International Review of Administrative Studies* 76(4), 676–701.

Fiske, E. and Ladd, H. F. (2004) *Education reform in post-apartheid South Africa*. Washington DC: Brookings Institute Press.

Fukuyama, F. (2014) *Political Order and Political Decay*. New York: Farrar, Straus and Giroux.

Grindle, M. S. (2012) *Jobs for the Boys: Patronage and the State in Comparative Perspective*. Cambridge, MA: Harvard University Press.

Hughes, O. (2003) *Public Management and Administration: An Introduction,* 3rd edn. Basingstoke and New York: Palgrave Macmillan, 17–43.

Huntington, S. P. (1991) *Political Order in Changing Societies*. New Haven: Yale University Press.

Keefer, P. and Khemani, S. (2005) 'Democracy, Public Expenditures and the Poor: Understanding Political Incentives for Providing Public Services', *World Bank Research Observer* 20(1).

[23] As Chapter 6 details, in Kenya, 55 per cent of parents assist with school buildings, and 42 per cent with maintenance.

Kelsall, T. and vom Hau, M. (2017) 'Beyond Institutions: A Political Settlements Approach to Development'. University of Manchester.

Khan, M. (2010) 'Political Settlements and the Governance of Growth-Enhancing Institutions', mimeo.

Khan, M. and Jomo, K. S. (2000) *Rents, Rent-seeking and Economic Development: Theory and Evidence in Asia.* Cambridge: Cambridge University Press.

Khemani, S. (2016) *Making Politics Work for Development: A Policy Research Report.* Washington DC: World Bank.

Levy, B. (2014) *Working with the Grain: Integrating Governance and Growth in Development Strategies.* New York: Oxford University Press.

Khan, M., Hirsch, A., and Woolard, I. (2015) 'Governance and inequality: Benchmarking and interpeting South Africa's evolving political settlement', ESID Working Paper No. 51. Manchester: The University of Manchester.

Lipset, S. M. (1959) 'Some Social Requisites of Democracy: Economic Development and Political Legitimacy', *American Political Science Review* 53, 69–105.

Lipsky, M. (2010) *Street-level Bureaucracy: Dilemmas of the Individual in Public Service.* New York: Russell Sage Foundation.

Lodge, T. (2014) 'Neo-patrimonial politics in the ANC', *African Affairs* 113/450, 1–23.

Manning N. (2001) 'The Legacy of the New Public Management in developing countries', *International Review of Administrative Sciences* 67(2), 297–312.

McLennan, A. and Fitzgerald, P. (eds) (1992) *The Mount Grace papers. The New Public Administration Initiative and the Mount Grace Consultation.* Johannesburg: Public and Development Management Programme, University of Witwatersrand.

Moore, B. (1966) *The Social Origins of Dictatorship and Democracy.* Boston: Beacon Press.

Pollitt, C. and Bouckaert, G. (2011) *Public Management Reform. 2011. A Comparative Analysis,* 3rd edn. Oxford: Oxford University Press.

RSA (2010) *The SACMEQ III Project in South Africa: A Study of the Conditions of Schooling and the Quality of Education.* Pretoria.

Sah, R. K. and Stiglitz, J. E. (1986) 'The architecture of economic systems: Hierarchies and polyarchies', *American Economic Review* 76(4), 716–27.

Schick, A. (1998) 'Why Most Countries Should Not Try New Zealand Reforms', *The World Bank Research Observer* 13(1), 123–31.

Schotte, S., Zizzamia, R., and Leibbrandt, M. (2017) 'Social stratification, life chances and vulnerability to poverty in South Africa', Southern Africa Labour and Development Research Unit, SALDRU Working Paper No. 208. University of Cape Town.

Schwella, E. (2000) 'Paradigms: Context and competencies'. In F. Theron and E. Schwella (eds), *The State of Public and Development Management in South Africa. The Mount Grace II Papers* (pp. 33–43). Stellenbosch: University of Stellenbosch.

Scott, J. C. (1998) *Seeing Like a State.* New Haven: Yale University Press.

Southall, R. (2004) 'Political change and the black middle class in democratic South Africa', *Canadian Journal of African Studies* 38, 3.

Southern and East Africa Consortium for Monitoring Educational Quality (SACMEQ) (2007) http://www.sacmeq.org/.

Streek, B. and Wickstead, R. (1981) *Render under Kaiser: A Transkei Dossier*. Johannesburg: Ravan Press.

The Presidency, Department of Performance Monitoring and Evaluation (2013) MPAT. *Management Performance Assessment 2012/13 Final scores Education Sector Feedback*. Pretoria.

Weber, M. (1922) *Economy and Society*. Berlin.

Wilson, J. Q. (1989) *Bureaucracy: What Government Agencies Do and Why They Do It*. New York: Basic Books.

Part III
Horizontal Governance

8

Case Studies of School-Level Governance Dynamics in the Western Cape

Ursula Hoadley, Brian Levy, Lawule Shumane, and Shelly Wilburn

8.1 Introduction

South Africa's public schools fall under the hierarchical control of the country's nine provincial departments of education, which vary widely from one another in their effectiveness. Chapters 4–7 analysed the causes and effects of this variation, focusing especially on the Western and Eastern Cape. As they show, variations in bureaucratic quality indeed affect educational outcomes. However within provinces, and controlling for the socio-economic circumstances of learners, there also are quite substantial variations in performance across schools. Why?

An extensive literature, summarized in Chapter 1 of this book, suggests that for services such as basic education where provision is dispersed, giving 'horizontal' actors at the service provision front line some autonomy vis-à-vis hierarchical control potentially can improve performance. South Africa's 1996 Schools Act delegated quite substantial formal authority to the school level, and assigned a major role to school governing bodies (SGBs) to exercise that authority. The South African education system thus offers an ideal opportunity to explore how the delegation of authority to the service provision front line affects performance. This chapter explores the question through a series of in-depth case studies of school-level governance in the Western Cape province. Chapter 9 focuses on schools in the Eastern Cape.

There are at least four distinct channels through which delegation of authority to the service provision front line might improve performance. One of these involves the customization of service provision; for education, this raises questions of approaches to pedagogy, which fall outside the scope of the present study. The other three work more directly through governance. They comprise:

- *A managerial channel*—improving motivation, with a 'zone of autonomy' at the service provision front line hypothesized to provide the opportunity for internal leaders to motivate their teams effectively, including by fostering an environment of continuing learning on the part of staff as well as students (Wilson, 1989; Lipsky, 2010).
- *An informational channel*—creating scope for the utilization of local-level information of a kind to which higher-level hierarchical authorities lack access—and thereby enhancing processes for the selection of good quality staff and leaders, and the efficacy of efforts to hold staff and leaders accountable for their performance (Sah and Stiglitz, 1986; North, 1990; and Aghion and Tirole, 1997).
- *An accountability channel*—enabling developmentally oriented local stakeholders (including professionally committed teaching staff) to hold school staff accountable for making their best effort. A necessary condition for 'empowerment' to be effective as a means of strengthening accountability is that developmentally oriented stakeholders indeed have sufficient influence to be able to 'trump' predatory actors seeking to capture school-level resources (teaching and administrative positions, contracts, other discretionary resources) for private purposes (Levy, 2014).

Figure 8.1, reproduced from Chapter 1 (with one adjustment, on which more below) illustrates schematically the multiple causal mechanisms through which stakeholders potentially might influence school-level governance, and thereby affect educational outcomes. The heavy bolded arrow from the school principal

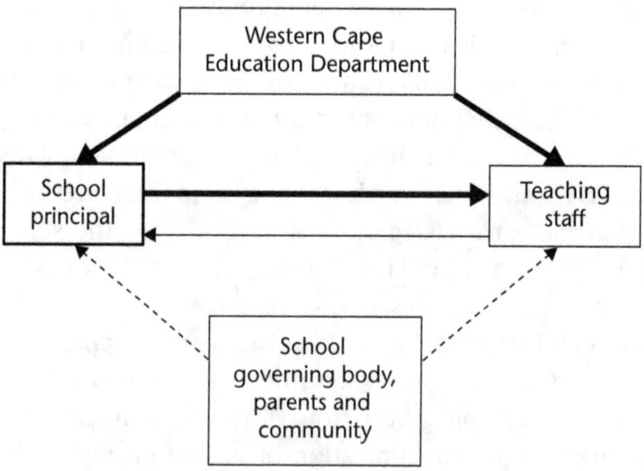

Figure 8.1. School-level governance interactions

to the teaching staff reflects a central finding of empirical research on the determinants of school performance—namely that the quality of school leadership is an important proximate explanatory variable (Hallinger and Heck, 1996; Leithwood, Patten, and Jantzi, 2010). The lighter arrow in the opposite direction points to the possibility of a two-way relationship, with the teachers' organizational culture affecting the approach to management of the school principal. The arrows linking the SGB, parents and community to the principal and teachers illustrate the potential role of local-level actors from outside the school. Although not included explicitly in Figure 8.1, the school-level research also probed the role and influence on school-level governance of the teachers' unions (SADTU and NAPTOSA) and political parties.

What differentiates Figure 8.1 from the equivalent figure in Chapter 1 is the heavily bolded lines linking the education bureaucracy to the principal and teachers. These bolded lines signify that, consistent with the in-depth analysis in Chapter 4, the Western Cape's bureaucratic hierarchy is relatively strong. (The lines linking the education bureaucracy to schools are drawn very differently in the parallel figure in Chapter 9's analysis of school-level governance in the Eastern Cape, where bureaucratic capabilities are much weaker.)

The contrasts between the Western Cape and Eastern Cape provinces provide an ideal opportunity to explore a central theme of this book, namely how 'good fit' works—how preferred approaches to policy design and implementation might vary according to the contexts in which they are being undertaken. Viewed from this perspective, the Western Cape school-level cases can be interpreted as exploring the potential role of horizontal governance as a *complement* to a well-functioning bureaucracy. By contrast, the Eastern Cape cases in chapter 9 explore horizontal governance's role as a potential *substitute* in a setting where hierarchy is weak.

8.2 Research Context and Methodology

This section introduces the research methodology used for the Western Cape school-level case studies. Our point of departure is the finding in the education literature that the quality of school-level leadership is an important proximate determinant of school performance. The school-level processes of principal selection are used as a lens through which to refract local governance dynamics, and thereby gain insight into the broader multi-stakeholder contexts within which the principal is embedded. This section provides some background on our sample schools; on the principal selection process in the Western Cape; and on our research methodology. Sections 8.3–8.5 delve in detail into the school-specific processes. Section 8.6 concludes.

8.2.1 *The Sample*

Our school-specific analysis builds on a prior research programme (the SPADE initiative[1]), which studied a stratified sample of fourteen Western Cape schools in relation to their *internal* governance dynamics and instructional regimes (Hoadley and Galant, 2015). For the present study we selected four schools from the SPADE sample. The schools fall within two of the Western Cape's eight educational districts. Though the sample is small, in-depth depiction of school-level governance within these schools may be suggestive of broader patterns that prevail in schools located within lower-income communities in the Western Cape. The present study thus provides a framework and direction for the exploration of the findings in a larger sample. The intention in the sampling is to explore positive possibilities, rather than to confirm findings of dysfunction reported widely.

The four schools that constitute our cases were initially selected for the SPADE research based on their performance on the Western Cape Education Department's (WCED) systemic tests in the early 2000s. Two schools were selected as 'above average' performers within their socio-economic profile; both schools had achieved an overall mean for the period that was at least 5 per cent above the predicted value, given their profile. These two schools were matched with two schools that had achieved 5 per cent below the expected value.

Two matched pairs, each with a high- and low-performing school, were thus established, one set in a former mixed-race area (coloured, in the South African vernacular), and the other located in a black township. Within each set are two differentially performing schools situated in the same community, about 2 km apart. Both communities can be described as urban, economically depressed, and affected by a range of social problems, such as violence, substance abuse, absent or young parents, and illiteracy. Each pair is thus similar in demographic composition and general functionality, but with different levels of academic performance.

The first matched pair is located in the settlement of Brandonville,[2] approximately 30 km outside the city of Cape Town. The broader community surrounding these schools originated in the late 1980s and is home to 25,364 residents, according to the 2001 national census. Of the total population, 82 per cent are Afrikaans-speaking, 94 per cent are coloured, and 44 per cent

[1] The SPADE (Schools Performing Above Demographic Expectations) project is interested in the factors that account for primary schools in disadvantaged communities performing above expectations. The focus of the SPADE project was on internal governance, pedagogy and home-school instructional practices and their contribution to differential performance.

[2] The name of the area is a pseudonym, given that it is a relatively small area, which may render the schools recognizable. The information, is however, provided for the actual area.

of the working age population are unemployed (Census, 2001). In the early 1990s the community's population began to expand, necessitating the establishment of additional primary schools in the area, including School 1 and School A. Local principals were requested to select particular teachers for transfer to these schools. School 1 was established in 1993 and currently serves 1,321 learners, drawn from its immediate community. School A opened in 1995 and provides for 1,204 learners. The majority of School A's learners reside in the local community, and about 200 of the learners are isiXhosa-speaking. Both schools offer Afrikaans and English as mediums of instruction. The broader community continues to grow steadily, with the construction of local housing projects.

The second matched pair is located in Khayelitsha. Khayelitsha Township was established in 1983, built under the principle of racial segregation executed by the apartheid government. The government envisaged Khayelitsha (meaning 'new home') as a relocation point to accommodate all 'legal' black residents of the Cape Peninsula in one new, purpose-built and easily controlled township. The government classified people as legal if they had already lived in the area for ten years. Due to the immense influx of people, it is the second biggest black township in South Africa after Soweto in Johannesburg, with a population of between 400,000 and 450,000 people. Khayelitsha is located approximately 35 km outside the city of Cape Town. Residents are 97 per cent isiXhosa-speaking, 99 per cent are black, and about 47 per cent of the working age population are unemployed (Census, 2001). Around 60 per cent of households are classified as shacks, predominantly constructed out of corrugated iron.

The two Khayelitsha Schools are located about 2 km apart. School 2 was established in 2000. The staff was largely made up of teachers who were declared excess in other schools where student numbers had declined. In 2012, School 2 had 1,175 learners. The entire student body is isiXhosa-speaking and the school has had a good reputation in the local community. School B was started in a community centre in 1991, without the formal permission of the provincial education department. In 1993 it was formally opened by the provincial department, a principal formally appointed and teachers paid. In 2012 it had 1,124 learners, all of whom were isiXhosa-speaking, residing locally. Both schools offer isiXhosa (from Grade R to Grade 3) and English (from Grades 4 to 7) as mediums of instruction.

Table 8.1 details the annual average (literacy and numeracy) scores obtained by each school for the Western Cape systemic tests between 2002 and 2013.[3] The SPADE research identified School 1 and School 2 as relatively high

[3] The scores comprise the percentage of children who achieve a passing score, averaging across annual WCED, externally administered literacy and numeracy systemic tests.

Table 8.1. Systemic Tests—Percentage of Cohort that Meets the Grade 3 Proficiency Standard

	School 1	School A	School 2	School B
2002	66	41	44	31
2004	60	39	54	33
2006	61	47	50	47
2008	61	53	55	45
2011	61	36	53	46
2012	62	36	33	44
2013	49	28	27	45

performers, and School A and School B as relatively low performers, relative to the median for their relevant demographic cohort. In practice, as the table suggests, the performance patterns turned out to be messier than those intended in the initial research design and school selection processes.

As Table 8.2 highlights, there turned out to be a strong correlation between turnover in leadership and school-level performance over time. (To disguise identities, but facilitate narrative flow in subsequent sections, the table includes a pseudonym for each school's principal during each period.) All four schools in our sample experienced a turnover in leadership (i.e. the school principal) over the period studied, with noteworthy consequences:

- In both of the hitherto better-performing schools (Schools 1 and 2) the change in principal resulted in subsequent performance declines.
- In the relatively low-performing School A, the change in principal was associated with a worsening of subsequent performance.
- The interaction between performance and leadership in School B is complex; we postpone discussion until section 8.5.

Consistent with the above patterns, the analysis which follows focuses centrally on the interactions between leadership, leadership change, and trends in performance in each of the schools highlighted in Table 8.2.

8.2.2 *The Principal Selection Process—De Jure and De Facto*

The South African Schools Act of 1996 and the Employment of Educators Act of 1998 specify an elaborate process for the appointment of principals. In Table 8.3, we use the public governance typology introduced in Chapter 1 to characterize the official, de jure ('ideal') process of principal selection. As per the discussion in Chapter 1, any specific governance arrangement is likely to be a hybrid combination of the four ideal types defined by the cells; we capture this heuristically in Table 8.3, and in subsequent tables in the chapter, by allocating 100 points across the four cells. As per the table:

Table 8.2. Governance Episodes Across Four Schools, 2002–14

	Earlier period	Change in principal	Later period
School 1	Relatively strong performance *Smit*	2010	Declining performance *Jooste*
School A	Relatively weak performance *Arendse*	2006–08	Continuing low-level equilibrium *Poole*
School 2	Relatively strong performance *Komape*	2007–10; 2011	Declining performance *Various*
School B	Mixed performance *Somana*	2009–11	Average performance *Rala*

Table 8.3. Governance of Principal Selection—The Policy 'Ideal'

Appointment of principal x		
Hierarchical		50%
Negotiated		50%
	Personalized	Impersonal

Source: authors

- Looking down the columns, in its official, de jure ('ideal') form) the entire process is impersonal—decisions are made following formal rules which apply impartially to all candidates, with no scope for more personalized deals.
- Looking across the rows, within the broadly impersonal framework there is a mix of hierarchical and negotiated processes. Higher political and bureaucratic levels set the parameters for appointments, provide some resources, and formally are responsible for actual appointments. Much of the actual decision-making is at the lower levels, in a negotiated form involving the SGB (which formally is responsible for principal selection) and the district office of the bureaucratic hierarchy.

We characterize this 'ideal' form in the table as 50 per cent impersonal/hierarchical and 50 per cent impersonal/negotiated.

The Western Cape process for appointing a principal formally involves the following steps:

- An interview panel is constituted, consisting of the SGB, a district official and a union representative. The district official and the union representative are intended to serve only as observers. The district official observing on the interview panel acts as advisor and representative of the WCED. The district official can call the SGB to order, but cannot make recommendations on their behalf. The SGB may co-opt additional members onto the interview committee, should they require additional expertise. Where the SGB in general lacks capacity, it is the district officer's role to provide support.

- The School Management Team[4] (SMT) defines criteria according to which the SGB assesses applicants.
- An advertisement is posted by the Western Cape Education Department (WCED). The advertisement contains information relating to: i) key results areas and duties; ii) job description; and iii) job competencies and qualifications. Schools are able to add items to the job description of the principal (according to the school's needs); however, the addition cannot be inconsistent with higher-level selection criteria negotiated and agreed upon at the national level.
- The WCED accepts applications, and screens the applications for educators who have misconduct charges against them, those who have been fired, and those who have retired due to poor health. It also indicates which applicants have the relevant qualifications. The applications are then put into a sealed envelope and sent to the school. This is done on the basis of a collective agreement with the unions to ensure no names are added or taken out the envelope.
- The SGB sets a date when the envelope will be opened. Unions are invited to attend. An initial screening takes place where the SGB shortlists five to six candidates. This list is sent to the WCED. Only established school principals and deputy principals are eligible to apply for principal posts. Currently equity and representation criteria are taken into account, but only at the early stages of the appointment process. At the shortlist stage, expertise, qualification and experience are the primary criteria for selection.
- The interview committee then conducts interviews. They may give assignments to candidates to complete, and they also make use of competency tests (paid for by the WCED if conducted by an external agency).
- Once the interviews are completed, the SGB provides a list of three candidates (in order of preference) to the provincial head of education. The provincial head of education makes their final selection from this list, although they are not compelled to select the SGB's most preferred candidate.

In practice, formal processes may or may not play out in the ways intended by those who write the formal rules. A variety of de facto alternatives are possible, including:

[4] The SMT consists of the heads of department, the deputy principals and the principal (or one fulfilling this role).

- A high quality de facto process that follows the de jure rules, with robust developmentally oriented decision-making on the part of the SGB, aligned with the WCED, and resulting in the selection of a well-qualified and committed principal.
- A process that follows the de jure rules, but that de facto is captured by influential, non-developmental factions—resulting in the selection of a principal who lacks the commitment and/or skill to prioritize good educational outcomes.
- A contested process, in which conflict among stakeholders entrusted with decision-making responsibilities results in a failure to agree on a candidate.
- A process where decision-making is inconsistent with the formal rules laid out above—perhaps because school-level stakeholders act outside the formal structures (this could be for developmental or predatory reasons), or perhaps because WCED intervention supersedes the formal rules. (In these instances, a variety of alternative possible outcomes are possible, each paralleling those listed above.)

Understanding which of the above processes of principal selection played out in each of our schools—and why—is a central goal of the present paper. Since these processes do not play out in a vacuum, we also examine the processes of decision-making that prevailed within each of the school in the period preceding the selection of a new principal—as shaped by the organizational culture established by the 'period 1' principal.

8.2.3 *Research Methodology*

Our research method is what George and Bennett (2005) refer to as 'process tracing'. Process tracing focuses on a very specific set of decisions. It 'attempts to trace the links between possible causes and observed outcomes' (p. 4). Often used to test the hypotheses of a theory of causation, process tracing considers the sequence and values of intervening variables in a case 'to see whether the causal process a theory hypothesizes or implies in a case is in fact evident in the sequence and values of the intervening variables in that case' (p. 6) The focus in gathering data, then, is on sequential processes within a particular historical case, not on correlations of data across cases. The aim is to achieve 'high internal validity and good historical explanations of particular cases versus making generalizations that apply to broad populations' (p. 22).

To learn about these decision processes, semi-structured, in-depth interviews were conducted with a number of key informants in each of the schools. A total of eleven in-depth interviews were conducted across the four schools, lasting between two and four-and-a-half hours each. These interviews were supplementary to the in-depth knowledge the researchers already had of each of the schools as a result of prior rounds of interviews and engagement in the context of the earlier SPADE research. Detailed field notes were kept by at least two interviewees on each occasion. These notes were integrated and a comprehensive record of each interview constituted the data for analysis. Responses between different informants were triangulated, and contradictions in accounts were identified, and examined further in subsequent interviews.

The interviews aimed at identifying dominant and influential stakeholders in the school, and mapping stakeholders in relation to the achievement of developmental goals (in the case of the school, improved student learning). In considering 'multi-stakeholder governance', we considered those setting the goals of school management and overseeing performance and the recruitment and management of staff in the school (school management team (SMT); school governing board (SGB); district administration). To understand the workings of the accountability channel, we were also interested in the existence of predatory and trumping coalitions and how these played out in the history of the schools. Section 8.3 focuses on these leadership dynamics in Schools 1 and 2, where performance initially was relatively strong. Section 8.4 seeks to account for the consistently weak performance in School A, notwithstanding a shift in leadership. Section 8.5 explores some of the more paradoxical leadership dynamics that underpinned School B's performance patterns over time.

8.3 Schools 1 and 2—Brittle Strengths

While Schools 1 and 2 had been included in the initial SPADE sample on the basis of their exemplary performance, as Table 8.3 signals both schools have seen their systemic test results decline radically subsequent to 2011. In both schools, a likely contributor to this decline was the replacement of an effective principal with a weak successor. The failure to appoint strong successors did not occur in a vacuum. Some of the reasons may be found in the ways in which, in the earlier period, the successful principals went about the tasks of school governance. So it is there that we begin.

8.3.1 *Two High-Performing Principals in Action*

Both Schools 1 and 2's episodes of relatively strong performance were characterized by a disproportionate emphasis on hierarchical modes of governance. Further, as Table 8.4 signals, using the heuristic device introduced earlier, in

Table 8.4. 'Intertwined', Predominantly Hierarchical Governance

Hierarchical	60–70	
Negotiated	0–10	30
	Personalized	Impersonal

Source: authors

both schools the hierarchical pattern took a very specific form, in which the personalized and impersonal dimensions of hierarchy were wholly intertwined. Each case was characterized by a principal who personally was strongly committed to achieving strong performance in their school—and leveraged the impersonal-hierarchical framework of rules provided by the WCED as a way of safeguarding the educational mission of the school from efforts at capture.

For School 1, interviewees attributed its steady and relatively good performance prior to 2013 to the principal at the time, Mr Smit, and his 'systems'. Smit was well-liked, respected, and extremely vigilant with respect to attendance and latecoming. He monitored teachers and 'drove performance'. Interviewees reported that:

> Mr Smit had a vision for the school... He knew what was going on in the classes and knew the curriculum. Teachers also did not have to fill in forms all the time, compared to now.

Smit concentrated on two issues: the appointment of strong staff, particularly in management positions, and the establishment of strong bureaucratic systems in the school. He sought to promote expertise in those managing the school, and was described as unafraid of challenges to his own authority. He developed and relied on clear systems and principles, which had bite at the level of staff appointment and management, particularly in relation to teacher performance. He set up school-level processes to ensure rigorous appointment processes, co-opting the circuit (WCED) in this regard to support decisions taken in the school. He also established a strong management committee (SMT) within the school, allowing for the establishment of rule-setting. He also addressed staff underperformance. Teachers were dealt with individually, and where problems arose, individual strategies were developed to deal with these. Smit developed strong administrative procedures for all activities in the school, and a filing system that kept a careful record of policies, decisions and processes. He also had a close relationship with the circuit office and with a professional network of teachers in the Brandonville area. According to interviewees, under Smit the SGB appeared to be entirely compliant with respect to the principal's directives.

In School 2, paralleling Mr Smit, Mrs Komape also laid down explicit rules and procedures for resolving disputes and making decisions. She used these to deal with a number of inherited disputes and contestations around teacher contract posts. She also inherited an SGB heavily involved in local politics and with strong influence over the former principal. Komape disciplined the SGB, thwarting a number of attempts by the SGB to capture school funds. In her words: 'If you create a space for your SGB to mess with you, you will lose control as principal'. Slowly the SGB was brought in line, and co-operated with the rules laid down by Komape.

Mrs Komape actively pursued attempts to make processes transparent. She spent a great deal of energy educating other school actors in legitimate processes and rules. She put in place strict observation of school hours—for both students and teachers; in her words, instilling 'a culture of diligence' in the school. She took the same transparent, bureaucratically driven approach to teacher underperformance. 'Progressive discipline' as recommended by the Department was followed. The tabling of a systematic record of the teachers' conduct, as well as regular meetings with the teachers ('the teachers were welcome to bring their union representatives to the meeting so that they didn't feel they were being victimized') provided a systematic basis on which to address underperformance and come to a mutual agreement on an improvement plan for the situation.

Mrs Komape acknowledged that there were risks associated with taking a strong developmental path: 'You do not know what will happen tomorrow.' She said it was always a possibility that unions or staff members could use parents to initiate an investigation of 'mismanagement of school funds' against a principal. It is for this reason that Mrs Komape used established bureaucratic processes to perform her role. As she put it, she did her tasks 'according to the requirements of government circulars'. According to her, this limited the points where fault could be found. She considers herself lucky to have never experienced such intimidation.

Again paralleling Mr Smit, Mrs Komape drove a deliberate, merit-based staff appointment process in the school. She invested substantial time and effort in educating the SGB in interview processes, including assisting in preparing questions and suitable answers ahead of time, candidate scoring procedures and minute keeping. Her own records of appointment processes were impeccable, anticipating the possibility of contestation of an appointment. In these ways, she attempted to safeguard the process from capture. While unions were a real threat to rule-bound school-level governance, Mrs Komape argued that they could only have a negative effect if the space was created for them to capture the decision-making processes.

The recruitment of an HOD position offers a striking example of how Mrs Komape leveraged formal rules—including the backing of the WCED hierarchy—to prevail in the face of an attempt at the capture. The position drew the interest of a branch chairperson of the South African Democratic Teachers Union (SADTU). The successful candidate would be required to teach music at the school. The branch chairperson was escorted to his interview by his vice chairperson. The union observer selected by the candidate to be part of the interview panel was the SADTU branch treasurer. In anticipation, the principal established one of the interview questions as requiring that the candidate play the melodica and 'teach' the panel a musical piece. It became evident that the branch chairperson had never been involved in music. He could neither play the instrument nor read the music piece. He ended up singing the piece incorrectly. Since the criteria and the questions were carefully established, the non-appointment of the SADTU candidate could not be contested.

8.3.2 *Principal Succession—Things Fall Apart*

In their efforts to achieve results, both Mr Smit and Mrs Komape relied on a combination of charismatic leadership and formal rules. But in neither case was the strengthened governance sustained once they exited. In both cases, things rapidly fell apart.

In 2009, Mr Smit retired from School 1 and Mr Jooste, who had been one of the deputy principals at School 1, was appointed acting principal, and subsequently principal. There were strong indications across the interviews of discontent about Jooste's appointment. At the time of the interviews, it was clear that the school had become split between those who supported and those who opposed Mr Jooste's principalship. Several argued that he had not been the best candidate in the application pool for the principal position. Rather, as Table 8.5 illustrates, the outcome appears to have been the result of personalized deal-making involving Mr Jooste, the SGB and circuit-level staff within the WCED.

According to interviewees, three SGB members were actively courted by Mr Jooste while he was acting principal. He granted rights to one member to sell food on the school property, and supported another's career progression in the school. In the interviews, it was claimed that Jooste intimidated some members of the SGB and co-opted others, such that they 'would never go against the principal'.

In addition, Jooste could rely on a historically established professional network in the Brandonville area. Jakobs, the circuit manager, had been a principal at one of the primary schools in the Brandonville area prior to taking

Table 8.5. Predominantly, Personalized Deal-Driven Governance

Hierarchical	45	10
Negotiated	45	0
	Personalized	Impersonal

Source: *authors*

up the job as circuit manager, and he had been friends with Mr Jooste for years. One interviewee claimed that Jakobs persuaded the SGB to appoint Jooste, another claimed that Jakobs influenced the interview process by 'assisting' the interview committee to craft questions that would favour Jooste.

An HOD, as union observer, wrote a report on the appointment process, arguing that two of the external candidates were better qualified for the post. Knowledge of Mr Jooste within the tight teacher professional network in the Brandonville area also prompted the report: 'We came together from [one of the more established primary schools in the Brandonville area]. I know his record. I know what he is like.' The report that was submitted by the HOD was never consulted, as this happened only in the case of a dispute, and none was formally declared in this appointment.

Interviews consistently described Mr Jooste's leadership at School 1 once he became principal as 'hands off', taking no action in relation to increasing underperformance and absenteeism of teachers. He was reported to comply strictly with bureaucratic procedure, but without consultation and negotiation with other staff. Relying on the systems and good reputation of the school established by Smit, he was not perceived as contributing to developing the school. Rather, he undermined it by eliminating strong teachers who challenged anti-developmental practices within the school. He was reported to have co-opted both the circuit and the SGB in supporting his decisions in the school. The negative consequences for the educational mission of the school were reflected in the declining test scores shown in Table 8.3.

School 2's process of principal selection was even more fragmented than that of School 1, along lines suggested by Table 8.6. In 2007, following seven years of strong management, Mrs Komape was seconded to WCED district-level administration to provide governance support across a number of schools. As an interim measure, School 2's SGB and principal made a decision for the school's two deputy principals to alternate in performing principal responsibilities on a quarterly basis. The deputies were aligned with the two phases in the school—a female deputy in the foundation phase (Grades R to 3) and a male deputy in the intermediate phase one (Grades 4 to 7). This was a temporary solution. In 2009, Komape was appointed formally at the district and vacated her position at the school.

Following Mrs Komape's formal appointment, the SGB held an internal application process for appointing an 'acting' principal, and the female

Table 8.6. Fragmented Governance

Hierarchical	10	30
Negotiated	60	0
	Personalized	Impersonal

Source: authors

deputy principal was appointed for the rest of 2009. The appointment process resulted in divisions in the staff, based on vested interests of individuals in line for promotion in the different phases. If the deputy principal from the intermediate phase was appointed as principal, this would open up promotion posts (potentially a deputy and HOD position) in that phase. The same would apply if the foundation phase deputy were to be appointed. A new SGB was appointed in 2010 that supposedly favoured a male candidate.

The conflict between the acting principal and the other deputy worsened, and came to a head when the acting principal (the female foundation phase deputy) reported the situation to the district office. There, she discovered that the male deputy had been compiling a case against her. The case was around alleged mismanagement of funds. The story given by the then acting principal (female deputy) was as follows:

> The school's choir had the opportunity to travel to Joburg for a competition. The SMT went to the school's book supplier and got 10 per cent of their payment back for books. This was done 'behind my back'. The SMT then used this money to buy air tickets for their travel.
>
> When I found out, I did not report this, even though I now see I should have. I was afraid that reporting them would have implications for their jobs ('their bread'). I also felt that I would start a battle that I had no chance of winning.

The district intervened in 2010, in order to address the conflict at the school and drive the appointment of a permanent principal. The acting female head applied for the post and the circuit manager, together with the SGB, managed the appointment process. After the interview process, the SGB declared a dispute, saying they had not been adequately trained to appoint the appropriate candidate. Some interviewees claimed that the SGB had been progressively captured by the male deputy. There were also claims that SADTU had become involved, and that the male deputy, one of the HODs, and the SADTU branch chairperson who had been an observer in this round, were influencing the SGB. The female deputy also stated that there were rumours at the time that the SMT had purchased a cell phone and groceries for the SGB chairperson, in order to receive information on the interviews.

During this process, conflict between the male deputy and the female head worsened, until finally they agreed to the appointment of a new acting principal, who stepped in for two years from 2010 to the end of 2011. The female deputy again applied for the job when it was advertised in 2011, but lost out to an external candidate, Mrs Madolo. In 2012, the new principal took over. From 2009 until 2012, then, a failed principal selection process resulted in School 2 experiencing troubled and disruptive governance and, as per Table 8.3, a collapse in its hitherto exemplary scores on systemic tests. As of the time of our interviews, there was little evidence that the new principal had been able to reverse the decline.

8.4 School A—Persistent Low-Level Equilibrium

In School A, as the systemic test scores in Table 8.3 show, things went from bad to worse, with a leadership transition exacerbating rather than reversing an earlier period of relatively weak performance.

The roots of School A's weaknesses can be traced to the way in which it was started. Interviewees gave two reasons given for teachers coming to the school at its start-up. One was that there were promises of opportunities for promotion. The other was that principals in neighbouring schools used the opportunity to rid themselves of teachers regarded as 'lazy' or as 'troublemakers'. As one interviewee put it, 'The problem cases landed at [School A]'.

Under the first principal, Arendse, there was a series of contestations around promotion posts at the school. Leaks from selection processes, suspicions of undue influence of the SGB, and relations of patronage were reported across the interviews. For example, in 1996 the appointment of an HOD was contested. The appointment process was carried out a second time and a different person was then appointed. Around 2005, a friend of Arendse was appointed into an HOD position. The process of shortlisting and interviews was undertaken without informing a potential candidate on the staff who had indicated interest in the position.

More generally, interviewees claimed that the best person for the job was not always appointed. Arendse had strong personal connections to his management team. Appointments were made according to family and friendship networks. One member, who had a significant drinking problem, remained in his post despite this problem, as he was a rugby referee who supplied tickets to major games to Arendse. Attempted capture of the SGB by potential appointees to posts occurred regularly. Interviewees pointed out parents' vulnerability towards influence, given their low literacy levels and poverty. Suggestions that bribes could be paid (though no direct evidence or cases were reported) were made. In sum, Arendse's approach to leadership was disproportionately personalized, anchored in horizontal deal-making along the lines illustrated by Table 8.5. In Mr Arendse's case, these deals had little developmental purpose—but rather (paralleling the selection of Jooste as School 1 principal) were predominantly centred around individual objectives.

In 2006, after twelve years of tenure, Arendse was removed following the bringing of criminal charges against him. Following Arendse's removal, the WCED played a central role in the principal appointment process which followed. It appointed a circuit manager, Mr Damonse, to serve as acting principal. Further, because of the school's history of contested appointments and a dysfunctional SGB, the WCED intervened to oversee the appointment of new deputies and a permanent principal. The WCED organized and chaired the interview process, including some parents in the process.

But the WCED's direct involvement did little to transform the prevailing culture in the school. School A, like School 1, is in an area characterized by longstanding personalized ties between WCED circuit staff and school staff. Given these ties, the likelihood was high from the first that the new principal would be hired from within School A's existing staff. At the time of Arendse's removal, there were two deputies—Poole and Arendse's nephew. The latter died of a heart attack shortly after the aforementioned criminal investigations of his uncle. A strong relationship developed between Damonse and Poole, which had historical roots, but which strengthened during Damonse's acting headship, with Damonse mentoring Poole to take over. In sum, School A's process of principal selection was overwhelmingly personalized—along the lines of Table 8.5, though more hierarchical.

Poole took over the school in 2008. He soon faced problems with the SGB and community over alleged misuse of school funds. An audit was held, and the main 'troublemakers' who had instigated the inquiry in the school left. The teachers involved in the incident were eventually charged with inciting and were fined. Two 'camps' have endured in the school, those for and those against the principal. In 2010 there was conflict between Poole and the community over the appointment of so-called 'mommy teachers'—parents who were brought in to supervise classes, given the high teacher absentee rate. Parents blockaded the entrance to the school and demanded the removal of the principal. They demanded to know who approved the employment of temporary educators whom they believed to be unqualified. A new SGB was appointed in 2012, with careful oversight from the principal. From interviews, it appears that the SGB currently functions to rubber stamp the principal's decisions.

Poole's management style is described at times as divisive, at other times as autocratic, but never as focused on issues of instruction. Significant problems of teacher absenteeism and large classes remain unaddressed in the school. There is distrust between management and teachers. Of the teachers, the principal says: 'They mainly come to earn a salary. This is their main driver.'

8.5 Unexpected Resilience—The Case of School B

Compared with the other Western Cape case study schools, School B is an outlier. Its patterns of governance have been participatory and personalized—along the lines illustrated in Table 8.5. But unlike the other instances of

Table 8.5-style governance, noted earlier, in the case of School B, participatory governance turns out to have been a source of resilience.

The school began as a community centre with seven 'volunteer' teachers. It consisted of ten rooms, no blackboards, and each teacher had a class of 160 learners. Mrs Somana began her tenure as the first principal of the school at this time. In 1993, the school was opened formally by the WCED, and they began providing teaching posts and funding.

Somana served as principal of School B for nearly twenty years. Interviewees repeatedly referenced her kind-hearted character towards students and their parents, and her positive impact on the community. Her management style was informal, and oriented towards a culture of 'looking after one's own'. Interviewees asserted that during her tenure as principal, the filling of promotion or senior posts (e.g. HOD, deputy principal) did not often follow bureaucratic procedure. In general, external candidates were not appointed. One interviewee put it thus in relation to an advertised HOD post:

> Some of the external applicants didn't attend their interview... they assumed an internal candidate would receive it. Appointments are up to the SGB and external candidates don't usually receive posts.

Viewed through a lens of rule-boundedness as a desirable pattern of governance, School B's relatively low scores in the initial systemic tests are unsurprising. Indeed, using the lens of the typology framework, School B's personalized and participatory governance patterns superficially are similar to the School A pattern. In School A, as we have seen, this pattern was associated with a persistent low-level equilibrium of mediocre performance. But what happened in School B once the initial systemic test results were released was very different, and within two years the school showed significant improvement in its test scores.

These test score gains were attributed in the interviews to the instituting of a number of developmentally oriented strategies: an afterschool programme, NGO involvement, home visits by Somana when learners had been absent, and support structures for orphans and vulnerable children (initiated by a parent). Although tentative, the data suggest that Somana's personalized leadership, embedded positively in the community, may have provided a 'floor' of sorts, constructively responsive at key moments.

Informality also had another consequence. In the later stages of Mrs Somana's tenure (2006–09) issues of financial mismanagement were brought to light. Teachers began to notice the poor condition of the school (e.g. no toilet paper, leaking taps, etc.); some did not receive salaries; and the prospective Grade R facility was at a standstill. Eventually a service provider and a number of teachers reported non-payment of funds to the WCED. The capturing of school funds threatened the school's developmental stability. In early 2010 the WCED launched a formal investigation. Department officials conducted an audit as well as a formal Whole School Evaluation. A few months later, Mrs Somana submitted a letter to the SGB and WCED for 'early retirement'. From the interviews, it did not emerge clearly who had been implicated in the financial mismanagement.

In selecting a successor to Mrs Somana, School B's legacy of strong community involvement and a developmentally oriented SGB turned out to be a source of resilience. Following Somana's departure, the SGB requested the WCED's assistance in selecting an acting principal so as not to negatively impact on the school's performance. Shortly thereafter, the department appointed a 'caretaker' principal—a coloured man who was at the time awaiting the outcome of his application for a permanent post elsewhere. An SGB member described the situation thus:

> He was a good guy. Things improved, but the teachers had a negative perception of him. They thought he wouldn't understand the challenges of the school. [The SGB] feared that his life was in danger. You see, he was good, but it was a cultural issue.

These serious threats in the broader school community led to the caretaker principal's departure; he took a permanent post at another school. The SGB decided to appoint one of the deputies as acting principal. After deliberation amongst parents and the SGB, the most senior or long-standing deputy, Mr Mayila, was appointed in January 2011.

Over the next few months, the permanent principal post was advertised publicly with clear criteria determined by the SGB, which focused on the development of the school. Because Mr Mayila, the acting principal at the time, was a candidate for the permanent position, a local high school principal oversaw the appointment process. Another internal staff member (an HOD) was considered for the post, as well as two external candidates, one male and one female. The primary stakeholders throughout the process were SGB members, the local high school principal, a union representative, and the circuit manager (the latter two as observers only). The process strictly followed the WCED's established policies. The appointment process was described as 'harmonious' and 'professional', with 'no discrepancies'. 'By the book' transparent processes (which closely approximated the principal selection 'ideal' of Table 8.3) allowed for the two most suitable (high-scoring) candidates to be shortlisted. The WCED made the final decision and offered Mr Rala, an external candidate, the principalship.

8.6 Patterns and Implications

Relative to other provinces in South Africa, public schools in the Western Cape are well-governed, and generally show better results. As Chapter 4 detailed, by and large the WCED hierarchy delivers effectively on the things hierarchies are expected to deliver. However, there are continuing challenges to improvement, including the hugely difficult socio-economic setting faced by many children in the Western Cape, a delayed effective curriculum regime, and continuing weaknesses in teachers' instructional capacity.

Might there also be some 'micro-governance' reasons? In this final section, we draw on our school-level case studies to reflect more broadly on the ways in which de facto hierarchical and horizontal governance arrangements might help explain why the effort to improve outcomes continues to be enormously challenging.

8.6.1 *Hierarchical Governance*

The WCED's well-functioning hierarchy is an important asset. Getting textbooks delivered; ensuring that teaching posts are filled with teachers who meet a minimum set of criteria; ensuring an optimal balance between personnel and non-personnel expenditure; tracking how schools use resources (including trends in performance); getting funding to the right places at the right times; pro-actively trying to fill leadership positions with the right people for the job—in contrast to many other departments of education in South Africa and elsewhere, the WCED does all of these things well. These are important strengths.

The focus of our research, though, has been on narrower micro-governance concerns. Our interest has been to understand at school-level (along lines suggested by Figure 8.1) both the potential benefits and the limits of a relatively well-performing hierarchy. We have focused especially on the position of principal—both how principals choose to exercise their authority, and the processes of principal selection.

Our case studies identified three distinct ways through which principals exercise their authority—each with different implications as to the influence of hierarchy on school performance:

i. Developmentally oriented governance through top-down leadership, underpinned by rules—illustrated by the leadership styles of Smit in School 1 and Komape in School 2.

Both principals gave strong emphasis to putting in place a framework of rule-boundedness within their schools. In doing so, both benefited hugely from confidence that the rules would indeed be enforced at higher levels of the WCED's bureaucratic ladder. Both used this platform of credible rules as a key buttress against pressures to act in ways that were inconsistent with the school's educational mission.

ii. 'Isomorphic mimicry'—the use of leadership authority to establish a seemingly desirable form (in this case hierarchical governance), but without the substance (accountability for performance) which the form is intended to deliver.

As recent work has explored globally, this pre-occupation with form, rather than the pursuit of concrete development results, is especially prevalent where 'entities are highly dependent on getting greater legitimacy from external constituencies in which 'best practices' are highly defined' (Andrews, 2013; Andrews, Pritchett, and Woolcock, 2012). In our case studies, School 1 under Jooste, and School A under Poole provide two examples of low-level equilibria of rule-following mediocrity along these lines.

iii. Participatory leadership—in which a principal governs the school by actively fostering a sense of participation and teamwork, underpinned by shared commitment to a framework of rules which supports co-operative decision-making.

While none of the schools in our sample provided an unequivocal example of 'good practice' along these lines, the participatory approach through which School B was governed (though without formal rules) provided a partial illustration. (School A1 in the Eastern Cape case study in Chapter 9 provides a good example of how participatory governance can work.)

Note that both (i) and (ii) are wholly consistent with institutional arrangements where schools are embedded within strong organizational hierarchies. Only (iii) requires for its effectiveness the presence of a 'zone of autonomy' at school level, which principals potentially can use to motivate teachers.

Given the centrality of school-level leadership in shaping outcomes, the process of principal selection offers one seemingly straightforward way of improving quality. Here our case studies are sobering (although it is important to qualify what follows by noting both that our sample size is too small to serve as a basis for generalization and that, as detailed below in our final sub-section, a variety of recent initiatives are under way within the WCED to improve principal selection). In three of the four cases in this paper (School B was the exception), the process of principal selection turned out to be retrogressive. In both of the initially high-performing schools (Schools 1 and 2), leadership transitions resulted in a clear subsequent decline in performance. In a third (School A), a change in leadership did nothing to disrupt a low-performance equilibrium. Though the specifics of why principal selection was so difficult varied across School 1, 2 and A, the case studies suggest three underlying patterns.

First, a key driver fuelling contestation in all three cases was the presence of in-house candidates for principal (i.e. from the incumbent deputy principals). In the culture prevailing in the schools, length of service and the occupation of a particular post are regarded as a natural conduit to promotion. Over 55 per cent of principals nationally are promoted from within schools (Wills, 2015). Further, when an internal candidate is promoted, it opens up a whole set of potential promotion posts below this position. In School 1, the presence of a well-networked internal candidate resulted in complaints (which were never formally followed through on) that better-qualified external candidates were passed over. In School 2, contestation for the top position between two competing deputies resulted in the process dragging on for almost four years.

Second, in two of the cases (both cases were in the Brandonville area, where, as noted, there were close linkages between school staff and officials in the WCED circuit office), the relevant WCED officials appear to have abetted an insider-driven and only partially competitive process. In one case, interviewees suggested that the circuit staff-person steered the SGB interview process towards a preferred, insider candidate. In the other, the circuit staff actively mentored an internal candidate, and then took direct leadership of the interview process, which resulted in the mentee's selection.

Third, in neither School 1 nor the 2007–10 contestation in School 2 did the SGB function as an impartial judge and overseer, with the best interests of the school at heart. Instead, the SGB became a focal point for lobbying by insider candidates, with multiple allegations from interviewees of efforts by candidates and their supporters to informally influence the SGB decision processes.

8.6.2 *Horizontal Governance*

As the evidence on principal selection signals, in three of our four case study schools (School B again being the exception), the patterns we observed provided little evidence that horizontal governance played a positive role. On the contrary, in these three schools, SGBs (school governing bodies) more often were sites for political contestation and personalized favour than they were part of the solution (though we feel it necessary to note that, contrary to a familiar narrative, we found very little evidence that contestation and the pursuit of favour were driven by teachers unions).[5] On occasion, developmentally oriented principals turned to non-governmental organizations outside their immediate communities for support, but mostly the involvement of these outside organizations was quite superficial. Indeed, in some of our cases, any positive potential of horizontal governance was confounded by the

[5] Although more present as a potential agent in the Khayelitsha context than in the other area studied, in none of our sample schools were unions found to be instrumental in contributing to or predating on school resources. In one case, School 2, attempted capture of the appointment process of an HOD was thwarted by commitment to official procedure.

strength of predatory influence networks. In such circumstances, neither the motivational nor the informational rationales for horizontal governance arrangements can have much, if any, positive effect.

While we recognize that our sample is small, and thus that our findings could be an artifact of sample selection, broader research (for the specific Western Cape demographic profile which is our focus) suggests that the pattern of the principal driving school performance, with relatively limited constructive input from the SGB, communities, or other non-governmental actors is a more general one (Hoadley, Christie, and Ward, 2009). In relatively affluent and stable communities with high social capital, negotiated governance could indeed be prevalent, and associated with strong performance. (Indeed, in such settings this may be the normatively preferred mode of governance.) However, where social capital is weaker and conflict over resources is acute, the absence of strong hierarchical governance could render a school especially vulnerable to predation. These patterns accord with recent work on management in resilient schools in South Africa: performance is driven from within, without reliance or support from external agents (Chikoko, Naicker, and Mthiyane, 2015).

Yet, for all of these evident weaknesses in horizontal accountability, our research cautions against focusing on hierarchical performance measures to the exclusion of the development of more sustained, horizontal relations between stakeholders at the school and community level. For reasons set out in the introduction to this chapter, the ability of any bureaucracy to exert strong control at the micro level is inevitably limited. Our results point to the real danger that surface compliance, or 'isomorphic mimicry', can mask underperformance, making the necessity and means for intervening in a school more opaque. And even where performance is good, insofar as it is dependent on top-down leadership from an incumbent principal, as our case studies of Schools 1 and 2 suggest, the risk of performance reversal is especially acute at moments of succession from one principal to another.

Against this backdrop, the patterns we observed in School B are striking. Though tentative, School B possibly indicates the potential of strong school-community ties to support developmentally oriented decision-making. This relationship, between the school and community, as a 'floor' or support for enhanced decision-making has been raised by Hoadley, Christie, and Ward (2009), though they argue that it derives from a support for, rather than direct action in, decision-making processes in the first instance.

8.6.3 *Some Policy Implications*

The evidence from our case studies raises a troubling dilemma. On the one hand, our results are consistent with a pattern that is evident in many parts of the world (Pritchett, 2013)—the reality of dysfunction beneath the surface of seemingly well-organized bureaucratic processes. The difference between a high-performing bureaucracy and 'isomorphic mimicry' can be difficult to discern. On the other hand, our results also are consistent with broader research which suggests that, for the specific Western Cape demographic profile which is our focus, the absence of constructive input from the SGB, communities, or other non-governmental actors is the norm, rather than the exception (Lewis and Naidoo, 2004; Karlsson, 2002).

Given these findings, one temptation for policymakers (at least in settings such as the Western Cape, where bureaucratic quality is relatively strong) is to try and 'double down'—to eliminate performance shortfalls by the introduction of seemingly more and more robust tools of top-down performance management. Our cases suggest the limitations of this.

What, then, is to be done? As discussed further in Chapter 10, we propose pragmatism and incrementalism—foreswearing bold reform initiatives in favour of relatively modest tweaks capable of achieving seemingly small (but potentially far-reaching in their consequences) improvements in the functioning of both hierarchical and horizontal systems of governance.

Our case studies suggest that the developmental returns may be especially high from an intensified focus on the selection of school principals. In the episodes of principal selection examined in our case study schools, neither hierarchical action by the WCED nor participatory engagement by SGBs was able systematically to assure the recruitment and placement of good principals. A better balance between hierarchical and horizontal governance is needed—one which is better able to leverage the strengths of each, while limiting the risks of local capture or of isomorphic mimicry in the face of the inevitable limitations of higher levels of the bureaucracy in accessing local-level information.

Part of the solution may lie in the WCED's recent intensification of efforts to influence principal selection, detailed in Chapter 4. Our case studies suggest that in settings such as the Western Cape, where a platform of capable bureaucracy is in place, pragmatic managerial interventions along these lines have the potential to yield substantial improvements in the process of principal selection.[6] Along with the ongoing intensified focus on putting in place strong, developmentally oriented school leaders, renewed focus on the structure of the relationship between SGB, principal and district (circuit), and what functions they should serve would be helpful.

[6] Note that in settings where bureaucracies are weak and/or captured (which, as Chapter 5 details, is the case in the Eastern Cape), initiatives to strengthen the authority of the bureaucracy in appointing school principals may simply shift the basis of contestation over capture to different terrain, with very uncertain consequences in terms of overall impact.

Excluding SGBs entirely from the processes of principal selection may not be an ideal solution. As our case study of School B (and our school-level case studies in the Eastern Cape) suggest, some involvement of SGBs can help limit the risks of capture, while maintaining a floor of support for developmental decision-making. But all too often the current relationships do not work well; and there also is a need for systemic support to enable SGBs to better play their developmental role.

In our view, rather than viewing the interaction between hierarchical and horizontal governance as zero-sum, the task for practitioners is to find ways to make more effective the 'both/and' balance, with an emphasis on impersonal forms of decision-making. Our cases have shown that effective hierarchical modes have the potential to create the conditions for fostering local initiative and developmental practice by the school to augment the work of the state. There is also a strong suggestion that informational and other inputs from developmentally oriented local stakeholders have the potential to contribute to the principal selection process—as long as the door is not opened for predatory capture. Finding a better balance is a fundamental challenge for practitioners—but one which, if addressed successfully, appears from our case studies to offer real opportunity for achieving quite substantial short- to medium-term gains in educational outcomes.

References

Aghion, P. and Tirole, J. (1997) 'Formal and real authority in organizations', *Journal of Political Economy* 105, 1–29.

Andrews, M. (2013) *The Limits of Institutional Reform in Development: Changing Rules for Realistic Institutions*. New York: Cambridge University Press.

Andrews M., Pritchett, L., and Woolcock, M. (2012) 'Escaping capability traps through problem-driven iterative adaptation', Working Paper No. 299. Washington DC: Center for Global Development.

Chikoko, V., Naicker, I., and Mthiyane, S. (2015) 'School leadership practices that work in areas of multiple deprivation in South Africa', *Educational Management Administration Leadership* 43(3), 452–67.

George, A. L. and Bennett, A. (2005) *Case Studies and Theory Development in the Social Sciences*. Cambridge, MA: MIT Press.

Hallinger, P. and Heck, R. H. (1996) 'Reassessing the principal's role in school effectiveness: A review of empirical research, 1980–1995', *Educational Administration Quarterly* 32(1), 5–44.

Hoadley, U., Christie, P., and Ward, C. (2009) 'Managing to learn: Instructional leadership in South African secondary schools', *School Management and Leadership* 29(4), 373–89.

Hoadley, U. and Galant, J. (2015) 'Specialization and school organization: Investigating pedagogic culture', *British Journal of Sociology of Education* 37(8), 1187–210.

Karlsson, J. (2002) 'The role of democratic governing bodies in South African schools', *Comparative Education* 38(3), 327–36.

Leithwood, K., Patten, S., and Jantzi, D. (2010) 'Testing a conception of how school leadership influences student learning', *Educational Administration Quarterly* 44(4), 455–7.

Levy, B. (2014) *Working with the Grain: Integrating Governance and Growth in Development Strategies*. New York: Oxford University Press.

Lewis, S. G. and Naidoo, J. (2004) 'Whose theory of participation? School governance policy and practice in South Africa', *Current Issues in Comparative Education* 6(2), 100–12.

Lipsky, M. (2010) *Street-level Bureaucracy: Dilemmas of the Individual in Public Service*. New York: Russell Sage Foundation.

North, D. W. (1990) *Institutions, Institutional Change and Economic Performance*. New York: Cambridge University Press.

Pritchett, L. (2013) *The Rebirth of Education: Schooling Ain't Learning*. Washington DC: Center for Global Development.

Sah, R. K. and Stiglitz, J. E. (1986) 'The architecture of economic systems: Hierarchies and polyarchies', *American Economic Review* 76(4), 716–27.

Wills, G. (2015) 'A profile of the labour market for school principals in South Africa: Evidence to inform policy'. Working Papers 12/2015, Stellenbosch University, Department of Economics.

Wilson, J. Q. (1989) *Bureaucracy: What Government Agencies Do and Why They Do It*. New York: Basic Books.

9

Case Studies of School-Level Governance Dynamics in the Eastern Cape

Brian Levy and Lawule Shumane

9.1 Introduction

This chapter explores governance dynamics in four case study schools in low-income communities in South Africa's Eastern Cape province. As Kota, Hendricks, Matambo, and Naidoo explored in Chapter 5, the performance of the Eastern Cape education bureaucracy is notoriously weak. Many of the core functions of an education bureaucracy—allocating personnel and finance; supporting teacher training; providing infrastructure, textbooks, and furniture; performance management—have not been done well.

Do bureaucratic weaknesses doom Eastern Cape schools to poor performance? Or, as was explored in Chapter 1, might horizontal governance function as an 'institutional substitute', with weaknesses in hierarchy offset, at least to some extent, by alternative (more horizontal and bottom-up) institutional arrangements for motivating school staff and assuring accountability for performance? The main purpose of this chapter is to explore, in the Eastern Cape context, the hypothesis that horizontal governance can be a partial institutional substitute for weaknesses in hierarchy.

Our analysis takes as its conceptual point of departure the classic distinction introduced in Chapter 1 between institutions (the 'rules of the game') and organizations (the 'players')—that is, between governance arrangements and stakeholder influences. As North (1990), North, Wallis, and Weingast (2009), and Ostrom (2005) explore theoretically, governance arrangements and stakeholder dynamics are interdependent: The rules of the game set the parameters for the interactions among stakeholders; stakeholders, in turn, work to try and (re-)shape the rules of the game to their advantage. This chapter explores how this interplay between institutions and stakeholders plays out at school level.

In part, school-level governance is shaped by the formal rules of the game that are prescribed by higher levels. Of particular salience here is the South African Schools Act of 1996 which gives a central role at school level to school governing bodies (SGBs), in which parents have a majority of voting (i.e. formal) power. However, as is well known, formal, de jure governance need not translate directly into de facto governance. Indeed, as the case studies in this chapter will illustrate, the gap between these can be wide indeed.

A necessary condition for delegated, horizontal accountability to be effective is that there exists a coalition of 'developmentally oriented' stakeholders engaged at or near the service provision front line, with sufficient influence to be able to 'trump' predatory actors seeking to capture school-level resources (teaching and administrative positions, contracts, other discretionary resources) for private or political purposes. This brings us to analysis of the stakeholders and their influence.

Figure 9.1 illustrates schematically the multiple causal mechanisms through which a variety of stakeholders interact with one another in ways that potentially can influence school-level performance. With one exception, the figure is identical to a parallel figure introduced in Chapters 1 and 8. The exception comprises the arrows linking the Eastern Cape Department of Education (ECDoE) and school-level actors. The arrows are drawn to signify the extreme weakness of the ECDoE, identified in Chapter 5 and (as we shall see) confirmed in the case study analysis.

In sections 9.2–9.5 below, we trace how the causal mechanisms in Figure 9.1 played out in the case study schools, with a particular focus on variations in the 'play of the game' (that is, in the balance between developmental and predatory stakeholders) both across schools and over time within schools.

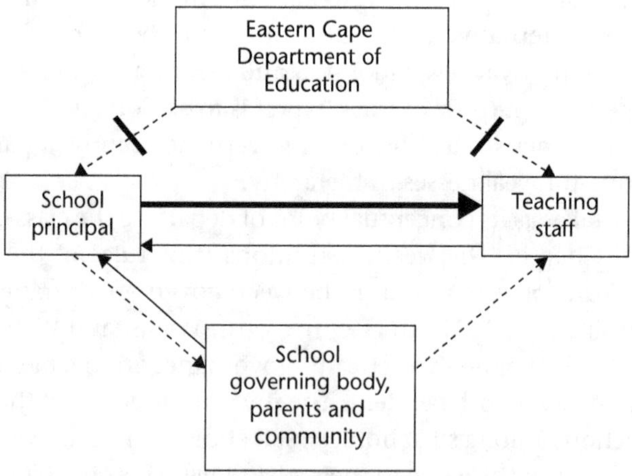

Figure 9.1. Governance interactions

Section 9.6 assesses more broadly the relationship between the divergent observed patterns of stakeholder influence, the prevailing school-level governance arrangements, and performance.

9.1.1 *Empirical Methodology and Sample Selection*

This sub-section lays out our methodological approach to assessing and evidencing the empirical relevance of each of the causal mechanisms delineated above. Paralleling the approach adopted in Chapter 8 for the analysis of Western Cape schools, the empirical point of departure was to select schools that were similar in their socio-economic contexts, but had different educational outcomes. The hypothesis to be explored was that these differences in outcomes could be explained by differences across the schools in their patterns of horizontal governance. The methodology comprised in-depth case studies of a small number of schools, rather than statistical analysis, with the aim of exploring the influence of the various causal mechanisms summarized in Figure 8.1 in accounting for variations in outcomes—both across schools, and over time within individual schools.

In selecting the sample of schools, a first step was to identify two matched pairs[1] of schools—geographically contiguous with one another, and thus with similar socio-economic profiles, with one relatively high-performing, and the other relatively weak. But it proved difficult to identify a robust indicator for school performance in the Eastern Cape that could be tracked over multiple years. In the Eastern Cape there was no provincial level standardized assessment at lower grades which paralleled the Western Cape systemic tests used in the Chapter 8 analysis. In 2012, the Department of Basic Education (DBE) launched the Annual National Assessments (ANA), which assess student performance from Grades 1 to 9. However, the ANA results are neither readily available, nor yet viewed to be reliable.[2] For this reason, rather than using the school-level ANA results as the basis for assessing performance, we distinguished between the schools on the basis of reputation.

One indicator of reputation comprises feedback from senior district officials. Schools A1 and B1 were selected from a list of schools that were deemed by the

[1] This 'matched pair' approach also was adopted in the Western Cape school-level case study—which had the advantage of the availability of robust standardized tests as a basis for school-level comparisons.

[2] School principals in the case study schools were reluctant to share their ANA results with the field researcher. More broadly, published ANA results have raised eyebrows in the academic community, due to the differences between self-reported school performance and independently moderated school performance. A significant discrepancy exists—especially for the Eastern Cape—between the results reported by schools and the verified results. For example, for the Eastern Cape as a whole, in 2013 the percentage of Grade 3 students with a score of 50 per cent or more was self-reported for numeracy as 54.9 per cent, but adjusted downward after external verification to 42.2 per cent; for literacy, the self-reported score was 50.2 per cent, and the adjusted score 27.0 per cent.

district officials to be top performers as of 2015, and matched to two other schools (Schools A2 and B2) in the same (or similar) community. To the extent possible, the aim was that each pair would have the same essential characteristics: school wealth quintile classification; language of teaching and learning; community; and school fee status.

School enrolment figures comprised our second indicator of reputation. Barriers to entry into individual Eastern Cape public schools are limited, in part because the total number of students in the Eastern Cape is declining as a result of outmigration to the Western Cape and elsewhere. Parents prefer to enrol their children in schools that have a reputation for performance, or in schools they perceive to have a high performance standard. All else constant, we thus expect schools with a reputation of high performance will have high or increasing student enrolment. The converse is true when parents perceive school performance to be low. Table 9.1 details the patterns of learner enrolment over time for our two matched pairs of schools. As will become evident in subsequent sections, the trends in enrolment track closely the perception of stakeholders interviewed as to the performance trends over time in each school—adding to our confidence that enrolments offer a useful proxy for school-level performance, at least as perceived by the parent community.

The patterns of learner enrolment in Schools A1 and A2 are largely consistent with the information provided by district officials—high and stable in School A1 and low (and declining) in School A2.[3] By contrast, enrolments in Schools B1 and B2 were more unstable over the period covered in Table 9.2—declining with a subsequent turnaround in School B1, and a precipitate decline with incipient signs of stability in School B2.

Our analysis combines cross-section and time-series inquiry into school-level variations in performance and their governance drivers. For the across-schools

Table 9.1. Trends in Learner Enrolment, 2008–15 (number of learners)

	School A1	School A2	School B1	School B2
2008	1048	650	611	1200
2009	1145	616	611	1031
2010	1022	639	521	777
2011	907	521	347	784
2012	950	455	433	758
2013	1030	489	464	720
2014	949	542	502	669
2015	1041	575	547	690

Source: Butterworth District Education Management Information System, 2015.

[3] School A2's capacity is large. In the mid-1990s, the school had a strong reputation, and close to 2,000 students. Then came more difficult times: by 2000, the number of students had fallen to about 1,000 and, as per the table, continued to fall subsequently.

analysis, variations in socio-economic contexts are controlled for through the matched-pair approach to sample selection. For the analysis of patterns within the same school over time, socio-economic conditions are controlled for by the fact that the socio-economic characteristics of a community change only little over the short-to medium-term.

A longitudinal focus on changes over time in patterns of governance and performance/reputation for the case study schools aligns well with the methodology for case study analysis laid out by George and Bennett (2005) and used for both the Western Cape and Eastern Cape school-level case studies. As detailed in Chapter 8, process tracing focuses on a very specific set of decisions. For these:

- It 'attempts to trace the links between possible causes and observed outcomes'.
- It considers the sequence and values of intervening variables in a case 'to see whether the causal process a theory hypothesizes or implies is in fact evident in the sequence and values of the intervening variables in that case'.

The aim is to achieve 'high internal validity and good historical explanations of particular cases versus making generalizations that apply to broad populations' (p. 22).

Information about the schools was gathered, where available, from online sources, the district office and semi-structured interviews with immediate stakeholders (school principals, deputy principals, SGB chairpersons, school teachers with long tenure at each school and parents). At least three stakeholders from each school participated in the interviews.[4] Where possible, individuals who were named in interviews and had left the school were also asked to participate. (See Appendixes A9.1 and A9.2 for details as to the positions of each person interviewed in each school, and their functions.)

Of course, with only four schools (each, as elaborated further below, with three distinct observations: earlier period; principal selection; later period), drawn from one geographic locale within a single district, the size of our sample is small. The results cannot be interpreted as representative of the Eastern Cape as a whole. We thus make no claims as to the relative importance across the province of each of the patterns observed in our cases; rather, our goal is to shed light on causal mechanisms.

Some characteristics of the sample schools

The four sample schools were all from a specific locality in the Butterworth District of the Eastern Cape. For reasons of confidentiality the specific locality

[4] Detailed notes of each interview have been retained in the research project's records.

within the district must remain anonymous. The Butterworth district is the third largest in the province with (as per official statistics published in 2015) 381 schools, 82,573 learners (down from 106,803 in 2010), and 3,342 teachers (ECDoE, 2015). Over 98 per cent of the population is Black African, with over 98 per cent in the bottom three quintiles of South Africa's socio-economic distribution. Based on high school (matric) pass rates, the district is one of the weaker performers in the Eastern Cape. Between 2011 and 2015, on average 54.1 per cent of those who wrote the matric exam passed, as compared with an average pass rate of 61.4 per cent for the Eastern Cape province. (South Africa's overall pass rate was 73.8 per cent.)

As was detailed in Chapter 8, the quality of school leadership has been identified by education researchers as a key proximate determinant of school performance. Strikingly, as Table 9.2 details, all four schools experienced a change in school leadership over the periods studied. Insofar as school-level leadership matters for performance, this directs attention to the selection of a new principal as a critical juncture for careful process tracing analysis—both in accounting for performance, and in revealing the micro-dynamics of school-level governance. How did School A1 navigate principal selection in a way that helped sustain relatively strong performance? Why did School A2's dysfunction reproduce itself? What were the relationships between governance dynamics, principal selection and the rollercoaster trends in performance of Schools B1 and B2?

Sections 9.2–9.5 provide 'thick' narrative descriptions of stakeholder interactions over time in each school, and the relationship between the observed patterns of interaction and school performance (as measured by our enrolment proxy). The narratives focus especially on the ways in which the teacher cadre was governed, the ways in which new principals were selected, and the ways in which the SGB, parents and the community engage with the school. Section 9.6

Table 9.2. School Performance Periods *(including pseudonym principals' names)*

	Earlier period	Change in principal	Later period
School A1	Relatively strong —*Mrs Mbala*	2004 (smooth)	Relatively strong —*Mr Zondi*
School A2	Relatively weak performance —*Mrs Kunta*	2012–2013 (contested)	Relatively weak performance (possibly with some initial turnaround) —*Mr Makhatini*
School B1	Weak performance —*Mrs. Dinga*	2009–2011 (contested)	Improving performance —*Mr Nkosi*
School B2	Good reputation to 2008; then rapid decline —*Mr Kramer*	2010–2012 (contested)	Ongoing efforts at turnaround —*Mr Risha*

Source: (for this and all following tables) authors.

builds on the narratives to distinguish more broadly among some divergent pattern of school-level governance, and their relationship to performance.

9.2 A Sustained High-Performer—School A1

School A1 is the only school in the sample with consistent, relatively strong performance over the long term—as evidenced by sustained high enrolments, its identification by the ECDoE Butterworth district office as a good performer, plus (as this section will detail) reports from interviewees of consistently robust internal processes. It thus offers especially clear insight into the kinds of 'good fit' institutional arrangements that facilitate relatively strong performance, notwithstanding the Eastern Cape's fragmented broader political and institutional arrangements.

Table 9.3 introduces a summary qualitative table that we use throughout the chapter. Building on the detailed narratives in the body of the chapter, each column of the table provides, for each of the case study schools, a summary overview of the relative influence on governance of each of the various stakeholders identified in Figure 9.1—either (if there is no change over time) over the full period studied, or for distinct sub-episodes within the case study schools. As Table 9.3 highlights, sustained leadership by the school principal has been central to the good performance of School A. A performance-driven vision was put in place by the school's first principal, Mrs Mbala (a pseudonym, as are all names throughout this chapter), who led the school from its founding in the early 1980s until her retirement in 2003. Mr Zondi, the current principal, who replaced Mrs Mbala upon her retirement in 2003, has sustained this vision.

Table 9.3. Stakeholder Engagement—High- and Low-Performing Equilibria

The influence on governance of...	A high-performing equilibrium	A low-performing equilibrium
	School A1	*School A2*
(i) Eastern Cape Department of Education	+	–
(ii) Principal	+++++	–/+
(iii) Teachers	++++	0
(iva) School governing body	+++	- - -
(ivb) Parents and broader community	++	–
(va) Political parties	0	- -
(vb) Unions	0	–

Key: +++++ = very positive; +++ = positive; + = marginally positive
0 = passive/neutral
- = marginally negative; --- = negative; ----- = very negative
n/a = no relevant information available

Succession from Mrs Mbala to Mr Zondi was smooth—indeed, as per Table 9.3, it was the only smooth principal succession process in any of the case study schools. Mr Zondi, a relatively junior post-level 1 educator was the first male educator in the school when he joined in 1992. He was mentored by Mrs Mbala, and committed himself to many school projects. This made him the favoured candidate to replace Mrs Mbala, even prior to the interviews for the position.

Both principals successfully inculcated School A's vision among teaching staff. They systematically promoted transparency between staff members and with other stakeholders, consistently followed formal processes when it came to appointing staff and the SGB, and systematically fostered a sense of community. The result is that, as one interviewee put it, 'the teachers all felt like family', with explicit rules governing professional conduct. All behaviour that escapes the borders of this conduct is addressed by school leadership.

The principal takes a leading role in the appointment processes in the school. When new senior positions become available, he carefully follows the formal processes laid out by the ECDoE, and calls a staff meeting and encourages all eligible staff members to apply. Interviews suggest that those who apply are given a fair chance, with (again, in stark contrast to the other case study schools) no informal lobbying efforts by staff to try and capture senior posts. An interviewee described how new staff are inducted into the school's organizational culture:

> The principal will call newly appointed staff to a meeting and introduce them to everyone. At this meeting the principal will welcome the new staff member to the team and inform them on school culture…he will often say 'Mr or Ms so and so, at this school we are a family and if we have problems we deal with them openly. If there is unrest, we will know it is you because it has never happened before'.

Beyond the appointments process, two examples volunteered by interviewees illustrate how the school handles personnel challenges that could compromise performance:

- To curb teacher absenteeism, the school requires all teachers to report to their senior (head of department, deputy principal or principal) before they take the day off and explain the reasons for the absence. Teachers are required to submit doctor's notes, report family emergencies, and in cases where they have 'taken their car in for service, they must provide a copy of the receipt'.
- The case of a staff member who was battling alcoholism, which greatly affected his work initially, was addressed by the principal and school

management team. Seeing little improvement, the SGB stepped in and finally approached the family and asked them to intervene. They forwarded the case to the district office; following this, he was treated as a 'displaced educator' by the department of education. After some time, his family found another school for him to transfer to.

Complementing this strong internal culture is a distinctive pattern of engagement with external stakeholders. Other than the teachers and principals themselves, the SGB is the most important player in school governance. As Table 9.3 signals, the school has very strong norms in place as to the role and functioning of the SGB, including (according to the SGB interviewee):

- SGB members are elected at an open meeting. The meeting chair ensures that there are more candidates than positions; each candidate is required to make the case to parents for voting for them.
- At the first SGB meeting, and as part of school policy, the principal 'adamantly discourages party or union politics from infiltrating school processes'.
- Parent members of the SGB sit on the school's finance and procurement committees, give input into how resources are used, and are responsible for reporting on resource use to the school community as a whole.

Beyond the SGB, the school also maintains strong networks externally—with parents, with the broader community, with non-governmental organizations, and other departments of government beyond the ECDoE. Examples include the following:

- Parents have always shown overwhelming support for the school, and attend parents' meetings in large numbers—'the school often needs to hire more chairs to accommodate them all'.
- The school has an extensive extramural programme, which is credited by staff as the reason for the school's high enrolment figures (soccer and netball, boy scouts and girl guides, gymnastics, choir). The school gymnastics team recently competed in Australia; its under-12 soccer team competed in a national soccer tournament.
- The school participates in corporate-sponsored competitions that enable them to gain more resources—for example, two recycling competitions, which the school won, and which generated funding to maintain the school building.
- Staff are required to support extramural programmes—this serves as a team-building activity.

- Government departments (health, social development, police, traffic) and a variety of NGOs (e.g. the Love Life Trust, Soul Buddies) all offer programmes to students.

The relationship between the school and the Eastern Cape Department of Education (ECDoE) is something of a delicate balance. The principal maintains good relationships with the district office—and thereby manages to ensure its support for the school, while keeping it at arm's length from involvement in governance at school level and thus keeping its influence modest. Key aspects/ illustrations of this relationship identified by interviewees include:

- The school is something of a showcase for the district; it was, for example, shown as a model school to the national minister of basic education in the course of a 2011 visit to the district.
- To maintain its teacher complement, and be responsive to parental demand, the school has kept its student numbers high. The ECDoE has accommodated this demand by providing portable classrooms.
- Textbook delivery has been reliable—but in large part because the school management team (SMT) is pro-active. 'The SMT chooses which school books to order and the best companies to order the books from, and when to order the books, in order that they may arrive on time'.
- At the same time, 'the school does not just sit back and wait for the government to provide; it is able to fundraise... As an example, the school was promised 16 laptop computers if it had a secure storage room. The school raised the funds to provide the room, but the laptops have not yet been delivered... Most of the things that the school has been able to acquire are a result of the efforts of school's leadership': the department is yet to provide for the school.
- A national policy states that pregnant teens attending school should be allowed to take tests and exams at home, and schools should ensure this happens. The principal reportedly spoke to the staff and the district office and suggested that this would create perverse incentive for young teens and decided not to implement it at the school.

Unions and political parties are kept at a careful distance from School A1's governance. School staff belong to two unions—SADTU and NAPTOSA—at a ratio of about 50:50. Teachers from the different unions co-operate: 'When SADTU teachers attend a meeting, they will provide information to all staff members' (and vice versa for NAPTOSA). While keeping politics at a distance, the school allows all political parties to use its classrooms for meetings, as it believes that 'the children's parents belong to different political parties, so the school must assist them all'.

9.3 Mired in a Toxic Governance Culture—School A2

The contrast between School A1 and School A2 is stark, as a comparison of the second and third columns of Table 9.3 highlights. School A2 has long been a fixture in the Butterworth area. Prior to the mid-1990s, the school had a strong reputation, and close to 2,000 students. Then came more difficult times: by 2000, the number of students had fallen to about 1,000; it then declined further to a low of 455 in 2012. Little information could be obtained from interviews about the earlier period; the focus here is on the period subsequent to 2009—when the school has been characterized by polarized contestation among competing factions within the SGB, among staff, and spreading into the broader community.

The current principal, Mr Zondi, offered a vivid picture of what he found when he began his tenure at the school in 2013:

- Infrastructure was poor and deteriorating. The building was not taken care of. There were no sports grounds, no computer lab, no staff room, and no offices for the principal and deputy principal.
- Classrooms were poorly stocked. Chalkboards were falling; students did not have enough desks and chairs; there was no storeroom for textbooks (which meant they would get lost).
- Vandalism had been a big problem at the school. Some students were involved in local gangs and substance abuse; many young girls would get pregnant and stay away from school.

Underlying this dysfunction was a passive parent community, and a politicized SGB. In part, the absence of parental engagement was because of the demographic profile of the school. The new principal reported that when he began at the school in 2013, over half of the students were orphans. But:

> The community did not neglect the school from out of the blue; they saw that the teachers appeared to not care... This is when they decided to take their children out of a school where the students were ill-disciplined to one where there were firm rules [School A2 is located within two kilometres of School A1].

An absent parent community and, it would seem, the absence of strong leadership from the principal from the mid-1990s onwards manifested (again in stark contrast to School A1, as per Table 9.4) in a dysfunctional SGB. This is illustrated vividly in the process that resulted in Mr Zondi's appointment. The post was advertised in 2012, following the retirement of Mr Zondi's predecessor. Mr Banda, the school deputy principal, serving as the acting principal at this time, applied. Controversy struck after the first interviews, when the SGB could not agree as to who would be their preferred candidate to recommend for the appointment. As a result, interviews were held two more times—there were strong supporters of Mr Banda and one SGB member who was adamantly opposed to his promotion.

Local-level politics appear to have been the reason Mr Banda did not receive the post. Mrs Peter, an SGB member who was against Mr Banda's appointment, was also an ANC councillor in the community. Mr Banda had previously been an ANC councillor in the same community and later changed his political affiliations to Congress of the People—a political party that broke away from the ANC during the 2008/09 political cycle. In her assessment of the candidates, Mrs Peter awarded Mr Banda very low scores to drag down his average (2 out of 20), while other SGB members gave him significantly higher scores (between 14 and 17 out of 20) for the same questions. Immediately following the interviews, the district official who was present (in his formal role as observer) did not allow the SGB to discuss the candidates; instead, he tallied the scores and ranked candidates according to their arithmetical average. Believing he had been unfairly treated, Mr Banda wrote a letter of complaint to the district office, but did not receive a response. The losing faction did not readily accept defeat. After Mr Zondi was appointed, parents and some SGB members staged protests for three weeks outside the school, preventing him from gaining access to the school.

Beyond the principal selection process, interviews offered further insight into the ways in which the SGB is a site for some of the ongoing political infighting over school resources:

- The two-term SGB member acknowledged that she knew little about either the school's history, or its current level of performance.
- The SGB is directly involved in decision-making on spending. Relative to other schools, an unusually high proportion of the budget is allocated to building maintenance—a budgetary line item, which, with the permission of the circuit office, can straightforwardly be diverted to other 'essential' uses. (Of all the schools studied, this school had the least well-maintained physical infrastructure.)
- SGB members are centrally involved in the appointment of teachers. According to one interviewee, in the selection of teachers for eight posts that became available subsequent to 2013, 'unions, local political structures and teachers within the school all tried to influence who would be appointed by the school'.
- As of the time of interviews, the mid-2015 SGB elections appeared to be becoming politicized:
    - According to one interviewee, 'within the community, organizations will mobilize from within parents' structures in order for them to have a role in school processes'.

- Against the backdrop of many unsubstantiated rumours, there was an unusually well-attended parents' meeting to discuss school finances.
- Mrs Peters (who exited the SGB in 2012) apparently was mobilizing parents to vote for her candidacy.

Mr Zondi, who is new to the Butterworth area, appears to be trying hard to turn around the school's toxic culture and reputation—both by reaching out to the community, and (as discussed further in section 9.6) by trying to begin to introduce a more rule-bound culture into the school. The district office finally intervened (after repeated requests) to signal its support for him. And he has managed to build a strong collegial relationship with the veteran teacher who was denied the principalship. But, insofar as the school continues to be enmeshed in community politics, it remains too soon to tell whether a sustained turnaround can be achieved.

9.4 Two Downward Spirals—Schools B1 and B2

We turn now to the two remaining case study schools, School B1 and School B2. As with School A2, both became trapped in cycles of decline. School B1's toxic governance culture dates back to the 1990s—but, by contrast to our research into School A2, the School B1 interviewees were able to shed valuable light onto the origins of the downward governance spiral. School B2's dysfunctional governance emerged more recently. However, by contrast to School A2 (and as will be discussed in section 9.5), both Schools B1 and B2 have been able to reverse these downward spirals.

Table 9.4 summarizes the patterns of stakeholder influence which prevailed in Schools B1 and B2 in the periods immediately prior to and during the downward spirals. As the table signals (and the narratives will detail), one striking difference between the schools is in the role played by each school's

Table 9.4. Two Downward Spirals—Stakeholder Roles

The influence on governance of...	A long, slow decline	A rapid downward spiral
	School B1	*School B2*
(i) Eastern Cape Department of Education	- -	**0**
(ii) Principal	- - - - -	++++/**0**
(iii) Teachers	- - -	+++/- - - - -
(iva) School governing body	+/**0**	+/**0**
(ivb) Parents & broader community	**0**	+/**0**
(va) Political parties	**n/a**	**n/a**
(vb) Unions	**n/a**	**n/a**

Key: See Table 9.3.

longstanding principal. In School B1 this role was deeply destructive over a long period of time. By contrast, in School B2 the principal's role was seemingly positive until just before the end of his tenure; indeed, for much of the relevant period, School B2 enjoyed a good reputation in the community.

This one difference aside, as the narratives below detail, there were some striking similarities in the patterns of governance across the two schools. Specifically:

- In both schools, the tone and mode of operation set by the principal was personalized, rather than bound by impersonal rules.
- In both schools, teaching staff played a central role in the downward spiral—integral to a long, slow decline in the case of School B1, and as instigators of a sudden, precipitous collapse of governance in School B2.
- In neither school did the ECDoE intervene to reverse the downward spiral; in School B1 it may even have hastened the decline.
- While parents in School B2 (but not B1) had a history of being generally supportive of the school's achievements, in neither school was the SGB active in the governance of the school in the periods prior to, or during, the downward spiral.
- In neither school did our interviews uncover evidence that either political parties or teacher unions contributed to the downward spiral, though we were alert to the possibility. (But we cannot rule out that hidden organizational allegiances and rivalries comprise a beneath-the-surface explanation for some of the patterns which are described below.)

9.4.1 *School B1*

Mrs Dinga, the principal who set in motion School B1's long decline, was appointed about a decade after the school's 1978 start-up. She remained in the post of principal for almost twenty-five years. But from the latter-1990s onwards, Mrs Dinga was, for much of the time, an absentee principal. According to an interviewee who had a long-time association with the school, 'she would be absent for periods of about two to three months'. This continued for about a decade(!).

Mrs Dinga would produce doctor's notes and apply for sick leave, but her colleagues in school management believed that there was another reason for her absence. Interviewees reported that she had purchased a home in East London (a town 100 km away from Butterworth) and this increased the cost of attending work, hence her absence from school. The school went into a downward spiral. The number of students fell from close to 1,000 in the early 1990s, to a low of 341 in 2011, the year in which a new principal was finally appointed.

The principal's behaviour set the tone more broadly for the behaviour of school staff. Teachers took advantage of her absence to tend to other business during school hours—some attended school only for specific periods when they were scheduled to teach, and others stayed away completely. In the instances Mrs Dinga attended school, it is reported that some teachers would not curb their behaviour; Mrs Dinga would remain in her office, not attending to what was happening around her, and ignored by staff.

Attendance by students was sporadic: 'Students would arrive at the school just to be marked for attendance – by the time the break came, you would see many of the students walking around the community in their uniforms'. Disregard for the school spilled out into the broader community. According to interviewees, the community did not seem to have any respect for school property, and the school was vandalized frequently: 'It became a night-time destination for local misfits'. Around the early 2000s, vandalism reached an all-time high, with the school losing much of its furniture. This occasioned some publicity from the SABC (South African Broadcasting Corporation) and a visit to the school by the then MEC of education in the Eastern Cape, but there was no follow-up.

While the SGB and the deputy principal made some effort to turn things around, Mrs Dinga showed blatant disregard for their efforts. The current head of the SGB (whose first term on the SGB was in 2001–04, when Mrs Dinga was principal) stated that:

> Mrs Dinga would even comment and say that she was not certain if I was appointed to antagonize her... we just did not see eye-to-eye.

(He was not re-elected in 2004, but midway through the 2004-07 term he returned as a co-opted member.)

The SGB would submit reports to the district office, expecting them to address the issue, but nothing materialized. In one episode, Mrs Dinga was reported to have forged the SGB chairperson's signature when she wanted to appoint an educator to the school. The district office failed to address this transgression.

One interviewee suggested that the reason for not sanctioning Mrs Dinga's behaviour was that 'some district officials are cowards'. (Another interviewee volunteered that Mrs Dinga's parents lived in the same location where the ECDoE district office was situated.) Finally, in 2009, the parents and the SGB took measures into their own hands. (More on that action, and the subsequent turnaround, later in the chapter.)

9.4.2 *School B2*

In stark contrast to School B1, prior to 2008 School B2 had a reputation of being a 'good' school. This reputation was shaped in large part by its longstanding principal, Mr Kramer, who was appointed to the position in 1990, three years after the school's founding. Mr Kramer enjoyed a high profile in the community. An interviewee explained:

> Mr Kramer lived in the local community and had been a church leader as well. He was able to hear what his students got up to, and would deal with them when they returned to school or when they met at church . . . He always availed the school and its resources to the Butterworth community at large. He would negotiate days with the municipal office when students could go into town and clear the litter. He encouraged the school's drum majorettes to perform whenever there were celebrations in town . . . He supported the school choir, which gained quite a reputation in Butterworth.

As per Table 9.1 earlier, enrolments in the school were high (above 1,200 students) up to 2008. But after 2008, enrolment dropped off precipitously—falling below 800 in 2010, and then continuing a slow decline into 2014. This collapse in enrolments was set in motion by the emergence of conflict among the teaching staff.

Prior to 2008, relations among staff seemed positive. According to interviewees, staff would have birthday celebrations each month for their colleagues and would travel to East London for strategic planning sessions to assess the school's strengths and weaknesses. Teachers had a buddy system and would help one another when they felt overwhelmed. But one interviewee reported that when the troubles began around 2008, 'some of these [activities] were thrown out like they never existed'.

The staff conflicts erupted over appointment decisions—initially over who would succeed two heads of department (HODs) who retired in 2008, and then over who would succeed Mr Kramer, following his death in 2010. The senior phase HOD position was hotly contested. The first time the interviews were conducted, a teacher disputed the process and that meant that a second session had to be scheduled. The second interview session did not even take place, as some teachers (in support of the candidate who filed a dispute) decided to stage a protest to prevent the interviews from progressing. The Eastern Cape Department of Education responded by freezing the post.

Appointing a new HOD for the foundation phase was equally challenging. In this case, though, opposition to the outcome did not surface until after the appointment had been made. Mr Kramer had encouraged all qualifying teachers to apply, regardless of years of service at the school—and, to the dismay of some of the teaching staff, the appointment went to a teacher who had only joined the school four years earlier. The backlash from some staff was large. The new HOD (one of the interviewees for this study) reports that in the years immediately following her appointment, she had to work very hard to achieve stability. While some teachers were supportive, others showed blatant disregard for her position, and would often not submit required work to her.

Then, in 2010, Mr Kramer died unexpectedly. As a stopgap measure, the SGB appointed the school's deputy principal, Mr Mavundla as acting principal. But, again, things unravelled. How this unravelling eventually was turned around is the subject of the next section. For now, the focus is on the dysfunctional dynamics surrounding the appointment of a new principal.

According to our interviewees, Mr Mavundla did not perform well. Said one: 'He was more concerned with being liked by the staff.' Under Mr Mavundla's leadership, school rules were relaxed significantly. Staff wanted to 'come and go' as they pleased. This was the genesis of the school's subsequent teacher absenteeism problem; even those teachers who attended school would often miss their classes.

After noting the decline in performance, the SGB decided that they could not appoint Mr Mavundla and encouraged a more junior staff member who had a reputation as a hardworking teacher at the school, Mr Risha, to apply for the position. (One interviewee believes Mr Mavundla lost the post after he shirked on his responsibility as principal and did not speak at a former SGB member's funeral; this was not well received by the SGB.) Some teachers at the school were in support of reforms and supported Mr Risha's appointment, while others fervently believed that Mr Mavundla deserved the post, as the most senior educator in the school.

Tension rose. The initial spark of controversy came after the principal interviews. A group of teachers in support of Mr Mavundla's appointment discovered that he would not receive the post. After meeting with a circuit official during school hours, these teachers proceeded to Butterworth district office in an attempt to dispute the process. A few weeks later, the ECDoE head of Butterworth district and some of his colleagues came to the school with the intention of announcing the outcome of the principal selection process. The teachers were called into the staffroom and as the district head started speaking, some teachers interrupted, protesting the outcome of the interviews. The team from the district office decided to leave, and the protesting teachers followed the officials to the district office. Subsequently, the protesting educators were fined by the ECDoE and deductions were made from their monthly salaries. Mr Risha took up his position as principal in 2012. Since then, as Section 9.6 will detail, the school has witnessed the beginnings of a turnaround, orchestrated by a close partnership between Mr Risha and the SGB.

Why did a school with a long, proud history slide so rapidly into destructive conflict? And why, in both the 2008 and 2010 conflicts, did the SGB seem taken by surprise and (at least initially) overwhelmed by the events that unfolded? One background factor surely was the weakness of the ECDoE. Another possibility (which we cannot rule out, but did not uncover in the course of interviews) may have been that political conflicts external to the school found their way within the school walls. But, based on the accounts provided by interviewees, we are inclined (in the absence of evidence to the contrary) to give more emphasis to internal school-level dynamics.

As of 2008, community engagement appears to us to have taken the form more of basking in the reflected glory of the school's achievements than of active engagement. Beyond a cheerleading role, in practice the SGB's role in school governance was a passive one. Here is a description from one interviewee of how the SGB operated during Mr Kramer's tenure:

> Those parents who were on the SGB did not want to step down. SGB members were actively involved in school programmes and were supportive of the school... There never was any reason to report to the SGB, because they were always involved... SGB members would even attend school extramural activities.

When the school's leader, Mr Kramer, suddenly lost his ability to control events, the weaknesses of the other pillars of governance (the ECDoE and the SGB) were starkly exposed.

9.5 Turnarounds via Participatory Governance

In recent years, both Schools B1 and B2 have (to varying degrees) turned around their downward spirals of decline. As this section details, the specifics of how the turnarounds were effected are different across the two schools. Even so, as Table 9.5 summarizes (and the narratives which follow will detail) there are some striking similarities in the influence of the various stakeholders.

The similarities in the causal mechanisms of turnarounds include:

- In both schools, the SGBs were the key actors in setting the turnaround in motion—initially via their roles in supporting a committed and competent

Table 9.5. Stakeholder Engagement in Two Turnaround Schools

The influence on governance of...	School B1	School B2
(i) Eastern Cape Department of Education	0	0
(ii) Principal	++++	++(+)
(iii) Teachers	0/+	- - -/0
(iva) School governing body	+++++	+++
(ivb) Parents and broader community	++++	++
(va) Political parties	+	n/a
(vb) Unions	0	+

Key: See Table 9.3.

school principal, and subsequently via their ongoing support for that principal.

- In both schools, the new principal and the SGBs reached out to the broader community (including parents) to support the turnaround.
- In both schools, a central (and ongoing) challenge was to turn around the pre-existing organizational culture among staff. School B1 aimed to do so by building a stronger sense of community, and School B2 by introducing a more rule-bound culture.
- In neither school did the ECDoE play more than a marginal role in supporting the turnaround—but in neither, once the turnaround was set in motion, was its role a negative one.
- There was some indication of involvement by elected officials and by the teachers' union, SADTU; according to interviewees, their roles were positive, but largely on the margin.

9.5.1 *School B1*

In 2009, frustration at the principal's continuing absence finally boiled over. A group of parents and some SGB members met, and jointly reached the view that Mrs Dinga should not continue as school principal. At the group's urging, the SGB took their decision to the ECDoE district office, which did not respond well. 'The district office did not accept this', said one interviewee. In response, as a last resort, the parent community staged a protest, preventing the principal from accessing the school, and thus forcing the district to respond. She was not dismissed; rather, the district office kept her on as a displaced teacher, reporting to the district office, until her retirement in 2010.

Between 2009 and the end of 2010, the deputy principal (who was close to retirement) served as the acting principal. When, finally, the principal post formally became available, the deputy/acting principal encouraged Mr Nkosi, a relatively junior post-level 1 teacher at the school who had proven his commitment by taking on some of Mrs Dinga's responsibilities during the period of her absence, to apply for the position. The SGB supported this recommendation as they had witnessed Mr Nkosi's work over the grim period in the school's history, including his efforts to improve the severed relations between the school, the SGB and the local community. While the teachers in the school belong to SADTU, the newly appointed principal was reported to belong to the rival union, NAPTOSA. Said the head of the SGB: 'I would be misleading you if I noted any role played by unions.'

Together with the SGB and the support of the local community, the principal has been successful in implementing turnaround policies that have supported school performance. Many of the staff members who took liberties under Mrs Dinga's leadership retired from the school; only four teachers (who welcomed the changes) remain at the school from this period. School B1 filled many of the vacant posts through the redeployment process—the district office provided the school with a list of educators that would be joining the staff. The school remained with three vacancies which were filled in collaboration with the SGB. A new SGB subcommittee was selected for each interview and SGB members were expected to report to the team after the interview.

According to interviewees, measures taken to turn the school around included the following:

- The SGB and new principal held a meeting with the community, requesting parents to enrol at the school, as conditions were sure to improve. The local ANC councillor assisted in organizing the parents.
- A 'school times policy' was introduced, with school-level stakeholders agreeing on setting new class times, assigning essential non-teaching duties to staff and agreeing on the school start time.
- A protocol was established so that the principal would be informed in advance when teachers planned to attend department-mandated workshops, and would in turn inform the SGB chairperson.
- The SGB volunteered to perform functions of non-teaching staff (such as cleaning and security) together with the teachers and students.
- With the help of their ward councillor, the school was able to gain funds from a local business towards renovating school premises. In the interim, until a new fence was put up, a community organization provided security services.
- As an additional step in improving its physical environment, and building on a connection provided by the ECDoE district office, the school joined the eco-schools project.

By 2015, the number of pupils in the school had risen to 547, up from a low of 341 in 2011. Indeed, the turnaround was sufficiently advanced that School B1 was recommended for this study by a district official in the ECDoE as an example of a 'better performing' school in Butterworth town.

9.5.2 *School B2*

The factionalized contestation that had turned School B2 upside down from 2008 onwards did not end when Mr Risha (the principal selected by the SGB against the wishes of some teachers) began his tenure in 2012. Mr Risha initially struggled to stabilize the school. Some educators deliberately stayed away from staff meetings, and even stated that, in their eyes, he was not their principal.

An interviewee described two cases of post-2012 teacher underperformance. The educators' offences included late-coming, absenteeism and disregarding school procedure when disciplinary action was taken against them. With the support of the SGB, school management wrote formal letters of warning to the teachers, but these went unread. Said one interviewee: 'We would leave them on their desks in the staff room, they would not take them . . . if we gave it to them personally, they would not read it.'

The SGB decided to intervene, involving parents in a discussion of the teachers' performance. Parents were outraged and staged protests outside the school, attempting to prevent the teachers from coming into the school. The school was advised by the ECDoE district office to submit a petition which detailed the dissatisfaction of the school management and parents with the teachers' performance. One teacher subsequently was redeployed to another school; the other teacher remains on the redeployment list.

With advice and support from his SGB, Mr Risha determinedly worked to transform school culture. Staff had worked with each other for a long period of time, and school processes had become personalized. In response, Mr Risha applied formal rules for everything. One interviewee notes that in staff meetings, he would recite department procedure in an effort to curb teacher underperformance. A 'no work, no pay' policy was implemented. After some time, the effects on salaries became visible and teachers began to co-operate.

To counteract a pattern where class attendance by some teachers had become sporadic, Mr Risha implemented what is known as a period register. The school appointed class monitors, who were also responsible for monitoring which teachers should be attending each of their periods. These students have been given the right to remind educators when they have forgotten about attending a specific session. Additionally, with the support of the SGB, the school hired a security guard stationed at the school gate. Teachers are expected to sign in in the mornings (adding their time of arrival). Teachers are expected to sign out of school in the principal's office at the end of each day.

The role of SADTU in this turnaround is worthy of note. SADTU is the only union represented in the school; eighteen of the school's twenty-three teachers are members; three staff members have, at different times, served as local SADTU chairpersons. According to one interviewee, SADTU's role was a constructive one:

> During the tumultuous period, the principal would approach the unions and ask them to speak to their members. The unions did not show preference to any side when teachers were contesting posts, rather they tried to show support to the school.

Another interviewee remarked, jokingly, that 'when SADTU are looking for leaders, they look to the school'.

Overall, through the application of department-mandated rules and regulations, calm is reported to have returned to the school. But it was clear from the interviews that the turnaround efforts remain a work-in-progress. One interviewee described the evolution of School B2's climate as follows:

> In 2011/2012, teachers were segregated into groups according to their alliance [those for or against the principal's appointment] and each group occupied a different staff room...Some teachers would not even greet the SGB when they came to the school...Things are fast on the mend and working relations between staff members have improved. Teachers appear to be congregating in one staff-room now, and even attend school extra-mural matches together.

9.6 School-Level Governance Institutions—A Comparative Assessment

In this section, we turn from a school-by-school exploration of the causal mechanisms through which stakeholders exerted their influence (positive or negative; strongly or weakly) on school-level outcomes to a more systematic comparative analysis of the governance arrangements, the 'rules of the game'. We use the public governance typology introduced in Chapter 1 to characterize and contrast the institutional arrangements prevailing in our case study schools across two dimensions:

- whether the arrangements are hierarchical (that is, organized around vertical relationships between 'principals' and 'agents'), or whether they are negotiated (that is, organized around horizontal 'principal-principal'/ peer-to-peer arrangements); and
- whether they are based on impersonal rules of the game, which are applied impartially to all who have standing, or whether they are organized among personalized 'deals' among influential actors.

Our goal is to assess the hypothesis that, as a platform for performance, horizontal governance can be a partial substitute for weaknesses in hierarchy.

As Figure 9.1 signalled, the school-level findings underscore the weaknesses of hierarchy in Eastern Cape education. Across all the schools, beyond the most basic tasks, such as ensuring that teachers are paid, the ECDoE is most notable for its absence. In three of the four schools (A2, B1 and B2) conflicts arose, and were addressed—or exacerbated—by school-level stakeholders; higher levels of the education bureaucracy seemed to have exceedingly limited power to help resolve them.

Strikingly, despite an effort to probe, we also did not find that either teachers' unions (including SADTU) or political parties exerted a decisive influence on school-level governance. It is, of course, plausible, that political economy factors have played a more decisive role than our case studies were able to uncover. The 'usual suspects' include patronage ANC politics, and anti-developmental interventions (including the sale of posts) by SADTU. While we cannot dismiss the relevance of these forces, our school-level observations have persuaded us that other, hyper-local governance dynamics play a more important role in accounting for educational outcomes than is usually acknowledged in discussions of the governance of education. In this, our findings build on Nick Taylor's observation (quoted in Jansen, 2015) that:

> When I entered NEEDU, I thought SADTU was a huge problem . . . But the more I got into the data . . . I began to realize that there is a bigger problem. The biggest problem is the poor management in many parts of the system. Where management is weak, unions do what they do.

We highlight three distinct patterns of school-level governance. A first pattern, illustrated heuristically in Table 9.6, is predominantly personalized and (within the school) hierarchical: the principal is dominant, and shapes school culture and expectations. As our findings underscore, hierarchical may or may not be developmental—whether the school uses its resources to pursue educational or more private/predatory goals depends almost wholly on the preferences of the principal. Indeed, as per the narrative in section 9.4, governance in School B1 under Mrs Dinga was personalized, hierarchical and predatory. In School B2, by contrast, Mr Kramer, whose approach to governance also was personalized and hierarchical, had long been perceived as an effective principal.

In addition to variations among principals in their goals and effectiveness, there is a further reason why personalized hierarchy may be capricious: insofar as the goals of a school are personality dependent, they potentially are volatile and can readily be reversed once the principal leaves (or loses authority for some other reason). School B2 illustrates this: its successful governance was dependent on Mr Kramer's personal authority; when that was lost, things fell apart. As Chapter 8 details, this governance pattern of strong performance under a charismatic principal, which was reversed once that principal left, was also evident in the two early-period successful schools analysed in the case studies of Western Cape schools.

Table 9.6. Personalized, Hierarchical Governance

Hierarchical	80–100	0
Negotiated	0–20	0
	Personalized	*Impersonal School-level rules*

Source: *authors*.

In our second and third patterns of governance, illustrated heuristically in Tables 9.7 and 9.8, authority is distributed among multiple stakeholders. These patterns bring us to the question of whether and how horizontal governance might serve as an institutional substitute for weaknesses in hierarchy. Our case studies signal that, as with hierarchy, distributed governance can be associated with either positive or negative outcomes. School A2's pattern of governance was along the lines characterized in Table 9.7—personalized and fragmented; it also was predatory. The (early period) principal, teachers, SGB and some community insiders colluded with one another, via informal/personalized rules, to capture school revenues for private purposes. The school seemed largely trapped in a low-level equilibrium.

Table 9.8 illustrates a more impersonal variant of multistakeholder governance, along lines evident in School A1. Similar to the Table 9.7 pattern, governance in School A1 had substantial negotiated, horizontal aspects, with authority distributed among multiple stakeholders (with the principal as *primus inter pares*)—but, in this instance, the focus was on building a shared commitment among the teacher cadre to a developmental culture within the school, on nurturing inclusive relationships externally with parent, community and bureaucratic stakeholders—all anchored (in the case of School A1, though not necessarily in all instances of collaborative governance) in the transparent and consistent application of a rule-bound culture. These allegiances provided, in turn, a relatively robust platform for resisting patronage and other predatory pressures. (Note Table 9.8's distinction between hierarchical-impersonal rules from outside the school—i.e. the ECDoE—and those established within, and by the school community itself; for School A1, the latter were the more salient rules.) It is, of course, plausible that collaborative governance could be associated with mediocre performance. Nonetheless, the experience of School A1 offers some cause for optimism that horizontal governance can, under some conditions, serve as an institutional substitute, offering a platform for improved performance, even where hierarchy is weak. We discuss this further in the final section.

One final point vis-à-vis horizontal governance: it is tempting to view the Table 9.7 pattern of personalized, fragmented governance as especially toxic. But the School B1 case study points to a more nuanced conclusion. The way in which School B1 turned itself around was via a bottom-up (Table 9.7-like) challenge by the SGB, parents, and communities to the pre-existing

Table 9.7. Personalized, Fragmented Governance

Hierarchical	5–40%	0%
Negotiated	60–95%	0%
	Personalized	*Impersonal*

Source: authors.

Table 9.8. Collaborative Governance

Hierarchical	10–20%	30%	5–10%
Negotiated	15–30%	15–30%	0%
	Personalized	*Impersonal: School-level rules*	*Impersonal: Department-level rules*

hierarchical, personalized and predatory (Table 9.6-style) governance arrangements. Bottom-up-induced chaos cannot, of course, provide a sustainable basis for school governance—but it can sometimes be (and was) a crucial step in unlocking a pre-existing predatory equilibrium.

9.7 Clouds with Silver Linings

In seeking to learn how governance plays out in practice at the school level, this study has given priority to case-study depth over statistical breadth. While we have confidence in the accuracy of our individual school-level narratives, as with all 'small-n' research designs, it is important to be aware of inevitable limitations in the broader applicability (the 'external validity') of the research. With only four schools, drawn from a single district, the size of our sample is small. We make no claims as to the relative importance across the province of each of the patterns observed in the cases. Further, across the province, there are almost surely additional patterns of school-level governance interaction other than the ones which we have observed. Rather, consistent with the methodological strengths of small-n case studies which use process tracing methodologies, our goal has been to identify causal mechanisms and refine hypotheses—to understand better the potential and limitations of horizontal governance as an institutional substitute in settings where (as with the ECDoE) hierarchy is weak.

School-level performance emerges in our analysis as an outcome of strategic interactions among the school principal, the teaching staff, the SGB and the broader community. Insofar as horizontal governance is prevalent, its effect on performance depends on the relative strength of developmentally-oriented stakeholders and stakeholders seeking to capture school-level resources for private or political purposes. A priori, the strategic interactions among stakeholders could result in a variety of potential outcomes, including:

- a low-level equilibrium of capture, centred around the principal and teaching staff in the short term, with the collusion of the SGB and the broader community, and reproduced via a captured process of principal selection;
- a high-performing equilibrium, with the parties converging on performance-oriented governance, with sufficient mutual commitment to effectively counter any efforts at predation by one or another party; or

- a disequilibrium, driven by determined efforts on the part of one or other of the actors to disrupt the pre-existing relationships.

Our case studies uncovered evidence of both vicious circles and virtuous spirals—with governance arrangements shaped (for good or ill) by interactions along the stakeholders. Our illustrations of virtuous spirals comprised:

- sustained, mutually supportive participatory governance (in School A1)—nurtured by an inclusion-oriented principal in the earlier period, providing a platform for seamless succession by another inclusion-oriented principal, and continuing into the present;
- activism (in School B1) by the SGB and broader community to turn around a prior period of dysfunction—forcing out a predatory principal in one school and (in both that school and in School B2) actively collaborating with a new principal to transform school culture by putting in place and consistently enforcing new school-level rules of conduct; and
- some effort in all the schools (varying in intensity and effectiveness) by developmentally oriented principals to enlist the SGB and community in support of the consolidation of a more performance-oriented, rule-bound internal culture.

Given the broader weakness of top-down governance in the Eastern Cape, these patterns are consistent with the 'silver lining' proposition suggested at the outset of this chapter—namely that, in settings where top-down governance is weak, horizontal governance sometimes can serve as a (partial) institutional substitute. The 1996 South African Schools Act has provided the country with an institutional framework that delegates significant authority to school governing bodies in which the majority of positions are held by parents. What has been lacking, however, has been systematic effort to support SGBs to take on this putative developmental role. On the contrary, the South African education discourse has focused almost exclusively on the failures of school-level governance, and has been pre-occupied with the exploration of options to recentralize authority.[5] In our view, the results in this chapter point in a very different direction.

Might there be ways of intervening to support SGBs that improve the odds that they will support developmental outcomes, rather than being part of some low-level, predatory equilibrium? Our findings underscore that the influence of horizontal governance on performance (for good or ill) depends on the relative influence of developmental and predatory stakeholders. It follows that, while it could perhaps be somewhat helpful to strengthen

[5] For a recent example, see the proposals along these lines, summarized in Republic of South Africa, Department of Basic Education (2016).

the capacities of individual SGBs, the crucial task for initiatives aimed at strengthening horizontal governance is their effect in empowering developmental actors within SGBs, parents and the broader community. Chapter 10 explores further how this might be achieved.

We are not proposing that support for SGBs is a magic bullet. But we believe that our findings offer encouragement that a non-hierarchical entry point for improving educational outcomes indeed has some potential to achieve gains. Perhaps it is time to complement ongoing efforts to strengthen hierarchy with something different.

Appendix A9.1: Interviewees

The following people were interviewed in each school. (To protect anonymity, names are not provided, and gender has sometimes been altered.)

Interviewees for School A1:

- Former SGB member, she was first served on the SGB from 2003 to 2006 and again from 2009 to 2012.
- Senior teacher, appointed in 1987.
- Deputy principal at School A1 since 2005, she was first appointed in 1984 as the head of department (HOD).

Interviewees for School A2:

- School principal; appointed to this position in 2013.
- SGB treasurer serving her second term on the SGB; was initially appointed onto the SGB in 2009.
- School deputy principal; he joined the staff in 1994 and was appointed deputy principal in 2003.

Interviewees for School B1:

- Deputy principal from 1983 until her retirement in 2011.
- Current chair of school governing body (SGB); has served four terms on SGB, beginning in 2001, with one break in between.
- SGB member and parent, has had children at school since 2022; been on SGB since 2012.

Interviewees for School B2:

- Head of department (HOD) at the school; she joined the school in 2004, and was appointed foundation phase head in 2008.
- Deputy principal at the school; he joined the school in 1990 as an HOD.
- Treasurer of the SGB; she has served on the SGB since 2009.

Appendix A9.2: Stakeholder Mapping

Immediate school stakeholders

Principal—School leader

School management team—consists of the principal, the deputy(ies) and the heads of department.

School staff—teaching and administrative staff employed by the school (and in some cases the SGB).

School governing body—mandatory members include the school principal, parents with children at the school (the parent body makes up 50 per cent plus one person on the SGB), teachers and non-teaching school staff).

Parent body—parents (or guardians) of children attending the school.

The hierarchy

Eastern Cape Department of Education—is responsible for administering public schooling in the province from Grades 1 to 12.

ECDoE district office—exercises the authority of the ECDoE in all day-to-day administrative and professional dealings with schools.

ECDoE circuit office—interacts with school to implement education policy effectively Department of Basic Education, 2014.

Unions—the two largest teacher unions are the South African Democratic Teacher's Unions (SADTU) and the National Professional Teachers Organization of South Africa (NAPTOSA).

Role of school principal

- Leading the learning school.
- Shaping the direction and development of the school.
- Managing quality and securing accountability.
- Developing and empowering self and others.
- Managing the school as an organization.
- Working with and for the immediate school community as well as the broader community.
- Managing human resources in the school.
- Management and advocacy of extra-curricular activities.

Government Gazette, 2014

Role of the SGB

- Develop a school mission statement.
- Adopt a code of conduct for learners at the school and determine the admission and language policy.
- Recommend teachers to the ECDoE for appointment or employ additional teachers.
- Supplement resources provided by the state in order to improve the quality of education offered by the school.
- Support school staff as they perform their professional tasks.
- Oversee the maintenance of school property and buildings.

South African Schools Act of 1996

References

George, A. and Bennett, A. (2005) *Case Studies and Theory Development in the Social Sciences*. Cambridge, MA: MIT Press.

Jansen, L. (2015) 'SADTU "exploits culture of chaos"'. IOL, http://www.iol.co.za/news/south-africa/kwazulu-natal/sadtu-exploits-culture-of-chaos-1902198.

North, D. W. (1990) *Institutions, Institutional Change and Economic Performance*. New York: Cambridge University Press.

North, D. W., Wallis, J., and Weingast, B. (2009) *Violence and Social Orders: A Conceptual Framework for Interpreting Recorded Human History*. New York: Cambridge University Press.

Ostrom, E. (2005) *Understanding Institutional Diversity*. Princeton, NJ: Princeton University Press.

Republic of South Africa, Department of Basic Education (2016) Report of the Ministerial Task Team Appointed by Minister Angie Motshekga to Investigate Allegations into the Selling of Posts of Educators by Members of Teachers Unions and Department Officials of Provincial Education Departments, http://www.education.gov.za/Portals/0/Documents/Reports/MTTJobsReport2016.pdf?ver=2016-05-20-173514-773.

10

'All for Education'—Meeting the Governance Challenge

Brian Levy

10.1 Introduction

Over the past quarter century, access to schooling has expanded rapidly the world over, but gains in literacy and numeracy have proven harder to come by. Transforming schooling into learning for all is a central challenge of our time. This book addresses the challenge through a focus on the governance of public education in South Africa, a country whose legacy of discrimination, inequality and poverty gives special urgency to the task of improving educational outcomes. Chapters 2–9 set out the empirical findings as to the relationship between governance and educational outcomes. This chapter explores some potential policy implications.

In any educational system, the crucial learning relationship is that between the learner and teacher—so research as to what pedagogical approaches are effective has, for good reason, been a central focus of efforts to strengthen educational outcomes. Attention to pedagogy has been of special salience in South Africa. As Chapter 2 of the book detailed, the post-apartheid transformation of South Africa's education system was multi-dimensional. Alongside far-reaching fiscal, equity and institutional changes, the country also had to re-orient teaching away from inherited master-servant patterns, put in place a wholly new post-apartheid curriculum and, more broadly, learn about the kinds of non-elitist pedagogical approaches which can achieve rapid gains for an historically oppressed population.

But the fact that pedagogy matters does not diminish the salience of governance. For one thing, though much has been learned about effective pedagogy, the gains have not yet spread broadly. Getting beyond pilot initiatives and working at scale by disseminating knowledge as to what works, and supporting teachers seeking to adopt new practices, is a central function of education bureaucracies—and thus how they are governed. More broadly, governance arrangements matter crucially for outcomes because they structure the incentives, constraints, rewards and sanctions of a system's participants—and thereby shape the efficiency and effectiveness with which resources are used to achieve the intended results.

All too often, governance challenges have been conceived in narrowly technocratic terms—with a presumption that, given enough 'capacity' and 'political will', shortfalls in governance can be addressed straightforwardly. However, as a classic report on *Making Services Work for Poor People* underscored:

> Too frequently those seeking improvement have focused only on internal organizational reforms—focusing on management of the frontline workers. If organizational failures are the result of deeper weaknesses in institutional arrangements . . . direct attacks on the proximate determinants (more money, better training, more internal information) will fail.[1]

Building on this critique, in recent years scholars and practitioners have explored in depth the relationships between context, governance and development outcomes. The nostrum that 'context matters' in shaping the efficacy of specific governance arrangements has become commonplace. The frontier challenge, explored in this book, is to probe *how* context matters—how the preferred ('good fit') approach to improving outcomes varies according to specific political and institutional contexts.

This book has explored the link between context and good fit in relation to a specific governance-related question: what should be the balance between hierarchical and horizontal institutional arrangements for the public provision of basic education? As Chapter 1 reviews, some scholars and practitioners argue that education should be tightly managed hierarchically—with strong, top-down control of recruitment, promotion, curriculum and the content of classroom-level instruction. But others argue for more horizontal approaches which delegate significant resources and responsibility to internal and community stakeholders at the school level, thereby allowing for the development of appropriate context-specific solutions. Following the logic laid out above, an obvious response to the hierarchical-horizontal debate is to argue that the appropriate balance between hierarchical and horizontal governance depends crucially on context. But how?

South Africa's far-reaching reforms of the education sector, laid out in the 1996 South African Schools Act (SASA), provide an ideal 'natural experiment' for exploring the interplay between context, hierarchical and horizontal

[1] World Bank (2004: 58).

governance. SASA replaced the pre-existing, fragmented and racially-ordered institutional arrangements with a unified, multi-tiered system:

- The national-level was assigned responsibility for policymaking, for resourcing the system, and for setting the overall regulatory framework.
- The provincial-level was assigned responsibility for implementation—for spending the budgetary resources made available from the centre, and employing the teachers, administrators and other personnel who comprised the vast majority of employees in the system.
- Substantial school-level responsibilities (including important roles in the recruitment of the school principal and senior teachers) were assigned to school-governing bodies (SGBs) in which parents were required to be in the majority.

Chapters 2–7 of the book explored how politics and institutions influence the structure and performance of South Africa's education bureaucracies at both the national level (Chapters 2 and 3), and the provincial level (Chapters 4–7). Chapters 8 and 9 detailed the results of school-level case studies conducted in South Africa's Western Cape and Eastern Cape provinces.

The current chapter explores the implications of the findings for action, situating the analysis within the broader context of the education system as a whole. Section 10.2 lays out the policy possibilities, limitations, synergies and constraints of hierarchical and horizontal governance in the South African context. Section 10.3 synthesizes the school-level case study findings, highlighting the links between hyper-local governance dynamics and performance. Section 10.4 explores why it has been so difficult, in South Africa and elsewhere, to address the challenges of governance (and other) reforms in the education sector—and how these challenges might be addressed more effectively.

10.2 Hierarchical and Horizontal Governance Revisited

Theory tells us that both hierarchical and horizontal governance have the potential to support good educational outcomes, in distinctive ways. A well-functioning hierarchy can undertake efficiently many of the logistical tasks (e.g. teacher post provisioning, payroll, infrastructure provisioning and maintenance, textbook and supplies management) associated with a large public educational system. Crucially for the South African context, a well-functioning bureaucracy potentially can also function as a transmission belt, investing in learning about pedagogical approaches which improve educational outcomes, and communicating the results throughout the school system.

Horizontal governance also has the potential to add value—both as a complement and as a substitute for hierarchy. As Chapter 1 explored in depth, in sectors such as education where service provision is diffused geographically, delegation of authority to local levels potentially can improve performance. Where bureaucracy is strong, horizontal governance potentially can function as a complement:

- helping to customize provision in ways which are responsive to the local context;
- improving motivation—with a 'zone of autonomy' at the service provision front line providing the opportunity for internal leaders to motivate their teams effectively, including by fostering an environment of continuing learning on the part of staff as well as students;
- creating scope for the utilization of local-level information of a kind to which higher-level hierarchical authorities lack access—and thereby enhancing processes for the selection of good quality staff and leaders, and the efficacy of efforts to hold staff and leaders accountable for their performance.

Where bureaucracy is weak, horizontal governance potentially can be useful in a different way. Along with the specifically local functions highlighted above, local participation could function as a potential institutional substitute—providing support for some of the logistical, managerial and oversight functions which in other contexts might be done hierarchically.

Figure 10.1 suggests one way of framing how hierarchical and horizontal governance might interact in different contexts. The horizontal axis distinguishes between settings where hierarchical governance is relatively strong, and settings where it is weak. The vertical axis distinguishes between settings where school governing body and community engagement is developmental, and those where it is weak or predatory. The barrier along the horizontal axis signals that (for reasons explored in detail in Chapter 7 and discussed further

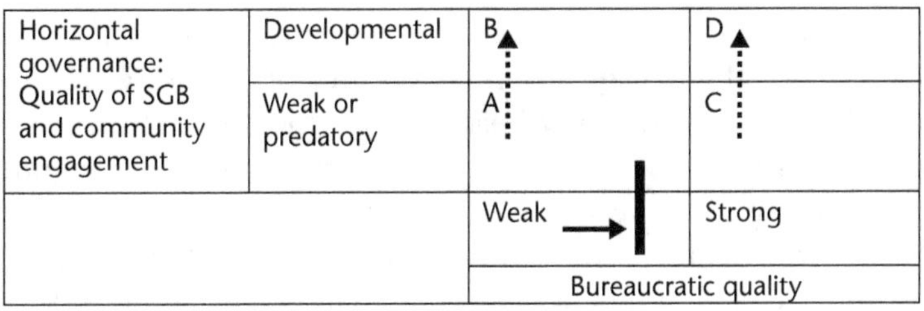

Figure 10.1. Governance options for improving school outcomes
Source: author

below) the potential to strengthen hierarchy is limited in contexts where politics and institutions are personalized, patronage-oriented and fragmented.

Three distinctive ways of leveraging governance to improve educational outcomes in different contexts are suggested by the figure:

- In settings where political and institutional constraints are such that weaknesses in bureaucratic capability are unlikely to be remediable—endeavouring to improve outcomes by moving from quadrant A to quadrant B, with participatory horizontal governance functioning as a potential institutional substitute.
- In settings illustrated by quadrant C where hierarchical governance is relatively strong, horizontal governance is weak, and educational outcomes are disappointing—endeavouring to identify targeted ways of leveraging and building on the pre-existing strengths of the hierarchy to improve outcomes (i.e. improving outcomes while remaining within quadrant C).
- (Also with quadrant C as a starting point): complementing hierarchical initiatives with efforts to strengthen horizontal governance—that is, trying to move from quadrant C to quadrant D.

The sections which follow elaborate on these options, drawing on both the results of the Western Cape and Eastern Cape case studies, and the broader comparative literature.

10.2.1 *Hierarchies in Practice*

The comparison of South Africa's Western Cape and Eastern Cape provinces illustrates vividly how divergent socio-economic, political and institutional contexts shape the performance of education bureaucracies. Table 10.1 summarizes some of the contextual differences between the two provinces. Chapter 7 provides more detailed information, and analyses in depth the causal mechanisms through which these distinctive contexts affect the behaviour of their bureaucracies.

The Eastern Cape provided a strikingly unpropitious political and institutional context for the consolidation of a results-oriented bureaucracy. The province inherited from the apartheid era a fragmented, patronage-oriented bureaucracy. Its weak middle class, and the electoral dominance of one political party, translated into weak demand-side pressure for better services. Fragmentation among elites within the dominant party fuelled further the predisposition to seek influence via patronage. The result was that, as Chapter 5 details, the Eastern Cape Department of Education (ECDoE) has been bedevilled by divergent and competing regional interests, organizational

Table 10.1. Two Divergent Contexts

	1. Socio-economic	2. Political	3. Inherited institutions
Western Cape	Diverse social composition—both ethnically & by economic class	- elites dispersed across multiple political parties with two broad groupings - competitive elections	Inheritance of 'impersonal' bureaucracy
Eastern Cape	Homogenous social composition—disproportionately poor & Xhosa-speaking	- ANC electorally dominant; - deep intra-party fragmentation	Inheritance of patronage bantustan bureaucracies

Source: chapter 7

cultures, and patronage ties which consistently defied centralized control. It has experienced repeated leadership turnover and a general flouting of centralized authority. Obstacles to enforcing management control and sustaining leadership continuity have contributed to chronic weaknesses in both financial and personnel management. This low-level equilibrium proved resistant to change, even when the provincial department of education was taken under administration by central government.

The question naturally arises as to whether, as per Figure 10.1, horizontal governance might serve in an Eastern Cape-type setting as at least a partial institutional substitute for hierarchical weakness. On this score, the research findings are somewhat encouraging. The comparative econometric analysis laid out in Chapter 6 found that including 'parental contribution to school construction and maintenance' as an explanatory variable had a positive and statistically significant effect on educational outcomes. The school-level case study analyses in Chapter 9 (on which more below) detailed the causal mechanisms through which participatory governance can (but need not) have a positive influence on school performance.

By contrast to the Eastern Cape, the Western Cape's socio-economic, political and institutional context provided a supportive platform for relatively strong bureaucratic capability, oriented towards public service provision. As Chapter 5 details, the Western Cape Education Department (WCED) does well the core tasks of a bureaucracy: managing resources; assigning personnel to where they are most needed; monitoring and managing on the basis of performance. In turn, as Chapter 6 explored econometrically, these bureaucratic strengths translated into gains in educational outcomes relative to other South African provinces, even once other determinants of outcomes are controlled for. But strikingly, the econometric analysis in Chapter 6 also showed that, for all of the strengths of its bureaucracy, when compared with some other African educational systems (notably Kenya), the outcomes achieved by the Western Cape were mediocre (paralleling quadrant C in Figure 10.1). Why this might be the case is considered further in section 10.4.

The above is not intended to imply that there is no scope for provincial-level leaders (both political and technocratic) to improve education bureaucracies. But it does imply that these individual efforts can be supported by (or confounded by) context. Note, though, that the Table 10.1 divergence in contexts between the two provinces is extreme. In such contexts, the status quo will be more tightly locked in (again, for good or ill), so change will be more constrained, and more incremental. Had the research been undertaken in other provinces, it is likely that in at least some of them, the exogenous variables would have aligned in a more mixed way. In these more mixed cases, the quality of public bureaucracy would be more of a knife edge, with scope for more rapid improvement (or more rapid decline).

10.2.2 *Horizontal Governance in Practice*

Plausibly, as Figure 10.1 suggests, horizontal governance can offset some of hierarchical governance's limitations: in settings such as the Eastern Cape, where the capabilities of hierarchies are weak, but where the broader context renders bureaucratic improvement infeasible, it might serve as an institutional substitute. In all settings, it could serve as an institutional complement, taking on specific hyper-local functions which fall below the radar even of relatively well-performing bureaucracies. But does this happen in practice?

SASA's assignment of substantial school-level responsibilities (including the recruitment of the school principal and senior teachers) to school governing bodies (SGBs) in which parents are required to be in the majority provides an excellent opportunity for exploring empirically the extent to which horizontal governance can indeed realize its potential as complement and/or partial substitute for hierarchies. But paradoxically SASA's seeming empowerment of the school-level cannot be taken as a signal that South Africa's education system has embraced horizontal governance.

As discussed further in the final section of this chapter, momentum for the empowerment of SGBs in SASA came via two sources: via the interests of affluent parents who had been beneficiaries of apartheid-era public schooling; and via those anti-apartheid activists who had embraced a participatory vision of democracy. While the latter influence weakened rapidly, the concerns of white South Africans that quality be maintained in the public[2] schools which historically had served their children shaped both the design

[2] In South Africa, public education dominates, both historically and to the present day; as of 2015, about 95 per cent of school-going children were enrolled in the public system.

and implementation of policy towards SGBs. The delegation of substantial authority to the school level, including the right to top-up public funds with self-financing by the parent body, was a way of assuaging these concerns.

However, while affluent families can relatively straightforwardly take on the enhanced school-level responsibilities assigned by SASA, the challenge is more formidable for poor families. Whether and how the rhetorical embrace of participation might translate into genuine empowerment of parents and communities, beyond the already-empowered elites, was a central question of the school-level case study research reported in Chapters 8 and 9 and is explored comparatively in section 10.3 below. To set the stage for that analysis, it is helpful first to lay out some of the relevant issues and evidence raised from the global comparative literature.

Research worldwide suggests that strengthened horizontal governance can (but need not) improve educational outcomes. Bruns, Filmer, and Patrinos (2011) offer rich detail on dozens of carefully evaluated horizontal reforms, including reforms to improve school-based management, to enhance information transparency, and to make teachers more accountable for performance. They find considerable variations in impact; some interventions turn out to make a significant positive difference, others have been ineffective. Mansuri and Rao's (2013) multi-sector and multi-country review of whether participation works finds a similarly variable set of effects. What accounts for these variations?

One possible explanation for the variation is that the potential for horizontal governance is inherently limited in settings where parents are poor and uneducated, and thus lack the requisite basic skills (let alone knowledge of pedagogy) to participate effectively in in school governance. This explanation is not consistent with the evidence of positive impact (including in poor communities with low levels of education) cited above. The school-level case studies summarized below add to the evidence by detailing the causal mechanisms through which horizontal governance can have a positive impact, even when parents themselves lack education.

A second possible explanation is that the cause of variations in performance lies not so much in governance as in divergent pedagogical and managerial practices. A pessimistic view would be that the technical constraints are binding, so there are no gains to be had from strengthening horizontal governance. A more optimistic view is that even in such circumstances enhanced participation can transform interactions at the school-level—strengthening accountability and commitment to results, and more broadly fostering mutual solidarity and a learning-oriented culture. The school-level findings in section 10.3 shed empirical light on this question.

A third common explanation for variation across locales is that the efficacy of horizontal governance depends on power—with parents in poor communities generally disempowered relative to teachers, school leadership and the organizational structures (bureaucracies and unions) of education. Thus, so the concern goes, even if horizontal governance can be shown to add value, efforts to strengthen it will be blocked by more powerful stakeholders with a vested interest in the status quo. Analytically, as Levy (2014) explores, this issue concerns the strength of developmentally oriented stakeholders relative to predatory actors seeking to capture school-level resources for private or political purposes—and whether these threat/trumping dynamics are rigid, or subject to change. Again, the school-level case studies in section 10.3 provide empirical insight.

10.3 Governance at the School Level

The school-level governance research detailed in Chapters 8 and 9 explored the causal mechanisms through which educational outcomes were shaped by interactions between school leadership and other stakeholders inside and outside the school. This section provides a comparative synthesis of some key findings.

The research focused on eight schools—four in the Western Cape and four in the Eastern Cape. The case studies adopted a process tracing methodology, which enabled them to drill into the details of the causal mechanisms through which horizontal governance influenced school-level outcomes.[3] To control for the influence of socio-economic conditions on performance, the initial intention was to target matched pairs of successful and less successful schools within the same community. While the eight schools indeed comprised four sets of geographically contiguous matched pairs, the patterns of success and weakness turned out to be more complex than initially had been expected. All eight schools had gone through a change in principal over the relevant period, making for the three distinct governance 'episodes' illustrated in Figure 10.2: an initial period; a transitional period, and associated process of selection of a new principal; and a later period. As detailed later, within-school variations in performance over time turned out to be strongly associated with changes in principal.

Table 10.2 summarizes the main findings from the case studies vis-à-vis the influence of hierarchical and horizontal governance in each school. The

[3] As detailed in Chapter 8, in the Western Cape, outcomes were measured by trends in school-level systemic tests conducted by the WCED. In the Eastern Cape no parallel test results were available; trends in enrolment were used as a proxy.

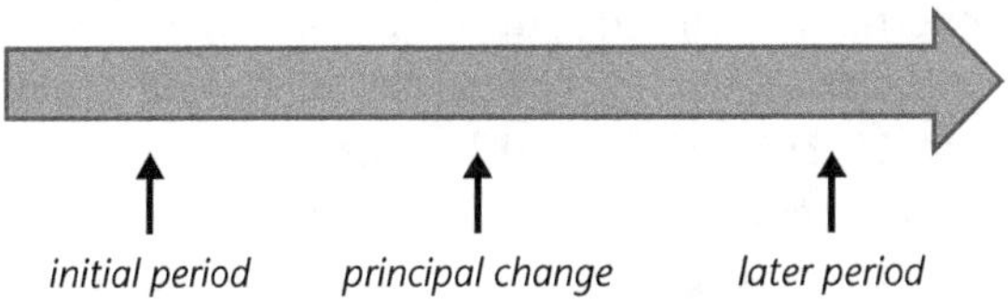

Figure 10.2. All case study schools experienced a change in leadership

Table 10.2. Governance and Performance in the Case Study Schools

	Eastern Cape	Western Cape
I: INFLUENCE OF HIERARCHICAL GOVERNANCE		
Role of provincial bureaucracy	- Protects dysfunctional status quo in two schools; - Offers modest support for school principals seeking turnaround in later period in two schools.	WCED buttresses authority of charismatic principals in initial period in two schools, but performance declined when the principals left.
Role of school-level leaders	How authority is exercised by school leaders consistently has a strong influence on governance and performance in all periods in all schools	
	Highly respected principal drives relatively strong performance in early initial period in one school.	Charismatic principals drive strong performance-orientation in initial period in two chools
II: INFLUENCE OF HORIZONTAL GOVERNANCE		
Positive influence	- Sustained performance-oriented multi-stakeholder governance in one school - Stakeholder initiated turnaround in two schools	- Stakeholder supported turnaround in one school
Negative influence	- Ongoing capture in one school - Capture during earlier period in two schools	- Ongoing capture in one school - Capture in latter period in one school - Conflictual principal succession disrupts performance in one school

table distinguishes between two facets of hierarchical governance: hierarchical influence exerted by the relevant provincial department, and leadership by the school principal. The school-level findings as to the role of provincial bureaucracies are consistent with the provincial-level evidence of Chapters 4–7. In none of the Eastern Cape case studies was there any evidence that the ECDoE offered more than very modest help to foster a performance orientation at the school-level. The Western Cape's WCED, by contrast, played a more pro-active role—but there are some paradoxical findings, which are best considered jointly in the discussion below of the role of the school principal.

As the table also summarizes, there were substantial variations across schools—and within schools over time—in the influence of horizontal governance. In some schools, for some periods of time, its influence was positive. In others, a variety of school-level stakeholders were complicit in the capture of school-level resources for more narrowly personalized purposes. The efficacy of horizontal governance turned out to be strongly associated with the approach to leadership of the school principal, with some striking interactions between the (Figure 10.2) initial period and later period patterns.

The centrality of the school principal has been identified in global research on school-level governance as an important proximate determinant of school performance (Hallinger and Heck, 1996; Leithwood, Patten, and Jantzi, 2010). The findings in the Chapter 8 and 9 case studies are consistent with this, but with a crucial addition. As they underscore, the principal does not function in isolation, but is embedded in a dense network of horizontal interactions with teachers, with the school governing body (SGB), with parents, and with the community more broadly. Over time, these relationships—and how the principal nurtures them (or fails to nurture them)—are key underlying determinants of school-level educational outcomes.

Table 10.3 applies the governance framework introduced in Chapter 1 and used throughout this volume to characterize some different ways in which school principals approach engagement with other stakeholders. The framework is organized around two dimensions of school-level governance arrangements. One dimension distinguishes between hierarchical and more horizontal, peer-to-peer modes of structuring authority—with the former organized around vertical relationships between 'principals' and 'agents', and the latter organized around negotiated understandings among multiple stakeholders. The second dimension distinguishes between impersonal and personalized governance arrangements—with the former built around rules which apply equally to all who have standing, and the latter structured around informal understanding among influential actors.

In practice, any specific governance arrangement is likely to be a hybrid combination of the resulting four cells, with the relative weight varying from school to school. A useful heuristic way of describing these hybrid patterns is to allocate 100 points across the four cells. Table 10.3 highlights three distinct patterns. Each builds on, but should not be interpreted as being identical to,

Table 10.3. Three Patterns of School-Level Governance

<table>
<tr><td colspan="3">A: Principal-centric governance</td></tr>
<tr><td>Hierarchical</td><td colspan="2">70</td></tr>
<tr><td>Horizontal</td><td>10</td><td>20</td></tr>
<tr><td></td><td>Personalized</td><td>Impersonal</td></tr>
<tr><td colspan="3">B: Collaborative governance</td></tr>
<tr><td>Hierarchical</td><td>25</td><td>25</td></tr>
<tr><td>Horizontal</td><td>25</td><td>25</td></tr>
<tr><td></td><td>Personalized</td><td>Impersonal</td></tr>
<tr><td colspan="3">C: Bottom-up governance</td></tr>
<tr><td>Hierarchical</td><td>0–50</td><td>5</td></tr>
<tr><td>Horizontal</td><td>40–90</td><td>5</td></tr>
<tr><td></td><td>Personalized</td><td>Impersonal</td></tr>
</table>

school-specific patterns of interaction among stakeholders described in depth in the Chapter 8 and 9 case studies.

The first pattern, illustrated heuristically in Table 10.3 panel A and evident in three schools, comprises strong top-down leadership by a charismatic, committed results-oriented principal. As Chapter 8 details, in the two Western Cape schools this leadership was underpinned by support from a well-functioning bureaucracy. This leadership style yielded good results—but (for reasons explored below) only in the initial period.

In a second pattern, illustrated by Table 10.3 panel B, the school principal's approach to leadership is strongly collaborative. Among the case study schools, the clearest illustration of strong, participatory leadership was a school in the Eastern Cape. The institutional culture of the school, established by its founding principal, was one where all stakeholders—teachers, the SGB, the extended community—felt included. Even with the ECDoE, which was carefully kept at arm's length, relationships remained cordial. This pattern of collaborative governance was underpinned by impersonal rules, collectively developed, collectively owned, and largely self-imposed.

The third pattern, evident in the initial period in four of the eight schools, was one of weak/captured leadership. In two cases (one in each province) this dysfunctional leadership can be linked directly to the predatory preferences of a 'strong' principal, who inculcated a culture of self-seeking and inattention to learning throughout their schools. In the remaining two schools (both in the Eastern Cape) leadership was relatively weak; in one of the two there was a low-level equilibrium of capture with the principal, teachers, and the SGB working in cahoots with one another; in the other the stakeholders were mired in endemic conflict.

The way in which school principals engaged with other stakeholders in the initial period had a powerful impact on the interactions in subsequent periods—with principal succession comprising the critical juncture. In three of the eight case study schools, the initial period equilibrium proved to be robust over time:

- A high-level equilibrium of strong performance persisted throughout the period of study in the Eastern Cape school which had successfully inculcated a set of collaborative governance arrangements in the first period. (Indeed, this was the only one of the eight case study schools which consistently sustained relatively[4] strong performance throughout the

[4] Both the trend in numbers of students and area feedback (and visual observation during fieldwork) identify the school as a relatively strong performer locally. But given the vast disparities between average performance in the Eastern and Western Cape, there is no basis for extrapolating this relative success into absolutely strong performance in relation to schools in low-income areas in both provinces.

period of study.) The school's inclusive culture supported a smooth process of principal succession. The successor principal, an internal candidate from within the teaching staff, had been mentored by the initial principal, enjoyed the support of the SGB and, once appointed, continued along the path that had been established.

- A low-level equilibrium persisted in two schools (one in each province), with captured/weak SGBs selecting school principals who (in one case) actively supported the continuation of the dysfunctional equilibrium and (in the other) seemed powerless to reverse the dysfunctions, despite what seemed to be good intentions.

In the remaining five schools, the inter-temporal dynamics were less stable.

Three schools went from relatively strong to weak performance. Strikingly, all three were schools where initially strong performance was based on charismatic leadership by the principal—with the subsequent declines pointing to the limitations of this 'heroic' style of leadership. Though in the short term, the determined efforts of a strong principal can yield success, at some point the time comes for succession. If succession turns out badly (as happened in both of the Western Cape schools), or if the principal loses authority for some other reason (as happened in the Eastern Cape example), then this successful performance is likely to be reversed. (Chapter 8's detailed depiction for two Western Cape schools of how the institutional vacuum that became evident following the exit of a charismatic principal resulted in conflict and a collapse of school performance is especially salient.)

The remaining two case study schools (one in the Western Cape, and one in the Eastern Cape) offer vivid examples of performance turnaround—with (as per Table 10.3 panel C) the turnarounds underpinned by active multistakeholder engagement. In the Western Cape turnaround school, poor results in a first cycle of standardized tests, conducted in 2002 and 2004 shocked the school community. In response, and building on close relationships between the principal and the community, an intensive effort was made to improve outcomes, which subsequently rose significantly (although, it must be noted, not to the level of becoming a high performer). This school also was the only one of the four Western Cape case studies where principal transition successfully proceeded by the book.

The role of participatory governance is even more striking in the Eastern Cape example of turnaround. This school had long been characterized by neglectful and predatory leadership on the part of an often-absent principal. The number of pupils had fallen from close to 1,000 in the early 1990s to a low of 341 in 2011. After over a decade(!) of ongoing dysfuntion, a group of parents and some SGB members met, and jointly reached the view that the principal needed to be replaced. At the group's urging, the SGB took their decision to the ECDoE district office. After failing to win support from the bureaucracy, the parent community staged a protest, preventing the principal from accessing the school, and forcing the appointment of a replacement, with whom they worked closely to turn around the school. By 2015, four years after the intervention by parents, the number of pupils in the school had risen to 547, up by 70 per cent from the trough.

In sum, and crucially for policy purposes, the school-level case studies show that stakeholder dynamics are not pre-ordained by either the broader local context or by the strength of the education bureaucracy, but turn out to be contingent and cumulative—with individual agency by stakeholders playing a significant role. This raises the possibility that pro-active interventions potentially could tilt the balance of threat-trumping interactions in some fraction of schools away from predatory and towards more developmental actors, with a positive impact on educational outcomes. This possibility is explored further in section 10.4.

Before concluding the discussion of the school-level case studies, one final empirical finding is worthy of note. Going into the research, the expectation was that the largest teachers' union, SADTU, would play a significant role in shaping school-level dynamics, using its power to influence appointments, and assert control more generally. We also expected to see evidence of political parties using the power of appointment for patronage purposes. While we did find a few instances, in general we found that in both provinces hyper-local school-level dynamics were decisive; generally, these were at most loosely linked to these broader union and political influences. For the Western Cape, this likely reflected the relatively robust role played by the WCED's industrial relations department, which engaged unions in a collaborative rather than top-down manner. For the Eastern Cape, it was perhaps more a symptom of the generalized fragmentation of the province's politics. Though surprising, this finding is consistent with the observation of a seasoned scholar/practitioner of South African education, Nick Taylor (quoted in Jansen, 2015) that:

> When I entered the National Education Evaluation Unit in South Africa's Department of Basic Education I thought SADTU was a huge problem ... But the more I got into the data ... I began to realize that there is a bigger problem. The biggest problem is the poor management in many parts of the system. Where management is weak, unions do what they do ...

10.4 Orchestrating Change

The research presented in this book has documented uneven governance at every level of South Africa's educational system. School-level governance turns out to be something of a 'hit or miss' affair, with outcomes dependent on hyper-local dynamics between developmental and predatory actors. Provincial-level education bureaucracies have been bogged down by systemic political and institutional constraints in some provinces, and caught up in a cycle of mediocrity in others where the broader constraints seem less binding. National-level policy compromises made to accommodate influential actors (explored in depth in Chapters 2 and 3) have resulted in the prioritization of 'rules of the game' which give little more than lip service to quality. The result is an education system in which all too many pupils go to school, but fail to learn.

At the same time, much is known in South Africa as well as elsewhere as to the kinds of pedagogy that can be effective in fostering learning among children from poor, historically deprived backgrounds. For governance, too, there are abundant studies which explore rigorously the efficacy or otherwise of specific interventions.[5]

Given the urgency of the task, and the seeming availability of knowledge as to how better outcomes can be achieved, the temptation is strong to embrace a 'just do it' approach to reform—to argue that getting better results is simply a matter of political will, of the consolidation of power, and mobilization of the will necessary to use that power. However, as both the global experience of efforts at education sector reform and the findings of this study underscore, a 'just do it' approach is misguided. Effective reform requires a more skilful way of engaging with the stubborn governance realities that have made it difficult to translate the global commitment to universal education into genuine gains in learning. This final section uses a systems perspective to explore why it has been so difficult, in South Africa and elsewhere, to address the challenges of governance (and other) reforms in the education sector—and how these challenges might be addressed more effectively.

10.4.1 *A Complex System*

In recent years, spurred by the proliferation of randomized controlled trials (RCTs) and other robust methods of impact evaluation, the discourse on policy reform (in education and elsewhere) often has proceeded along the following lines: identify robustly what works, then scale it up. Yet translating micro-level findings into reforms that make a difference at scale has proven elusive. The central reason, suggests the 2018 World Development Report,

[5] However, for reasons explored throughout this section, all of this evidence should be interpreted through Pritchett's (2015:7) dictum that 'pretty much everything everyone believes is the key element of better schools has, by now, been rigorously disproved to have an impact on student learning somewhere. Of course, many of these same notions have also been rigorously proven to have an impact on student learning'.

Learning to Realize Education's Promise, is that agendas for 'scaling-up' generally are derived from linear extrapolation of specific cause-effect relationships. However, the challenge of working at scale looks very different once education is considered from a broader, systemic perspective.

Pritchett (2015: 11) defines a 'system' as '*a collection of elements or actors, each of which has its own objectives and a collection of feedback loops connecting the elements/actors'*. Figure 10.3, taken from the 2018 World Development Report, illustrates for education. It distinguishes among three levels of the system. At the centre is learning. In the middle level are the proximate drivers of learning: learners, and the extent to which they are prepared (nutritionally, by their family environment, and otherwise) to learn; teachers, and the distinctive skills and motivations they bring to the endeavour; the availability of the inputs (infrastructure, textbooks and other teaching materials) which support the learning environment); and school management. At the outer level are the very many actors who influence the proximate drivers, and thus learning. The different parts are linked through myriad relationships which shape the incentives and constraints on learning.

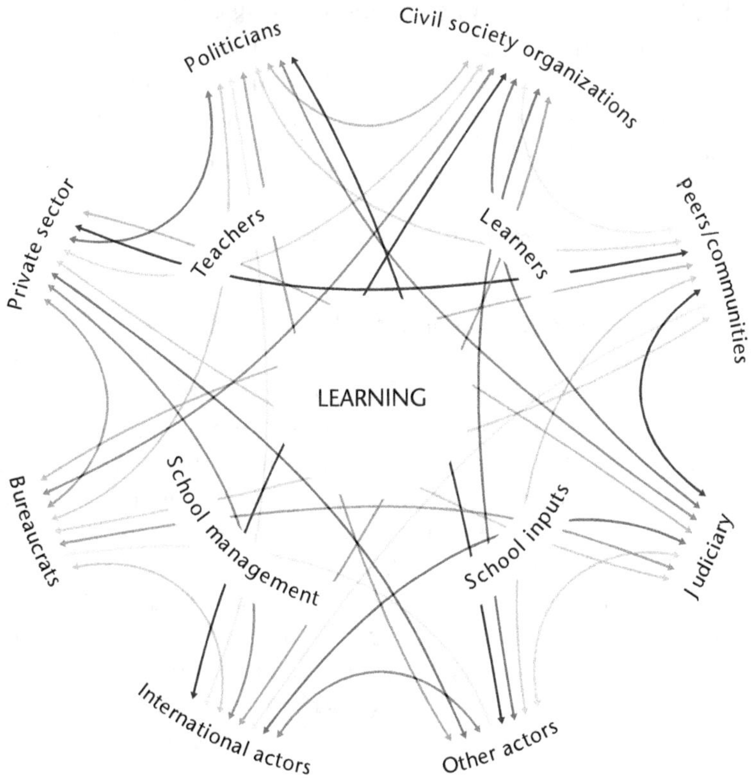

Figure 10.3. The education system

For a system to be 'coherent' (that is, in balance/equilibrium), the goals and incentives of the various actors need to be aligned with one another. This complicates the challenge of education sector reform. As the 2018 World Development Report puts it:

> The multiplicity of actors and institutions in an education system makes the outcomes of efforts to improve learning unpredictable... Many systems are stuck in low-learning traps [in which] actors lack either the incentives or the support needed to focus on learning... As actors juggle multiple objectives... it often is in the interest of each to maintain the status quo—even if society, and many of these actors, would be better off if they could shift to a higher-quality equilibrium.[6]

Ideas as well as interests shape how a system functions. Each of the many actors identified in Figure 10.3 have particular interests. But interests do not function in an ideational vacuum. As Lavers (2016), Lavers and Hickey (2015), World Bank (2015) and Evans (2017) explore in depth, they commonly are accompanied by a set of ideas which offer a narrative as to what goals are desirable, and what means are plausible. Where this underlying narrative varies widely among stakeholders, conflict can be endemic. Where a system is in equilibrium (high or low), the ideas are likely to be widely shared, explicitly or implicitly. Understanding how low-level equilibrium traps take hold and are sustained thus requires careful attention to both the interests of the stakeholders who influence the system, and the ideas which they hold vis-à-vis the system's functioning.

10.4.2 *Hierarchical and Horizontal Governance—Some Low-Level Equilibrium Traps*

Questions as to the potential and limits of hierarchical and horizontal governance turn out to be especially deeply intertwined with normative ideas as to how a 'good' society should be organized. Thus, while to this point the principal focus of the study has been on the interactions between interests and governance, to understand the potential and obstacles to reform, it is helpful to also bring ideas into the picture. Building on the research findings laid out earlier, this subsection explores how interests and ideas can result in continuing low-level equilibrium traps, vis-à-vis both hierarchical and horizontal governance.

To begin with hierarchical governance, as summarized earlier in this chapter, differences in socio-economic and political contexts and in institutional legacies from the apartheid era emerged in the present research as central in accounting for differences in bureaucratic performance in South Africa's Western Cape and Eastern Cape provinces. The Eastern Cape's Department of

[6] World Bank (2018: 12, 13, 15, 178).

Education performed poorly, but deep-seated political and institutional constraints rendered infeasible the prospect of more than marginal improvements in its functioning. In the Western Cape, the contextual constraints are less binding, but educational outcomes remain disappointing.

But notwithstanding the evidence as to its limitations, in countries where education has long been organized around public bureaucracies, the ideational commitment runs deep to targeting improvements in hierarchical management as the key to better outcomes. Argumentation along these lines can point to multiple examples of successful, hierarchical systems—from (historically) France, to Russia, to Japan and Vietnam—as illustrations of what can be achieved. But the arena of education reform also is replete with examples of hierarchical systems whose performance fails to improve, notwithstanding cycle after cycle of ambitious efforts at reform. To cite just two of many possible examples: Malaysia's educational outcomes continue to lag its South East Asian peers, notwithstanding five major curricular and pedagogy reforms within the past two decades, none of which addressed the hyper-centralized way in which the country's system is organized.[7] Morocco's hyper-centralized system also has been the focus of repeated, high-profile reform efforts which, again, neither addressed the hyper-centralized structure, nor yielded the hoped-for results.[8]

As the 2018 World Development Report suggests, one reason why so many countries become trapped in endless cycles of bureaucratic reforms which lead nowhere is a failure to distinguish between the 'coherence' of reforms and whether or not they are aligned towards learning. As Pritchett (2015: 33) argues, bureaucratic reform often centres around 'process compliance', a pattern of

> bureaucratic management in which teachers/principals' accountability is basically for enrolments and the operation of 'schooling'... While there might be some vague reference to children actually acquiring needed competencies... 'process

[7] Tzu Lyn Phang provided the background research for Malaysia. The Malaysian reforms are: the 1997 Malaysia Smart School Project; the 2003 curriculum, English in the Teaching of Mathematics and Science; the 2006 National Education Blueprint; the 2011–15 new Standard Primary School Curriculums, and the 2013 Malaysian Education Blueprint 2013–25, with the latter part of the broader Big Fast Results initiative facilitated by the Performance Management and Delivery Unit established in the Prime Minister's office; there currently is optimism that the last of these might yield better results than the earlier efforts.

[8] Sarah Kouhlani-Nolla provided the background research for Morocco. One reform was initiated in 1999 shortly after King Mohammed VI came to power, when a new Ministry of National Education was established and initiated curricular, pedagogical and examination changes under the rubric of a National Charter of Education. Disappointment with the results led to the launch in 2009 of a National Education Emergency Plan. Disappointment with this effort led to a new reform initiative in 2012, and then a new long-term, fifteen-year perspective, launched in 2015 by the Ministry of National Education.

compliance is, in and of itself and with no reference to outcomes, completely adequate for discharging accountability.

Process compliance can be useful as a veneer which covers the reality of a patronage-driven bureaucracy. It can also take on an ideational life of its own. Indeed, one plausible explanation for the continuing limitations of the WCED is that it has been so deeply immersed in 'hierarchy as process compliance' for so long that repeated efforts at fostering performance management have repeatedly been re-interpreted through a process-compliance lens, undercutting their potential for re-orienting the bureaucracy towards learning.

For horizontal governance, too, interests and ideas interact in accounting for the patterns which persist in South Africa, but with some unusual features relative to other countries. Grindle (2004), taking a broad, systemic perspective, explores in depth for Latin America how efforts to decentralize the governance of education to subnational and school levels were resisted by interests who derived their power from control over bureaucratic hierarchies. In Mexico, Bolivia and Ecuador, resistance by alliances of the bureaucracy and teachers' unions to efforts to shift authority downwards resulted in a scaling back of the reform agenda. By contrast, reform progressed rapidly, and resulted in major gains in quality in the Brazilian state of Minas Gerais, where teachers' unions were less relentlessly opposed to a decentralization of responsibilities down the system.

In South Africa, by contrast, there might seem at first glance to be a more open path for leveraging horizontal governance to improve educational outcomes. For one thing, by contrast to the struggles and only partial gains achieved in Latin America, the 1996 South African Schools Act accords substantial authority to school governing bodies (SGBs). For another, the case study evidence summarized in section 10.3 highlights the potential of horizontal governance as an entry point for improving educational outcomes. The case studies show that strong developmental coalitions can provide a 'floor' or support for enhanced decision-making[9]—supporting performance-oriented school principals, and serving as a counterweight to capture. Further, the evidence suggests that school-level dynamics are fluid, raising the possibility that, for at least a subset of schools, pro-active interventions can tilt the balance between developmental and predatory influences in favour of the former. As discussed further below, there is abundant experience from around the world of successful interventions to support horizontal governance. Yet the potential largely has been ignored.

[9] For this point, see also Hoadley, Christie, and Ward (2009).

A review conducted for this study (Eberhard, 2016) found that outside of the small minority of historically elite, English and Afrikaans medium schools, the South African government has made almost no effort, successful or unsuccessful, to support participatory governance. Further, a 2003 review of school governance (Soudien, 2003) commissioned by the national Minister of Education, and led by an eminent and experienced scholar and educator, identified some key obstacles to horizontal governance in poor communities and put forward a series of proposals as to how the obstacles might be overcome; the report was never released. Even more troubling has been the policy response to a more recent ministerial review report (Department of Basic Education, 2016) which explored corruption in the recruitment of teachers. The report identified a variety of weaknesses in the recruitment processes, but only one of its recommendations found its way into an amendment proposed in late 2017 to amend SASA (RSA, 2017)—namely a proposal to sharply circumscribe the role of school governing bodies (SGBs) in school-level recruitment and appointments processes.

A plausible explanation for this continuing neglect can be found in the ways in which interests, power and ideas interact with one another. As noted earlier, momentum for the empowerment of SGBs came via two sources: the interests of affluent parents who had been beneficiaries of apartheid-era public schooling; and those anti-apartheid activists who had embraced a participatory vision of democracy. While the former comprised influential stakeholders with a compelling personal interest in SGB policies, the impetus from the latter turned out to be weak.

To be sure, as of the mid-1990s, popular democracy might have appeared to be part of the DNA of South Africa's liberation struggle: hundreds of community groups had come together under the umbrella of the United Democratic Front (UDF); their efforts helped bring down apartheid. Indeed, participatory governance was embraced by the Reconstruction and Development Programme (RDP) which served as the ANC's election manifesto in 1994. But within a few years, the participatory vision receded into the background. Why?

One common explanation is that, with the announcement of the Growth, Employment and Redistribution (GEAR) strategy in 1996, this participatory democratic vision was hijacked by 'neoliberal', technocratic interests. Hijackings aside, there were multiple other reasons why the momentum for popular democracy declined with the ANC's accession to power. A practical reason is that, having won the election, the ANC needed to govern. To staff its government, it turned to many of the activist-intellectuals who had been part of the UDF. The consequence, in the education sector as well as elsewhere was to deplete the leadership of the organizations which had been at the vanguard of the push for popular democracy (Woolman and Fleisch, 2009: 111).

There also were more fundamental reasons for a narrow embrace of hierarchical, less participatory approaches to governing:

> Black civil society... had emerged and developed in a context of extreme repression and absolute exclusion, and had as such little experience of transacting with the state. The transition to majority rule thus represented both a political and institutional rupture. The vacuum of authority was quickly filled by the ANC. As an organization in exile that was constantly threatened by the apartheid state, the ANC had developed extremely disciplined organizational structures, including clear lines of command that proved far more effective in establishing its power in the transition period than the decentralization and flat organizational structures of civil society. (Heller, 2009: 142)

This 'had devastating consequences for ideological and organizational diversity represented by grassroots organizations affiliated to the UDF' (Madlingozi, 2007: 85).

The ANC's predispositions aligned well with the deeply-rooted hierarchical culture of the apartheid-era bureaucracy inherited by the new government:

> Confronted with an unruly reality as they attempted to place their stamp on society after assuming office, government strategists who had expected office to confer the power to remake society often saw centralization and 'co-ordination' as a means of ensuring the predictability and certainty after which they hankered... These approaches, which were repeatedly buttressed by a public policy debate which repeatedly insisted that it is the prime function of government to 'deliver' to citizens rather than articulate their voice, imply that, because citizens value the fruits of 'delivery' more than intangibles such as voice or participation, the latter are at best a luxury to be enjoyed when they do not impede the technical supply of services, at worst a hindrance because the substitute talk for urgently required action. (Friedman, 2005: 766–7)

In the context of a culture of 'process compliance', and in the face of the inevitable political pressures of patronage, 'delivery' has not worked out as planned. In consequence, there has indeed been something of a resurgence of civic activism. Perhaps unsurprisingly given South Africa's history of political struggle, this activism has expressed itself principally through the oppositional discourse of 'social movements'—a discourse which, in the early 2010s, earned South Africa something of a renewed reputation as 'the protest capital of the world'.[10]

[10] The quote is from Habib (2013: 60); see also Madlingozi (2007).

10.4.3 *Cumulative Incrementalism*

The findings of this book pose a dilemma for education reform. At all levels (national, provincial, and school), the quality of governance is shown to have a strong influence on educational outcomes. But the observed governance patterns turn out to be shaped by the broader institutional and political context—with the potential for 'fixing' governance weaknesses constrained by that context. This final subsection suggests a way of dealing with this dilemma.

The suggested approach combines two complementary aspects of reform—practical initiatives which take into account the role of interests in constraining reform, plus a broader reframing of the ideas surrounding how the provision of education and other public services might be improved. The overall aim is to initiate a process which proceeds deliberately, and incrementally, maintaining stability, while cumulatively building momentum for re-orientating the system as a whole towards learning.

For many decades, South Africa's education system has been buffeted by wave after wave of change. The 1976 uprising of school pupils initiated a grass-roots struggle for political change, with the slogan 'no education before liberation' characterizing at least part of the struggle. As Chapter 2 details, between 1994 and 1998, far-reaching institutional and fiscal transformations (unprecedented globally in their scope) were undertaken. Curriculum and pedagogical transformations also were set in motion, with adjustments (some major) continuing to 2012. Only since the mid-2000s could the new system be described as broadly stable—and there is some evidence that, with stability, outcomes are beginning to improve, albeit from an astonishingly low base. Table 10.4 illustrates, with data on South Africa's performance in the Trends in Mathematics and Science Study (TIMSS); added information is provided in Chapters 2 and 7.

The risks are high that a new round of 'transformational' reform would short-circuit the process of consolidation, and reverse the limited gains which have been achieved. Indeed, experience the world over suggests that the longer-run impacts of 'bold' efforts to achieve reform by confronting vested interests (notably including teachers' unions) can be highly uncertain. As Grindle (2004) shows for Latin America, such confrontations rarely result in 'victory', but instead usher in a period of considerable turbulence. The 2018 World Development Report takes a similarly cautious view. It contrasts reforms in Poland and in Chile. In Poland, large-scale changes in the structure of the education sector remained unpopular, with ongoing pressures to scrap them, notwithstanding evidence of success. In Chile, by contrast, incremental cumulative reforms over a decade, beginning in 1996, built strong momentum

Table 10.4. TIMSS Performance—Provincial Comparisons Across Years

Province	TIMSS 2003 (Gr 8 & 9)	TIMSS 2011 (Gr. 9)	TIMSS 2015 (Gr. 9)
	Average math. score	Average math. score	Average math. Score
Western Cape	414	404	391
Gauteng	303	389	408
Eastern Cape	250	316	346
Free State	291	359	367
KwaZulu-Natal	278	337	369
Limpopo	244	322	361
Mpumulanga	287	344	370
Northern Cape	341	366	364
North West	280	350	354
South Africa	**285**	**348**	**368**

Source: See Chapter 6 for details and discussion

for change, including support from the teachers' union. Based on these and other experiences, the World Development Report concludes that:

> A gradual, negotiated approach to reform may work better than confrontation. Where coalitions of system actors foster collaboration among shared goals, reforms are more likely to succeed... Even if evidence shows that the reforms improve learning, their sustainability is at risk when they are misunderstood or unpopular among system actors. (2018: 204)

The evidence in this book points to a variety of practical, incremental reforms vis-à-vis both hierarchical and horizontal governance. For hierarchical governance, one crucial task is to continue to strengthen the 'transmission belt' through which emerging lessons about effective pedagogy are disseminated throughout the system. A second task is to fine-tune the interactions between the bureaucracy and SGBs in appointments processes, especially for school principals. In recent years, operating within the framework set by SASA, the WCED has introduced psychometric competency assessments for candidates for principal, used early retirement options to encourage principals in poorly-performing schools to retire, and ensured (informally) that successor principals in poorly performing schools come from outside the school. But note that efforts to use strengthened hierarchy to improve principal selection are likely to add value only in settings where hierarchy already works relatively well—in settings where hierarchies are more politicized, the consequence could simply be to create new risks of school-level capture with patronage-oriented decision-making upstream in the bureaucracy.

Turning to horizontal governance, the findings in this book suggest that it can be a useful complement in settings where education bureaucracies are relatively capable—and can also be a value adding institutional substitute in settings where bureaucracies are dysfunctional. As discussed earlier, South

Africa's point of departure for leveraging the potential benefits of horizontal governance are more favourable than Grindle's Latin American cases as it already has in place (via the 1996 Schools Act) an institutional architecture which fully empowers SGBs. What has been missing are efforts from either public sector or non-governmental stakeholders to breathe life into that architecture—especially in low-income communities which (given the country's apartheid history and political struggle) lack experience of participatory, collaborative approaches to service provision.

How might such initiatives be designed? As the school-level case studies suggest, the core challenge is less one of 'capacity' than of empowering developmentally-oriented stakeholders at the school-level. Given the large number of schools, a school-by-school approach would be too demanding of the limited capacity available. An alternative might be to focus on interventions capable of influencing the dynamics of multiple schools in a more 'wholesale' way—linking developmentally-minded SGBs and other local stakeholders with one another, rather than working one-by-one. The aim would not be to transform all schools: in some schools, positive governance dynamics might already be in place; in others, predatory capture might be too powerfully locked-in to dislodge.

Experience in other countries points to a wide range of approaches through which countries have successfully worked at scale to improve participatory governance, with (as shown in some impact evaluations) a positive effect on learning outcomes. Some of these approaches focus directly on training parents and communities; others train trainers, with the process cascading down to the school level; others work with clusters of schools; and others focus on learning-by-doing, combining training with finance and support for implementation of small-scale school projects.[11] What seemingly holds South Africa back from embracing approaches along these lines is their disjuncture with prevailing ideas as to what it takes for a society to successfully engage in the challenges of public service provision.

To complement the pragmatic reforms highlighted above, what might be the potential of broader reframing of the ideas surrounding how the provision of education and other public services can be improved? Such a reframing would re-engage from a pragmatic perspective, some of the participatory ideas

[11] Among programmes implemented at scale, Ghana provides an example of direct training support (Social Impact, 2014); Guinea of a training of trainers approach (Garnier et al., 2005; Midling et al., 2006); Haiti (American Institutes for Research, 2001; 2004) and Nigeria (Healey, 2016) examples of cluster-based approaches; and Honduras (World Bank, 2009) of an approach which combine training with finance and support for implementation of small-scale school projects. Bruns, Filmer, and Patrinos (2011) synthesize the results of the impact evaluations of a rich array of approaches to strengthen school-level transparency and participatory management, some robust (but small-scale) randomized controlled trials, and other interventions at scale.

which had currency in mid-1990s South Africa. Inevitably, the discussion is somewhat speculative—but to provide both inspiration and a sense as to what might be the possible impact on education it is helpful to look at experience elsewhere, specifically that of Kenya.

A useful point of departure is the striking fact that, controlling for a variety of exogenous factors, the performance of the Western Cape education system lags substantially behind that of Kenya, notwithstanding the Western Cape having almost five times the level of human resources. Figure 10.4 illustrates the extent to which Kenya is a positive outlier. The country's success can hardly be attributed to the quality of its education bureaucracy: Kenya is notorious for its high levels of corruption; patronage permeates the public sector. What seems to have made the difference are the 'softer' dimensions of governance. Consider the following description from a long-time practitioner/observer of the Kenyan education system:

> What one sees in rural Kenya is an expectation for kids to learn and be able to have basic skills... Exam results are far more readily available in Kenya than other countries in the region. The 'mean scores' for the Kenya Certificate of Primary Education (KCPE) and equivalent KCSE at secondary school are posted in every school and over time so that trends can be seen. Head teachers are held accountable for those results

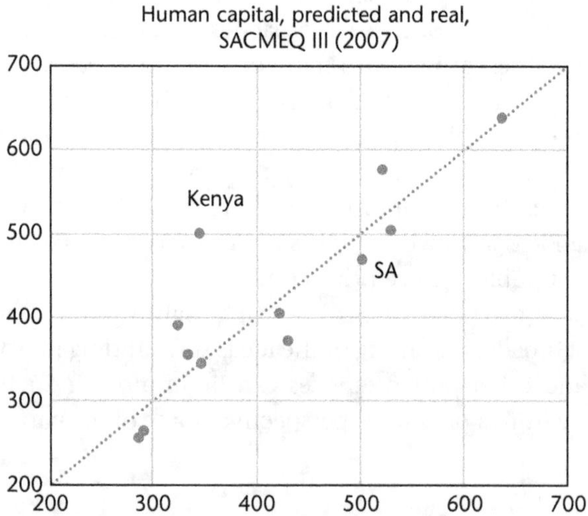

Figure 10.4. Kenya's educational outcomes in comparative perspective

Note: The x-axis of the figure shows predicted scores for 2007 on the Southern African Consortium for Monitoring Education Quality (SACMEQ) test controlling for a variety of exogenous factors. The y-axis shows actual scores.

Source: Chapter 2

to the extent of being paraded around the community if they did well, or literally banned from school and kicked out of the community if they did badly.[12]

As Appendix A10.1 explores in detail, the roots of active civic engagement in the education sector run deep in the foundational ideas which shaped modern Kenya: in a decades-long effort to resist British colonial influence; in the vision of the country's liberation struggle leader and first president, Jomo Kenyatta, of an educated population as the central manifestation what it means to be a proud independent nation; in the inclusion of education as top priority in the country's first national plan; and in an abiding commitment in the first decade of the country's independence to *Harambee*—'self-help'—as the pathway to development, with education holding pride of place within the Harambee movement. The contrast could not be starker between this Kenyan vision and the South African vision of service 'delivery' by government.

Against that backdrop, consider the call for 'active citizenship' in South Africa's 2012 National Development Plan:

> Active citizenship requires inspirational leadership at all levels of society . . . Leadership does not refer to one person, or even a tight collective of people. It applies in every aspect of life . . . To build an inclusive nation the country needs to find ways to promote a positive cycle, where an effective state, inspirational leadership across all levels of society, and active citizens reinforce and strengthen each other. (The Presidency, National Planning Commission, 2012)

If South Africa were actually to embrace active citizenship as the path to improving outcomes, the consequences for the education system could be far-reaching. In many schools, an activated citizenry could decisively shift the balance between developmental and predatory actors in favour of the former. Within the bureaucracy, new momentum could emerge for learning-oriented engagement, surfacing the limits of pre-occupations with 'process compliance' for its own sake, or for fostering access without an explicit focus on actual learning. Teacher unions might increasingly embrace a vision of teaching as a profession, as a calling, and move decisively away from a narrow pre-occupation with the rights of teachers as employees. New possibilities would arise for adapting national policies in ways that enhance a focus on educational outcomes. Civil society activism might more systematically target those aspects of education-sector governance which have strong impacts on learning.

[12] Personal communication, 9 January 2017 from Benjamin Piper, RTI Senior Director of Africa Education, based in Nairobi, Kenya. Quoted by permission. In an econometric analysis, Bold et al. (2010) show that high levels of parental and community support were indeed associated with persistently better support in the KCPE exams.

The glow of South Africa's political miracle has long faded. But as of the time of completing this book, it seems just possible that the country may perhaps be beginning to confront the reality that the end of apartheid was just one (giant) step along the path of meeting the challenge of inclusive, economic as well as political liberation for all. To move forward, South Africa could do much worse than—learning from Kenya at the time of its independence—putting education at the centre of a vision of people-centred development, in a way in which realizing the potential becomes the task of all of the country's citizens. A top-down vision of 'education for all' is insufficient to meet the frontier challenge of improving outcomes. What is called for now is 'all for education'.

Appendix A10.1: Accounting for Kenya's Educational Performance[13]

This appendix provides some historical background to the assertion in the chapter that 'soft governance' accounts for Kenya being a positive outlier (at least through to 2007) relative to its Southern and East African comparators—with these soft governance strengths rooted in large part in the country's struggle to shake off the shackles of colonialism. Four aspects of this struggle appear especially salient.

First, dating back to the 1920s, an independent schools movement had emerged as a weapon in resistance to colonial influence. Early resistance came from the Kikuyu Central Association (KCA), founded in 1921 to protest against colonial land policies. Within a decade, education had become an effective new arena for struggle:

> The Kikuyu Independent Schools Association (KISA), and the African Independent Pentecostal Church, which fused orthodox Christianity with Kikuyu tribal traditions, became the focal points for the growing anti-European feeling of young Africans...Legal means of getting their rights—the endless unsuccessful lawsuits and the pointless petitions the government ignored—had been fruitless and frustrating. The law was a dead end: the settlers and the colonial administration were too strong and were set against them. Now they had a platform based on culture and religion, and the public was ready to move. The new schools and the new church bred others; another school movement and another church group, even more militant and aggressive, formed in competition. But if they couldn't agree with each other, they all agreed in opposing the missions. In the next couple of years the effects were spectacular. The KCA's inflammatory speeches drew natives away from the mission schools and congregations in droves. The Church of Scotland mission in Kikuyu province lost 90% of its members, and the Africa Inland Mission even more. (Wepman, 1985: 47–8)

Following World War Two, conflict between the independent schools movement and the colonial authorities erupted afresh, culminating in the forced closure of the

[13] This appendix draws on very useful background research by Sarah Pfund, plus helpful informal inputs from David Throup.

schools (which were perceived to be a source of the Mau Mau rebellion) for much of the 1950s (Wepman, 1985; Fischer, 1977).

Second, the personal history of Jomo Kenyatta (Kenya's first president and a major figure in the country's liberation struggle) was deeply intertwined with education as a form of resistance:

- Born in the 1890s, he was educated in mission schools.
- In the 1920s, he became active in the KCA, which (building on his mission school experience, and fluency in English) he used as a platform to advocate for better-quality education for Africans, within a framework of cultural nationalism.
- Upon returning to Kenya in the later 1940s (after fifteen years living in Europe) to take up leadership of the Kenya African Union (later the ruling party, KANU), he also became director and principal of the Kenya African Teachers College, founded by his brother-in-law, and run by the independent schools movement (Fischer, 1977).
- He was jailed in 1952, and released in 1961 resuming active leadership of KANU, becoming the first president of independent Kenya in December, 1963.

Third, education emerged as among the very top early priorities of independent Kenya. Thus:

> In 1964, a special Education Commission was established to review how the education system could be used to build national identity, encourage racial and ethnic intermixing and support development. (Hornsby, 2012)

Education featured centrally in Kenya's 1966 development plan, which asserted that 'education is more than simply preparation for the university or training for clerical jobs. Our farmers need education and so do the workers' (Fischer, 1977: ii–iii).

Fourth, in June 1963, Kenyatta offered a vision of an independent Kenya imbued with *Harambee* ('let us pull together') (Kenyatta, 1964); in December, the country adopted the term as its official national motto. By the early 1980s, over 20,000 Harambee associations had registered with government; these associations had become 'the principal vehicle through which local communities exerted claims on the state . . . the most important arena of rural political life . . . Over time, the emergence of Harambee, combined with the regular holding of elections, established a measure of national political accountability by linking state and society together'. (Barkan, 1994: 19). Engagement with education held pride of place within the Harambee movement:

> In an upsurge of protest, Africans mobilized during colonial rule to launch an underground educational movement in order to vie for increased social power and status. This movement latter became known as the Harambee school movement . . . Harambee or self-help schools became a vital aspect of Kenya's secondary school system. (Dinavo, 1990: 4)

> Harambee was not just a political slogan, a rallying point, or an idea looking for an occasion to manifest itself. For education in particular, Harambee had a meaning all of its own; it was a very influential reality, especially in the area of secondary education . . . Politicians, concerned with their public image and their re-electability, yielded to public demands for more education . . . Available funds were running short . . . The demand and pressure for more schools continued

> to grow. In this spiral of conflict between demand and ability to supply, Kenyatta's call for Harambee—let's pull together—seemed to contain the answer. (Fischer, 1977: 81–3)

Along with the above, two subsequent developments must also be noted. One is the introduction in 1978 of the standardized countrywide test, the Kenya Certificate of Primary Education, under the leadership of Kenyatta's successor Daniel Arap Moi, himself a former schoolteacher; this test provided the information platform through which communities hold school staff to account, as described in the body of the chapter. The second is the repeated pressure for free primary education, which culminated in a new policy in 2003 which went beyond exhortation and banned the imposition of school levies and other cost-sharing mechanisms (Somerset, 2009). The policy resulted in a sudden increase in the number of pupils; Grade 1 enrolments rose from 970,000 in 2002 to 1.3 million in 2003. But it also had the unintended consequence of reducing the commitment of parents to schools, resulting in a subsequent exit of children to low-fee private schools (Bold et al., 2010).

References

American Institutes for Research (2001) 'Formative evaluation of USAID/Haiti Education Portfolio: Final Report', Improving Educational Quality Project.

American Institutes for Research and Centre de Formation et Decrement Technique, (2004) 'Haiti: Education 2004 Project Impact Evaluation Study'. USAID.

Barkan, J. D. (1994) *Beyond Capitalism vs. Socialism in Kenya and Tanzania.* Boulder: L. Rienner.

Bold, T., Sandefur, J., Kimeny, M., and Mwabu, G. (2010) 'Education for prosperity: improving access and quality'. In C. Adam, P. Collier, and N. Ndung'u (eds), *Kenya: Policies for Prosperity,* Oxford: Oxford University Press, 293–308.

Bruns, B., Filmer, D., and Patrinos, H. (2011) *Making Schools Work: New Evidence on Accountability Reforms.* Washington DC: World Bank.

Dinavo, T. R. (1990) 'Educational policy change in postindependent Kenya: The case of harambee and government secondary school.' PhD dissertation.

Eberhard, F. (2016) 'A preliminary review of School Governing Body support initiatives in South Africa', mimeo. Cape Town.

Evans, A. (2017) 'Politicizing inequality: the power of ideas'. Working paper. London.

Fischer, H. (1977) 'The Influence of Jomo Kenyatta and Julius K. Nyerere on Education and Development in Kenya and Tanzania.' PhD dissertation, University of Southern California, *Proquest LLC,* 1–234.

Friedman, S. (2005) 'Getting better than "world class": The challenge of governing post-apartheid South Africa', *Social Research* 72(3), 757–84.

Garnier, M., Diallo, M., Diallo, T., Koivogui, A., Leno, P., and Sako, M. (2005) 'Community Participation, Quality and Equity in Guinea's Schools: Evaluation Report of the PACEEQ project: 2001–2005'. PACEEQ/RTI International.

Grindle, M. S. (2004) *Despite the Odds: The Contentious Politics of Education Reform.* Cambridge, MA: Harvard University Press.

Habib, A. (2013) *South Africa's Suspended Revolution: Hopes and Prospects*. Johannesburg: Wits University Press.

Hallinger, P. and Heck, R. H. (1996) 'Reassessing the principal's contribution to school effectiveness: A review of empirical research, 1980–1995', *Educational Administration Quarterly* 32(1).

Healey, F. H. (2016) 'Social Acccountability in Education: The Northern Education Initiative in Nigera'. In A. Wetterberg and D. Brinkerhoff (eds), *Governance and Service Delivery: Practical Applications of Social Accountability Across Sectors*. Raleigh: RTI Press.

Heller, P. (2009) 'Democratic deepening in India and South Africa', *Journal of Asian and African Studies* 44(1), 123–49.

Hoadley, U., Christie, P., and Ward, C. (2009) 'Managing to learn: Instructional leadership in South African secondary schools', *School Management and Leadership* 29(4), 373–89.

Hornsby, C. (2012) *Kenya: A History Since Independence*. London: I. B. Tauris.

Kenyatta, J. (1964) *Harambee! The Prime Minister of Kenya's Speeches 1963–1964, From the Attainment of Internal Self-Government to the Threshold of the Kenya Republic*. Nairobi: Oxford University Press.

Lavers, T. (2016) 'The role of ideas in the politics of development', mimeo. University of Manchester.

Lavers, T. and Hickey, S. (2015) 'Investigating the political economy of social protection expansion in Africa: At the intersection of transnational ideas and domestic politics'. ESID Working paper no. 47. University of Manchester.

Leithwood, K., Patten, S., and Jantzi, D. (2010) 'Testing a conception of how school leadership influences student learning', *Educational Administration Quarterly* 44(4), 455–7.

Levy, B. (2014) *Working with the Grain: Integrating Governance and Growth in Development Strategies*. New York: Oxford University Press.

Madlingozi, T. (2007) 'Post-apartheid social movements and the quest for the elusive "new" South Africa', *Journal of Law and Society* 34(1), 77–98.

Mansuri, G. and Rao, V. (2013) *Localizing Development: Does Participation Work?* A World Bank Policy Research Report, Washington DC.

Midling, M., Filion, L., Gnahoui, E. David, Gassama Mbaye, M., Diallo, A. T., and Diallo, A. (2006) 'Program evaluation for USAID/Guinea Basic Education Program Portfolio', Devtech Systems.

Piper, B., 9 January 2017, Personal communication.

Pritchett, L. (2015) 'Creating education systems coherent for learning outcomes: Making the transition from schooling to learning', *Research on Improving Systems of Education,* Working Paper RISE-WP-15/005.

Pritchett, L., Woolcock, M., and Andrews, M. (2010) 'Capability traps? The mechanisms of persistent implementation failure', Centre for Global Development, Working Paper 234.

RSA (2017) Draft Basic Education Laws Amendment Bill. Pretoria: Department of Basic Education.

Social Impact (2014) 'Final Performance Evaluation of USAID/Ghana's Partnership for Accountable Governance in Education (PAGE) Project: Final Report'. USAID.

Somerset, A. (2009) 'Universalizing Primary Education in Kenya: The Elusive Goal', *Comparative Education* 45, 2.

Soudien, C. (2003) 'Review of school governance in South African public schools'. Final draft report of the ministerial review committee on school governance. Department of Education. Pretoria.

The Presidency, National Planning Commission (2012) *National Development Plan, 2030: Our Future—Making it Work*. Pretoria.

Wepman, D. (1985) *Jomo Kenyatta*. New York: Chelsea House Publishers.

Woolman, S. and Fleisch, B. (2009) *The Constitution in the Classroom: Law and education in South Africa, 1994–2008*. Pretoria: Pretoria University Law Press.

World Bank (2004) *Making Services Work for Poor People. World Development Report 2004*. Washington DC: World Bank.

World Bank (2009) 'Implementation Completion and Results Report on a Credit in the Amount of SDR32.3 Million (US$ 41.5 Million Equivalent) to the Republic of Honduras for a Community-Based Education Project'. Report No. ICR0000714.

World Bank (2015) *Mind, Society and Behavior. World Development Report 2015*. Washington DC: World Bank.

World Bank (2018) *Learning to Realize Education's Promise. World Development Report 2018*. Washington DC: World Bank.

Index

Note: Tables and figures are indicated by an italic *t* and *f*, respectively, following the page number.

The manufacturer's authorised representative in the EU for product safety is Oxford University Press España S.A. of el Parque Empresarial San Fernando de Henares, Avenida de Castilla, 2 – 28830 Madrid (www.oup.es/en or product.safety@oup.com). OUP España S.A. also acts as importer into Spain of products made by the manufacturer.

www.ingramcontent.com/pod-product-compliance
Lightning Source LLC
LaVergne TN
LVHW011914200926
848484LV00002B/620
* 9 7 8 0 1 9 8 8 2 4 0 5 3 *